International Juridical Double Taxation from an Ability-to-Pay Perspective under EU Law

Maria Júlia Ildefonso Mendonça

Wolters Kluwer

Published by:
Kluwer Law International B.V.
PO Box 316
2400 AH Alphen aan den Rijn
The Netherlands
E-mail: lrs-sales@wolterskluwer.com
Website: www.wolterskluwer.com/en/solutions/kluwerlawinternational

Sold and distributed by:
Wolters Kluwer Legal & Regulatory U.S.
920 Links Avenue
Landisville, PA 17538
United States of America
E-mail: customer.service@wolterskluwer.com

ISBN 978-94-035-0298-4

e-Book: ISBN 978-94-035-0308-0
web-PDF: ISBN 978-94-035-0318-9

Para a Avó Bia.
Obrigada, Pai e Mãe.

Table of Contents

List of Abbreviations

AG	Advocate General
CJEU	Court of Justice of the European Union
Directive on tax dispute resolution mechanisms	Council Directive (EU) 2017/1852 of 10 October 2017 on tax dispute resolution mechanisms in the European Union.
EEA	European Economic Area
EU	European Union
EU Multilateral Arbitration Convention	Convention on the elimination of double taxation in connection with the adjustment of profits of associated enterprises (90/463/EEC)
Interest and Royalty Directive	Council Directive 2003/49/EC of 3 June 2003 on a common system of taxation applicable to interest and royalty payments made between associated companies of different Member States
Merger Directive	Council Directive 2009/133/EC of 19 October 2009 on the common system of taxation applicable to mergers, divisions, partial divisions, transfers of assets and exchanges of shares concerning companies of different Member States and to the transfer of the registered office of an SE or SCE between Member States
MLI	Multilateral Convention to Implement Tax Treaty Related Measures to Prevent Base Erosion and Profit Shifting.
OECD	Organisation for Economic Co-operation and Development
OECD MC	OECD Model Tax Convention on Income and on Capital
Parent-Subsidiary Directive	Council Directive 2011/96/EU of 30 November 2011 on the common system of taxation applicable in the case of parent companies and subsidiaries of different Member States
SEA	Single European Act
TEU	Treaty on European Union
TFEU	Treaty on the Functioning of the European Union

UN	United Nations
UN MC	United Nations Model Double Taxation Convention between Developed and Developing Countries
VCLT	Vienna Convention on the Law of Treaties

Foreword

International double taxation and ability-to-pay are not two technically related concepts in the current state of development of Tax Law. Both concepts move in two clearly differentiated territories. International double taxation belongs to the field of attracting foreign investment and establishing tax incentives, while ability-to-pay has its place in the foundations of domestic taxation. Eliminating international juridical double taxation and legitimising the tax system, respectively, are the historical functions that correspond to the development of these concepts, which are today converted into solid legal categories.

However, it is a well-known fact that social evolution puts the legal categories and the Law, which is responsible for regulating economic and social relations to ensure stability and justice, under constant stress. This gives rise to various phenomena: new principles, new rules and, sometimes, authentic mutations of the traditional legal categories and the relationship between them.

In this sense, there is no doubt that the creation of the European Union (EU) has represented an enormous challenge for the Law that continues to bear fruit in many areas. This book is clear proof of that, as it establishes a possible technical relationship between international juridical double taxation and ability-to-pay under EU law.

I was the supervisor for Júlia Mendonça's excellent doctoral thesis on 'International Juridical Double Taxation from an Ability-to-Pay Perspective under EU Law' at the Pompeu Fabra University in Barcelona, which I am extremely grateful to preface at the courteous express request of the author. This work falls firmly within the framework of the challenge mentioned above, and the author tackles a classic and nuclear problem of international tax law and EU law – the issue of the compatibility of international juridical double taxation in the EU, which is of growing importance today as a consequence of globalisation – with courage, extraordinary rigour and uncommon soundness. This problem is the object of an innovative reformulation at the end of the book, in which a clear link between international juridical double taxation and the ability-to-pay principle is established by making use of instrumental concepts of unquestionable value, such as 'artificial economic strength', 'intangible economic strength' or 'overall ability to pay'.

Throughout this book, the author examines the trajectory of international juridical double taxation and the ability-to-pay principle in academic literature, regulations and, above all, in the Court of Justice of the European Union's (CJEU) case law, which is the object of rigorous, systematic, and exhaustive critical analysis. It is precisely this in-depth case law analysis that allows the author to propose a reformulation of the problem.

According to the author, the issue is no longer about whether international juridical double taxation is compatible with EU law but whether disregarding taxpayers' overall ability in cross-border situations is in accordance with EU law. The author asserts that, from such a perspective, the tax disadvantage deriving from international juridical double taxation may also be perceived as resulting from a Member State's exercise of taxing powers in a discriminatory or restrictive manner, which constitutes a forbidden obstacle to free movement under EU law.

The road to such a conclusion is not easy, nor is its effective implementation, as the author herself points out in what she rightly calls 'the challenges' of the proposed thesis. However, the long and complex journey towards this conclusion is a pleasant one thanks to the author's careful writing, the accuracy of her observations and findings at every step, and the soundness of her arguments.

As the author notes, the approach followed by the CJEU in its case law places the problem of international juridical double taxation within the scope of the definition of Member States' tax jurisdiction and not within the scope of the exercise of Member States' taxing powers, in which the prohibition of tax restrictions and discrimination operates. Nevertheless, even though there is no contradiction in the reasoning followed by the CJEU in its case law, it is paradoxical that the CJEU considers that, in the author's words, 'the Member States do not breach EU law if they do not eliminate international juridical double taxation, even though it undermines taxpayers' ability to pay. However, the Member States breach EU law if they undermine taxpayers' ability to pay in the process of eliminating international juridical double taxation'.

Such an observation is the starting point for in-depth research into the role of the ability-to-pay principle in the CJEU's case law, which leads to valuable results. In particular, and very briefly summarised, this research makes it possible to identify the existence of the protection of taxpayers' ability to pay in cross-border situations in the field of direct taxation at an EU law level.

This formulation of case law on the protection of taxpayers' ability to pay, arising from situations where discrimination or a restriction is found regarding the consideration of expenses related to economic activity and personal and family circumstances, could also apply to cases of international legal double taxation essentially, because international juridical double taxation may imply taxing an 'artificial economic strength' that does not represent those taxpayers' overall ability to pay, resulting in a tax disadvantage unilaterally created by one Member State with respect to taxpayers in a cross-border situation when compared to taxpayers in a purely domestic situation.

Since the Schumaker decision, CJEU's case law has been extending the scope of the comparability test, as well as the criteria that allow for the inclusion of a tax measure within the scope of the exercise of taxing powers and not within the definition of tax jurisdiction, as demonstrated throughout the book. These considerations represent a turning point in the recognition of the role that the ability-to-pay principle can play in the determination of restrictive or discriminatory tax disadvantages and allow its consideration in the field of international juridical double taxation. A certainly brilliant and innovative contribution, even though, as already mentioned, it has its challenges.

By way of final reflection, it only remains for me to add that inserting the perspective of ability-to-pay in the taxation of taxpayers in a cross-border situation within the EU is one of those late fruits of the European project that represents a giant leap in the evolution of Tax Law and whose careful consideration is worth every effort. Delving into this field implies taking on a considerable challenge, which, in any case, is deserving of praise. If, in addition, the study carried out involves rigorously systematising the case law that adopts this perspective, constructing instrumental categories and critically reviewing their content in order to end up with a possible reformulation of the serious and growing problem of international juridical double taxation, as this work does, and all this is done with a doctrinal and bibliographical mastery and an extraordinary capacity for synthesis, the praise must turn into thankfulness.

A thankfulness that is joined by best wishes for the author's brilliant future academic and professional career.

In Barcelona, 6 October 2023
Antonia Agulló Agüero
Full Professor of Financial and Tax Law,
Pompeu Fabra University, Barcelona

Introduction

International juridical double taxation has been a concern since the beginning of the last century. The reason is evident: it represents an additional burden to cross-border activities. As affirmed in the first paragraph of the introduction to the OECD Model Tax Convention on Income and on Capital (hereinafter 'OECD MC'), 'its harmful effects on the exchange of goods and services and movements of capital, technology and persons are so well known that it is scarcely necessary to stress the importance of removing the obstacles that double taxation presents to the development of economic relations between countries'.[1]

If the phenomenon of international juridical double taxation is disquieting regarding international trade, it brings an even more profound concern regarding the EU because the EU integration project relies on constructing the internal market.[2] The EU internal market should comprise an area without internal frontiers where the free movement of goods, persons, services and capital is ensured.[3]

In this regard, it has been asked whether there is 'any better method of restricting the freedom of movement than legal double taxation'.[4] After all, 'the very existence of double juridical taxation contradicts the essence of the European Union'[5] since, as clearly stated by Advocate General (AG) Ruiz-Jarabo Colomer, 'the fact that a taxable event might be taxed twice is the most serious obstacle there can be to people and their capital crossing internal borders'.[6]

1. OECD Model Tax Convention on Income and on Capital: Condensed Version (OECD Publishing 2017), Introduction, para. 1.
2. Article 3(3) Treaty on European Union (TEU).
3. Article 26(2) Treaty on the Functioning of the European Union (TFEU).
4. M. Wathelet, *The Sovereignty of the Member States and the European Court of Justice: New Trends or Confirmation?*, in *A Vision of Taxes Within and Outside European Borders* (L. Hinnekens & P. Hinnekens eds, Kluwer Law International 2008), 916.
5. D. Gutmann, *How to Avoid Double Taxation in the European Union?*, in *Allocating Taxing Powers Within the European Union* (I. Richelle et al. eds, Springer 2013), 67.
6. Opinion of AG Ruiz-Jarabo Colomer in Case C-376/03 (*D.*), para. 85. Moreover, according to the European Commission, 'double taxation in a cross-border context as a result of inconsistent interaction of different domestic tax systems, is a major impediment and a real challenge for the

The issue of international juridical double taxation within the EU is far from being a novelty. Indeed, 'the question whether unresolved double taxation constitutes a violation of the fundamental freedoms is nearly as old as the EC Treaty itself'.[7]

The compatibility with the EU law of international juridical double taxation has been intensely examined and discussed in the academic literature for many years, and the Court of Justice of the European Union ('CJEU' or 'the Court')[8] has already ruled on it.

According to the CJEU case law, the disadvantages that could arise from the parallel exercise of tax competences by different Member States – to the extent that such an exercise is not discriminatory – do not constitute a prohibited obstacle to free movement under the EU law.[9] Therefore, despite being a hindrance to free movement, international juridical double taxation is not, per se, considered incompatible with EU law.

Nevertheless, whether international juridical double taxation leads to unequal tax treatment deriving from disregarding taxpayers' overall ability to pay has not been pondered. Most Member States build their tax systems around the ability-to-pay principle, the taxpayers' economic strength being the primary ground to ascertain each taxpayer's fair amount of taxes due. International juridical double taxation means taxpayers must bear the tax burden on the same taxable event in different States. That double tax burden reduces the taxpayers' economic strength, but the loss of ability to pay is not considered in any of those States.

Ultimately, this research aims to address international juridical double taxation from an ability-to-pay perspective in the EU context. From this perspective, the issue is no longer whether international juridical double taxation is compatible with EU law rather than whether disregarding taxpayers' overall ability in cross-border situations complies with EU law.

For such a purpose, the present research is organised into seven chapters.

In Chapter 1, international juridical double taxation is explained: its definition, causes, cases and the foundations for its elimination.

Chapter 2 addresses the legal means and methods designed to eliminate international juridical double taxation. Emphasis is put on the legal instruments existing in the EU.

In Chapter 3, the EU general tax law framework is analysed, highlighting how EU law limits the exercise of Member States' taxing powers.

---

internal market' – *see* Communication from the Commission to the European Parliament, the Council and the European Economic and Social Committee, *Double Taxation in the Single Market*, COM(2011)712 final, p. 3.

7. G. Kofler, *Double Taxation and European Union Law: Analysis of the Jurisprudence*, in *Double Taxation Within the European Union* (A. Rust ed., Kluwer Law International 2011), 104.
8. To designate the Court of Justice of the European Union or its predecessor the European Court of Justice, the abbreviations 'CJEU' or 'the Court' will be used indistinctly.
9. *See, e.g.*, CJEU, Case C-513/04 (*Kerckhaert & Morres*), para. 20; Case C-298/05 (*Columbus Container Services*), para. 43; Case C-194/06 (*Orange European Smallcap Fund*), para. 37; Case C-67/08 (*Block*), para. 28; Case C-128/08 (*Damseaux*), para. 27; Case C-540/11 (*Levy and Sebbag*), para. 18.

Chapter 4 approaches the relevance of individuals' ability to pay in light of EU law.

In Chapter 5, the CJEU's case law on cases in which international juridical double taxation is not eliminated is examined together with the academic literature in this regard.

In Chapter 6, the CJEU's case law on cases in which taxpayers' ability to pay was undermined in the process of eliminating international juridical double taxation is addressed, highlighting the forbidden tax obstacles to free movement created by the Member States.

In Chapter 7, a final assessment is conducted to examine whether there is a contradiction in the CJEU's case law and whether international juridical double taxation may be perceived from an ability-to-pay perspective in light of EU law.

Conclusions are presented at the end.

From the outline drawn, the limitations of this research are apparent: it only deals with international juridical double taxation suffered by individuals in the EU context without considering legal persons.

Such restraint of analysis is explained, on the one hand, by the fact that the ability-to-pay principle has its most remarkable expression regarding individuals; consequently, the validity of arguments presented in this research is more suitable regarding natural persons. On the other hand, international juridical double taxation suffered by legal persons is more in the line of sight of the EU legislator, as demonstrated by the few EU Directives that aim to avoid double taxation of undertakings[10] and the Commission's proposals for a Council Directive on Business in Europe: Framework for Income Taxation (BEFIT),[11] for a Council Directive on transfer pricing,[12] and for a Council Directive establishing a Head Office Tax system for micro, small and medium-sized enterprises.[13]

Falling outside the scope of this research are also the problems related to international economic double taxation and domestic double taxation. Hence, any reference made to 'double taxation' should be deemed as concerning 'international juridical double taxation' related to individual taxpayers.

10. Council Directive 2011/96/EU of 30 November 2011 on the common system of taxation applicable in the case of parent companies and subsidiaries of different Member States (hereinafter 'Parent-Subsidiary Directive'), the Council Directive 2003/49/EC of 3 June 2003 on a common system of taxation applicable to interest and royalty payments made between associated companies of different Member States (hereinafter 'Interest and Royalty Directive'), and the Council Directive 2009/133/EC of 19 October 2009 on the common system of taxation applicable to mergers, divisions, partial divisions, transfers of assets and exchanges of shares concerning companies of different Member States and to the transfer of the registered office of an SE or SCE between Member States (hereinafter 'Merger Directive').
11. European Commission, *Proposal for a Council Directive on Business in Europe: Framework for Income Taxation (BEFIT)*, COM(2023) 532 final.
12. European Commission, *Proposal for a Council Directive on transfer pricing*, COM(2023) 529 final.
13. European Commission, *Proposal for a Council Directive establishing a Head Office Tax system for micro, small and medium sized enterprises, and amending Directive 2011/16/EU*, COM(2023) 528 final.

CHAPTER 1

International Juridical Double Taxation

– Analysis of the concept of international juridical double taxation under the OECD MC and the Council Directive (EU) 2017/1852 of 10 October 2017 on tax dispute resolution mechanisms in the EU.

– Examination of the causes leading to international juridical double taxation and the cases where it occurs.

– Reflection on the grounds for eliminating international juridical double taxation. The EU as being a breeding ground for exploring international juridical double taxation as entailing a problem regarding the exercise of taxing powers and for pondering the taxpayers' overall ability to pay as a ground for requiring its elimination.

1.1 APPROACHING THE CONCEPT OF INTERNATIONAL JURIDICAL DOUBLE TAXATION

1.1.1 The Traditional Notion

Double taxation may be seen as a broad phenomenon covering a multiplicity of different events. In broad terms, and as stated by Seligman, it is the 'taxation of the same person or the same thing twice over'.[14]

In this broad definition, the emphasis is on the repetition of taxation over the same event. It encompasses all sorts of duplicated taxation, even if it regards different kinds of taxes or taxes owed to different authorities of the same State or of different States.

However, not all kinds of double taxation, understood broadly, raise questions demanding an in-depth reflection, as it is widely accepted. For instance, taxpayers bear a combination of taxes on income, property and wealth consumed, yet this is not

14. E. Seligman, *Essays in Taxation* (The Macmillan Company 1921), 95.

problematic or wrong. As Seligman puts it, 'it is double taxation, but it is not unjust double taxation'.[15]

If different taxes have different objects, the imposition triggered attains distinct manifestations of the taxpayers' economic strength.[16] Griziotti calls this sort of duplicate taxation 'multiple taxation'.[17]

The kind of double taxation addressed in this research derives from the juxtaposition of autonomous direct tax systems, which is known as juridical double taxation.[18]

It may occur within the same State due to the competing taxing powers of different authorities, causing internal or domestic juridical double taxation. It may also occur between different States, constituting a case of international juridical double taxation, which is the object of study of this research.

International juridical double taxation is explained generically as a manifestation of a conflict of laws[19] or, as some authors consider more accurate, a concurrence of rules.[20]

Two or more States, when exercising their taxing powers within their own jurisdiction, may subject the same taxpayer to tax regarding the same taxable event without interfering with the taxing powers of the other States. This occurs because the States' tax systems are entirely independent, and each State ignores the other's tax system.[21] This way, the rules of each tax system at stake are equally applied without being alternatives or subsidiaries of each other.[22]

The juxtaposition of tax jurisdictions that ignore one another may lead to positive or negative conflicts. International juridical double taxation represents a manifestation

15. *Ibid.*, at 98.
16. The perception of the accumulation of different taxes as double taxation implies a particular understanding of the ability-to-pay principle, which ideally could only be respected through the establishment of a single tax. For Kaldor, this single tax would be an expenditure tax – *see* N. Kaldor, *An Expenditure Tax* (Allen & Unwin 1955); for Tipke, the single tax would be on income. For the author, taxes on wealth should not exist since they are ultimately supported by income – *see* K. Tipke, *Die Steurrechtsordnung* II (Verlag Dr. Otto Schmidt 1993), 778, cited by S. Vasques, *Capacidade Contributiva, Rendimento e Património*, 23 Fiscalidade 15 (2005), 38-39. Although the tax object is deemed as a manifestation of ability to pay, the ability-to-pay principle must not be identified with the object of taxation. Outlining the autonomy between the definition of income and the concept of ability to pay, *see* A. Agulló Agüero, *Estructura de la imposición sobre la renta y el principio de capacidad contributiva*, 37 REDF 23 (1983).
17. Cf. B. Griziotti, *L'imposition fiscale des étrangers*, 13 Recueil des Cours 1 (1926), 43; B. Griziotti, *Principios de política, derecho y ciencia de la hacienda* (E. Mata trans., Editorial Reus 2d ed. 1958), 307.
18. Alongside juridical double taxation, economic double taxation is often identified as a type of double taxation that raises numerous issues. Notwithstanding, the particular problems concerning this sort of double taxation fall outside the scope of this research.
19. J. P. Niboyet, *Les doubles impositions au point de vue juridique*, 31 Recueil des Cours 5 (1930), 12; B. Griziotti (E. Mata trans., Editorial Reus 2d ed. 1958), 301-302. *See also* A. Borras, *La doble imposición: problemas jurídico-internacionales* (Instituto de Estudios Fiscales 1974), 21.
20. M. Udina, *Il diritto internazionale tributario* (CEDAM 1949), 251-252. *See also* M. Pires, *International Juridical Double Taxation of Income* (Kluwer Law and Taxation Publishers 1989), 35-36; A. Xavier, *Direito tributário internacional* (Almedina 2d ed. 2011), 31.
21. J. P. Niboyet, 31 Recueil des Cours 5 (1930), 12.
22. M. Pires (Kluwer Law and Taxation Publishers 1989), 36.

of positive conflict, while international juridical double non-taxation manifests a negative conflict, remaining certain taxable events untaxed by any State.[23]

The OECD MC defines international juridical double taxation as 'the imposition of comparable taxes in two (or more) States on the same taxpayer in respect of the same subject matter and for identical periods'.[24]

As presented today, this definition gathers the common points developed by the doctrinal studies approaching the issue of international juridical double taxation over the years.[25]

This definition is usually explained as demanding the overall identity of the different States' tax systems juxtaposed. Such an overall identity is found in four elements: *(i)* the identity of the taxable event; *(ii)* the identity of the taxable person; *(iii)* the identity of the tax; and *(iv)* the identity of the period of taxation.

The analysis and discussion of the definition of international juridical double taxation and its elements, always subject to much controversy, was thoroughly conducted by scholars.[26] Therefore, these definition elements will subsequently be only briefly enunciated without claiming to be exhaustive.

Identity of the taxable event: International juridical double taxation occurs when a given fact or event triggers taxes in two different States because it fulfils a provision enacted by the law of each of those States. That fact or event is deemed a taxable event in both those States.

23. J. P. Niboyet, 31 Recueil des Cours 5 (1930), 13-14; A. Borras (Instituto de Estudios Fiscales 1974), 21-22. Regarding international double non-taxation, *see* specifically C. Marchgraber, *Double (Non-)Taxation and EU Law* (Kluwer Law International 2018), and A. Van de Vijver, *International Double (Non)taxation: Comparative Guidance from European Legal Principles*, 24(5) EC Tax Rev. 240 (2015) DOI: 10.54648/ecta2015025.
24. OECD MC, Introduction, para. 1.
25. For an overview of the various definitions of international juridical double taxation put forward by the doctrine, *see* A. Borras (Instituto de Estudios Fiscales 1974), 27-30, who highlights that most of them starts from the almost classic definition presented by Dorn. Indeed, the definition provided by the OECD MC embodies Dorn's, moving away from the definition provided in the London and Mexico Model Tax Conventions Commentary and Text approved by the Fiscal Committee of the League of Nations in 1946. According to Dorn, *'la doppia (multipla) imposizione si verifica, allorchè più titolari di sovranità tributaria indipendenti (in ispecie più Stati indipendenti) sottopongono lo stesso contribuente per lo stesso oggetto contemporaneamente ad un'imposta della stessa specie'* – H. Dorn, *Diritto finanziario e questioni fondamentali sulle doppie imposizioni*, 2(1) Rivista di Diritto Finanziario e Scienza delle Finanze 115 (1938), 131.
26. P. Guggenheim, *L'imposition des successions en droit international et le problème de la double imposition* (Mémoires publiés par la Faculté de droit de Genève 1928), 18-37; A. Spitaler, *Das Doppelbesteuerungsproblem bei den direkten Steuern* (Reichenberg 1936), 105 et seq.; H. Dorn, 2(1) Rivista di Diritto Finanziario e Scienza delle Finanze 115 (1938), 134-142; M. Udina (CEDAM 1949), 254-257; A. A. Knechtle, *Basic Problems in International Fiscal Law* (Kluwer 1979), 29-30. Besides these four elements, Knechtle emphasises a fifth: '(T)he imposition of a tax by different original, i.e., sovereign tax jurisdiction (taxing powers) whose holders are either (nation-) States or member of different States (i.e., sovereign provincial States of different countries).' This element is seen by many authors as a precondition, being inherent to the juxtaposition of the tax systems of several States. *See* O. Bühler, *Principios de Derecho internacional tributario* (F. Cervera Torrejón trans., Editorial de Derecho Financiero 1965), 223-226. For a detailed study of these elements and the diverse positions in this regard, *see* PIRES, Manuel (1989). *See also* A. Xavier (Almedina 2d ed. 2011), 31-49.

Identity of the taxable person: The person performing said taxable event must also be the same. Such a person is subject to taxation under those provisions in two different States.

It may be the case that the identity of the taxable person is not met when the other identities are. In such circumstances, two different taxpayers are taxable regarding the same income or capital. It would configure a case of international economic double taxation rather than international juridical double taxation.

Identity of the tax: The taxes levied on the same taxable event upon the same taxable person by each State must be similar, that is to say, comparable. They must have an equivalent nature or scope despite not having the same features – e.g., the same formula for assessing the tax base or the same tax rates. Otherwise, if taxes are not comparable, that is a case of multiple taxation rather than double taxation, as already observed.

Identity of the period of taxation: The similar taxes levied on the same taxable event upon the same taxable person by each State must regard the same period of taxation. That is to say, the prior three *identities* must be reunited at the same relevant moment.

Some authors consider this definition component to play a secondary role, and others do not even mention it.[27] However, following Udina, it may be argued that this requirement has an ancillary function of clearly differentiating between taxable events within periodic taxes.[28]

In short, what has been traditionally understood as international juridical double taxation is the imposition of comparable taxes by different States on the same taxpayer regarding the same taxable event and tax period.

1.1.2 The Notion Provided by the Directive on Tax Dispute Resolution Mechanisms

Recently, EU law defined double taxation in the Council Directive (EU) 2017/1852 of 10 October 2017 on tax dispute resolution mechanisms in the EU (hereinafter 'Directive on tax dispute resolution mechanisms').

Under Article 2(1)(c) of this Directive, double taxation is 'the imposition by two or more Member States of taxes covered by an agreement or convention referred to in Article 1 in respect of the same taxable income or capital when it gives rise to either: *(i)* an additional tax charge; *(ii)* an increase in tax liabilities; or *(iii)* the cancellation or reduction of losses that could be used to offset taxable profits'.

As can be observed, some differences exist between the traditional notion of international juridical double taxation and the Directive one.

27. *See* further, M. Pires (Kluwer Law and Taxation Publishers 1989), 19.
28. M. Udina (CEDAM 1949), 256. In contrast, Ismer and Ruß argue that the concept of double taxation should be extended to cover intertemporal double taxation, i.e., the imposition of comparable taxes at different times on the same taxable object or closely connected objects. Cf. R. Ismer & J. Ruß, *What Is International Double Taxation?*, 48(6/7) Intertax 555 (2020), 560-561 DOI: 10.54648/taxi2020052.

First, and more obviously, the notion of double taxation provided by the Directive only refers to the phenomenon taking place between the Member States, not including any other State, which is a logical consequence of its scope of application.

Second, the concept of double taxation foreseen in the Directive does not refer to the identity of the taxable person, not requiring the same person to be subject to comparable taxes levied by two or more Member States. That is to say that the concept of double taxation foreseen in the Directive covers juridical double taxation and economic double taxation.

Third, the definition provided by the Directive does not refer to the identity of the period of taxation. However, if the period of taxation is understood as having an ancillary function of clearly differentiating between taxable objects, the lack of reference to it does not have further consequences.

Last but not least, the definition of double taxation established by the Directive includes the consequences of double taxation as an element of the concept. Accordingly, double taxation must give rise to 'either: *(i)* an additional tax charge; *(ii)* an increase in tax liabilities; or *(iii)* the cancellation or reduction of losses that could be used to offset taxable profits'.[29]

The reference to these consequences denotes that, under EU law, stress is on the extra tax burden derived from having comparable taxes levied by two or more Member States regarding the same taxable income. Such an approach is not a complete novelty, as it can also be found in the old Mexico and London Model Tax Conventions, Commentary and Text, approved by the Fiscal Committee of the League of Nations in 1946.[30]

In these Model Tax Conventions, it was explained that 'international double or multiple taxation arises when the taxes of two or more countries overlap in such a manner that persons liable to tax in more than one country bear a higher tax burden than if they were subject to one tax jurisdiction only. The additional burden so incurred must, of course, be due not merely to differences in tax rates for the countries concerned but to the fact that two or more jurisdictions concurrently impose taxes having the same bases and incidence without regard to the claims of the other tax jurisdictions'.[31]

This approach to the notion of double taxation thus includes a quantitative element related to the tax burden derived from the overlap of taxing jurisdictions. As noted by Ismer and Ruß, 'parallel taxation is a necessary but not sufficient condition for double taxation' as envisaged by the Directive on tax dispute resolution mechanisms.[32] In that sense, the relevant double taxation covers only situations in which the tax burden is increased without this increase resulting from differences in tax rates.[33]

Therefore, due to the quantitative element, the notion of double taxation does not cover certain situations. It is the case when double taxation initially existed but was

29. *See* Art. 2(c) of the Directive on tax dispute resolution mechanisms.
30. League of Nations Fiscal Committee, London and Mexico model tax conventions: commentary and text: official no. C.88.M.88.1946.II.A. (1946).
31. *Ibid.*, p. 7.
32. R. Ismer & J. Ruß, 48(6/7) Intertax 555 (2020), 557-558.
33. M. Pires (Kluwer Law and Taxation Publishers 1989), 13.

then eliminated by the action of one of the States. It is also the case when double taxation was potentially existent but did not occur in practice due to a qualification conflict or because a State applied a zero rate to the taxable event, as exemplified by Debelva and Luts.[34]

In short, the notion of double taxation introduced by the Directive seems to be, on the one hand, broader than the traditional notion, as it covers both juridical and economic double taxation, and, on the other hand, narrower because it addresses only cases in which the Member States have failed to avoid double taxation through bilateral or multilateral agreements. The reason for this difference is addressed in the next section.

1.1.3 The Relevant Notion for This Research Purpose

As observed, the traditional notion of international juridical double taxation is not entirely coincident with the notion provided by the Directive on tax dispute resolution mechanisms. Notwithstanding, the main difference between the two notions lies in the fact that they do not describe the same issue.

The traditional notion seeks to describe the problem resulting from the juxtaposition of tax jurisdictions: the imposition of comparable taxes by different States on the same taxpayer regarding the same taxable event and tax period. The statement of this problem paved the way for the development of substantive measures to eliminate juridical double taxation. Indeed, the OECD MC, which aims to establish mechanisms for avoiding international juridical double taxation between States, adopts the traditional notion of juridical double taxation.

Due to its purpose, the traditional notion formulates the problem of double taxation on its original terms, that is to say, based necessarily on the assumption that double taxation has not been previously eliminated. Hence, this notion is not concerned with ascertaining whether substantive measures are in place to avoid such double taxation.

Conversely, the notion of double taxation foreseen in the Directive on tax dispute resolution mechanisms seeks to describe a second-layer problem resulting from the juxtaposition of tax jurisdictions: the occasional failure of bilateral or multilateral substantive measures adopted within the EU to avoid the imposition of comparable taxes by different Member States on the same taxable object.

The premise of this notion is the pre-existence of bilateral or multilateral substantive measures to eliminate double taxation and their failure to accomplish it. The cases of double taxation covered by the Directive's scope are those of unrelieved double taxation, which are manifested in '*(i)* an additional tax charge; *(ii)* an increase in tax liabilities; or *(iii)* the cancellation or reduction of losses that could be used to offset taxable profits'.[35]

34. F. Debelva & J. Luts, *The European Commission's Proposal for Double Taxation Dispute Resolution: Turning the Tide?*, 71 Bull. Int'l Tax'n 5 (2017), para. 3.2.4.2.
35. Article 2(1)(c) of the Council Directive (EU) 2017/1852 of 10 October 2017.

The Directive's aim is, thus, to provide, through the adoption of procedural measures, a solution for those cases of unrelieved double taxation.

Therefore, the traditional notion of double taxation, which is foreseen in the OECD MC, and the notion provided in the Directive on tax dispute resolution mechanisms envisage and define double taxation according to the specific problem of tax jurisdictions juxtaposition each one tries to resolve.

The relevant notion of double taxation for the present research purposes must also be shaped following the problem it seeks to resolve. The problem identified is the effective imposition within the EU of comparable taxes by different Member States on the same individual regarding the same taxable object and tax period without any relief being provided.

The premise of this notion is the occasional failure or non-existence of substantive and procedural measures in force within the European context to avoid juridical double taxation of individuals. Our concern is, thus, the cases where, within the EU context, there are no substantive measures in place, or where they exist, those measures have failed their purpose, and the procedural measures (eventually) applicable were ineffective.

As a preliminary note for understanding this premise, the causes and cases of international juridical double taxation must be analysed, followed by examining the grounds for its elimination.

1.2 CAUSES AND CASES OF INTERNATIONAL JURIDICAL DOUBLE TAXATION

1.2.1 Cause: The Juxtaposition of Tax Jurisdictions

Inherent to State sovereignty is the power to tax.

Nowadays, the States' power to tax is taken for granted because, after all, 'taxes are what we pay for civilized society'[36] or 'the dues we must pay for the privileges of membership in an organized society'.[37]

However, justifying taxation is not straightforward, and several theories exist in this regard. Such theories follow the evolution of the concepts of state and sovereignty.[38] In this regard, two leading theories are worth highlighting: the benefit theory and the sacrifice theory.

In the benefit theory, the older one, taxes were conceived as a consideration for the benefits provided by the State to people. In turn, the sacrifice theory results from a change in the conception of the State. The State is no longer seen as an autonomous entity that provides some services to people but as a superior unity of which all citizens

36. As stated by the US Supreme Court Judge Oliver Wendell Holmes in *Compañía General de Tabacos de Filipinas v. Collector of Internal Revenue.*
37. As stated by Franklin D. Roosevelt.
38. *See* K. Vogel, *The Justification for Taxation: A Forgotten Question*, 33 Am. J. Juris. 19 (1988), 33 DOI: 10.1093/ajj/33.1.19.

form part. Therefore, taxes could not be conceived as consideration for the services individually received by people but as a contribution as a whole to all State services. Thus, taxes would demand equal sacrifice from all citizens, regardless of the public services each receives.[39]

As noted by Vogel, it would be more accurate to speak of two groups of theories since they cover various conceptions.[40] Authors, such as Martha, Debelva and Albrecht, refer to other major theories to justify taxation: the realistic theory, the ethical or retributive theory, the contractual theory, and the theory of sovereignty.[41] However, these theories lead back somehow to the benefit theory and the sacrifice theory or justify taxation simply on the State's power (or sovereignty).

Furthermore, the benefit theory and the sacrifice theory are sometimes discussed not as the basis for justifying taxation in itself – in the abstract – but rather for justifying concrete taxes and as standards for distributing the tax burden among taxpayers. In other words, the discussion is not centred on the *why* but on *how* taxes are applied.[42]

In any case, taxation is the basic formula for financing the own existence of the State as we know it today, and the power to impose taxes depends inevitably on the State's tax jurisdiction.[43]

39. For an overview of the evolution of these theories, as well as their precedents, *see* K. Vogel, 33 Am. J. Juris. 19 (1988) DOI: 10.1111/raju.1988.1.issue-2; K. Vogel, *Observaciones acerca de la teoría de la justificación del impuesto*, 100 Hacienda Pública Española 149 (1986); M. Steward, *The Tax State, Benefit and Legitimacy*, in *Studies in the History of Tax Law* (P. Harris & D. Cogan eds, Hart Publishing 2015); S. Vasques, *O Princípio da Equivalência como Critério de Igualdade Tributária* (Almedina 2008), 251-305.
40. K. Vogel, 33 Am. J. Juris. 19 (1988), 24.
41. *See* R. Martha, *The Jurisdiction to Tax in International Law: Theory and Practice of Legislative Fiscal Jurisdiction* (Kluwer Law and Taxation 1989), 18-23; F. Debelva, *International Double Taxation and the Right to Property: A Comparative, International and European Law Analysis* (IBFD 2019), 43-52. Mentioning only the ethical, contractual, and sovereignty theories, *see* A. R. Albrecht, *The Taxation of Aliens under International Law*, 29 Brit. Y.B. Int'l L. 145 (1952),145-149.
42. *See, e.g.*, R. Musgrave & P. Musgrave, *Public Finance in Theory and Practice* (McGraw-Hill 1989), 219-233. In this regard, the benefit theory is usually linked to the principle of equivalence, and the sacrifice theory is usually linked to the ability-to-pay principle. However, as Neumark noted, there may be certain reluctance in basing the ability to pay as a criterion to distribute the tax burden among taxpayers on the theory of sacrifice. The concept of sacrifice, due to its dogmatic matter, is not suitable to typify the nature of the tax obligations of our days – cf. F. Neumark, *Principios de la imposición* (L. Gutiérrez Andrés trans., Instituto de Estudios Fiscales 2d ed. 1994), 138. On the ability-to-pay principle, *see infra* section 4.1.
43. Jurisdiction '*denominates primarily, but not exclusively, the lawful power to make and enforce rules*' – B. Oxman, *Jurisdiction of States*, in *Max Planck Encyclopedia of Public International Law* (R. Wolfrum ed., Oxford University Press 2012). For an overview on tax jurisdiction, *see*: A. H. Qureshi & A. Kumar, *The Public International Law of Taxation: Text, Cases and Materials* (Kluwer Law International 2d ed. 2019); S. Gadžo, *Nexus Requirements for Taxation of Non-residents' Business Income: A Normative Evaluation in the Context of the Global Economy* (IBFD 2018); S. Gadžo, *The Principle of 'Nexus' or 'Genuine Link' as a Keystone of International Income Tax Law: A Reappraisal*, 46(3) Intertax 194 (2018) DOI: 10.54648/taxi2018022; W. Schön, *Persons and Territories: On the International Allocation of Taxing Rights*, 6 Brit. Tax Rev. 554 (2010); R. Avi-Yonah, *International Tax as International Law*, 57(4) Tax L. Rev. 483 (2004) DOI: 10.2139/ssrn.516382; R. Martha (Kluwer Law and Taxation 1989); J. H. Beale, *Jurisdiction to Tax*, 32(6) Harv. L. Rev. 587 (1919).

The concept of tax jurisdiction can be synthetically explained as the 'State's competence to tax persons, property and transactions, or events'[44] or as the 'law-making and law-enforcing powers of the state in the specific area of taxation'.[45]

As Bühler observed, ascertaining States' tax jurisdiction implies answering a fundamental question: *to what extent* may a State exercise its taxing power?[46] Unfortunately, there is no smooth answer since States' tax jurisdiction limits are not clearly defined under international law.

Two schools of thought have been identified in the doctrine.[47] On the one hand, it has been argued that international law does not limit States' tax jurisdiction, and consequently, the only existent limitations are of practical order, such as enforcement.[48]

On the other hand, it has been advocated that international law constrains the States' tax jurisdiction by imposing a 'reasonable connection' between the State and the taxable event.[49]

As Guggenheim emphasises, the fact that the States never tax beyond certain limits – i.e., in the absence of a genuine connection – is a sign that a mandatory requirement under international law is at stake rather than a self-limitation of States.[50] It seems intuitive that some connection between the State and the person performing the taxable event must exist for that State to exercise its taxing powers over that person.

For a long time, the jurisdictional connection between a State and a person was found in political allegiance. Citizens would be held responsible for their country, and citizenship would encompass rights and duties such as paying taxes. However,

44. A. H. Qureshi & A. Kumar (Kluwer Law International 2d ed. 2019), 33.
45. S. Gadžo (IBFD 2018), 38; S. Gadžo, 46(3) Intertax 194 (2018), 198.
46. O. Bühler, *Les accords internationaux concernant la double imposition et l'évasion fiscale*, 55 Recueil des Cours 433 (1936), 458: '*Existe-i-il des normes, de droit international commun qui limitent les pouvoirs nationaux d'imposer?*'; or in a more practical way, R. Avi-Yonah, 57(4) Tax L. Rev. 483 (2004), 498: 'Can a country simply decide to tax non-residents that have no connection to it on foreign source income?'.
47. For an overview on the different doctrinal positions, *see* A. H. Qureshi & A. Kumar (Kluwer Law International 2d ed. 2019), 35-93; S. Gadžo (IBFD 2018), 39-42.
48. M. Norr, *Jurisdiction to Tax and International Income*, 17(3) Tax L. Rev. 431 (1962), 431; A. A. Knechtle (Kluwer 1979), 37; A. Q. Qureshi, *The Freedom of a State to Legislate in Fiscal Matters under General International Law*, 41 Bull. for Int'l Fiscal Documentation 14 (1987), 21; J. Monsenego, *Taxation of Foreign Business Income Within the European Internal Market* (IBFD 2012), 60. *See* further O. Bühler, 55 Recueil des Cours 433 (1936), 458-459, and H. W. Kruse, *Derecho tributario: parte general* (P. Yebra Martul-Ortega & M. Izquierdo Macías-Picavea trans., Edersa 3d ed. 1978), 115.
49. A. R. Albrecht, 29 Brit. Y.B. Int'l L. 145 (1952), 153; F. A. Mann, *The Doctrine of Jurisdiction in International Law*, 111 Recueil des Cours 1 (1964), 110-111; M. Akehurst, *Jurisdiction in International Law*, 46 Brit. Y.B. Int'l L.145 (1972-1973), 179-180; F. A. Mann, *The Doctrine of International Jurisdiction Revisited after Twenty Years*, 186 Recueil des Cours 9 (1984), 29-31; R. Martha (Kluwer Law and Taxation 1989), 43; W. Schön, 6 Brit. Tax Rev. 554 (2010), 554; A. Rust, *Double Taxation*, in *Double Taxation Within the European Union* (A. Rust ed., Kluwer Law International 2011), 3; M. Lang, *Introduction to the Law of Double Taxation Conventions* (Joint publication of IBFD & Linde 2013), 23; E. Reimer & A. Rust eds, *Klaus Vogel on Double Taxation Conventions* (Kluwer Law International 4th ed. 2015), 'Introduction', m.no. 8; S. Gadžo (IBFD 2018), 39; P. Hongler, *Justice in International Tax Law: A Normative Review of the International Tax Regime* (IBFD 2019), 75-80.
50. P. Guggenheim (Mémoires publiés par la Faculté de droit de Genève 1928), 10.

political allegiance was progressively abandoned since national non-residents may not have political ties with the country of their citizenship, and foreigners may actively participate in a State's economic and social life other than that of their nationality.[51]

This way, economic allegiance is more suitable to ascertain tax jurisdiction, easing the task of justifying aliens' taxation.[52] Accordingly, all who have a relevant economic interest in a State – deriving income from that State or consuming and saving in that State – are under its jurisdiction.[53]

Nevertheless, the economic and social bond with a State may vary in intensity. Personal and territorial attachment are expressions of the range of such intensity.

In personal attachment, a relationship between the State and the person is established. The link is found in nationality and residence.

As observed, *nationality* (citizenship), as the manifestation of political allegiance, was a classic connection factor for ascertaining jurisdiction. Nowadays, a mere political attachment may not justify taxation. Globalisation eases migration, increasing the number of people residing and working in a country other than the one of their nationality.[54] In such a case, the relationship between a State and its nationals is weak. Furthermore, as Avi-Yonah observes, it would be enough to abandon a nationality in exchange for another to counter this ground for taxation.[55]

Residence followed *nationality* as a connection factor in order to broaden personal attachment and give it a substantial reality. This substantial reality[56] is embodied by the physical presence within the State's territory for a minimum number of days, by the location of the taxpayers' permanent home, the centre of their vital interests or habitual abode.[57] Choosing residence as a connecting factor for taxation is essential to prevent discrimination between resident nationals and non-nationals, as

51. League of Nations, Report on Double taxation presented to the Financial Committee by Professors Bruins, Einaudi, Seligman and Sir Josiah Stamp (1923), 19.
52. *See* M. E. Lehr, *Quelques mots sur les doubles impositions en droit international*, 31 Revue de Droit International et de Législation Comparée 554 (1899); B. Griziotti, 13 Recueil des Cours 1 (1926), passim; E. Seligman, *La double imposition et la coopération fiscale internationale*, 20 Recueil des Cours 460 (1927), passim; L. Einaudi, *La coopération internationale en matière fiscale*, 25 Recueil des Cours 1 (1928), 44-58; E. Allix, *La condition des étrangers au point de vue fiscal*, 61 Recueil des Cours 545 (1937).
53. The Report on Double taxation presented to the Financial Committee by Professors Bruins, Einaudi, Seligman and Sir Josiah Stamp identifies four bases for economic allegiance: the origin of wealth; the *situs* of wealth; the place of enforcement of the rights to wealth and the place where wealth is consumed or disposed (place of residence). Source and residence were identified as the most important. *See* League of Nations (1923), pp. 22 et seq.
54. W. Schön, 6 Brit. Tax Rev. 554 (2010), 556.
55. R. Avi-Yonah, 57(4) Tax L. Rev. 483 (2004), 485.
56. In turn, regarding undertakings, both formal and substantial criteria for ascertaining personal attachment are used. A legal person will be deemed as having a personal attachment with a State when it is incorporated under the law of that State (place of incorporation) and/or when its effective management is carried out in that State (place of management).
57. States may adopt different criteria ascertaining residence. The criteria mentioned are some of those enunciated in Art. 4 (a)(b) of the OECD MC as tiebreaker rules. For the analysis of those criteria, *see* K. Dziwiński, *Dual Residence and Treaty Entitlement of Individuals*, in *Tax Treaty Entitlement* (M. Lang et al. eds, IBFD 2019), 149-163.

Bühler and Seligman have already noted.[58] Additionally, it allows avoiding schemes to abandon nationality of a particular State despite residence within that State.[59]

Most countries have adopted residence as the relevant connection factor regarding personal attachment. However, nationality is still used in some countries to ascertain tax jurisdiction, as it happens in the United States, and it has particular relevance regarding diplomats or other persons in government service. Furthermore, other countries use this criterion with an anti-avoidance purpose, treating expatriated citizens as tax residents for a certain period upon emigration.[60] Additionally, nationality may also be used as a tiebreaker rule when a person is considered a resident of two States.[61]

In turn, territorial attachment derives from the existence of a link between one State and the activities performed or carried on within its territory. The State is entitled to tax the income or wealth derived from its own territory as the source State.

In this case, attachment is not found in the person owning the income or wealth but in the economic benefit derived from that State.[62]

The economic benefit derived from a State's territory entitles it to tax non-residents. Indeed, such an economic benefit does not depend on a physical presence therein. The physical presence may or may not exist, as it happens in the case of a temporary residence, not fulfilling the minimum period required for a person to be deemed as a resident of a State.[63]

The idea behind territorial attachment is relatively simple. The challenge is ascertaining where the source of income or wealth is located. It may refer to the place where income is produced or services are performed, where property generating income is located, where the payor of income is established, or where the value is added to a good.[64] The digital transformation of the economy is making this task even more problematic.

Although tax jurisdiction - and consequently the power to tax - depends on connecting factors stemming from personal and territorial attachment, the truth is that the degree of connection required varies significantly from one State to another.[65]

58. O. Bühler (F. Cervera Torrejón trans., Editorial de Derecho Financiero 1965), 216; E. Seligman (The Macmillan Company 1921), 117-118.
59. R. Avi-Yonah, 57(4) Tax L. Rev. 483 (2004), 485-486.
60. *See* further G. Beretta, *Cross-Border Mobility of Individuals and the Lack of Fiscal Policy Coordination among Jurisdictions (Even) after the BEPS Project*, 47(1) Intertax 91 (2019) DOI: 10.54648/taxi2019006.
61. Article 4(2)(c) of the OECD MC.
62. R. Martha (Kluwer Law and Taxation 1989), 54; A. A. Knechtle (Kluwer 1979), 36.
63. R. Martha (Kluwer Law and Taxation 1989), 54.
64. K. Vogel, *Worldwide vs. Source Taxation of Income: A Review and Re-evaluation of Arguments (Part I)*, 8/9 Intertax 216 (1988), 223 et seq. DOI: 10.54648/taxi1988043; M. Pires (Kluwer Law and Taxation Publishers 1989), 121 et seq.; E. Kemmeren, *Source of Income in Globalizing Economies: Overview of the Issues and A Plea for an Origin-Based Approach*, 60(11) Bull. Int'l Tax'n 430 (2006), 432; R. Avi-Yonah, 57(4) Tax L. Rev. 483 (2004), 490-491.
65. *See* J. Monsenego (IBFD 2012), 54-55, who notices that the connecting factors vary greatly between countries, they change from one type of tax to another, they also change over time, and that States may limit their connecting factors voluntarily through agreements between them.

There are no uniform criteria for assessing tax residence and the source of income; the States have the power to define these in their domestic law.

The lack of a homogeneous application of the connecting factors by all States may generate, per se, the juxtaposition of tax jurisdictions.

Additionally, the cases of the juxtaposition of tax jurisdictions are increased by the establishment of tax liability. Tax liability is the total sum of obligations undertaken by a person that results from the (personal or territorial) fiscal relationship with a State.[66]

Primarily, tax liability relies on the existence of tax jurisdiction. Secondly, the extent of tax liability depends on the connecting factor that gives rise to tax jurisdiction. Thus, tax liability varies according to the type of attachment with a State.

Personal attachment generally triggers full tax liability, meaning the State of residence (or nationality, if it is of relevance) has the power to tax its residents' (or nationals') income or wealth irrespectively from where such income or wealth derives. Full tax liability leads to worldwide taxation.[67]

In turn, territorial attachment usually triggers limited tax liability, meaning the State of the source of income or wealth has the power to tax such benefits because they are derived from its territory. Limited tax liability leads to territorial/source taxation.

The overlap of diverse sorts of tax liabilities in different States gives rise to international juridical double taxation.

The combined use of full and limited tax liability is usual in most countries, which could be seen as a rule of customary international law.[68] However, its reasoning is not indisputable[69] and has changed over time.

In the first moment, the theoretical grounds for full tax liability could be found in the services provided by a State to its nationals (when political allegiance is or was of relevance)[70] and to its residents.[71] Such taxpayers should contribute to the costs of society. Then, this theorisation was pragmatically transposed into the very own structure of income taxes, which were designed to be comprehensive taxes on taxpayers' global income.[72]

66. A. A. Knechtle (Kluwer 1979), 35.
67. According to the commentary on Art. 4, para. 3, of the OECD MC, 'Generally the domestic laws of the various States impose a comprehensive liability to tax – "full tax liability" – based on the taxpayers' personal attachment to the State concerned (the "State of residence"). This liability to tax is not imposed only on persons who are "domiciled" in a State in the sense in which "domicile" is usually taken in the legislations (private law). The cases of full liability to tax are extended to comprise also, for instance, persons who stay continually, or maybe only for a certain period, in the territory of the State. Some legislations impose full liability to tax on individuals who perform services on board ships which have their home harbour in the State.'
68. R. Jeffery, *The Impact of State Sovereignty on Global Trade and International Taxation* (Kluwer Law International 1999), 33. *See also* A. R. Albrecht, 29 Brit. Y.B. Int'l L. 145 (1952), 158; M. Kobetsky, *International Taxation of Permanent Establishments: Principles and Policy* (Cambridge University Press 2011), 25.
69. K. Vogel, 8/9 Intertax 216 (1988), 216; W. Schön, 6 Brit. Tax Rev. 554 (2010), 556.
70. Cf. B. Griziotti, 13 Recueil des Cours 1 (1926), 19-20; J. P. Niboyet, 31 Recueil des Cours 5 (1930), 26.
71. *Ibid.*, 34.
72. Cf. O. Bühler (F. Cervera Torrejón trans., Editorial de Derecho Financiero 1965), 220.

Nowadays, worldwide taxation is still justified because it is in the State of residence where taxpayers use most public infrastructures and services (*inter alia*, water services, waste management, health, education, social care, transport) and fully enjoy the State's public functions (*inter alia*, public security, justice, diplomacy). Consequently, it is in their residence State where they must contribute most.[73] However, such an argument may be used inversely to justify source taxation, as Debelva points out.[74] Indeed, in a globalised world, residents of one country may partially centralise their life cross-borders, use public infrastructures and enjoy States' public functions indiscriminately. The EU is an excellent example of these practices, which are increasing with remote work in the digital era.[75]

However, precisely due to globalisation in the digital era and the inherent risk of income not being sourced in any specific jurisdiction, Wattel finds the reason for worldwide taxation on the need to ensure the residual competence to tax a person.[76] For such cases, the State of residence is in a better position because it has easy access to the complete information on the taxpayer and, in return, that State has to ensure that the taxpayer's overall ability to pay is duly taken into account, as noted by Schön.[77]

Source taxation is less questionable than worldwide taxation. Usually, priority is given to source taxation because the income derived has a close connection with a State since it is within its territory that the opportunity for obtaining income and wealth is found. The reason for source taxation is precisely the creation of the conditions for that opportunity.[78]

1.2.2 Cases of International Juridical Double Taxation

From the previous analysis, it is possible to summarise in three case scenarios the situations in which two or more States regard themselves as simultaneously entitled to tax the same taxable event performed by the same taxpayer at a specific moment.[79]

---

73. J. Monsenego (IBFD 2012), 47. *See also* Opinion of AG Geelhoed in Case C-374/04 (*Test Claimants in Class IV of the ACT Group Litigation*), para. 50: '[T]he State of residence of the taxpayer has in principle tax jurisdiction over its total income ('worldwide' taxation). A principal rationale behind this is that the place where the taxpayer uses most facilities (e.g., public services, social security, infrastructure etc.) is his State of residence.' *See* further P. Wattel et al., *Terra/Wattel European Tax Law* I (Kluwer Law International 7th ed. 2018), 612.
74. F. Debelva (IBFD 2019), 93.
75. *See* Joint Research Centre, *Telework in the EU before and after the COVID-19: where we were, where we head to*, European Commission's science and knowledge service – Science for Policy Briefs (2020). Confronted with the new realities of the digital world, States have now started to take action regarding taxation of individuals.
76. P. Wattel et al. (Kluwer Law International 7th ed. 2018), 612.
77. W. Schön, 6 Brit. Tax Rev. 554 (2010), 556-557. In turn, Knechtle argues that worldwide taxation just occurs because a State may bring to bear the whole pressure of its administration on the residents in its territory – A. A. Knechtle (Kluwer 1979), 36.
78. *See* J. P. Niboyet, 31 Recueil des Cours 5 (1930), 26; P. Wattel et al. (Kluwer Law International 7th ed. 2018), 612-613. *See also* Opinion of AG Geelhoed in Case C-374/04 (*Test Claimants in Class IV of the ACT Group Litigation*), para. 50.
79. OECD MC, Commentary to Art. 23A and B, paras 3 and 4. *See*, for example: F. Debelva (IBFD 2019), 100-103; A. H. Qureshi & A. Kumar (Kluwer Law International 2d ed. 2019), 474; A. Rust,

The first case scenario occurs when a State A resident carries out some activity or investment in State B. State A is entitled to subject its residents to full tax liability. Consequently, the taxpayer's worldwide income will be subject to taxation in State A, regardless of its source. Conversely, State B is entitled to subject the non-residents to limited tax liability, that is to say, to tax the income they derive from the activity or investment performed within its territory. The overlap of these tax liabilities leads to international juridical double taxation. Such is a case of *worldwide versus source taxation*.

The second case scenario happens when a person is deemed resident in two different States, and such States tax their residents on their worldwide income. It also occurs when a State taxes based on nationality and its citizens reside in another State that taxes based on residence. Such cases, where a taxpayer is subject to full tax liability in two different States, give rise to international juridical double taxation, configuring a case of *worldwide versus worldwide taxation*.

The third case scenario arises when two States consider that the taxpayer's income is derived from their territory. This situation occurs because the domestic income definition may be very comprehensive and may differ from one State to another. In such cases, limited tax liability in two States also gives rise to international juridical double taxation, constituting a case of *source versus source taxation*.

1.3 GROUNDS FOR THE ELIMINATION OF INTERNATIONAL JURIDICAL DOUBLE TAXATION

Once ascertaining the causes and cases of international juridical double taxation, it is appropriate to explore why the elimination of double taxation is promoted among States.

The fact is that, under international law, international juridical double taxation is not illegal or illegitimate. Consequently, it is not forbidden, and the States have no obligation to avoid or eliminate it.[80] As explained by Vogel and Rust, 'customary international law does not forbid double taxation. Double taxation, resulting from the interaction of the domestic laws of two (or more) States, will be consistent with international law as long as each legislation is consistent with international law'.[81]

Although it is not forbidden under international law, international juridical double taxation is a burden for international operations. As affirmed in the OECD MC, 'Its harmful effects on the exchange of goods and services and movements of capital, technology and persons are so well known that it is scarcely necessary to stress the

(A. Rust ed., Kluwer Law International 2011), 1-2; K. Vogel, *Double Tax Treaties and Their Interpretation*, 4(1) Int'l Tax & Bus. Law 1 (1986), 5-6.

80. According to Bühler, such an obligation, which is far from existing, would be equivalent to the transfer *mutatis mutandis* of the principle ne bis in idem into the international tax law, which is far for being recognized. Cf. O. Bühler, 55 Recueil des Cours 433 (1936), 459.

81. E. Reimer & A. Rust eds, *Klaus Vogel on Double Taxation Conventions* (Kluwer Law International 4th ed. 2015), 'Introduction', m.no. 11; *see also* J. H. Beale, 32(6) Harv. L. Rev. 587 (1919), 588; H. Dorn, 2(1) Rivista di Diritto Finanziario e Scienza delle Finanze 115 (1938), 125; M. Norr, 17(3) Tax L. Rev. 431 (1962), 431; J. P. Niboyet, 31 Recueil des Cours 5 (1930), 25.

importance of removing the obstacles that double taxation presents to the development of economic relations between countries.'[82]

International juridical double taxation may induce taxpayers to act according to taxation rather than economic criteria.[83] A double tax burden always reduces the total potential profitability of a given economic activity. Nevertheless, such activity may still be profitable. The problem arises when international double taxation truly inhibits cross-border activities, impacting international flows.

By preventing cross-border activities, international juridical double taxation obstructs the global economy's growth, impairing both the States seeking foreign investment and the States willing to expand their markets.[84]

Therefore, in order to allocate economic resources efficiently on a worldwide basis, some relief from double taxation must be provided.

As stated in the United Nations Model Double Taxation Convention between Developed and Developing Countries (hereinafter 'UN MC'), 'the growth of investment flows between countries depends to a large extent on the prevailing investment climate. The prevention or elimination of international double taxation in respect of the same income – the effects of which are harmful to the exchange of goods and services and to the movement of capital and persons, constitutes a significant component of such a climate'.[85]

Aware of the benefits of promoting an international environment where investment may flow, States started to include unilateral measures into their domestic law and enter into bilateral and multilateral agreements with each other.

While providing some relief from double taxation, these measures and agreements offer legal certainty regarding what the taxpayer can expect in terms of taxation when deciding to carry out cross-border activities. Therefore, these instruments encourage cross-border activities.

Additionally, tax treaties bring further benefits to the States.[86]

On the one hand, through them, States may allocate taxing powers to each other, ensuring a share in the revenue derived from cross-border activities. Although dividing taxing rights may not seem appealing at first sight, it is better to guarantee less revenue derived from cross-border activities than not having revenue at all, as those cross-border activities would probably not be performed due to the associated high tax costs.

On the other hand, tax treaties are crucial to enforcing worldwide taxation. It is of little use for a State to be entitled to subject its residents to full tax liability but not be able to gather information on the income they earn abroad. This way, tax treaties are

82. OECD MC, Introduction, para. 1.
83. *See* M. Pires (Kluwer Law and Taxation Publishers 1989), 75-86; A. A. Knechtle (Kluwer 1979), 46-47.
84. M. Pires (Kluwer Law and Taxation Publishers 1989), 77.
85. Model Double Taxation Convention between Developed and Developing Countries (United Nations 2021), p. vii, para. 5.
86. *See* further F. Barthel et al., *The Relationship Between Double Taxation Treaties and Foreign Direct Investment*, in *Tax Treaties: Building Bridges Between Law and Economics* (M. Lang et al. eds, IBFD 2010), 3-20.

helpful in terms of fighting against fiscal avoidance and evasion,[87] mainly by facilitating information exchange between States.[88]

Unilateral domestic tax provisions and tax treaties thus have the positive effect of relieving taxpayers from international juridical double taxation.

Nevertheless, protecting taxpayers from such double taxation is not the States' primary concern, rather a consequence of their aims, which encompass the promotion of foreign investment, safeguarding their taxing rights over such investment and preventing tax evasion.

As explained by Kemmeren, 'Double tax conventions on income and capital (DTC) build bridges between the economies of the contracting States. They play an important role in promoting the economic well-being of the contracting States. DTCs stimulate foreign direct investments. The rationale of DTCs is not the avoidance of international juridical double taxation, which is only a means in order to realise the real goal. As explicitly expressed in the OECD Commentary, DTCs remove the obstacles that international juridical double taxation presents to the development of economic relationships between countries. International juridical double taxation harmfully affects the exchange of goods and services and movements of capital, technology and persons.'[89]

Symptomatic of this is the fact that, since 1992, the title of the OECD MC lacks a reference to the 'elimination of double taxation'.[90]

It is, then, worth pondering whether the protection of taxpayers against international juridical double taxation could be considered, per se, as a ground for its elimination.

---

87. OECD MC, Commentary on Art. 1, para. 54.
88. The concerns about double taxation and tax evasion were patent in the early League of Nations' report from 1925 [League of Nations, Double Taxation and Tax Evasion Document – Report and Resolutions submitted by the Technical Experts to the Financial Committee – F.212. (1925), pp. 23-26]. In 1927, the League of Nations Report on double taxation and tax evasion presented by the Committee of Technical Experts on Double Taxation and Tax Evasion clearly stressed the connection between the elimination of double taxation and the prevention of tax avoidance: 'It is highly desirable that States should come to an agreement with a view of ensuring that a taxpayer should not be taxed on the same income by a number of different countries, and it seems equally desirable that such international co-operation should prevent certain incomes from escaping taxation altogether.' [League of Nations, Double Taxation and Tax Evasion: Report, C. 216. M.85 (1927), p. 23; *see also* M. Norr, 17(3) Tax L. Rev. 431 (1962), 445-446]. Therefore, the League of Nations presented in 1927 a 'Draft of a Bilateral Convention on Administrative Assistance in Matters of Taxation' alongside with a 'Draft of a Bilateral Convention for the Prevention of Double Taxation' [League of Nations, Double Taxation and Tax Evasion: Report, C. 216. M.85 (1927)]. Later, the Mexico and London Model Tax Conventions also contained a model on the prevention of the double taxation alongside with a model on the reciprocal administrative assistance for the assessment and collection of taxes [League of Nations Fiscal Committee, London and Mexico model tax conventions: commentary and text: official no. C.88.M.88.1946.II.A. (1946)]. In 1963, a provision on information exchange was inserted in the OECD Draft Double Taxation Convention on Income and Capital [*see* Draft Double Taxation Convention on Income and Capital 1963 (OECD Publishing 1963)]. Since then, the OECD Models of Tax Treaties have included such provision. For a historical overview of the provisions regarding the exchange of information in the Model Tax Conventions, *see* V. Wöhrer, *Data Protection and Taxpayers' Rights: Challenges Created by Automatic Exchange of Information* (IBFD 2018), 12-53.
89. E. Kemmeren, *Double Tax Conventions on Income and Capital and the EU: Past, Present and Future*, 21(3) EC Tax Rev. 156 (2012), 156 DOI: 10.54648/ecta2012016.
90. Cf. OECD MC, Introduction, para. 16. *See also* A. H. Qureshi & A. Kumar (Kluwer Law International 2d ed. 2019), 473.

After all, the lack of elimination of juridical double taxation means that a taxpayer in a cross-border situation must bear equivalent tax burdens in different States. Because the taxpayer interacts with tax systems that ignore one another, those States calculate the tax due, disregarding the tax also due on the same income in the other State. However, the economic strength of the taxpayer is one and the same, regardless of where he/she has performed his/her activity.

For instance, if the taxpayer derives income from just one State, the tax burden may be ascertained, in principle, according to the taxpayer's ability to pay taxes. Consequently, the tax burden is commensurate with his/her economic strength.

By contrast, where the taxpayer derives income from more than one State, even if all the States involved ascertain the tax burden according to that taxpayer's ability to pay, the taxpayer's overall ability to pay is considered in none of those States because, as said, they ignore the tax one another levy. This way, in none of those States is the tax burden commensurate to the taxpayer's economic strength.

It must be noted that the taxpayers' economic strength is linked to the *total amount* of income earned, and it does not change according to the *place* where that income is earned. As taxes represent a burden on that economic strength, taxes inevitably reduce taxpayers' economic strength.

Therefore, when international juridical double taxation is not eliminated, the overall taxation suffered by the taxpayer is not commensurate to his/her economic strength because that economic strength has been mitigated by the tax burden borne in the other State.

Moreover, this will happen even if each State treats taxpayers engaged in cross-border activities and taxpayers engaged in domestic activities in the same way. Despite offering equal treatment to cross-border and purely internal situations, the States disregard the taxation suffered in the other State by the taxpayer engaged in cross-border activities, overlooking his/her loss of economic strength.

The fact that the overall taxation suffered by the taxpayer is not applied according to the taxpayer's overall ability to pay taxes has led authors such as Pires,[91] Knechtle[92] and Guggenheim[93] to qualify international juridical double taxation as a violation of tax justice.[94]

91. M. Pires (Kluwer Law and Taxation Publishers 1989), 86-87: 'Double taxation violates tax justice, because overall taxation is not applied according to taxable capacity. Although equal taxation may be applied in each State from the national point of view to taxpayers in equal situations, a second taxation will exist due to the fact that they receive income abroad.'
92. A. A. Knechtle (Kluwer 1979), 46: 'IDT [International Double Taxation] is a breach of the postulate of fiscal justice, since it is incompatible with equal taxation of all tax subjects in accordance with their economic capacity. Each conflicting tax system, when looked at in isolation, may have due regard to the subject's ability to pay. Where IDT exists, however, the second requirement of just taxation, equal treatment of all taxpayers in comparable economic circumstances, is not fulfilled. One taxpayer who has only domestic property and income, and another who also owns foreign property and enjoys a foreign income, are not taxed equally.'
93. P. Guggenheim (Mémoires publiés par la Faculté de droit de Genève 1928), 16-17: '*Il y a désavantage évident subi par le contribuable imposé pour un même objet d'imposition par différents Etats, vis-à-vis du contribuable grevé seulement par un Etat pour un objet d'imposition identique et par un impôt identique. Il peut donc être question d'une multiple imposition non*

Indeed, affirming that international juridical double taxation is not forbidden under international law amounts to analysing the issue from only the perspective of tax jurisdictions. In other words, international juridical double taxation is not forbidden under international law because States have the power to define their tax jurisdictions; tax jurisdictions may overlap; insofar as States do not exceed their own tax jurisdiction - whose limits are not clearly defined under international law - the taxation levied on a taxpayer is legitimate even if it overlaps with the taxation levied by another State that is acting under its own tax jurisdiction.

However, tax jurisdiction only establishes *the extent to which* States may exercise their taxing powers: what persons they may tax and with what intensity such taxation may be exercised (full or limited tax liability). Tax jurisdiction says nothing about *how* the taxing powers are exercised, and international law is of no help in this regard.

The understanding of international juridical double taxation as implying the overall taxation of a taxpayer that is discrepant from her/his overall ability to pay taxes comprises a problem regarding *how* the States' taxing powers are exercised. In fact, if the States' direct tax systems apply the ability-to-pay principle as a standard for distributing the tax burden among taxpayers, why do States mitigate such principle when their tax system overlaps with another that uses the same principle? In such cases, should not taxpayers' overall ability to pay be deemed an adequate ground for promoting the elimination of double taxation?

Since within the EU the exercise of taxing powers by the Member States is not entirely free as they have to comply with the EU law, the particular context of the EU is a breeding ground for exploring international juridical double taxation as entailing a problem regarding the exercise of tax powers and to ponder the taxpayers' overall ability to pay as a ground for requiring its elimination.

1.4 CONCLUDING AND SUMMARISING REMARKS

This chapter begins with an analysis of the concept of international juridical double taxation.

The OECD MC adopts the traditional notion of international juridical double taxation that scholars have developed over time. Accordingly, international juridical double taxation is 'the imposition of comparable taxes in two (or more) States on the same taxpayer in respect of the same subject matter and for identical periods'.

---

conforme à la justice économique, dans le cas où le même contribuable se trouve imposé par le même impôt et pour un même objet à la fois dans différents Etats faisant partie de la Communauté du droit des gens.'

94. Notwithstanding, Pires warns that the idea of tax justice is challenging to concretise [M. Pires (Kluwer Law and Taxation Publishers 1989), 88]. About tax justice, Agulló Agüero highlights the fact that its concretisation must be made according to the historical-social awareness in each moment [cf. A. Agulló Agüero, *Una reflexión en torno a la prohibición de confiscatoriedad del sistema tributario*, 36 REDF 555, 560-561 (1982)], and Sáinz de Bujanda stresses that without fair taxation, the human dignity loses its pivotal position in the system [F. Sáinz de Bujanda, *Reflexiones sobre un sistema de derecho tributario español*, 7 (16/17) Rev. Fac. Derecho Universidad de Madrid 7 (1963), 78].

Recently, the Directive on tax dispute resolution mechanisms enshrined a definition with slightly different wording, under which double taxation is 'the imposition by two or more Member States of taxes covered by an agreement or convention [...] in respect of the same taxable income or capital when it gives rise to either: *(i)* an additional tax charge; *(ii)* an increase in tax liabilities; or *(iii)* the cancellation or reduction of losses that could be used to offset taxable profits'.

This way, the notion of double taxation introduced by the Directive on tax dispute resolution mechanisms is not entirely coincident with the traditional notion enshrined in the OECD MC.

For instance, the Directive's concept of double taxation only covers cases where the Member States have not successfully eliminated double taxation through bilateral or multilateral agreements. Moreover, it includes a quantitative element related to the tax burden increase derived from the overlap of taxing jurisdictions, which prevents certain situations from being covered by the concept. It is the case where double taxation existed and was then eliminated by the action of one of the States involved or where double taxation potentially existed but did not occur in practice, for instance, due to a qualification conflict or because a zero rate was applied under national rules.

These differences between the two definitions analysed may be explained by the difference in the problem they describe and for which they seek a solution.

The traditional notion seeks to pave the way for adopting substantive measures to eliminate international juridical double taxation. Consequently, it formulates the problem of double taxation in its original form, that is to say, based on the assumption that there are no measures in place to avoid it. In contrast, the notion foreseen in the Directive on tax dispute resolution mechanisms is thought to describe a second-layer problem: the occasional failure of bilateral or multilateral substantive measures adopted by the Member States to avoid the imposition of comparable taxes on the same taxable event within the EU. The Directive's aim is thus to provide, through the adoption of procedural measures, a solution for those cases of unrelieved double taxation.

Like those notions, the relevant notion of double taxation for the present research's purposes must envisage and define double taxation according to the specific problem for which it seeks a solution. The problem that this research aims to address is the international juridical double taxation suffered by individuals within the EU because there are no substantive measures in place, or when they exist, they fail their purpose, and the procedural measures (eventually) applicable are ineffective. Therefore, the relevant notion of double taxation for this research is the effective imposition within the EU of comparable taxes by different Member States on the same individual regarding the same taxable event and tax period without this double taxation being eliminated.

After approaching the concept, the causes and cases of international juridical double taxation are examined to clarify the problems described.

International juridical double taxation is a consequence of the juxtaposition of States' tax jurisdictions. Ascertaining tax jurisdiction implies determining *to what extent* a State may exercise its taxing powers.

There is no unanimity in the doctrine on whether international law limits the States in defining their tax jurisdiction. However, the fact that the States never tax beyond certain limits indicates that some connection between the State and the person performing the taxable event must exist for that State to exercise its taxing powers over that person.

That connection was, for long, found in political allegiance, which was progressively replaced by economic allegiance. Economic allegiance entails that those who have a relevant economic and social interest in a State – deriving income from that State or consuming and saving in that State – are under its jurisdiction. The economic and social bond with the State may vary in intensity. Personal and territorial attachment are expressions of the range of such intensity.

On the one hand, personal attachment, which is found in residence and nationality, implies a relationship between the State and the taxpayer. Although most States adopt residence as the relevant connection factor regarding personal attachment, nationality still has a certain relevance.

On the other hand, territorial attachment requires a link between the State and the activities carried out within its territory by taxpayers. In other words, attachment is found in the economic benefit taxpayers derive from that State, regardless of their physical presence there.

The lack of uniform criteria among States for assessing these connecting factors may give rise to the juxtaposition of tax jurisdictions, causing international juridical double taxation.

Moreover, the establishment of tax liability – which varies according to the connecting factors – increases those cases of the juxtaposition of tax jurisdictions. Usually, personal attachment triggers full tax liability, leading to worldwide taxation, while territorial attachment triggers limited tax liability, leading to territorial/source taxation. That is to say that a State may tax its residents (or nationals, if nationality is relevant) on their income or wealth regardless of the source, and it may tax non-residents on the income or wealth derived from its territory.

The grounds for worldwide taxation are generally found in the fact that it is in the State of residence where taxpayers use most public infrastructures and services and fully enjoy the State's public functions. Thus, it is there where they must contribute most. Furthermore, the State of residence is better positioned to assess the taxpayers' overall social and economic situation and consider it, ensuring that the taxpayers' overall taxation is according to their overall ability to pay.

In turn, the grounds for source taxation are based on the source State providing the conditions for taxpayers to obtain income and wealth.

The combined use of full and limited tax liability is usual in most States, which means that the overlap of different sorts of tax liabilities in different States is common, giving rise to international juridical double taxation.

In short, the cases of international juridical double taxation occur in three case scenarios. First, it occurs when more than one State considers itself to be the State of residence of the taxpayer (or the State of nationality), taxing her/him on her/his worldwide income, configuring a case of *worldwide versus worldwide taxation*. Second, it occurs when two States consider the taxpayer's income derived from their territory, taxing her/him on that income, constituting a case of *source versus source taxation*. Third, it occurs when one State considers the taxpayer's income derived from its territory, taxing her/him on that income, and another State taxes his/her worldwide income because it is her/his residence State. Such is a case of *worldwide versus source taxation*.

This chapter ends with a reflection on the grounds for eliminating international juridical double taxation.

States eliminate double taxation because they aim to promote foreign investment, safeguard their taxing rights over such foreign investment, and prevent tax evasion. Protecting the taxpayer against double taxation is a consequence of attaining those aims but not an end in itself.

Double taxation is not deemed illegal or illegitimate under international law, and States are not obliged to eliminate it. However, analysing the legality or legitimacy of international juridical double taxation under international law amounts to analysing the issue just from the perspective of tax jurisdiction: insofar as a State does not exceed its own tax jurisdiction (whose limits are not clearly defined under international law), the taxation imposed on a taxpayer is legitimate even if it overlaps with the taxation levied by another State.

Tax jurisdiction only establishes *the extent to which* States may exercise their taxing powers; it says nothing about *how* the taxing powers are exercised, an issue outside the scope of international law.

The lack of elimination of juridical double taxation means that a taxpayer engaged in a cross-border situation must bear the tax burden in different States. Those States disregard the tax paid on the same income by the taxpayer in the other State. Because taxes represent a burden on taxpayers' economic strength, taxes inevitably reduce that economic strength. Consequently, the taxpayer's economic strength is not the same as it would be if his/her income is derived from just one of those States.

Indeed, where a taxpayer derives income from just one State, the tax burden is, in principle, ascertained according to the taxpayer's ability to pay taxes. Consequently, the tax burden is commensurate with the taxpayer's economic strength.

By contrast, where the taxpayer derives income from more than one State and international juridical double taxation is not eliminated, the taxpayer's overall ability to pay is considered in none of those States because they ignore the tax one another levy. The overall taxation suffered by the taxpayer is not commensurate to the taxpayer's economic strength because that economic strength has been mitigated by the tax burden born in the other State. That is to say, the taxpayer's overall ability to pay taxes, which stems from the taxpayer's economic strength, is not commensurate with the overall taxation suffered.

The understanding of international juridical double taxation as implying the overall taxation of taxpayers discrepant from their overall ability to pay comprises a problem regarding *how* the States' taxing powers are exercised. After all, if a State's direct tax system applies the ability-to-pay principle as a standard for distributing the tax burden among taxpayers, is that principle not mitigated when its tax system overlaps with another that enshrines the same principle?

The particular context of the EU is a breeding ground for exploring international juridical double taxation as entailing a problem regarding the exercise of taxing powers and for pondering the taxpayers' overall ability to pay as a ground for requiring its elimination because, within the EU, the exercise of taxing powers by the Member States is not entirely free since they have to comply with EU law.

In order to analyse such a hypothesis, some preliminary study must be conducted. In the first place, it is relevant to examine how international juridical double taxation is eliminated in general terms and, in particular, within the EU (Chapter 2). In the second place, the EU legal framework must be studied to ascertain how EU law limits the exercise of taxing powers by the Member States (Chapter 3). In third place, the relevance of taxpayers' overall ability to pay in light of EU law must be assessed (Chapter 4). Lastly, it is pertinent to analyse the CJEU's stance in cases in which international juridical double taxation was not eliminated (Chapter 5) and in cases in which it was eliminated, but taxpayers' ability to pay was undermined in the process (Chapter 6).

CHAPTER 2

Legal Means and Methods Designed to Eliminate International Juridical Double Taxation

– Overview of the legal means and methods for eliminating international juridical double taxation.

– Examination of the existing legal instruments, particularly within the EU, that set substantive and procedural measures to eliminate international juridical double taxation.

– Analysis of the concrete methods used by substantive measures to avoid such double taxation.

2.1 LEGAL MEANS DESIGNED TO ELIMINATE INTERNATIONAL JURIDICAL DOUBLE TAXATION

Regardless of why international juridical double taxation is eliminated, the benefits deriving from such elimination are undeniable, and States have been increasingly adopting means in this regard.

Such means involve the application of both substantive and procedural measures, which we briefly examine below.

2.1.1 Substantive Measures

States have introduced into their domestic law unilateral measures to avoid international juridical double taxation. Accordingly, in certain circumstances, a State waives the tax that would be due, preventing the taxpayer from bearing a double burden. However, taxpayers cannot always rely on the elimination of double taxation through unilateral measures since, on the one hand, not all States have them, and on the other hand, when they have them, the scope of application of such measures may not cover all situations. Moreover, due to their unilateral nature, those measures do not form a coherent whole at the international level, leading to gaps and loss of effectiveness.

States have also entered into bilateral and multilateral agreements to eliminate double taxation. Through these treaties, States agree on rules for allocating taxing powers between them, which have the effect of excluding or limiting the application of domestic tax rules. Hence, States bind themselves not to tax when the applicable tax treaty does not entitle them to do so, allowing taxpayers to benefit from mutually consistent rules for avoiding double taxation.

In all those cases (i.e., unilateral, bilateral and multilateral measures), States refrain from taxing by applying specific methods to avoid double taxation. Such methods are analysed in section 2.2.

Within the EU, the tax treaty network on income taxes is vast, and almost all Member States have entered into tax treaties with each other. However, there are some exceptions, as in the cases of Denmark–Spain,[95] Portugal–Finland,[96] and Portugal–Sweden.[97] There is no tax treaty between these States because it was unilaterally terminated, which illustrates how much the elimination of international juridical double taxation depends on the States' willingness.[98]

Regarding inheritance and gift taxation, the network of tax treaties between the Member States is far from complete. According to the report produced by Copenhagen Economics following the commissioning of a study by the European Commission, in the field of inheritance and gift taxation, 351 bilateral treaties between the Member States would be needed to secure complete coverage for all citizens.[99] In 2010, only 33 of those treaties were in force. The same data was used in the EU Commission expert group's report 'Ways to tackle inheritance cross-border tax obstacles facing individuals within the EU', mentioning that the situation had not changed by 2015.[100] More recent data was not found.

There is also a multilateral tax treaty between some EU Member States and third countries: the Nordic Multilateral Tax Treaty. The Contracting States of this multilateral treaty are Denmark, the Faroe Islands, Finland, Iceland, Norway and Sweden.

95. Terminated unilaterally by Denmark in 2008.
96. Terminated unilaterally by Finland in 2018.
97. Terminated unilaterally by Sweden in 2022.
98. For instance, the tax treaty between Denmark and France was unilaterally terminated by Denmark in 2008. A new tax treaty was only signed in 2022 and approved by the Danish Parliament and French Senate in 2023. It must also be noted that, until recently, there was no tax treaty between Cyprus and the Netherlands. This tax treaty, the first of its kind between the two Member States, was signed in 2021 and only entered into force on 30 June 2023.
99. Copenhagen Economics, *Study on inheritance taxes in EU Member States and on possible mechanisms to resolve problems of double inheritance taxation in the EU*, European Commission – Directorate-General for Taxation and Customs Union (2010/11), p. 49. *See also* J. Calvo Vérgez, *El papel de los CDI ante la doble imposición internacional en el ámbito del ISD*, in *La tributación de las sucesiones transfronterizas en España y en la Unión Europea: problemas actuales* (J. Ramos Prieto et al. eds., Aranzadi 2018), 479, who notes that, in the field of inheritance and gift taxation, the unilateral measures in place are clearly insufficient and the only way to tackle double taxation is through tax treaties.
100. European Commission expert group, *Ways to tackle inheritance cross-border tax obstacles facing individuals within the EU*, Directorate-General for Taxation and Customs Union (2015), p. 14.

Additionally, on the EU level, some Directives also allow the avoidance of international juridical double taxation. It is the case of the Parent-Subsidiary Directive,[101] the Interest and Royalty Directive,[102] and the Merger Directive.[103] However, as these Directives have a limited scope of application, they only allow for the avoidance of double taxation regarding certain operations carried out by certain undertakings resident in different Member States.

2.1.2 Procedural Measures

The failure to adequately apply the existing substantive measures to avoid international juridical double taxation leads to tax disputes between taxpayers and tax administrations. Procedural measures play a crucial role in resolving cases where double taxation was not avoided through the substantive measures in place.

Where a tax dispute arises from applying unilateral measures to eliminate double taxation, taxpayers may only rely on the national remedies provided by their States' national laws.

In turn, where a tax dispute arises from the interpretation and application of bilateral or multilateral tax treaties, taxpayers may rely on additional mechanisms for settling cross-border disputes foreseen in different legal instruments. Essentially, such mechanisms are the mutual agreement procedure and arbitration.[104]

The mutual agreement procedure allows the States' tax authorities involved in the tax dispute to reach an agreement. In arbitration, an agreement is achieved between the States' tax authorities involved through the empowerment of a third party. Generally, these mechanisms operate in a two-tier procedure, where arbitration follows the mutual agreement procedure.

The legal instruments providing mechanisms for settling cross-border disputes are *(i)* the tax treaties, *(ii)* the Multilateral Convention to Implement Tax Treaty Related Measures to Prevent Base Erosion and Profit Shifting (hereinafter 'MLI'), and within the EU, *(iii)* the Convention on the elimination of double taxation in connection with the adjustment of profits of associated enterprises (90/463/EEC) (hereinafter 'EU

101. According with its recital 3: 'The objective of this Directive is to exempt dividends and other profit distributions paid by subsidiary companies to their parent companies from withholding taxes and to eliminate double taxation of such income at the level of the parent company.'
102. According with its recitals 2 and 3: '(...) Council Directive 2003/49/EC of 3 June 2003 on a common system of taxation applicable to interest and royalty payments made between associated companies of different Member States'. According with recitals 2 and 3: '(2)(...) national tax laws coupled, where applicable, with bilateral or multilateral agreements may not always ensure that double taxation is eliminated, and their application often entails burdensome administrative formalities and cash-flow problems for the companies concerned. (3) It is necessary to ensure that interest and royalty payments are subject to tax once in a Member State.'
103. According with its recital 14: 'One of the aims of this Directive is to eliminate obstacles to the functioning of the internal market, such as double taxation. In so far as this is not fully achieved by the provisions of this Directive, Member States should take the necessary measures to achieve this aim.'
104. *See* P. Pistone et al., *Fundamentals of Taxation: An Introduction to Tax Policy, Tax Law and Tax Administration* (IBFD 2019), 193-142.

Multilateral Arbitration Convention'), and *(iv)* the Directive on tax dispute resolution mechanisms.[105]

Tax treaties usually include a provision on dispute resolution mechanisms, as suggested in Article 25 of the OECD MC. However, as the effectiveness of this provision has not always been satisfactory because the procedures were not transparent, could take too much time and reaching an agreement was not mandatory, the MLI played a key role in this tax treaty provision.[106]

The MLI,[107] of which all Member States are signatories, improves the mutual agreement procedure foreseen in this provision and includes it as a minimum standard. The changes cover all MLI signatories' tax treaties. The MLI also introduced a mandatory binding arbitration procedure, which is optional (Part VI of the MLI). It is only applicable when both States involved in a tax dispute have made such a choice and notified the Depositary accordingly.[108] In these cases, the mandatory binding arbitration procedure provided by the MLI is applicable in place of the arbitration procedures provided by the tax treaties at issue.[109] Within the EU, up to now, 16 Member States have chosen to apply Part VI of the MLI. These Member States are Austria, Belgium, Denmark, Finland, France, Germany, Greece, Ireland, Italy, Luxembourg, Malta, the Netherlands, Portugal, Slovenia, Spain and Sweden.[110]

The EU Multilateral Arbitration Convention is a multilateral treaty signed by all the EU Member States. It has a limited application scope, dealing only with double taxation on transfer pricing. It is designed to overcome tax disputes arising from including a Contracting State enterprise's profit in the profit of an enterprise of another Contracting State.[111] Under the EU Multilateral Arbitration Convention, resolving the tax dispute is mandatory.[112]

The Directive on tax dispute resolution mechanisms is an EU legal instrument designed to resolve disputes between the Member States when those disputes arise from the interpretation and application of agreements and conventions providing for

105. For an analysis of these legal instruments and the relationship between them, *see* further P. Wattel et al. (Kluwer Law International 7th ed. 2018), 331-379. *See also* S. Govind & L. Turcan, *Cross-Border Tax Dispute Resolution in the 21st Century: A Comparative Study of Existing Bilateral and Multilateral Remedies*, 19 Deriv. & Fin. Instruments 5 (2017).
106. *See* H. M. Pit, *Arbitration under the OECD Multilateral Instrument: Reservations, Options and Choices*, 71(10) Bull. Int'l Tax'n 568 (2017), 568-591.
107. The MLI modifies the tax treaties it covers but does not replace them. It rather coexists with such tax treaties being applied together. *See* MLI Explanatory Statement, para. 13. Regarding the relationship between the MLI and tax treaties covered, *see* N. Bravo, *A Multilateral Instrument for Updating the Tax Treaty Network* (IBFD 2020), 101-168; D. W. Blum, *The Relationship Between the OECD Multilateral Instrument and Covered Tax Agreements: Multilateralism and the Interpretation of the MLI*, 72(3) Bull. Int'l Tax'n 131 (2018).
108. Article 18 MLI.
109. Article 26(1) MLI.
110. The positions of these Member States are detailed in the 'Signatories and Parties to the Multilateral Convention to Implement Tax Treaty Related Measures to Prevent Base Erosion and Profit Shifting', available at https://www.oecd.org/tax/treaties/beps-mli-signatories-and-parties.pdf.
111. Article 1(1) EU Multilateral Arbitration Convention.
112. Article 12(1) EU Multilateral Arbitration Convention.

the elimination of double taxation.[113] Although the scope of this Directive overlaps with the other legal instruments analysed, it enhances the position of taxpayers affected by the tax dispute, granting them rights within the procedures and demanding for binding solution for the tax dispute at issue.[114]

2.2 METHODS DESIGNED TO ELIMINATE INTERNATIONAL JURIDICAL DOUBLE TAXATION

After this brief review of the existing substantive and procedural measures to eliminate double taxation, it is worth examining the concrete methods used by substantive measures to avoid such double taxation.

In bilateral and multilateral instruments, double taxation is avoided by distributive rules and methods to eliminate double taxation, i.e., the exemption and credit methods.[115]

Distributive rules may prevent one of the Contracting States from taxing in absolute terms by using the expression 'shall be taxable only'. In such a case, international juridical double taxation is avoided without the need for further measures.[116]

Conversely, where both Contracting States conserve their taxing rights over an item of income, the residence State is responsible for applying one of the methods specially designed to eliminate double taxation.[117]

Article 23(A) and (B) of the OECD MC - and also of the UN MC - describe the exemption method and the credit method, respectively. This provision does not include the deduction method as a method suitable for eliminating international juridical double taxation because, under this method, the tax paid in the other State is just treated as a deductible expense.

As pointed out in the Commentary to the OECD MC, the fundamental difference between the exemption and the credit methods is that in eliminating double taxation,

113. Article 1 of the Directive on tax dispute resolution mechanisms.
114. Article 15(2) of the Directive on tax dispute resolution mechanisms. *See also* K. Perrou, *Taxpayer Rights and Taxpayer Participation in Procedures under the Dispute Resolution Directive*, 47(8/9) Intertax 715 (2019), 716-719 DOI: 10.54648/taxi2019070. For an extensive analysis of the EU Multilateral Arbitration Convention and the Directive on tax dispute resolution mechanisms, *see* H. M. Pit, *Dispute Resolution in the EU: The EU Arbitration Convention and the Dispute Resolution Directive* (IBFD 2018), 31-1148; and J. Calvo Vérgez, *Últimas actuaciones en materia de arbitraje tributario dentro de la Unión Europea: la Directiva (UE) 2017/1852 del Consejo, de 10 de octubre de 2017, relativa a los mecanismos de resolución de litigios fiscales*, 11(2) Econ. Analysis L. Rev. 3 (2020), 3-29.
115. For a historical perspective of these two methods, *see* J. Avery Jones, *Avoiding Double Taxation: Credit Versus Exemption – The Origins*, 66(2) Bull. Int'l Tax'n 67 (2012).
116. In these cases, where double taxation is avoided through distributive rules, although the methods described in Art. 23 of the OECD MC (exemption and credit methods) are not applied directly, the rules generally applicable to exemption may be used – *see* E. Reimer & A. Rust eds, *Klaus Vogel on Double Taxation Conventions* (Kluwer Law International 4th ed. 2015), 'Article 23: Exemption Method/Credit Method', m.no. 3 and 19.
117. OECD MC, Commentary on Art. 23A and B, para. 6.

the exemption method looks at income, while the credit method looks at tax.[118] Both methods may be applied following diverse configurations. The credit method may assume the form of 'full credit' and 'ordinary credit'. Regarding the exemption method, it may be applied in the form of 'full exemption', 'exemption with progression' and 'modified exemption'.[119]

When eliminating double taxation, States may apply one or the other method in their different forms, depending on the item of income at stake.[120]

Furthermore, these methods may also be foreseen in States' domestic law, in their different forms, to ensure the unilateral elimination of international juridical double taxation in the cases where there is no international agreement in place or to implement and concretise the relief provided by the tax agreements.[121]

2.2.1 The Credit Method

Under the credit method, the residence State computes its tax based on the taxpayer's total income, regardless of where it is obtained. This way, the income taxed in the other State may also be taxed by the residence State. To eliminate double taxation, the residence State allows the tax paid in the other State to be deducted against its own tax.[122]

If States grant relief from double taxation through *full credit*, taxpayers are entitled to deduct from the tax determined in their residence State an amount equal to the tax paid in the other State. Such deduction is made regardless of whether the tax paid in the other State is higher than the tax due in the residence State. Thus, the full

118. *Ibid.*, para. 17.
119. Modified exemption is the term used by Vogel – E. Reimer & A. Rust eds, *Klaus Vogel on Double Taxation Conventions* (Kluwer Law International 4th ed. 2015), 'Article 23: Exemption Method/Credit Method', m.no. 21. Avery Jones prefers the term 'so-called credit' – J. Avery Jones, *What Is the Difference Between Schumacker and Gilly?*, 39(1) Eur. Tax'n 2 (1999). In the OECD MC Commentary on Art. 23A and B, it does not have an exact denomination, being treated as an 'alternative formulation of the Article'. Cf. OECD MC, Commentary on Art. 23A and B, para. 37.
120. Both methods are compatible with EU law. Cf. S. van Thiel, *Double Burdens on Cross-Border Economic Activity Within the European Union*, in *Comparative Fiscal Federalism* (R. Avi Yonah and M. Lang eds, Kluwer Law International 2016), 122-124; S. van Thiel, *Avoiding a Double Burden Within the European Union: Comments on Kofler and Rust's Analysis*, in *Double Taxation Within the European Union* (A. Rust ed., Kluwer Law International 2011), 181-183; E. Kemmeren, *The Internal Market Approach Should Prevail over the Single Country Approach*, in *A Vision of Taxes Within and Beyond European Borders* (L. Hinnekens & P. Hinnekens eds, Kluwer Law International 2008), 575. However, some scholars argue that preference must be given to one method over the other in the internal market context. Cf. K. Vogel, *Which Method Should the European Community Adopt for the Avoidance of Double Taxation?*, 56 Bull. for Int'l Fiscal Documentation 4 (2002); P. Pistone, *Double Taxation: Selected Issues of Compatibility With European Law, Multilateral Tax Treaties and CCCTB*, in *Double Taxation Within the European Union* (A. Rust ed., Kluwer Law International 2011), 206; M. Helminen, *The Principle of Elimination of Double Taxation under EU Law – Does It Exist?*, in *Principles of Law: Function, Status and Impact in EU Tax Law* (C. Brokelind ed., IBFD 2014); P. Wattel et al. (Kluwer Law International 7th ed. 2018), 708-709.
121. E. Reimer & A. Rust eds, *Klaus Vogel on Double Taxation Conventions* (Kluwer Law International 4th ed. 2015), 'Article 23: Exemption Method/Credit Method', m.no. 14.
122. OECD MC, Commentary on Art. 23A and B, para. 15.

credit may have the effect of reducing the residence State's tax on a taxpayer's domestic income. Ultimately, that would amount to the taxes of other countries being paid by the public treasury of the residence State. Therefore, full credit is hardly used.

If States grant relief from double taxation through *ordinary credit*, taxpayers are entitled to deduct the smaller of the following amounts: *(i)* the tax paid in the other State; or *(ii)* the part of domestic tax attributable to the income derived from the other State. To determine *(ii)*, the following formula is usually used:

$$\frac{\text{Foreign income}}{\text{Total income (worldwide)}} \times \text{Tax due in the residence State}$$

The application of the ordinary credit implies that the taxpayers always bear the highest tax rate in play regarding their foreign income: their residence State's tax rate or the other State's tax rate. Since the aggregate tax that taxpayers have to bear does not exceed the higher of the two taxes at stake (i.e., that of the residence State or that of the other State), double taxation is considered eliminated.

2.2.2 The Exemption Method

Under the exemption method, the State of residence does not tax the income that may be taxed in the other State.[123]

If the exemption method is applied in its form of *full exemption*, the taxpayer's foreign income is not taken into account in the residence State. In other words, when determining the tax imposed on the taxpayer's domestic income, the residence State completely ignores the income derived from the other State.[124]

In the case of *exemption with progression*, the taxpayer's foreign income is taken into account to determine the tax rate to be imposed on the taxpayer's domestic income.[125] This way, the taxpayer's foreign income is included in the residence State's tax base, allowing the determination of the average tax rate that would apply to the taxpayer's worldwide income. Then, the taxpayer's foreign income is excluded from the tax base, and the tax rate so determined is applied to that taxpayer's domestic income. Therefore, even when taxpayers' taxable income is spread over several countries, those taxpayers are subject to progressive taxation in their State of residence.

In turn, the *modified exemption* has a particular configuration, being halfway between the exemption with progression and the credit method.

On the one hand, the modified exemption is a variation from the exemption with progression.[126] The taxpayer's foreign income is included in the State of residence's tax base. Once the total tax due on the taxpayer's worldwide income has been established,

123. *Ibid.*, para. 13.
124. *Ibid.*, para. 14(a).
125. *Ibid.*, para. 14(b).
126. Sometimes the modified exemption is designated as exemption with progression, although the technique employed to eliminate double taxation corresponds to the modified exemption.

the residence State grants a deduction from the total tax so determined of an amount equivalent to the part of the total tax corresponding to the taxpayer's foreign income.[127]

On the other hand, it works as a tax credit since, when eliminating double taxation, the focus is on the tax, not on the income. Indeed, the formula to calculate the part of total tax corresponding to the income derived from the other State is the same one used to determine the deduction limitation in the ordinary credit.

However, whereas in the ordinary credit, the tax due in the other State tax is credited - albeit to a limited extent - against the tax due in the residence State, in the modified exemption, it is the tax due in the residence State on taxpayer's foreign income that is credited against the total tax due in the resident State.[128] Thus, the deduction granted by the residence State under the modified exemption may be higher than the tax due in the other State.

The rationale for the modified exemption lies in the fact that the application of the other exemption methods implies excluding the foreign income from the taxpayer's tax base in the residence State. Therefore, when States use the taxpayers' tax base for other purposes, such as granting social benefits, applying the full exemption or exemption with progression may lead to granting such benefits to taxpayers who ought not to receive them.[129] Applying the modified exemption overcomes this issue since taxpayers' tax base always comprises their worldwide income.

2.2.3 The Policies Underlying the Two Methods

The OECD MC and UN MC provide two different methods to eliminate international juridical double taxation because the economic considerations underlying those methods vary significantly.

Traditionally, the credit method has been considered to promote capital export neutrality, while the exemption method promotes capital import neutrality. Musgrave seems to be the first to develop these international tax neutrality concepts, based on the idea that taxes should not interfere with or affect taxpayers' choices on investing domestically or abroad.[130] These concepts have also been extended to cover labour as a factor of neutrality, referred to as capital and labour export neutrality and capital and labour import neutrality.[131]

According to Musgrave, 'export neutrality means that the investor should pay the same total (domestic plus foreign) tax, whether he receives a given investment income from foreign or from domestic sources', and 'import neutrality means that capital funds

127. OECD MC, Commentary on Art. 23A and B, para. 37.
128. D. Kleist, *Methods for Elimination of Double Taxation under Double Tax Treaties – With Particular Reference to the Application of Double Tax Treaties in Sweden* (Iustus Förlag AB 2012), 198.
129. OECD MC, Commentary on Art. 23A and B, para. 37.
130. R. Musgrave, *Criteria for Foreign Tax Credit*, in *Taxation and Operations Abroad: Symposium* (R. Baker et al. eds, Princeton: Tax Institute 1960), 83-93.
131. E. Kemmeren, *Legal and Economic Principles Support an Origin and Import Neutrality-Based over a Residence and Export Neutrality-Based Tax Treaty Policy*, in *Tax Treaties: Building Bridges Between Law and Economics* (M. Lang et al. eds, IBFD 2010), 491-493.

originating in various countries should compete at equal terms in the capital market of any country'.[132]

Therefore, while the credit method, associated with worldwide taxation, is better suitable for ensuring export neutrality because it equalises the tax burden among the resident taxpayers, the exemption method is more appropriate for ensuring import neutrality since priority is granted to territorial taxation, the source State being considered in a better position to tax.[133]

As noted by Musgrave, 'these two approaches to neutrality are mutually exclusive, unless the capital-exporting and the capital-importing countries have the same tax structure. Since this is not the case, a choice must be made. (...) Moreover, it is not clear which of the two objectives should be made the major criterion'.[134]

This is evidenced by the fact that the OECD MC and the UN MC give States the freedom to choose between one or the other methods for avoiding double taxation, depending on what they consider most appropriate. And, in general, the States adopt one or the other method, depending on the item of income at stake.

2.2.4 Some Specific Problems Regarding the Application of the Two Methods

Applying credit and exemption methods may generate the loss of personal and family deductions that are usually provided by most countries to individuals residing within their territory. That loss occurs because the methods for eliminating double taxation are applied in such a way that leads to those deductions only being granted in proportion to the domestic income obtained by taxpayers.[135]

An express and uniform solution for this issue is not provided in the OECD MC, given the wide variety of fiscal policies and techniques in the different States regarding determining deductions, allowances and similar benefits.[136]

Another problem arising from applying the two methods is the treatment of losses, as residence States may or may not allow the deduction of losses incurred in the other State. Again, an express and uniform answer for this issue is not provided in the OECD MC, and the solution depends on the Contracting States' domestic laws.[137]

132. R. Musgrave (Princeton 1960), 84-86.
133. K. Vogel, *Worldwide vs. Source Taxation of Income: A Review and Re-evaluation of Arguments (Part II)*, 10 Intertax 310 (1988), 311 DOI: 10.54648/taxi1988043. *See also* C. Checa González, *Medidas y métodos para evitar la doble imposición internacional,* 5 Anuario Fac. Derecho Universidad de Extremadura 151 (1987), 164-165.
134. R. Musgrave (Princeton 1960), 86. In further studies, R. Musgrave, following P. Musgrave, assumed that only capital export neutrality allows economic efficiency - P. Musgrave, *United States Taxation of Foreign Investment Income: Issues and Arguments* (Harvard Law School 1969), 119-121; R. Musgrave & P. Musgrave, *Inter-nation Equity*, in *Modern Fiscal Issues: Essays in Honour of Carl S. Shoup* (R. Bird & J. Head eds, University of Toronto Press 5th ed. 1972), 68-69. For a critical analysis and against their position, *see* K. Vogel, 10 Intertax 310 (1988); also against the preference for capital export neutrality, *see* E. Kemmeren (M. Lang et al. eds, IBFD 2010), 491-493.
135. For a more detailed analysis of this issue, *see infra* Chapter 5.
136. OECD MC, Commentary on Art. 23A and B, paras 43 and 62.
137. *Ibid.*, paras 44 and 65.

Notwithstanding, in the EU context, the Member States' power to deal with these issues is not as broad as it could be assumed from the OECD MC. As discussed in detail in the following chapter, the Member States must comply with EU law when exercising their taxing powers, which substantially impacts how these problems are treated within the EU.

2.3 CONCLUDING AND SUMMARISING REMARKS

After examining the international juridical double taxation concept in Chapter 1, an overview of the legal means and methods for eliminating such double taxation was needed.

Chapter 2 is therefore intended to briefly approach how international juridical double taxation is eliminated, being divided into two points. First, attention is paid to the existing legal instruments, particularly within the EU, that set substantive and procedural measures to eliminate double taxation. Second, given their relevance throughout this research, the concrete methods used by substantive measures to avoid such double taxation are examined.

The substantive measures to eliminate international juridical double taxation have been adopted unilaterally by States or through bilateral or multilateral agreements.

Unilateral substantive measures imply that a state renounces by its own initiative to tax cross-border situations in certain circumstances. Notwithstanding, taxpayers cannot always rely on unilateral substantive measures to avoid double taxation because those measures do not cover all situations; not all States have them, and even when they have them, the unilateral nature of those measures implies that they are not applied in a coordinated way.

Bilateral and multilateral measures are, therefore, more effective in ensuring the elimination of double taxation, as the Contracting States agree on distributive rules of taxing powers, allowing the taxpayers to rely on mutually consistent provisions.

Within the EU, the tax treaty network on income taxes is vast, and only a small number of Member States have not concluded or have terminated them. It is the case of Denmark–Spain, Portugal–Finland and Portugal–Sweden. The situation is different regarding inheritance and gift taxes, where the network of tax treaties between the Member States is far from being completed.

As far as EU law is concerned, it provides substantive measures to eliminate international juridical double taxation in very particular areas of corporate taxation within the EU, covering only certain operations carried out by certain undertakings resident in different Member States. Such measures are provided for by the Parent-Subsidiary Directive, the Interest and Royalty Directive and, to a lesser extent, the Merger Directive. No EU law substantive provision in force promotes the elimination of international juridical double taxation regarding individuals nor obliges the Member States to adopt and maintain substantive provisions on the elimination of double taxation.

This overview allows us to conclude that although the Member States have been promoting the elimination of international juridical double taxation, individuals engaged in cross-border situations within the EU cannot always count on the elimination of double taxation since substantive measures in this regard may not exist. The elimination of double taxation within the EU depends on the willingness of the Member States to adopt unilateral measures or conclude tax treaties between them. It is also subject to the possibility of Member States revoking those measures or terminating those tax treaties discretionarily.

Regarding procedural measures to avoid international juridical double taxation, it is pointed out that their application depends on the prior application of substantive measures. In other words, procedural measures are applicable only when substantive measures have failed their purpose. Therefore, procedural measures are not available where there are no substantive measures in place to avoid double taxation.

When unilateral substantive measures fail their purpose, taxpayers may only rely on procedural measures provided domestically. The situation is different when bilateral or multilateral measures fail their purpose. In that case, taxpayers may rely on the mutual agreement procedure and arbitration foreseen in legal instruments such as the tax treaties applicable to the case, the BEPS MLI, the EU Multilateral Arbitration Convention and the Directive on tax dispute resolution mechanisms.

In what concerns the concrete methods used by substantive measures to avoid international juridical double taxation, it is observed that bilateral and multilateral instruments apply them in parallel with distributive rules. Those methods may also be foreseen in the States' national law to ensure the elimination of double taxation unilaterally or to implement and concretise the relief provided in a bilateral and multilateral agreement.

Following the OECD MC and the UN MC, the methods to eliminate double taxation are the credit and exemption methods, which may assume different forms, namely the form of full credit, ordinary credit, full exemption, exemption with progression or modified exemption. These forms are characterised by the particular techniques used for avoiding double taxation, which are designed to favour certain interests of States. For instance, the ordinary credit aims to ensure that the credit for the tax paid in the other country does not affect the taxation of taxpayers' domestic income. In turn, the exemption with progression intends to ensure that taxpayers do not escape tax progressivity despite part of their income being obtained abroad, while the modified exemption aims to ensure that the tax base corresponds to the taxpayer's total income.

In essence, in their several forms, the credit and the exemption methods differ from each other regarding the point of reference for eliminating double taxation and the policy that underlies them.

The point of reference for eliminating double taxation under the credit method is the tax paid in the other State, while under the exemption method, it is the income derived from the other State.

The credit method aims to promote export neutrality, meaning that all taxpayers residing in a given country must bear equal taxation regarding their income, regardless of its source. In contrast, the exemption method aims to promote import neutrality, which implies that taxpayers deriving income from a given country must bear equal taxation regarding that income, regardless of their residence.

Finally, reference is made to some specific problems affecting individual taxpayers that may arise from applying the credit and exemption methods. Those problems concern personal and family deductions, deduction of other expenses and deduction of losses, which may partially be dropped when applying those methods. It is noted that the OECD MC offers no solution for these issues, leaving it to the discretion of States. However, the situation is entirely different within the EU since the Member States must comply with EU law, which substantially impacts how these problems are treated.

The next chapter examines the EU legal framework to clarify how EU law limits the exercise of taxing powers by the Member States.

CHAPTER 3
EU Law and the Exercise of Member States' Taxing Powers

– Analysis of the EU legal framework to clarify how EU law limits the exercise of taxing powers by the Member States.

– Study of the CJEU approach for assessing whether a national tax provision conflicts with EU law.

– Analysis of the three categories of obstacles that are likely to hinder free movement: discrimination, restrictions and disparities.

3.1 THE IMPACT OF THE INTERNAL MARKET ON THE MEMBER STATES' TAX SYSTEMS

One of the EU's goals is to establish an internal market, as enshrined in Article 3(3) of the TEU. It has been a goal since the beginning of the European integration project.

In fact, the Treaty of Rome placed the creation of a common market at the centre stage, although it did not offer any explicit definition of this term. The CJEU then clarified that the concept of a common market 'involves the elimination of all obstacles to intra-Community trade in order to merge the national markets into a single market bringing about conditions as close as possible to those of a genuine internal market'.[138]

The term 'common market' was gradually replaced by the term 'internal market', which was first introduced by the Single European Act (SEA) in 1987, providing a definition that has remained unchanged since then. Currently, that definition is foreseen in Article 26(2) of the TFEU, according to which 'internal market' means 'an area without internal frontiers in which the free movement of goods, persons, services and capital is ensured in accordance with the provisions of the Treaties'. The replacement of the terms is not meaningless: rather than demanding just the elimination of obstacles to intra-community, the 'internal market' is intended to impose the

138. CJEU, Case C-15/81 (*Schul*), para. 33.

creation of the conditions to ensure the free movement of goods, persons, services and capital in an area without internal frontiers.[139]

The internal market is conceived to operate as a national market as near as possible. In a domestic market, economic activities flow and internal borders do not exist. An internal market among 27 Member States requires the same fluidity, with activities being carried out without border restraints.

Taxation is thus an internal market matter since it may affect intra-Union movements, particularly cross-border trade, employment, services and investment, impelling taxpayers to stay in their home markets to avoid additional tax burdens. And, as Kemmeren notes, the economic openness required by the internal market should entail the highest possible level of tax neutrality, which means that, ideally, tax considerations should not prevail over economic or any other purposes when pursuing EU cross-border activities.[140]

Consequently, one of the essential tools for establishing the internal market since the beginning of the European project was a fiscal one: the customs union.[141] The abolition of import and export duties between the Member States and any other charges having the equivalent effect and the adoption of a common customs tariff at the Union's outside borders were among the first steps for establishing an EU market closer to a genuine internal market.[142]

Subsequently, the harmonisation of all indirect taxes was another logical step toward accomplishing an internal market. In this regard, discriminatory and protective

139. C. Ehlermann, *The Internal Market Following the Single European Act*, 24(3) Common Market L. Rev. 361 (1987), 369-370 DOI: 10.54648/cola1987020. In contrast, Pescatore argues that the adoption of the 'internal market' term represented a step back: 'For the well-balanced and complex notion of a 'Common Market', the Single Act substitutes the one-sided notion of an 'internal market' – cf. P. Pescatore, *Some Critical Remarks on the Single European Act*, 24 Common Market L. Rev. 9 (1987), 11 DOI: 10.54648/cola1987002. On the terms 'common market' and 'internal market' *See also* R. De La Feria, *The EU VAT System and the Internal Market* (IBFD 2009), 28-34; R. Barents, *The Single Market and National Tax Sovereignty*, in *Fiscal Sovereignty of the Member States in an Internal Market: Past and Future* (S. Jansen ed., Kluwer Law International 2011), 52-53; C. Marchgraber (Kluwer Law International 2018), 65-68.

140. In this regard, *see* E. Kemmeren, *The CJEU and the Internal Market Concept in Direct Taxation*, in *EU Tax Law and Policy in the 21st Century* (W. Haslehner et al. eds, Kluwer Law International 2017), 6-9; however, Schön stresses that 'the Internal Market does not require tax neutrality in all possible ways' and that 'According to the EU Treaties, the concept of international tax neutrality is not the single goal of EU tax law. Rather, this must be balanced with other objectives of the European Union. One of these political objectives is the preservation of fiscal sovereignty of the Member States' – W. Schön, *Neutrality and Territoriality – Competing or Converging Concepts in European Tax Law?*, 68(4/5) Bull. Int'l Tax'n 271 (2015), 276. Indeed, tax neutrality is far from being achieved in the EU and tax purposes may be determinant when deciding to pursue cross-border activities. For instance, recent studies have shown that income and wealth-rich individuals are highly sensitive to tax incentives. Aware of that, Member States have adopted preferential tax arrangements in the area of personal income and wealth taxation to tax-induce mobility – *see* Directorate-General for Internal Policies, *Harmful Practices and Competition in the Area of Personal Income and Wealth Taxation*, European Parliament (2022).

141. Under Art. 28 TFEU, 'the Union shall comprise a customs union which shall cover all trade in goods and which shall involve the prohibition between Member States of customs duties on imports and exports and of all charges having equivalent effect, and the adoption of a common customs tariff in their relations with third countries'.

142. Articles 30 and 31 TFEU.

taxes on products were prohibited, implying that other Member States' products must not be taxed less favourably than national products.[143] As Wattel explains, 'indirect taxes have been harmonized at the EU level because they are conspicuous and direct obstacles to free trade (...). If one is to have free trade, one has no choice but to either abandon such taxes altogether (taxes on the intra-EU border crossing of goods and services: customs duties), or to harmonize them to make them internationally neutral'.[144]

This way, Article 113 of the TFEU provides for 'the harmonisation of legislation concerning turnover taxes, excise duties and other forms of indirect taxation to the extent that such harmonisation is necessary to ensure the establishment and the functioning of the internal market and to avoid distortion of competition'.

In turn, such harmonisation does not exist regarding direct taxation, which concerns taxes on income and wealth. There is no direct tax that the Member States should implement, nor is there an EU framework establishing the main features with which the Member States' direct taxes should comply. Hence, the Member States have the power to design their direct tax systems freely.

The lack of specific provisions in the EU Treaties for harmonising direct taxes may be explained by two interconnected reasons: *(i)* Member States are reluctant to lose their tax sovereignty,[145] and *(ii)* direct taxation plays a central role in national economic policies.

Any attempt to promote harmonisation regarding direct taxes must be made under the general provision of Article 115 of the TFEU, aimed at establishing the internal market, which requires unanimity for the approval of Directives in the field of direct taxation.

Article 114 of the TFEU also provides for legislative approximation on the grounds of ensuring the internal market, requiring only a qualified majority. However, according to Article 114(2), this *shall not apply to fiscal provisions*. The CJEU has already clarified that 'those words cover not only all areas of taxation, without drawing any distinction between the types of duties or taxes concerned, but also all aspects of taxation, whether material rules or procedural rules'.[146]

Although enacting Directives in the field of direct taxation encompasses a complicated process, it does not mean that this path has not been followed. Indeed, there are a few EU Directives adopted on the grounds of Article 115 of the TFEU that establish substantive measures in the field of direct taxation: the Parent-Subsidiary Directive, the Interest and Royalty Directive, the Merger Directive and the Council Directive (EU) 2016/1164 of 12 July 2016 laying down rules against tax avoidance practices that directly affect the functioning of the internal market (the Anti-Tax

143. Articles 110-113 TFEU.
144. P. Wattel et al. (Kluwer Law International 7th ed. 2018), 5.
145. P. Wattel et al. (Kluwer Law International 7th ed. 2018), 5. *See also* P. Farmer, *Direct Taxation and the Fundamental Freedoms*, in *The Oxford Handbook of European Union Law* (A. Arnull & D. Chalmers eds, Oxford 2015), 810-811.
146. CJEU, Case C-338/01 (*Commission v. Council*), para. 63.

Avoidance Directive).[147] In the particular areas covered by these Directives, EU law shapes the Member States' national tax rules.

This kind of harmonisation of Member States' tax laws, made through legislation, coordination and cooperation at the EU level, is known as *positive integration*. Such integration is essential for achieving an internal market with the same characteristics as a national market.

Nevertheless, relying exclusively on positive integration and spontaneous convergence of the Member States' direct tax regimes[148] for achieving and maintaining the proper functioning of the internal market – as one of the main goals of the EU – would be insufficient and lengthy.

Hence, the realisation of the internal market has also been ensured through a process of *negative integration*. As Pistone and Szudoczky observe, the negative integration process 'gives rise to a convergence of national tax systems, leading to a large extent to effects similar to those of positive integration'.[149] That convergence of national tax systems is based on interpreting the prohibitions laid down in the EU Treaties, which are liable to limit the Member States' exercise of taxing powers.[150] Accordingly, the CJEU has stated numerous times that: '[A]lthough, as Community law stands at present, direct taxation does not as such fall within the purview of the Community, the powers retained by the Member States must nevertheless be exercised consistently with Community law.'[151]

---

147. There are also the Directives concerning administrative assistance in the assessment and recovery of taxes that are based both on Arts 113 and 115 of the TFEU, since they regard direct and indirect taxes: Council Directive 2011/16/EU of 15 February 2011 on administrative cooperation in the field of taxation and repealing Directive 77/799/EEC; and the Council Directive 2010/24/EU of 16 March 2010 concerning mutual assistance for the recovery of claims relating to taxes, duties and other measures.
148. Agulló, through concrete examples, remarks that beyond the positive integration carried out by the EU legal action, there is a phenomenon of spontaneous approximation of the direct taxes of the Member States. Cf. A. Agulló Agüero, *El Impuesto de Sociedades ante el Derecho Comunitario*, 2 Impuestos 895 (1986), 903.
149. P. Pistone & R. Szudoczky, *Coordination of Tax Laws and Tax Policies in the EU*, in *Introduction to European Tax Law on Direct Taxation* (M. Lang et al. eds, Linde Verlag 2018), 36-37. Herrera Molina and Villar Ezcurra explain negative integration as a harmonisation resulting from obligations to refrain from acting, while De Juan Casadevall explains it as a de facto harmonisation. Cf. P. Herrera Molina & M. Villar Ezcurra, *Ayudas fiscales y Derecho comunitario: un ejemplo de armonización fiscal negativa*, in *Estudios de derecho financiero y tributario: en homenaje al profesor Calvo Ortega* (I. Martín Dégano et al. eds, Lex Nova, 2005), 2427; J. De Juan Casadevall, *El principio de no discriminación fiscal como instrumento de armonización negativa* (Aranzadi 2010), 72.
150. According to Pistone, 'although taxation remains the domain of the Member States, the exercise of powers in this field may in no way conflict with the supremacy of the internal market. Accordingly, when the ECJ interprets its own law, with a view to ascertaining whether the supremacy of European law is effectively enforced, it does not aim at interfering with what Member States do in the framework of their own prerogatives, but rather it aims at setting the limits to the exercise of such prerogatives' – P. Pistone, *The Requirements of the EU Internal Market: Steering the Development of Direct Taxes Towards a Fair Mix of Positive and Negative Integration*, in *Horizontal Tax Coordination* (M. Lang et al. eds, IBFD 2012), 337.
151. *See, e.g.*, CJEU, Case C-279/93 (*Schumacker*), para. 21; Case C-80/94 (*Wielockx*), para. 16; Case C-107/94 (*Asscher*), para. 36; Case C-391/97 (*Gschwind*), para. 20; Case C-385/00 (*De Groot*), para. 75; Case C-346/04 (*Conijn*), para. 14; Case C-513/04 (*Kerckhaert & Morres*), para. 15; Case C-329/05 (*Meindl*), para. 21.

This way, there is no such thing as tax sovereignty in the sense that Member States' tax systems fall entirely outside the EU law's scope[152] because, as explained by Bizioli and Sacchetto, '[t]he national (tax) interests are recessive when compared with the common European value: the establishment and functioning of the internal market'.[153]

The EU freedoms of movement - which are set forth by the EU Treaties, prevailing over national law[154] - play a fundamental role in limiting the exercise of taxing powers by the Member States, as they entail a prohibition of discrimination and restriction in cross-border activities. Consequently, if a Member State's tax provision constrains an EU freedom of movement, that provision may be repealed by an EU law.

Within this process of negative integration, the Court's case law has a 'destructive effect' on national tax measures colliding with EU law, which has been described as 'harmonisation through the back door' since 'the ECJ cannot act in a constructive manner to improve the compatibility of the national taxation systems of the Member States with each other'.[155]

Nevertheless, the Member States still have full power to define their direct tax systems under the political and technical choices they consider the most appropriate, as long as those choices do not hinder free movement in a prohibited way.

3.2 THE FREEDOMS OF MOVEMENT AS PROHIBITIONS THAT LIMIT THE EXERCISE OF MEMBER STATES' TAXING POWERS

The freedoms of movement are an essential part of the internal market concept, working as its 'building blocks'.[156] The internal market's main idea is to merge the national markets into only one broad European market, where free movement throughout the EU is ensured.

As 'legal tools for opening national systems to the demands of the internal market',[157] the free movement provisions claim neutrality for cross-border activities.

152. R. Barents (S. Jansen ed., Kluwer Law International 2011), 59.
153. G. Bizioli & C. Sacchetto, *European Constitutional Integration: The Case of Direct Taxation*, in *Comparative Fiscal Federalism* (R. Avi Yonah & M. Lang eds, Kluwer Law International 2d ed. 2016), 16.
154. The EU freedoms of movement are foreseen in Arts 21, 28, 45, 49 and 56 of TFEU. The principle of EU law primacy over national law results from the Court's settled case law: Case C-6/64 (*Costa v. ENEL*). Despite of not being foreseen in the TEU, this principle was reaffirmed in the 17th declaration annexed to the Final Act of the Intergovernmental Conference which adopted the Treaty of Lisbon: 'The Conference recalls that, in accordance with well settled case law of the Court of Justice of the European Union, the Treaties and the law adopted by the Union on the basis of the Treaties have primacy over the law of Member States, under the conditions laid down by the said case law. [...].'
155. Cf. R. Seer, *The Jurisprudence of the European Court of Justice: Limitation of the Legal Consequences?*, 46(10) Eur. Tax'n 470 (2006), 471, with further references.
156. R. Lyal, *Nondiscrimination and EU Direct Tax Law*, in *Comparative Fiscal Federalism* (R. Avi Yonah & M. Lang eds, Kluwer Law International 2d ed. 2016), 48.
157. A. Cordewener, *The Prohibitions of Discrimination and Restriction Within the Framework of the Fully Integrated Internal Market*, in *EU Freedoms and Taxation: 2004 EATLP Congress* (F. Vanistendael ed., IBFD 2006), 8.

To this end, they compel the Member States not to treat cross-border activities worse than comparable domestic activities, both in *inbound* and *outbound* situations.

In addition to being anti-protectionist rules, the freedoms of movement comprise subjective rights conceded to individuals and legal persons exercising cross-border activities.[158] They are directly applied, meaning that EU individuals and legal persons - and also individuals and legal persons belonging to the European Economic Area (hereinafter 'EEA')[159] - may immediately invoke the provisions on free movement before a national or EU court without the need for additional measures transposing them into national law.[160]

Each fundamental freedom has its own scope of protection, settled in the TFEU and developed by the CJEU. However, their scope of protection has been interpreted in a convergent way since all freedoms of movement pursue the same goal: establishing and properly functioning the internal market.[161]

The scope of protection of each fundamental freedom is analysed further in the following points. Since the free movement of goods has scarce relevance for direct tax purposes, it is not an object of study.

3.2.1 Free Movement of Persons

The free movement of persons is especially relevant for direct tax purposes, as demonstrated by the many decisions of the CJEU in this regard.

158. A. Zalasiński, *The Role of the European Court of Justice in Taxpayer Protection in the Field of Direct Taxation*, in *Protection of Taxpayer's Rights: European, International and Domestic Tax Law Perspectives* (W. Nykiel & M. Sek eds, Wolters Kluwer Polska 2009), 64. According to some authors, the EU freedoms of movement may be analysed from a triple perspective: as being anti-protectionist rules, individual rights and allocating rules. In this regard, *see* E. Traversa & A. Pirlot, *Tax Sovereignty and Territoriality under Siege: How Far Should the EU Freedoms of Movement Impact on the Territorial Allocation of Taxing Powers Between Member States?*, in *Principles of Law: Function, Status and Impact in EU Tax Law* (C. Brokelind ed., IBFD 2014), 133-138; J. Snell, *Who's Got the Power? Free Movement and Allocation of Competences in EC Law*, 22(1) Y.B. Eur. L. 323 (2003), 323-351 DOI: 10.1093/yel/22.1.323; M. Poiares Maduro, *We the Court: The European Court of Justice and the European Economic Constitution* (Hart Publishing 1998), 166-169.
159. The EEA States not belonging to the EU are Norway, Liechtenstein and Iceland. The Agreement on The European Economic Area (OJ L 001 3.1.1994, p. 3) provides for the inclusion of the EU law covering the freedoms of movement throughout the EEA States. According to Art. 6 of this Agreement, its provisions should be interpreted in conformity with the judgments of the CJEU, in so far as those provisions are identical in substance to the EU Treaties.
160. The Court ruled for the first time about the direct effect of fundamental freedoms, concretely on the free of movement for workers, in Case C-41/74 (*Van Duyn*). Regarding tax matters, *see, e.g.*, Case C-18/95 (*Terhoeve*), paras 55 and 56: '55. [...] [the freedom of movement for workers] has direct effect in the legal orders of the Member States and confers on individuals rights which the national courts must protect. 56. It is also settled case law that every national court must apply Community law in its entirety and protect rights which the latter confers on individuals, where necessary disapplying any provision of national law which may conflict with it.'
161. *See, e.g.*, J. Englisch, *The European Treaties' Implications for Direct Taxes*, 33(8/9) Intertax 310 (2005), 313 DOI: 10.54648/taxi2005056; A. Cordewener (F. Vanistendael ed., IBFD 2006), 39; J. Lang & J. Englisch, *A European Legal Tax Order Based on Ability to Pay*, in *International Tax Law* (A. Amatucci ed., Kluwer Law International 2d ed. 2012), 273.

This freedom encompasses three dimensions with a different scope of protection: *(i)* free movement of workers, *(ii)* freedom of establishment, and *(iii)* free movement of EU citizens.

3.2.1.1 Free Movement of Workers

According to Article 45 of the TFEU, 'the freedom of movement for workers shall be secured within the Union'[162] and 'shall entail the abolition of any discrimination based on nationality between workers of the Member States as regards employment, remuneration and other conditions of work and employment'.[163] Subsequently, it is explained that it entails the right to accept employment offers, move freely within the territory of Member States for employment purposes, stay there for the same purpose and remain there afterwards.[164]

Article 45 of the TFEU requires two elements: a cross-border element, as it does not protect purely internal situations, and an economic element materialised in an employment relationship. This article thus covers all situations in which a national of a Member State is/was/will be employed (economic element) in the territory of another Member State (cross-border element).

The concept of *worker* is not defined in the EU treaties, but its interpretation should be done in light of the EU legal order principles and not by reference to the Member States' laws. Otherwise, this freedom's scope of protection could be frustrated since the Member States would have the power to change the meaning of that term unilaterally.[165]

Furthermore, according to the CJEU, because the term *worker* defines the field of application of one of the fundamental freedoms guaranteed by the Treaty, such a term must be interpreted broadly.[166]

The employment relationship's main feature is that during a period, a person performs services for and under the direction of another person, receiving remuneration

162. Article 45(1) TFEU.
163. Article 45(2) TFEU.
164. Article 45(3) TFEU.
165. *See, e.g.*, CJEU, Case C-53/81 (*Levin*), paras 11 and 12 (not regarding specifically tax issues): '11. [T]he terms "worker" and "activity as an employed person" may not be defined by reference to the national laws of the Member States but have a Community meaning. If that were not the case, the Community rules on freedom of movement for workers would be frustrated, as the meaning of those terms could be fixed and modified unilaterally, without any control by the Community institutions, by national laws which would thus be able to exclude at will certain categories of persons from the benefit of the Treaty. 12. Such would, in particular, be the case if the enjoyment of the rights conferred by the principle of freedom of movement for workers could be made subject to the criterion of what the legislation of the host State declares to be a minimum wage, so that the field of application ratione personae of the Community rules on this subject might vary from one Member State to another. The meaning and the scope of the terms "worker" and "activity as an employed person" should thus be clarified in the light of the principles of the legal order of the Community.'
166. CJEU, Case C-53/81 (*Levin*), para. 13: 'In this respect it must be stressed that these concepts define the field of application of one of the fundamental freedoms guaranteed by the Treaty and, as such, may not be interpreted restrictively.'

in return. Any person performing an effective and genuine activity in such terms, excluding those activities purely marginal and ancillary, is to be treated as a worker.[167] The fact that employment is part-time[168] or temporary, lasting only a few weeks,[169] does not exclude such situations from this freedom's scope of protection.

The application of this provision entails: *(i)* the right of the EU workers to move freely within the Union to pursue activities as an employed person; and *(ii)* the abolition of any discrimination based on nationality between workers of the Member States as regards employment, remuneration and other conditions of work and employment.

In effect, Article 7(2) of Regulation (EU) No. 492/2011 of the European Parliament and of the Council of 5 April 2011 on freedom of movement for workers within the Union, which requires equality of treatment, specifies that nationals of a Member State working in another Member State's territory must enjoy the same social and tax advantages as national workers. As the CJEU has explained, if the same tax advantages were not granted to all EU workers, the principle of equal treatment in terms of remuneration would be rendered ineffective.[170]

Although the wording of Article 45 of the TFEU only refers to discrimination based on nationality, the corresponding prohibition has been interpreted more widely, embracing all covert forms of discrimination that lead to the same result by applying other differentiation criteria.[171] This issue is analysed further in section 3.4.1.1.

Last but not least, according to the case law of the CJEU, the free movement of workers and the consequent prohibition of discrimination address the host Member State (where the employment is performed) and the Member State of origin, both being prevented from precluding cross-border employment.[172]

---

167. CJEU, Case C-107/94 (*Asscher*), para. 25: 'It is settled law that any person who pursues an activity which is effective and genuine, to the exclusion of activities on such a small scale as to be regarded as purely marginal and ancillary, is to be treated as a "worker" within the meaning of Article 48 of the Treaty. According to the case law, the essential characteristic of the employment relationship is that for a certain period of time a person performs services for and under the direction of another person in return for which he receives remuneration.'
168. CJEU, Case C-53/81 (*Levin*), para. 17: 'It should however be stated that whilst part-time employment is not excluded from the field of application of the rules on freedom of movement for workers […].'
169. *See* CJEU, Case C-169/03 (*Wallentin*), concerning a German student working in Sweden during a few weeks in summer who could rely on this freedom to claim a refund of the Swedish wage withholding tax.
170. CJEU, Case C-175/88 (*Biehl*), para. 12: 'The principle of equal treatment with regard to remuneration would be rendered ineffective if it could be undermined by discriminatory national provisions on income tax. […].'
171. CJEU, Case C-175/88 (*Biehl*), para. 13: 'According to the case-law of the Court, the rules regarding equality of treatment forbid not only overt discrimination by reason of nationality but also all covert forms of discrimination which, by the application of other criteria of differentiation, lead to the same result.'
172. *See, e.g.*, CJEU, Case C-18/95 (*Terhoeve*), para. 39: 'Provisions which preclude or deter a national of a Member State from leaving his country of origin in order to exercise his right to freedom of movement therefore constitute an obstacle to that freedom even if they apply without regard to the nationality of the workers concerned.'

3.2.1.2 Freedom of Establishment

The freedom of establishment is foreseen in Articles 49 to 54 of the TFEU.

It includes, under Article 49, 'the right to take up and pursue activities as self-employed persons and to set up and manage undertakings, in particular companies or firms (...) under the conditions laid down for its own nationals by the law of the country where such establishment is effected'. Moreover, 'restrictions on the freedom of establishment of nationals of a Member State in the territory of another Member State shall be prohibited. Such prohibition shall also apply to restrictions on the setting-up of agencies, branches or subsidiaries by nationals of any Member State established in the territory of any Member State'.

The freedom of establishment also encompasses two elements. First, it only covers intra-EU cross-border situations, meaning a transnational connecting factor must be present. Second, it requires the performance of entrepreneurial activities (economic element). Accordingly, the freedom of establishment covers all Member State nationals aiming to pursue entrepreneurial activities in another Member State territory.

Individuals have three possible ways of pursuing entrepreneurial activities cross-borders under the protection of this freedom of movement: *(i)* they have the right to establish directly in the other Member State territory to perform activities as a self-employed person, meaning that there is no subordination, in contrast with employment activities;[173] *(ii)* they can pursue such activities via an undertaking set up in the territory of the other Member State; and *(iii)* they also can pursue the activities mentioned by setting up in the territory of the other Member State agencies, branches or subsidiaries of an existing undertaking.

The freedom of establishment also covers legal persons resident in the EU, which means they must have their registered office, central administration or principal place of business within the Union.[174] Under the CJEU case law, a company's corporate seat 'serves as the connecting factor with the legal system of a particular State, like nationality in the case of natural persons'.[175]

The CJEU has interpreted the concept of establishment in a broad sense, as including the participation, on a stable and continuous basis, in a Member State's

173. Regarding the distinction between the scope of application of the freedom of establishment and the freedom of movement for workers, the Court has already stated that it is not very significant since they are based on the same principles. In this regard, the CJEU affirms, in Case C-107/94 (*Asscher*), para. 29, that: 'In any event [...], a comparison of Articles 48 [free movement of workers] and 52[freedom of establishment] of the Treaty shows that they are based on the same principles both as regards entry into and residence in the territory of the Member States by persons covered by Community law and as regards the prohibition of all discrimination against them on grounds of nationality. The same applies to the pursuit of an economic activity in the territory of the Member States by persons covered by Community law.'

174. Article 54, para. 2, TFEU: '"Companies or firms" means companies or firms constituted under civil or commercial law, including cooperative societies, and other legal persons governed by public or private law, save for those which are non-profit-making.'

175. CJEU, Case C-270/83 (*Commission v. France* – 'Avoir Fiscal'), para. 18.

economic life other than the Member State of origin and to profit therefrom.[176] Therefore, it presupposes a fixed establishment in that State, pursuing genuine activities there.[177]

The provisions on the freedom of establishment address both the host Member State and the Member State of origin. In this regard, the CJEU observed that '[e]ven though, according to their wording, the provisions concerning freedom of establishment are directed to ensuring that foreign nationals and companies are treated in the host Member State in the same way as nationals of that State, they also prohibit the Member State of origin from hindering the establishment in another Member State of one of its nationals or of a company incorporated under its legislation'.[178]

Therefore, individuals and undertakings have the right to leave a Member State (the Member State of origin) to establish themselves in another Member State to pursue or start pursuing an economic activity in that State. The other Member State (the host Member State) must ensure that these individuals and undertakings established there are not treated worse than its own nationals and domestic undertakings.

3.2.1.3 Free Movement of EU Citizens

Under Article 21(1) of the TFEU, every citizen of the EU has the right to move and reside freely within the territory of the Member States.

This provision, together with the general provision on the prohibition of any discrimination on the grounds of nationality established in Article 18 of the TFEU, protects the right of residence and movement of non-economically active persons, such as pensioners, students, children, or anyone else not carrying on activity and moving from one Member State to another.[179] Accordingly, it only applies where there is no

176. CJEU, Case C-646/15 (*Trustees of the Panayi Accumulation & Maintenance Settlements*), para. 27: 'The concept of establishment within the meaning of the Treaty is a very broad one, allowing an EU national to participate, on a stable and continuous basis, in the economic life of a Member State other than his State of origin and to profit therefrom, so contributing to economic and social interpenetration within the European Union.' *See also* Case C-55/94 (*Gebhard*), para. 25.
177. CJEU, Case C-196/04 (*Cadbury Schweppes*), para. 54: 'Having regard to that objective of integration in the host Member State, the concept of establishment within the meaning of the Treaty provisions on freedom of establishment involves the actual pursuit of an economic activity through a fixed establishment in that State for an indefinite period [...]. Consequently, it presupposes actual establishment of the company concerned in the host Member State and the pursuit of genuine economic activity there.'
178. *See, e.g.*, CJEU, Case C-446/03 (*Marks & Spencer*), para. 31.
179. CJEU, Case C-413/99 (*Baumbast*), paras 83 and 84 (not specifically regarding tax issues): '83. Moreover, the Treaty on European Union does not require that citizens of the Union pursue a professional or trade activity, whether as an employed or self-employed person, in order to enjoy the rights provided in Part Two of the EC Treaty, on citizenship of the Union. Furthermore, there is nothing in the text of that Treaty to permit the conclusion that citizens of the Union who have established themselves in another Member State in order to carry on an activity as an employed person there are deprived, where that activity comes to an end, of the rights which are conferred on them by the EC Treaty by virtue of that citizenship. 84. As regards, in particular, the right to reside within the territory of the Member States under Article 18(1) EC, that right is conferred directly on every citizen of the Union by a clear and precise provision of the EC Treaty. Purely as a national of a Member State, and consequently a citizen

economic element present. Otherwise, the situation falls within the scope of the free movement of workers or freedom of establishment.

Furthermore, Article 21 only covers cross-border situations involving EU citizens willing to move or reside within any Member State territory other than that of their nationality. Citizens of other States belonging to the EEA[180] and legal persons – who are not regarded as EU citizens[181] – fall outside the scope of application of this freedom. Therefore, in cases involving citizens of other States belonging to the EEA or legal persons, an economic element must always be present to invoke the right to free movement.

This freedom and the consequent prohibition of discrimination foreseen in Article 18 of the TFEU address the host Member State and the Member State of origin, both being prevented from hindering migration.[182] The prohibition of discrimination embraces all covert forms of discrimination that, by applying other differentiation criteria, lead to the same result of discrimination based on nationality.[183]

3.2.2 Freedom to Provide Services

Under Article 56 of the TFEU, 'restrictions on freedom to provide services within the Union shall be prohibited in respect of nationals of Member States who are established in a Member State other than that of the person for whom the services are intended'.

Like the other economic freedoms, the freedom to provide services entails a cross-border and an economic element.

Regarding the cross-border element, the freedom to provide services only covers intra-EU cross-border situations, not being applied to purely internal situations. This way, this freedom encompasses three situations.[184]

---

of the Union, Mr Baumbast therefore has the right to rely on Article 18(1) EC.' Regarding tax issues falling under Art. 21 TFEU, *see, e.g.*, Case C-224/02 (*Pusa*); Case C-520/04 (*Turpeinen*); Case C-632/13 (*Hirvonen*).

180. The EEA Agreement does not have a provision corresponding to Art. 21 of the TFEU, which may lead to restrictions in cases of cross-border non-economic activities involving nationals of non-Member States belonging to the EEA. *See* M. Helminen, *EU Tax Law – Direct Taxation* (IBFD 2017), 75.
181. The definition of citizenship of the Union is provided by Art. 20(1) of the TFEU. Accordingly, 'every person holding the nationality of a Member State shall be a citizen of the Union. Citizenship of the Union shall be additional to and not replace national citizenship'.
182. CJEU, Case C-224/02 (*Pusa*) paras 18 and 19: '18. In that a citizen of the Union must be granted in all Member States the same treatment in law as that accorded to the nationals of those Member States who find themselves in the same situation, it would be incompatible with the right of freedom of movement were a citizen, in the Member State of which he is a national, to receive treatment less favourable than he would enjoy if he had not availed himself of the opportunities offered by the Treaty in relation to freedom of movement. 19. Those opportunities could not be fully effective if a national of a Member State could be deterred from availing himself of them by obstacles raised to his residence in the host Member State by legislation of his State of origin penalising the fact that he has used them.'
183. *See* further section 3.4.1.1.
184. C. Barnard & S. Peers, *European Union Law* (Oxford University Press 2014), 410; I. Lazarov, *The Relevance of the Fundamental Freedoms for Direct Taxation*, in *Introduction to European Tax Law on Direct Taxation* (M. Lang et al. eds, Linde Verlag 2018), 63.

Firstly, it covers the providers of services. Accordingly, EU nationals and undertakings[185] have the right to move to another Member State to provide services there.

Secondly, it covers the recipients of the service. Consequently, the persons for whom the services are intended have the right to go to another Member State, where the provider is, to enjoy the services there.[186]

Thirdly, it also covers situations where neither the provider nor the recipient moves, but the service is provided from one Member State to another. Such a case occurs when the service is offered via the Internet, telephone or other electronic means of data transmission.[187]

As regards the economic element, Article 57 of the TFEU establishes that 'services' within the meaning of the Treaties are those usually provided for remuneration. An enumeration of what activities are included in that term is provided: activities of an industrial or commercial character, activities of craftsmen, and professions.

The last paragraph of Article 57 of the TFEU evinces that the situation where a provider of services moves to another Member State to render services falls within the scope of this freedom insofar as the activity is pursued *temporarily*. Otherwise, this situation falls within the scope of the freedom of establishment.

As the CJEU explains, to determine the temporary nature of an activity, the duration, regularity, periodicity or continuity of the provision of the service must be taken into account. The temporary nature of the activity does not have to do with the existence of infrastructures for providing the service.[188]

Additionally, Article 57 of the TFEU refers that services are those provided for remuneration *in so far as they are not governed by the provisions relating to freedom of*

185. Meaning companies or firms formed in accordance with the law of a Member State and having their registered office, central administration or principal place of business within the Union – *see* Art. 54 TFEU applicable *ex vi* Art. 62 TFEU.
186. CJEU, Case C-56/09 (*Zanotti*), para. 26: 'In that regard, it should first be noted that, whilst the third paragraph of Article 50 EC refers only to the active provision of services, where the provider moves to the beneficiary of the services, it is apparent from well-established case-law that the freedom to provide services includes the freedom of the persons for whom the services are intended to go to another Member State, where the provider is, in order to enjoy the services there.'
187. CJEU, Case C-243/01 (*Gambelli*), paras 53 and 54: '53. The Court has also held that, on a proper construction, Article 49 EC covers services which the provider offers by telephone to potential recipients established in other Member States and provides without moving from the Member State in which he is established. 54. Transposing that interpretation to the issue in the main proceedings, it follows that Article 49 EC relates to the services which a provider such as Stanley established in a Member State, in this case the United Kingdom, offers via the internet – and so without moving – to recipients in another Member State, in this case Italy, with the result that any restriction of those activities constitutes a restriction on the freedom of such a provider to provide services.'
188. CJEU, Case C 55/94 (*Gebhard*), para. 27: '[T]he temporary nature of the activities in question has to be determined in the light, not only of the duration of the provision of the service, but also of its regularity, periodicity or continuity. The fact that the provision of services is temporary does not mean that the provider of services within the meaning of the Treaty may not equip himself with some form of infrastructure in the host Member State (including an office, chambers or consulting rooms) in so far as such infrastructure is necessary for the purposes of performing the services in question.'

movement for goods, capital and persons. In this regard, the CJEU clarified that the interpretation under which the TFEU establishes a priority order between the freedoms of movement is incorrect. On the contrary, the wording of the article seeks to include in the notion of services all the economic activities not covered by the other freedoms. This way, it ensures that all economic activities fall within the scope of fundamental freedoms.[189]

These provisions on the free movement of services aim to forbid national laws that hinder the rendering of services between the Member States, applying to both inbound and outbound situations.

3.2.3 Free Movement of Capital and Payments

Under Article 63 of the TFEU, all restrictions on the movement of capital and payments between the Member States and between the Member States and third countries shall be prohibited.

As the TFEU does not define the notion of *capital* and *payments* movement, the CJEU has been using Directive 88/361/EEC as an interpretative guideline.[190]

Annexe I of the Directive contains a non-exhaustive list of transactions representing capital movements, which include direct investments; investments in real estate; operations in securities; operations in units of collective investment undertakings; operations in current and deposit accounts with financial institutions; credits related to commercial transactions or the provision of services; financial loans and credits; sureties, other guarantees and rights of pledge; transfers in performance of

189. CJEU, Case C-452/04 (*Fidium Finanz*), paras 31 and 32: '31. It has been argued before the Court that [...] in the light of the wording of the first paragraph of Article 50 EC [Art. 57 of TFEU], the provisions concerning the freedom to provide services apply as an alternative to those which govern the free movement of capital. 32. That argument cannot be accepted. Although in the definition of the notion of "services" laid down in the first paragraph of Article 50 EC it is specified that the services "are not governed by the provisions relating to freedom of movement for goods, capital and persons", that relates to the definition of that notion and does not establish any order of priority between the freedom to provide services and the other fundamental freedoms. The notion of "services" covers services which are not governed by other freedoms, in order to ensure that all economic activity falls within the scope of the fundamental freedoms.'

190. Council Directive 88/361/EEC of 24 June 1988 for the implementation of Art. 67 of the Treaty. The Directive had limited scope, covering only the Member States. With the Treaty of Maastricht, the free movement of capital was extended (unilaterally) to third countries. Therefore, the Directive became obsolete, but the Court still relies on it regarding the meaning of capital. *See, e.g.*, CJEU, Case C-386/04 (*Centro di Musicologia Walter Stauffer*), para. 22: 'The Treaty does not define the notions of "capital movements" or "payments". However, it is established case-law that, in as much as Article 73b of the EC Treaty [Article 63 of TFEU] substantially reproduces the contents of Article 1 of Directive 88/361, and even though that directive was adopted on the basis of Articles 69 and 70(1) of the EEC Treaty (Articles 67 to 73 of the EEC Treaty having been replaced by Articles 73b to 73g of the EC Treaty, now Articles 56 EC to 60 EC), the nomenclature in respect of "movements of capital" annexed to Directive 88/361 still has the same indicative value, for the purposes of defining the notion of capital movements, as it did before the entry into force of those provisions, subject to the qualification, contained in the introduction to the nomenclature, that the list set out therein is not exhaustive.'

insurance contracts; personal capital movements, comprising loans, gifts and endowments, dowries, inheritances and legacies; physical import and export of financial assets; and other capital movements.

Thus, this freedom has a broad scope, covering any rights transferred concerning movable and immovable assets. The transfer of rights configures the economic element required by this freedom. A cross-border element must also be present since purely internal situations are not covered.

There is a unique feature regarding this freedom's scope of application: it also coverers operations involving third States. Nevertheless, the freedom of movement of capital and payments in operations involving the third States is not as liberalised as in operations between Member States. In fact, under Article 64 of the TFEU, significant restrictions may be applied by the Member States in the movement of capital or payments to or from non-Member States. Under Article 66 of the TFEU, temporary safeguard measures concerning third countries are admitted when, in exceptional circumstances, movements of capital to or from third countries cause or threaten to cause serious difficulties for the operation of the economic and monetary union.

Restrictions are admissible in this context because third States are neither bound by EU law nor by reciprocal obligations, being placed in a different legal context, as stressed by the Court.[191]

The fact that, unlike the other freedoms, the scope of the free movement of capital and payments extends to third countries raises a particular concern. In this regard, it should be noted that the freedoms of movement are defined comprehensively and complementary, aiming to cover and protect all economic activities carried out cross-borders; consequently, their scope of application is liable to overlap. This overlap occurs especially between the free movement of capital and payments and the other freedoms since, as pointed out by the CJEU, the freedom to move certain types of capital is, in practice, a precondition for the effective exercise of other EU freedoms.[192]

191. CJEU, Case C-135/17 (*X – Sociétés intermédiaires établies dans des pays tiers*), paras 90 and 92: '90. [I]t must be recalled that the case-law concerning restrictions on the exercise of the freedoms of movement within the European Union cannot be transposed in its entirety to movements of capital between Member States and third countries, since such movements take place in a different legal context. [...] 92. It is also apparent from the Court's settled case-law that, where the legislation of a Member State makes entitlement to a tax advantage dependent on the satisfaction of conditions, compliance with which can be verified only by obtaining information from the competent authorities of a third country, it is, in principle, legitimate for that Member State to refuse to grant that advantage if, for example, because that third country has no treaty obligation to provide information, it proves impossible to obtain that information from that third country.'

192. CJEU, Case C-203/80 (*Casati*), para. 8. *See also* A. P. Dourado, *The EU Free Movement of Capital and Third Countries: Recent Developments*, 45(3) Intertax 192 (2017), 194 DOI: 10.54648/taxi2017016; A. P. Dourado, *Free Movement of Capital: The European Union Anti-Tax Avoidance Package and Brexit*, 44(12) Intertax 870 (2016), 872 DOI: 10.54648/taxi2016081; D. Smit, *The Relationship Between the Free Movement of Capital and the Other EC Treaty Freedoms in Third Country Relationships in the Field of Direct Taxation: A Question of Exclusivity, Parallelism or Causality*, 16(6) EC Tax Rev. 252 (2007) DOI: 10.54648/ecta2007043, where it is discussed whether the free movement of capital may be applied simultaneously with other freedoms or whether the other freedoms restrict its substantive scope. Furthermore, Kiekebeld and Smit defend that the question of the concurrence of the fundamental freedoms of movement should not be a question of exclusivity or parallelism, but rather a question of causality between the contested direct tax measure and the movement of capital – *see* B. Kiekebeld & D. Smit, *EU Free*

The overlap between fundamental freedoms is not problematic in cases involving only the Member States. After all, a strict distinction between operations falling within the scope of one or another freedom is not essential,[193] as all the freedoms of movement pursue the same goal, which is the establishment and proper functioning of the internal market.

However, the situation is different in cases involving third countries because the EU treaties do not extend the territorial scope of the other freedoms to third countries, preventing economic operators from those countries from profiting from them.[194] In these cases, determining whether the operation falls within the free movement of capital and payments or within the other freedoms is not irrelevant and is particularly difficult when, on the table, are also the freedom of establishment or the freedom to provide services.

According to the CJEU, to determine whether one or another freedom of movement is at stake, the purpose of the national provision regulating the situation at issue must be taken into account.[195] As Dourado notes, the purpose test acts as a tiebreaker rule that allows deciding in favour of one or the other fundamental freedom.[196]

Thus, as regards the overlap between the freedom of establishment and the free movement of capital and payments, it must be taken into account whether the national provision in question is intended to regulate a professional or commercial activity or whether it is intended to regulate investment.[197] As Schön explains, these freedoms illuminate different aspects of economic behaviour: the freedom of establishment is activity-related, while the free movement of capital is investment-related.[198]

Regarding the overlap with the freedom of providing services, the analysis is centred on whether the national measure primarily addresses the rendering of services. In such a case, because any restriction on the free movement of capital would be merely a consequence, the freedom to provide services is of application.[199]

Movement of Capital and Corporate Income Taxation: The Relationship Between the Free Movement of Capital and the Other TFEU Freedoms and Justification Grounds in a Third Country Context, in *Fiscal Sovereignty of the Member States in an Internal Market. Past and Future* (S. Jansen ed., Kluwer Law International 2011), 123-129.

193. A. P. Dourado, 45(3) Intertax 192 (2017), 194; A. P. Dourado, 44(12) Intertax 870 (2016), 872.

194. CJEU, Case C-35/11 (*Test Claimants in the FII Group Litigation*), para. 100, alluding specifically to the freedom of establishment: 'Since the Treaty does not extend freedom of establishment to third countries, it is important to ensure that the interpretation of Article 63(1) TFEU as regards relations with third countries does not enable economic operators who do not fall within the limits of the territorial scope of freedom of establishment to profit from that freedom.'

195. *See, e.g.*, CJEU, Case C-464/14 (*SECIL*), para. 31; Case C-35/11 (*Test Claimants in the FII Group Litigation*), paras 89 and 90. *See* further A. P. Dourado, 45(3) Intertax 192 (2017), 194, who defends that the purpose of the law has absorbed other arguments which in the past were used by the Court to resolve overlaps between EU freedoms.

196. A. P. Dourado, 45(3) Intertax 192 (2017), 197.

197. For instance, where the national measure addresses the cases in which a shareholder has a decisive influence on a company's decisions, the freedom of establishment is at stake [*see, e.g.*, CJEU, Case C-251/98 (*Baars*), para. 22]. Conversely, where the national measure addresses the cases of portfolio investments, the free movement of capital is at stake.

198. W. Schön, *Free Movement of Capital and Freedom of Establishment*, 17(3) Bus. Org. L. Rev. 229 (2016), 259.

199. CJEU, Case C-452/04 (*Fidium Finanz*), para. 49: 'It is apparent that, in the circumstances of the main case, the predominant consideration is freedom to provide services rather than the free

Lastly, it must be noted that under Article 65(1)(a) of the TFEU, the protection of free movement of capital and payments shall be without prejudice to the right of Member States to apply their tax provisions which distinguish between taxpayers who are not in the same situation with regard to their place of residence (i.e., between residents and non-residents) or with regard to the place where their capital is invested (i.e., between domestic and foreign-source capital income). However, according to Article 65(3), those measures cannot constitute a means of arbitrary discrimination or a disguised restriction on the free movement of capital and payments.

In this respect, the Court has clarified that Article 65(1) must be interpreted strictly, as it is a derogation from the fundamental principle of the free movement of capital and payments. Accordingly, a distinction must be drawn between unequal treatment permitted under Article 65(1) of the TFEU and arbitrary discrimination prohibited by Article 65(3) of the TFEU. It follows from the Court's settled case law that for a national provision to be compatible with the free movement of capital and payments, any difference in treatment must concern situations which are not objectively comparable or justified by overriding reasons in the general interest.[200]

3.3 THE MECHANISMS FOR CONTROLLING THE EXERCISE OF MEMBER STATES' TAXING POWERS

By joining the EU, which has the establishment of an internal market among its objectives, Member States have agreed to limit their margin of discretion to some extent.[201] In tax matters, this is particularly evident in harmonised areas, where an EU law shapes national tax rules. This limitation is also present even in non-harmonised areas, as is generally the case of direct taxation. As mentioned, the Member States must comply with EU law when exercising their taxing powers, and the CJEU plays a fundamental role in controlling so.

---

movement of capital. Since the rules in dispute impede access to the German financial market for companies established in non-member countries, they affect primarily the freedom to provide services. Given that the restrictive effects of those rules on the free movement of capital are merely an inevitable consequence of the restriction imposed on the provision of services, it is not necessary to consider whether the rules are compatible with Article 56 EC [Art. 63 of TFEU] et seq.'

200. CJEU, Case C-45/17 (*Jahin*), paras 32 and 34: '32. It is apparent from settled case-law of the Court that that provision, in so far as it is a derogation from the fundamental principle of the free movement of capital, must be interpreted strictly. Accordingly, it cannot be interpreted as meaning that all tax legislation which draws a distinction between taxpayers on the basis of their place of residence is automatically compatible with the Treaty. [...] 34. A distinction must therefore be drawn between unequal treatment which is permitted under Article 65(1) TFEU and arbitrary discrimination which is prohibited by reason of Article 65(3) TFEU. In that respect, it follows from settled case-law of the Court that, in order for a national provision, such as that at issue in the main proceedings, to be capable of being regarded as compatible with the Treaty provisions on the free movement of capital, the difference in treatment must concern situations which are not objectively comparable or be justified by overriding reasons in the general interest.'

201. F. Vanistendael, *The ECJ at the Crossroads: Balancing Tax Sovereignty Against the Imperatives of the Single Market*, 46(9) Eur. Tax'n 413 (2006), 419.

The Court is the EU's institution responsible for ensuring that 'in the interpretation and application of the Treaties the law is observed'.[202] The Court guarantees the effectiveness of EU law through the several safeguard mechanisms foreseen in the TFEU.[203] In tax matters, the most relevant ones are the infringement procedure and the preliminary ruling, which allow the CJEU to analyse the compatibility of national measures with EU law.

Through the infringement procedure, the European Commission[204] or any Member State[205] may take legal action against another Member State failing to implement EU law. The issue may be brought before the CJEU, which decides on the Member State's compliance with the EU law.[206]

In turn, the preliminary ruling is a procedure exercised by national courts before the CJEU, which enables them to question the CJEU about the interpretation or validity of an EU law and, therefore, on national law's conformity with the EU law.[207] It aims to ensure a uniform interpretation and application of EU law in all the Member States.

Although these procedures are essential to ensure, *inter alia*, the subjective rights granted under an EU law to individuals and undertakings engaged in cross-border activities, taxpayers only have indirect access to them.

For instance, regarding the infringement procedure, taxpayers may file a complaint against a Member State's breach of an EU law. The European Commission follows up on the complaint but is not obliged to open a formal infringement procedure.[208] The eventual judgment of the CJEU does not confer any right to the complainants, who must safeguard their interests domestically before a national court.[209] In turn, regarding the preliminary ruling, taxpayers may challenge domestic law's compatibility with an EU law by raising the issue in proceedings before national courts.[210] National courts from which decisions there is no higher appeal are obliged to refer the question to the CJEU.[211] Such obligation ceases in cases of *acte clair*,[212]

202. Article 19(1) TEU.
203. The safeguard mechanisms are the infringement procedure (Arts 258 to 260 TFEU), the action for annulment (Arts 263 and 264 TFEU), the action for failure to act (Arts 265 and 266 TFEU), the preliminary ruling (Art. 267 TFEU) and the EU non-contractual liability (Art. 268 TFEU).
204. Article 258 TFEU.
205. Article 259 TFEU.
206. *Ibid.*
207. Article 267 TFEU, paras 1 and 2.
208. Point 2 of the Annex 'Administrative procedures for the handling of relations with the complainant regarding the application of European Union law' to the Communication from the Commission, *EU law: Better results through better application*, (2017/C 18/02) OJ C 18, 19.1.2017, p. 10-20.
209. P. Schonewillet, *Eliminating Tax Barriers via the Infringement Procedure of Article 226 of the EC Treaty*, 15(3) EC Tax Rev. 147 (2006), 147 DOI: 10.54648/ecta2006027.
210. In this regard, *see* A. Di Pietro, *Justice fiscale et intégration européen: le rôle des juges fiscaux*, 2 Cluj Tax Forum Journal 7 (2019), 10, who stresses national courts' importance in the EU integration process, as they are responsible for interpreting national law in line with EU law and CJEU decisions.
211. Article 267, para. 3, TFEU.
212. The *acte clair* doctrine refers to the circumstances under which the last instance national courts are dismissed from the obligation of referral EU law interpretation questions to the CJEU. The

meaning that: *(i)* the question is not relevant because the answer to that question, regardless of what it may be, can in no way affect the outcome of the case;[213] or *(ii)* the question raised is materially identical with a question which has already been the subject of a preliminary ruling in a similar case (*acte éclairé*);[214] or *(iii)* correct application of the EU law is so evident as to leave no scope for any reasonable doubt (*acte clair*).[215]

Nonetheless, these procedures are still a powerful tool in taxpayers' hands, by which the laws of Member States may be challenged.[216] As affirmed by Poiares Maduro, 'the Treaties are not simply to be interpreted as an agreement between States, but as having been created for the "peoples of Europe": Community rules are directed towards individuals and can be invoked by them. The "subjectivation" of Community law provided a particularly strong instrument for ensuring the implementation and the effectiveness of Community law in national legal orders. It also presented Community law as a source of new rights for nationals of all Member States. Decisions of the Court are not seen as deciding conflicts among states, but as protecting individuals from states: even, in some cases, from their own home-state'.[217]

The CJEU, therefore, has a vital and challenging role regarding, in particular, direct taxation: it is responsible for protecting taxpayers against Member States' breaches of EU law and balancing the internal market imperatives with the Member States' interests.

CJEU introduced these circumstances in Case C-283/81 (*Cilfit*). Before, in the Joined Cases C-28/62 to 30/62 (*Da Costa*), the Court had already accepted an exception to the obligation of referral.

213. CJEU, Case C-283/81 (*Cilfit*), para. 10: '[...] Accordingly, those courts or tribunals are not obliged to refer to the Court of Justice a question concerning the interpretation of Community law raised before them if that question is not relevant, that is to say, if the answer to that question, regardless of what it may be, can in no way affect the outcome of the case.'
214. *Ibid.*, para. 14: 'The same effect, as regards the limits set to the obligation laid down by the third paragraph of Article 177 [now Art. 267 of TFEU], may be produced where previous decisions of the Court have already dealt with the point of law in question, irrespective of the nature of the proceedings which led to those decisions, even though the questions at issue are not strictly identical.' Before, in CJEU, Joined Cases C-28/62 to 30/62 (*Da Costa*): '[T]he authority of an interpretation under Article 177 already given by the Court may deprive the obligation of its purpose and thus empty it of its substance. Such is the case especially when the question raised is materially identical with a question which has already been the subject of a preliminary ruling in a similar case.' The referral obligation of the last instance national court ceases due to the existence of precedent (settled case law on the issue).
215. CJEU, Case C-283/81 (*Cilfit*), para. 16: 'Finally, the correct application of Community law may be so obvious as to leave no scope for any reasonable doubt as to the manner in which the question raised is to be resolved. Before it comes to the conclusion that such is the case, the national court or tribunal must be convinced that the matter is equally obvious to the courts of the other Member States and to the Court of Justice. Only if those conditions are satisfied, may the national court or tribunal refrain from submitting the question to the Court of Justice and take upon itself the responsibility for resolving it.' The referral obligation of the last instance national court ceases even without the existence of a previous decision of the CJEU on the issue.
216. I. Lazarov (M. Lang et al. eds, Linde Verlag 2018), 64, making reference to the preliminary ruling.
217. M. Poiares Maduro (Hart Publishing 1998), 9.

3.4 THE LIMITS TO THE EXERCISE OF MEMBER STATES' TAXING POWERS

The exercise of Member States' taxing powers is limited by the prohibitions set forth by the EU Treaty provisions. The CJEU is responsible for assessing whether or not a national provision conflicts with an EU law and, consequently, whether or not the Member State in question must repeal that provision. As it results from its case law in the field of direct taxation, the CJEU follows a step-by-step approach to this end.

The steps tendentially followed by the CJEU may be summarised as follows:[218] *(i)* ascertaining the freedom of movement affected by the national tax provision; *(ii)* ascertaining the obstacle to that freedom of movement caused by the national tax provision; *(iii)* ascertaining the possible justifications for the obstacle caused; and *(iv)* controlling the proportionality between the obstacle and the justification reason presented.

Since step *(i)* has already been addressed when studying the scope of protection of each freedom of movement in section 3.2., only steps *(ii)*, *(iii)* and *(iv)* are analysed in more detail in the following sections.

3.4.1 Obstacles to the EU Freedoms of Movement

An obstacle to the freedom of movement may be categorised as a discriminatory restriction (or simply discrimination), a non-discriminatory restriction (or simply restriction) or a disparity.

It is not always easy to determine under which category each obstacle falls, despite the critical consequences such a characterisation implies.

As analysed further below, only discriminations and restrictions are considered incompatible with the internal market, as expressly laid down, in general terms, in Article 18 of the TFEU, and particularly in Articles 45, 49, 56 and 63 of the TFEU regarding the freedoms of movement. Disparities, although undesirable within the EU context, are not prohibited in light of EU law.

3.4.1.1 Discriminations and Restrictions

The general prohibition of discrimination is laid down in Article 18 of the TFEU, first paragraph. Accordingly, 'within the scope of application of the Treaties, and without

218. We follow the systematic presented by Nogueira. The author stresses that the four typical moments mentioned above constitute a tendential framework that is followed by the Court with certain stability – *see* J. F. Nogueira, *Direito Fiscal Europeu – o paradigma da proporcionalidade* (Wolters Kluwer Portugal 2010), 204-205. In turn, in P. Wattel et al. (Kluwer Law International 7th ed. 2018), 74-75, the authors point out only three steps: comparability test, justification test and proportionality test. The comparability test is divided in two moments: ascertaining whether the national tax measure distinguishes between cross-border and domestic comparable situations; and whether there is an objective difference between the two situations which explains the difference in treatment.

prejudice to any special provisions contained therein, any discrimination on grounds of nationality shall be prohibited'.[219]

The provisions on freedom of movement (i.e., Articles 45, 49, 56 and 63 of the TFEU) are specific rules that render this principle effective in a concrete context. As Papadopoulou explains, the freedom of movement and the non-discrimination principle complement each other within the EU juridical order, as they cannot be effective without one another.[220]

Non-discrimination is an instrumental principle in attaining the EU internal market.[221] Because such a market must be established among 27 States, the principle of non-discrimination prescribes a rule of national treatment. Consequently, the Member States must offer national treatment to other Member States' nationals exercising their right to free movement.

In this sense, the non-discrimination provision is a manifestation of the equality principle (formulated as equal treatment) stated in its negative form (prohibition of discrimination).[222] The Court, resorting to the Aristotelian concept of equality, defines discrimination as applying different rules to comparable situations or applying the same rule to different situations.[223]

However, despite being closely connected with the equality principle, non-discrimination does not demand strict equal treatment. In other words, it does not demand that individuals or undertakings exercising their right to free movement within the EU be treated in the same way as those who, in a comparable situation, do not exercise that right. As Bammens explains, it is enough that individuals or undertakings exercising an EU freedom of movement not be treated less favourably.[224] For that

219. This way, due to the principle *specialia generalibus derogant*, the non-discrimination rule enshrined in the free movement articles has priority over the general rule established in Art. 18 TFEU. This article is only applied independently to situations governed by EU law concerning which the Treaty does not lay down any specific prohibition of discrimination, as it is the case analysed in section 3.2.1.3. *See, e.g.*, CJEU, Case C-336/96 (*Gilly*), para. 37; *see also* Opinion of AG Darmon in Case C-112/91 (*Werner*), para. 52.

220. R. Papadopoulou, *Principes généraux du droit et droit communautaire: origines et concrétisation* (Bruylant 1996), 81.

221. A. García Prats, *Imposición directa, no discriminación y derecho comunitario* (Tecnos 1998), 27-29.

222. CJEU, Case C-224/00 (*Commission v. Italy*), para. 14 (not regarding tax issues): 'First, it should be recalled that Article 6 of the Treaty, which is a specific expression of the general principle of equality, prohibits any discrimination on grounds of nationality.' *See also* M. C. Barreiro Carril, *Los impuestos directos y el Derecho de la Unión Europea: la armonización negativa realizada por el TJUE* (Instituto de Estudios Fiscales 2012), 173; G. González García, *Una aproximación al contenido de los conceptos de discriminación y restricción en el derecho comunitario*, 8 Documentos IEF 1 (2004), 9-10; A. García Prats (Tecnos 1998), 19-20.

223. *See, e.g.*, CJEU, Case C-279/93 (*Schumacker*), para. 30: 'It is also settled law that discrimination can arise only through the application of different rules to comparable situations or the application of the same rule to different situations.' The European Court of Human Rights (ECtHR) adopts an identical formulation, according to which the prohibition of discrimination (Art. 14 of the European Convention of Human Rights) 'not only requires that persons in a similar situation must be treated in an equal manner but also requires that persons whose situations are significantly different must be treated differently' – *see, e.g.*, ECtHR, Application No. 58641/00, *Hoogendijk v. The Netherlands*, 6 Jan. 2005, para. 2.

224. N. Bammens, *The Principle of Non-discrimination in International and European Tax Law* (IBFD 2012), 527. *See also* R. Papadopoulou (Bruylant 1996), 72-73. It must be noted that the

reason, Santa-Bárbara Rupérez defends that tax equality and tax non-discrimination are not interchangeable terms.[225]

This way, a Member State breaches the principle of non-discrimination when it treats another Member State's nationals worse than its own nationals when they are in a comparable situation.

However, this formulation - resulting in essence from the wording of the fundamental freedoms' provisions - presents a significant limitation, as it seems to target only the discriminatory treatment by one Member State vis-à-vis the nationals of another Member State. The CJEU overcame this shortcoming by interpreting the fundamental freedoms' provisions according to their context and purposes.

On the one hand, as mentioned above in section 3.2, when analysing the scope of application of the freedoms of movement, despite the express reference to nationality in Articles 18, 45, 49 and 56 of the TFEU, the Court has considered that the principle of non-discrimination would be rendered ineffective if it could be undermined by applying differentiation criteria other than nationality that led to the same result.[226]

For example, regarding direct taxation, *residence* has a more significant role than nationality as a connecting factor for triggering taxation. Therefore, the CJEU holds that a tax measure treating worse non-resident taxpayers than resident taxpayers in a comparable situation is liable to operate mainly to the detriment of nationals of other Member States since non-residents are, in most cases, foreigners.[227]

This way, the prohibition of discrimination on the grounds of nationality (usually referred to as 'overt discrimination' or 'direct discrimination') evolved in the CJEU case law to cover also forms of discrimination operating through the application of other criteria of differentiation (referred to as 'covert discrimination' or 'indirect discrimination').

On the other hand, the CJEU has had to deal with the issue of measures that hinder free movement without specifically targeting nationals (or residents) of other Member States, as those measures apply equally to both internal and cross-border situations.

---

protection against discrimination in this context is only operative regarding individuals or undertakings exercising freedom of movement.

225. J. Santa-Bárbara Rupérez, *La no discriminación fiscal* (Edersa 2001), 246.

226. This line of reasoning started in the CJEU, Case C-152/73 (*Sotgiu*), para. 11: 'The rules regarding equality of treatment [...] forbid not only overt discrimination by reason of nationality but also all covert forms of discrimination which, by the application of other criteria of differentiation, lead in fact to the same result. This interpretation, which is necessary to ensure the effective working of one of the fundamental principles of the Community, is explicitly recognized by the fifth recital of the preamble to Regulation No 1612/68 which requires that equality of treatment of workers shall be ensured "in fact and in law". It may therefore be that criteria such as place of origin or residence of a worker may, according to circumstances, be tantamount, as regards their practical effect, to discrimination on the grounds of nationality, such as is prohibited by the Treaty and the Regulation.'

227. *See, e.g.*, CJEU, Case C-175/88 (*Biehl*), para. 14: 'Even though the criterion of permanent residence in the national territory [...] applies irrespective of the nationality of the taxpayer concerned, there is a risk that it will work in particular against taxpayers who are nationals of other Member States. It is often such persons who will in the course of the year leave the country or take up residence there.'

This problem was first detected regarding the free movement of goods.[228] For instance, the legal requirements established by each Member State apply indiscriminately to all goods, regardless of their origin. However, the products produced and sold within the same Member State have only to fulfil the legal requirements of that country, while the products produced in one Member State and sold in another Member State have to comply with two different regulatory systems. Thus, despite being applied without distinction, those measures hinder free movement, which is incompatible with the very idea of the internal market.

In direct tax matters, the problem of measures that hamper free movement despite being applied without distinction is usually created by the Member State of origin – i.e., of which the taxpayer is a resident.[229] This State prevents its residents from exercising free movement by applying an apparently neutral measure that creates an additional burden on outbound situations. In other words, despite the Member State of origin applying the same tax treatment to residents pursuing a purely internal activity and to residents pursuing a cross-border activity, the cross-border activity becomes less attractive. This loss of attractiveness happens because the apparently neutral measure implies a limitation applied only to activities that do not take place exclusively within the borders of the Member State of origin.[230] Such a limitation occurs, for example, regarding personal tax deductions[231] or loss deductions.[232]

The Court dealt with this shortcoming of the principle of non-discrimination by resorting to the concept of restriction, which is also foreseen in the free movement provisions. Indeed, the TFEU uses open wording, employing the terms 'discrimination' and 'restriction' when stating that certain national measures are forbidden. The free movement of goods prohibits quantitative restrictions between the Member States and

228. CJEU, Case C-8/74 (*Dassonville*).
229. For a further analysis of the obstacles created by the Member State of origin, *see* M. C. Barreiro Carril (Instituto de Estudios Fiscales 2012), 210-225.
230. *See, e.g.*, Case C-18/95 (*Terhoeve*), para. 39: 'Provisions which preclude or deter a national of a Member State from leaving his country of origin in order to exercise his right to freedom of movement therefore constitute an obstacle to that freedom even if they apply without regard to the nationality of the workers concerned.'
231. CJEU, Case C-204/90 (*Bachmann*), para. 31: 'It is to be noted that provisions such as those contained in the Belgian legislation at issue constitute a restriction on freedom to provide services. Provisions requiring an insurer to be established in a Member State as a condition of the eligibility of insured persons to benefit from certain tax deductions in that State operate to deter those seeking insurance from approaching insurers established in another Member State, and thus constitute a restriction of the letter's freedom to provide services.'
232. *See, e.g.*, CJEU, Case C-414/06 (*Lidl Belgium*), paras 23-26: '23. As regards the tax regime at issue in the main proceedings, it must be pointed out that a provision which allows losses incurred by a permanent establishment to be taken into account in calculating the profits and taxable income of the principal company constitutes a tax advantage. 24. However, the provisions of that tax regime do not grant such a tax advantage where the losses are incurred by a permanent establishment situated in a Member State other than that in which the principal company is established. 25. In those circumstances, the tax situation of a company which has its registered office in Germany and has a permanent establishment in another Member State is less favourable than it would be if the latter were to be established in Germany. By reason of that difference in tax treatment, a German company could be discouraged from carrying on its business through a permanent establishment situated in another Member State. 26. It must be held that the tax regime at issue in the main proceedings involves a restriction on the freedom of establishment.'

measures having an equivalent effect (Articles 34 and 35 of the TFEU). The free movement of workers dictates the abolition of any discrimination based on nationality (Article 45(2) of the TFEU). The freedom of establishment and the freedom of providing services prohibit any restriction using nationality as the parameter (Articles 49 and 56 of the TFEU). The free movement of capital and services forbids restrictions (Article 63(1) and (2) of the TFEU), stressing that any differentiation in treatment cannot constitute a means of arbitrary discrimination or a disguised restriction (Article 65(3) of the TFEU).

The concept of restriction gained special relevance in the free movement of goods because nationality was of little use, and, as said, the perverse effect on the internal market of measures applied without distinction was more evident. In fact, in the *Dassonville* case, the Court began to interpret broadly the meaning of 'measures having equivalent effect', establishing that 'all trading rules enacted by Member States which are capable of hindering, directly or indirectly, actually or potentially, intra-Community trade are to be considered as measures having an effect equivalent to quantitative restrictions'.[233] The prohibition of restrictions was thus interpreted as a right to market access. This interpretation was then transposed to the other freedoms of movement due to their convergent scope of protection.

In their pure form, the prohibition of discriminatory and restrictive measures entails a different approach to the problem.

The prohibition of discriminatory measures has a *relative* structure. As Cordewener explains, the prohibition of discrimination requires comparative assessment, where the relevant *tertium comparationis* is the hypothetical purely domestic activity, which is equivalent to the cross-border activity except that it lacks the cross-border element.[234] This way, a measure is deemed discriminatory if it provides different treatment for equivalent domestic and cross-border situations, the latter being treated worse than the former.

In turn, the prohibition of restrictive measures has an *absolute* structure connected with the right to market access or, more broadly, the *right to freedom of movement*.[235] In this case, a comparative assessment between cross-border and domestic treatment is unnecessary since the cornerstone of the prohibition of restriction is the national rule's potential to hinder cross-border trade or activities. The restrictive national measure constitutes, per se, an obstacle to exercising the freedom of movement. As affirmed by AG Bobek, the restriction approach 'obviates, in theory

233. CJEU, Case C-8/74 (*Dassonville*), para. 5.
234. A. Cordewener (F. Vanistendael ed., IBFD 2006), 12. The author states that non-discrimination 'is a relative concept which cannot exist in a vacuum but always requires *a tertium comparationis* as point of reference. Since the legal protection of cross-border economic transactions and the abolition of discrimination as compared to transactions taking place merely within the Member State concerned are at issue, the relevant *tertium comparationis* is the hypothetical purely domestic transaction which is equivalent to the cross-border transaction except for the fact that it lacks the cross-border element'. *See also* R. Papadopoulou (Bruylant 1996), 64; P. Pistone, *The Impact of Community Law on Tax Treaties: Issues and Solutions* (Kluwer Law International 2002), 42-43.
235. A. Cordewener (F. Vanistendael ed., IBFD 2006), 26; P. Pistone (Kluwer Law International 2002), 46.

at least, the need for any comparison or identification of relatively disadvantageous treatment'.[236]

Although the prohibition of restriction is much more far-reaching than the prohibition of discrimination, in both analyses, what is at stake is allowing the use of an EU-wide internal market without the Member States inducing its nationals and residents to *stay at home* or *stay away*, as Cordewener notes.[237]

Nevertheless, the wideness of the restriction approach led the Court, on the one hand, to accept justification reasons other than those explicitly mentioned in the EU Treaties for restrictive national measures[238] and, on the other hand, to narrow the scope of the prohibition of restrictions in its case law through a more tightened interpretation of 'measures having equivalent effect'.[239]

Moreover, the restriction approach's wideness was never entirely transposed to the direct tax field. After all, on the one hand, the Member States remain sovereign regarding direct taxation; on the other hand, by nature, all taxes are restrictive and, therefore, make any economic activity less attractive.[240]

In direct tax cases, the Court resorts to a conception of restriction based on the right to freedom of movement[241] without dismissing a comparative assessment between the cross-border situation and the equivalent hypothetical purely internal

---

236. Opinion of AG Bobek in Case C-382/16 (*Hornbach-Baumarkt*), para. 36.
237. A. Cordewener (F. Vanistendael ed., IBFD 2006), 16-17.
238. CJEU, Case C-120/78 (*Rewe-Zentral – 'Cassis di Dijon'*). In this case, the Court established for the first time the rule of reason. *See* further section 3.4.2.
239. *See* CJEU, Case C-267/91 (*Keck and Mithouard*), where the CJEU began to differentiate between measures applied without distinction regarding product requirements (i.e., the physical characteristics of the product, such as those relating to designation, form, size, weight, composition,) and regarding selling arrangements (i.e., the way products are sold, such as resale at a loss). The former measures, when creating a restriction, are prohibited under Art. 34 or 35 of the TFEU. Measures regarding selling arrangements will be prohibited as per those articles only when they treat products coming from the other Member States less favourably. In this regard, the Court (at para. 16) explains that: 'The application to products from other Member States of national provisions restricting or prohibiting certain selling arrangements is not such as to hinder directly or indirectly, actually or potentially, trade between Member States within the meaning of the Dassonville judgment, so long as those provisions apply to all relevant traders operating within the national territory and so long as they affect in the same manner, in law and in fact, the marketing of domestic products and of those from other Member States.'
240. P. Wattel et al. (Kluwer Law International 7th ed. 2018), 65; R. Lyal (R. Avi Yonah & M. Lang eds, Kluwer Law International 2d ed. 2016), 53; J. Snell, *Non-discriminatory Tax Obstacles in Community Law*, 56(2) Int'l & Compar. L.Q. 339 (2007), 355-358. *See also* Opinion of AG Kokott in Case C-385/12 (*Hervis Sport- és Divatkereskedelmi*), para. 83: '[I]n the area of tax law an examination based on that criterion [restriction test] is not possible, otherwise all national duties would always have to be examined against EU law.'
241. As explained by AG Poiares Maduro in Case C-446/03 (*Marks & Spencer*), paras 28 and 35: '28. In all the subsequent judgments in which the Court considered it necessary to go beyond the rule on national treatment, the non-discrimination rule is not absent. Yet it is no longer linked to the criterion of nationality. It is based on the use of the right to freedom of movement. What is called in question in the national measure concerned is that it imposes a specific disadvantage on operators desirous of moving or establishing themselves within the Community. It is therefore a matter of pursuing *discrimination against Community nationals wishing to assert their rights derived from the freedoms of movement.* [...] 35. All these reasons explain the need to retain in tax matters the same concept of restriction on freedom of establishment which is applicable in the other areas. Thus "all measures which prohibit, impede or render less

situation. In this regard, Englisch observes that 'there is always a comparative or "relative" element inherent to the "restriction" analysis, which is indicating that the ECJ is really looking for a discrimination of cross-border activities as compared to purely national activities that are carried out within the boundaries of one and the same Member State'.[242]

Since the CJEU always applies the comparative assessment, the difference between the concept of *discrimination* and *restriction* has been relativised in direct taxation. As affirmed by AG Geelhoed, 'in the direct taxation sphere, there is no practical difference between these two manners of formulation, i.e., "restriction" and "discrimination"'.[243] Indeed, the Court labels national tax rules as 'discriminatory' or 'restrictive' in an oscillatory way[244] without further consequences.[245] Still, as Dourado observes, the Court, in its case law, often employs the term 'discrimination' to deal with obstacles to the free movement created by the host Member State while using the term 'restriction' to deal with the obstacles raised by the Member State of origin.[246]

With regard to the comparative assessment, it requires establishing objective comparability between the cross-border and the equivalent hypothetical purely internal situation. If that objective comparability is not established, the different treatment is not incompatible with the Treaty's provisions, and the Member States do not need to justify the difference in treatment.

Notwithstanding, releasing the Member States altogether from justification for the difference in treatment when objective comparability is not established has been advocated not to be the best approach in light of fundamental freedoms.

In this regard, AG Kokott argues that the examination of the objective comparability should be dispensed with since the lack of comparability makes it 'impossible to strike an appropriate balance between the fundamental freedom and the reason for the difference in treatment in the case concerned'.[247] The AG's critics regarding the objective comparability examination have to do with the fact that there are no criteria for determining those cases in which situations must be said not to be objectively comparable, and there are no criteria that allow delimiting the comparative assessment from the justification grounds. Indeed, looking at the Court's case law, in certain cases,

attractive the exercise of that freedom" must be regarded as restrictions.' For an analysis on the relationship between the concept of discrimination and restriction in direct taxation and its evolution, *see* N. Bammens (IBFD, 2012), 534-568.

242. J. Englisch, *Taxation of Cross-Border Dividends and EC Fundamental Freedoms*, 38(4) Intertax 197 (2010), 203 DOI: 10.54648/taxi2010025. *See also* A. Zalasiński, *The Limits of the EC Concept of 'Direct Tax Restriction on Free Movement Rights', the Principles of Equality and Ability to Pay, and the Interstate Fiscal Equity*, 37(5) Intertax 282 (2009), 288 DOI: 10.54648/taxi2009030.
243. Opinion of AG Geelhoed in Case C-374/04 (*Test Claimants in Class IV of the ACT Group Litigation*), para. 36.
244. A. Cordewener (F. Vanistendael ed., IBFD 2006), 3; F. Vanistendael, *General Report on the Fundamental Freedoms and National Sovereignty in the European Union*, in *EU Freedoms and Taxation: 2004 EATLP Congress* (F. Vanistendael ed., IBFD 2006), 170.
245. M. C. Barreiro Carril, *National Tax Sovereignty and EC Fundamental Freedoms: The Impact of Tax Obstacles on the Internal Market*, 38(2) Intertax 105 (2010), 107 DOI: 10.54648/taxi2010010.
246. A. P. Dourado, *Governação Fiscal Global* (Almedina 2d ed. 2020), 211-212; M. C. Barreiro Carril (Instituto de Estudios Fiscales 2012), 287.
247. Opinion of AG Kokott in Case C-48/13 (*Nordea Bank Danmark*), para. 22.

justification reasons are used to deny comparability of situations; in other cases, the lack of comparability is seen as a justification in itself for different treatment.

Such oscillation in the CJEU's analysis can be traced back to the primitive difference between 'discrimination' and 'restriction' approaches. In the early discrimination approach, the Court only accepted grounds of justification expressly foreseen in the Treaty (*see* section 3.4.2.), which implied that other grounds to justify the difference in treatment between cross-border and domestic situations could only be examined within the objective comparability analysis of those situations. By contrast, now that unwritten grounds of justification are widely acceptable, it is always possible to justify the difference in treatment between situations.

However, whereas the analysis of the grounds for justification opens the door to weighing the proportionality regarding the difference in treatment, the comparative assessment does not allow proportionality control. Consequently, in the AG's view, 'a balanced solution is therefore guaranteed only where the ground for a difference in treatment is considered in the context of the examination of a ground of justification',[248] as the 'examination of the objective comparability of situations cannot [...] be exhaustive without considering the reason for the different treatment'.[249]

Lang also defends that even where the objective comparability between the cross-border and the equivalent hypothetical purely internal situation is lacking, examining the possible justifications and assessing their proportionality may still be relevant in determining how differently different situations should be treated. In this author's opinion, 'different treatment should depend on how different the legal situations are. Accordingly, if the legal situations are neither alike nor completely different, the treatment should not be completely different either, but only different insofar as the situations are actually different'.[250]

Conversely, Wattel argues that not requiring objective comparability between the cross-border and the equivalent hypothetical purely internal situation in order to examine justification grounds and proportionality of national measures would require justifying and weighting virtually all the Member States' tax measures.[251]

Nevertheless, Wattel also defends that proportionality may still be assessed when ascertaining comparability. According to this author, 'the Court thus does not seem to

248. *Ibid.*, para. 27.
249. Opinion of AG Kokott in Case C-123/11 (*A Oy*), para. 41.
250. M. Lang, *Direct Taxation: Is the ECJ Heading in a New Direction?*, 46(9) Eur. Tax'n 421, (2006), 422. In another place, the author also points out that releasing the Member States from further justifications where objective comparability was not established 'may lead to the result that arguments are considered at the level of comparability, which had been considered at the level of proportionality in other cases. However, the alternative would be that in cases where the legal situation is not completely comparable, domestic rules could not be examined by the ECJ at all. Furthermore, the different levels of analysis in freedom cases are to a certain extent exchangeable, as has been seen in earlier cases where the Court already dealt with justifications at the level of comparability' – M. Lang, *Recent Case Law of the ECJ in Direct Taxation: Trends, Tensions, and Contradictions*, 18(3) EC Tax Rev. 98 (2009), 100 DOI: 10.54648/ecta2009015. Likewise, C. Marchgraber (Kluwer Law International 2018), 116-119; J. Englisch, 38(4) Intertax 197 (2010), 204.
251. P. Wattel, *Non-discrimination à la Cour: The ECJ's (Lack of) Comparability Analysis in Direct Tax Cases*, 55(12) Eur. Tax'n 542 (2015), 544.

realize that it may test directly whether incomparable cases are treated differently in proportion to their relevant incomparability'.[252]

In his turn, Bammens looks at the problem from a conceptual perspective, observing that 'comparability refers to the identity of the relevant characteristics. And it is clear that identity is not a matter of degree; either two characteristics are identical or they are not'.[253] Therefore, the author submits that 'the comparability test should be a binary analysis, as it is in the Court's traditional interpretation, such that situations are either comparable or incomparable'.[254]

Following the CJEU case law, objective comparability must be examined by considering the aim pursued by the national provisions at issue,[255] the legal framework applied to internal and cross-border situations[256] and the factual circumstances of the case.[257]

As already mentioned, a tax measure is deemed contrary to the right to free movement if the taxpayer exercising that right is treated worse than a taxpayer pursuing an objectively comparable activity domestically.[258] The *worse treatment* manifests in two ways: through a *tax advantage* denied to the taxpayer exercising a cross-border activity or through a *tax disadvantage* that affects only the taxpayer pursuing an activity cross-border.

3.4.1.2 Disparities

Disparities are distortions that result from differences between the Member States' legal systems and their coexistence.

252. *Ibid.*, 550.
253. N. Bammens (IBFD 2012), 989.
254. *Ibid.*, at 990.
255. *See, e.g.*, CJEU, Case C-337/08 (*X Holding BV*), para. 22: 'In that context, it is settled case-law of the Court that the comparability of a Community situation with an internal situation must be examined having regard to the aim pursued by the national provisions at issue.' *See also* Case C-39/10 (*Commission v. Estonia* para. 51: 'There could be discrimination within the meaning of the Treaty between residents and non-residents only if, notwithstanding their residence in different Member States, it were established that, having regard to the purpose and content of the national provisions in question, the two categories of taxpayers are in a comparable situation.'
256. *See, e.g.*, CJEU, Case C-270/83 (*Commission v. France* - 'Avoir Fiscal'), para. 20: '[...] By treating the two forms of establishment in the same way for the purposes of taxing their profits, the French legislature has in fact admitted that there is no objective difference between their positions in regard to the detailed rules and conditions relating to that taxation which could justify different treatment.'
257. *See, e.g.*, CJEU, Case C-80/94 (*Wielockx*), para. 20: 'However, a non-resident taxpayer, whether employed or self-employed, who receives all or almost all of his income in the State where he works is objectively in the same situation in so far as concerns income tax as a resident of that State who does the same work there. Both are taxed in that State alone and their taxable income is the same.'
258. As explained by Lyal: '[W]hat is important is market access, understood in this context as equal treatment of domestic and cross-border activities' - R. Lyal (R. Avi Yonah & M. Lang eds, Kluwer Law International 2d ed. 2016), 54.

In the case of disparities, the disadvantage (or advantage[259]) suffered by the taxpayer is not caused by the rules of just one Member State's tax system, as it happens in the case of discrimination or restrictions.[260] Instead, it results from the interaction between Member States' tax systems to which the taxpayer is exposed in a cross-border situation.[261]

The disadvantage caused by disparities also constitutes an obstacle to the internal market's proper functioning, hindering cross-border activities. However, unlike discrimination and restrictions, disparities are not forbidden under the EU Treaties' provisions on free movement. Moreover, no Member State is directly responsible for causing them, and no Member State can resolve them alone. Therefore, disparities can only be overcome through EU legislative action toward harmonisation.

Disparities may result: *(i)* from the configuration of Member States' tax system and *(ii)* from the definition of Member States' tax jurisdiction.

Disparities resulting from the configuration of Member States' tax systems derive from the differences between Member States' tax laws, particularly regarding tax rates,[262] tax base assessment,[263] and the existence or not of certain taxes.[264]

259. These distortions are not always negative. In some instances, they also provide advantages for taxpayers. *See* Opinion of AG Geelhoed in Case C-374/04 (*Test Claimants in Class IV of the ACT Group Litigation*), para. 43: '[...] In certain cases, these distortions provide disadvantages for economic actors; in other cases, advantages. While in the first case they are 'restrictive', in the second case they stimulate cross-border establishment activity. [...] In the latter case, the taxable subject concerned does not generally invoke Community law.'
260. D. Weber, *In Search of a (New) Equilibrium Between Tax Sovereignty and the Freedom of Movement Within the EC*, 34(12) Intertax 585 (2006), 588 DOI: 10.54648/taxi2006086; G. Bizioli & C. Sacchetto (R. Avi Yonah & M. Lang eds, Kluwer Law International 2d ed. 2016), 21.
261. Opinion of AG Geelhoed in Case C-374/04 (*Test Claimants in Class IV of the ACT Group Litigation*), para. 46.
262. An example of this is the *Gilly* case, where the German tax rate was higher than the French. Consequently, a French resident exercising her job in Germany would pay higher taxes than a French resident exercising the same job in France. The ordinary tax credit employed to eliminate double taxation could not erase the different tax rates applied in each Member State. In this regard, CJEU, Case C-336/96 (*Gilly*), para. 47: 'However, it is common ground that any unfavourable consequences entailed in the present case by the tax credit mechanism set up by the bilateral convention, as implemented in the context of the tax system of the State of residence, are the result in the first place of the differences between the tax scales of the Member States concerned, and, in the absence of any Community legislation in the field, the determination of those scales is a matter for the Member States.'
263. An example of this is the *Schempp* case. The German tax regime established that maintenance payments to a divorced or separated spouse would be deductible by the debtor when such payment forms part of the recipient's taxable income. Schempp could not fulfil this requirement since his former spouse is a resident in Austria, where maintenance payments are not taxable nor deductible. In this regard, CJEU, Case C-403/03 (*Schempp*), para. 32: 'In those circumstances, it is apparent that the unfavourable treatment of which Mr Schempp complains in fact derives from the circumstance that the tax system applicable to maintenance payments in his former spouse's Member State of residence differs from that applied in his own Member State of residence.' *See also* Case C-250/95 (*Futura Participations and Singer*), where the Court affirms clearly that, 'As yet, no provision has been made for harmonizing domestic rules relating to determination of the basis of assessment to direct taxes. Consequently, each Member State draws up its own rules governing the determination of profits, income, expenditure, deductions and exemptions as well as the amounts in respect of each of them which may be included in the calculation of taxable income or of losses which may be carried forward' (para. 33).

The differences between Member States' tax laws are inevitable without further harmonisation. Indeed, the Member States' tax systems are tailored to their macroeconomic circumstances, which differ from one State to another.[265] As explained by AG Geelhoed, economic policy decisions may vary considerably and entail a political choice. For instance, higher tax rates may have the reverse side of more and better public services being provided, or those higher tax rates may pursue a redistributive function.[266]

In order to identify a disparity resulting from differences between the Member States' tax laws, it must be assumed that all the Member States apply the challenged rule.[267] If the tax disadvantage (or advantage) disappears, it stems from this type of disparity, as this type of disparity would not exist if national tax systems were precisely the same in design and content.[268]

264. For instance, not all Member States have the same taxes, namely wealth taxes. In the *D* case, a German resident held most of his wealth in Germany (90%) and the rest (10%) in the Netherlands. Germany did not impose any wealth tax. In turn, according to the Dutch tax regime, resident taxpayers were subject to tax on their net worldwide assets and were entitled to an allowance. Non-resident taxpayers were taxed only on their net assets in the Netherlands but not entitled to any allowance (at least when 90% of their wealth was not held in the Netherlands). Consequently, D was neither entitled to the Dutch allowance nor any allowance in his residence State, where wealth tax was not imposed. In this regards, CJEU, Case C-376/03 (*D*), para. 41: 'The different treatment of residents and non-residents by the Member State in which the person concerned holds only 10% of his wealth and the lack of an allowance in that case can be explained by the fact that the person concerned holds only a minor part of his wealth in that State and that he is accordingly not in a situation comparable to that of residents. The circumstance that that person's State of residence has abolished wealth tax has no bearing on this factual situation. Since he holds the major part of his wealth in the State where he is resident, the Member State in which he holds only a proportion of his wealth is not required to grant him the benefits which it grants to its own residents.'

265. Opinion of AG Geelhoed in Case C-374/04 (*Test Claimants in Class IV of the ACT Group Litigation*), para. 43: '[...] That these disparities are inevitable is evident when one considers that national tax systems are tailored to the specific macroeconomic circumstances existing in that Member State at any given time. In the present state of integration of national economies, these circumstances vary considerably between Member States. For example, a number of important factors of production differ greatly between Member States (e.g., the structure and size of Member States' labour and capital markets). Member States with a large labour force relative to capital may, for instance, choose to place a greater tax burden on labour than capital'.

266. *Ibid.*, para. 44: 'Likewise, choices of economic policy may differ substantially between Member States. These choices are reflected in, for example, tax rates: Member States may choose to levy relatively higher tax in order to provide more and better public services, or because they wish to redistribute more income to lower levels of society. Each of these choices is a policy decision central to Member States' direct tax competence. In turn, these choices may be a factor contributing to other differences between national tax systems, such as the approach to relief of economic double taxation – for example, States with relatively lower tax rates may opt for a classical system of double tax relief, while States with higher tax rates may prefer an imputation system.'

267. Such a test is equivalent to the 'internal consistency test' applied by the US Supreme Court to evaluate taxes imposed by US states. *See* further, G. Kofler & R. Mason, *Double Taxation: A European 'Switch in Time'?*, 14 Colum. J. Eur. L. 63 (2007), 83-98; R. Mason, *Made in America for European Tax: The Internal Consistency Test*, 49 Bost. Coll. L. Rev. 1277 (2008), 1282-1283.

268. Opinion of AG Geelhoed in Case C-374/04 (*Test Claimants in Class IV of the ACT Group Litigation*), para. 48. P. Wattel et al. (Kluwer Law International 7th ed. 2018), 96; R. Mason, 49 Bost. Coll. L. Rev. 1277 (2008), 1309.

Disparities may also result from the Member States' tax jurisdiction definition. These disparities may lead to international juridical double taxation, where tax systems overlap, or to international juridical double non-taxation, where a given situation does not fall within any tax jurisdiction. Following the terminology employed by the CJEU, these disadvantages (or advantages) result from the 'exercise in parallel by two Member States of their fiscal sovereignty'.[269]

Contrary to disparities resulting from the Member States' tax system configuration, disparities resulting from the definition of Member States' tax jurisdiction occur even if all States apply the same rules for determining their tax jurisdiction.[270] For instance, even if all States tax their residents on their worldwide income and non-residents on source income, tax jurisdiction over the same taxpayer will overlap when that taxpayer resides in one State and carries out economic activities in another, causing international juridical double taxation.[271]

Despite this slight difference between disparities resulting from the configuration of Member States' tax systems and the definition of Member States' tax jurisdiction, the CJEU does not treat them as separate or autonomous categories of disparities, using the term 'disparities' to refer to both.[272] After all, both arise from the very existence of the power to tax, which allows the Member States to define their tax jurisdiction and configure their tax systems.

In the direct tax field, the Member States' power to tax is virtually unlimited in light of the EU law, except for a few Directives in particular areas.[273] Consequently, the CJEU cannot interfere with the existence of Member States' power to tax, that is to say, with the way the Member States define their tax jurisdiction and configure their tax systems.

Nevertheless, as the Court has stated numerous times,[274] although direct taxation does not as such fall within the purview of the EU, the powers retained by the Member States must be

269. *See, e.g.*, CJEU, Case C-513/04 (*Kerckhaert and Morres*), para. 20; CJEU, Case C–67/08 (*Block*), para. 31. Some authors use the terms 'dislocation of the tax base', 'division of tax jurisdiction' and 'tax base compartmentalisation'.
270. Opinion of AG Geelhoed in Case C-374/04 (*Test Claimants in Class IV of the ACT Group Litigation*), para. 48; P. Wattel et al. (Kluwer Law International 7th ed. 2018), 97 et seq.; W. Schön, 68(4/5) Bull. Int'l Tax'n 271 (2015), 274; D. Weber, 34(12) Intertax 585 (2006), 588 and n. 17; G. Kofler (A. Rust ed., Kluwer Law International 2011), 106-107.
271. W. Schön, 68(4/5) Bull. Int'l Tax'n 271 (2015), 274. The same is true if all Member States adopt worldwide taxation for both residents and non-residents. If, in turn, all Member States subject both residents and non-residents to source taxation, this would lead to the splitting of positive and negative income over two or more jurisdictions without the possibility of cancelling each other, meaning a tax overcharge – *see* P. Wattel et al. (Kluwer Law International 7th ed. 2018), 97 et seq., and 625; M. C. Barreiro Carril (Instituto de Estudios Fiscales 2012), 305 et seq.
272. Indeed, the CJEU refers to 'the exercise in parallel by two Member States of their fiscal sovereignty' as a disparity. *See, e.g.*, Case C–487/08 (*Commission v. Spain*), para. 27: '[T]hat results from the exercise in parallel by two Member States of their fiscal sovereignty. In accordance with the case-law of the Court, the adverse consequences arising from the disparities between the rules of the Member States cannot be criticised for that reason by the law of the European Union.'
273. *See* section 3.1.
274. *See, e.g.*, CJEU, Case C-279/93 (*Schumacker*), para. 21; Case C-80/94 (*Wielockx*), para. 16; Case C-107/94 (*Asscher*), para. 36; Case C-391/97 (*Gschwind*), para. 20; Case C-385/00 (*De Groot*), para. 75; Case C-346/04 (*Conijn*), para. 14; Case C-513/04 (*Kerckhaert & Morres*), para. 15; Case C-329/05 (*Meindl*), para. 21; Case C-182/06 (*Lakebrink and Peters-Lakebrink*), para. 14.

exercised consistently with EU law, namely, with the fundamental freedoms' provisions. Therefore, the CJEU must ensure that the way such a power to tax is *exercised* does not create unilateral disadvantages to taxpayers making use of free movement because, in that case, a discriminatory or restrictive measure may be at stake.

As Dourado notes, objective comparability between cross-border and internal situations necessarily entails the *exercise* of taxing powers.[275]

Therefore, the Member States do not need to adopt all the same taxes, apply all the same tax rates or assess the tax base in the same way, as those aspects are part of the Member States' power to configure their tax systems. In effect, a Member State is not bound by the tax policy choices of another Member State, and it has no obligation to mimic another Member State's tax system configuration.[276] Consequently, the disadvantage suffered by a taxpayer engaged in cross-border activities derived from, for example, having to bear higher tax rates in the host Member State than those applicable in the Member State of origin cannot be overcome by the action of the CJEU as it lacks the competence to interfere with Member States' power to configure their tax systems. In this regard, it is settled case law that the EU Treaties offer no guarantee to EU citizens that transferring their activities or residence to another Member State is neutral regarding taxation.[277]

However, the situation is different when a Member State applies, for example, a heavier tax rate to taxpayers carrying out an activity cross-borders (i.e., making use of free movement) than that applied to taxpayers carrying out the same activity domestically. In that case, the CJEU has the competence to examine the difference in treatment, as it leads to a disadvantage unilaterally created by a Member State, which only affects taxpayers making use of free movement. This last case concerns the *exercise* of taxing powers by a Member State.

The same applies to the Member States' power to define their tax jurisdiction. Tax jurisdiction establishes *to what extent* a State may exercise its taxing power, which falls outside the Court's scrutiny, as the EU Treaties do not establish anything in this regard. The CJEU's competence only regards *how* taxing powers are exercised within a Member State's tax jurisdiction.

This way, for instance, the Member States cannot be prevented from taxing their residents on worldwide income and non-residents on source income because, with that decision, the Member States are establishing *to what extent* they are willing to exercise

275. A. P. Dourado, *Governação Fiscal Global* (Almedina 2d ed. 2020), 219. As the author clearly explains, the CJEU differentiates between the *allocation* of taxing powers and the *exercise* of taxing powers. Only the latter can be considered to be discriminatory. Comparability of cross-border and internal situations can only occur regarding the exercise of taxing powers.

276. Bizioli and Sacchetto explain that 'Member States have no obligation, according to the fundamental freedoms, to adapt their tax regulations to those of the other Member States' [G. Bizioli & C. Sacchetto (R. Avi Yonah & M. Lang eds, Kluwer Law International 2d ed. 2016), 21] and Birk observes that there is no principle of equal taxation in EU law. Therefore, EU law does not demand all taxpayers to be subject to equal tax burdens across the EU [D. Birk, *Besteuerungsgleichheit in der Europäischen Union*, in *Steuerrecht im europäischen Binnenmarkt* (M. Lehner ed., Verlag Dr. Otto Schmidt 1996), 67 and 80].

277. CJEU, Case C-365/02 (*Lindfors*), para. 34; Case C-403/03 (*Schempp*), para. 45; Case C-67/08 (*Block*), para. 35; Case C-240/10 (*Schulz-Delzers and Schulz*), para. 42; Case C-371/10 (*National Grid Indus*), para. 62; Case C-405/18 (*AURES Holdings*), para. 32.

their taxing powers over taxpayers. However, the situation becomes different when the Member States decide to tax their residents, taking their personal and family circumstances into account while not doing the same regarding non-residents or residents obtaining income abroad. Since this case is liable to entail a disadvantage unilaterally created by a Member State that affects only taxpayers making use of free movement, this case concerns the Member States' *exercise* of taxing powers, not the definition of their tax jurisdiction nor the configuration of their tax systems. Consequently, the Court is competent to examine such a difference in treatment, which may be deemed incompatible with EU law insofar as those taxpayers are considered to be in a comparable situation, and there is no acceptable reason that justifies it or (if there is) it is not considered as proportional.

Establishing the line between the *definition* of tax jurisdiction and the *exercise* of taxing powers gives rise to another challenge: ascertaining whether international juridical double taxation – which stems from the definition of tax jurisdiction[278] – also poses a problem concerning the exercise of Member States' taxing powers.[279] This issue is further analysed throughout this research.

In brief, disparities represent a limit to the Court's own competence, as Dourado observes.[280] Despite being an obstacle to the internal market's proper functioning, the harmful effects of disparities are tolerated within the EU because the EU Treaties do not forbid them, and the CJEU may only intervene where the exercise of Member States' taxing powers creates a unilateral disadvantage to taxpayers making use of free movement.

3.4.2 Justification Reasons

If a forbidden obstacle to the exercise of the fundamental freedoms of movement is found, the CJEU examines the reasons put forward by the States to justify it. As affirmed by Nogueira, the EU freedoms of movement do not grant absolute rights and may be narrowed by justified reasons.[281]

There are reasons expressly provided in the Treaties that can be invoked by the Member States as justification, as is the case of public policy, public security or public health.[282] Because justifications on these grounds are of little use in the tax field, the

278. As yet, the CJEU has rejected to 'intervene in cross-border situations in which double tax burdens result from the simultaneous operation of two distinct tax systems', although, as Vanistendael argues, 'juridical double taxation may be against the basic rules of an internal market' – F. Vanistendael, *Denkavit Internationaal: The Balance Between Fiscal Sovereignty and the Fundamental Freedoms?*, 47(5) Eur. Tax'n 210 (2007), 213.The CJEU stance on international juridical double taxation is analysed further in Chapter 6, alongside scholars' approach in this regard.
279. Herrera Molina points out that what is relevant is ascertaining whether or not a provision hinders free movement rather than ascertaining whether that provision concerns the definition of tax jurisdiction or the exercise of taxing powers – cf. P. Herrera Molina, *Convenios de Doble Imposición y Derecho Comunitario* (Instituto de Estudios Fiscales 2009), 42.
280. A. P. Dourado (Almedina 2d ed. 2020), 202.
281. J. F. Nogueira (Wolters Kluwer Portugal 2010), 236.
282. Article 45(3) TFEU on the free movement of workers, Art. 52(1) TFEU on the freedom of establishment and on the freedom to provide services (*ex vi* Art. 62 TFEU) and Art. 65(1)(b) TFEU on the free movement of capitals and payments.

Court has begun to accept justifications not explicitly mentioned in the Treaties based on overriding reasons in the public interest.

Indeed, in the first moment, the CJEU adopted a strict approach, according to which, while discriminatory measures could only be justified based on reasons expressly foreseen in the Treaties, restrictive measures could be justified by overriding reasons in the public interest.[283] However, the Court gradually abandoned such a strict approach to adopt a more flexible one, under which both discriminatory and restrictive measures can be justified based on overriding reasons in the public interest.[284]

Therefore, the rule of reason[285] – under which justifications based on the public interest may be accepted and the proportionality test must be applied – is liable to be used in all tax cases where a forbidden obstacle to free movement is found.[286]

Despite the openness of the formula 'overriding reasons in the public interest', the CJEU has been cautious in accepting justifications on these grounds, refusing some of the arguments put forward by the Member States,[287] accepting others[288] and within

283. As explained by Lyal, the prohibition of restrictions gives the Court a more extensive power of reviewing Member States national legislation assessing its potential to hinder market access. An appropriate safeguard logically accompanied the Court's power. Cf. R. Lyal (R. Avi Yonah & M. Lang eds, Kluwer Law International 2d ed. 2016), 51.

284. The adoption of a flexible approach was in line with the blurred limits between 'discrimination' and 'restriction' and the oscillatory way the CJEU is labelling national tax rules that hinder the fundamental freedoms.

285. Regarding the concept and the origins of the 'rule of reason' principle, *see* A. Schrauwen, *In Defence of Public Interest: The Rule of Reason; Genesis of a Principle of Law*, in *The Rule of Reason: Rethinking Another Classic of European Legal Doctrine* (A. Schrauwen ed., Europa Law Publishing 2005), 3-18; and L. Gormley, *The Genesis of the Rule of Reason in the Free Movement of Goods*, in *The Rule of Reason: Rethinking Another Classic of European Legal Doctrine* (A. Schrauwen ed., Europa Law Publishing 2005). Schrauwen explains that the 'protection of these public interests against negative corollaries of a free liberal market was not included in the Treaty. The ECJ settled case-law provided protection of these interests, as long as it was "reasonable". It developed the concept of "mandatory requirements" to exempt public interest measures from the prohibitions and commandments of the market. This case-law is also known under the name of Rule of Reason. The word 'reason' is not taken in the sense of "ratio" but of "reasonable"' (p. 3); and Gormley observes that 'the real concept behind the rule of reason is the recognition that Community law does not yet offer at a legislative level guarantees in respect of certain interests or values. [...] The definition of the rule of reason is thus the recognition by the Court of the need, pending action at the Community level, to allow the Member States to act to ensure that certain interests and values are guaranteed in the general interest' (pp. 23-24).

286. *See* L. Hinnekens, *Basis and Scope of Public Interest Justification of National Tax Measures Infringing Fundamental Treaty Freedoms*, in *EU Freedoms and Taxation: 2004 EATLP Congress* (F. Vanistendael ed., IBFD 2006), 75 and 78-79; S. van Thiel, *Justifications in Community Law for Income Tax Restrictions on Free Movement: Acte Clair Rules That Can Be Readily Applied by National Courts – Part 1*, 48(6) Eur. Tax'n 279 (2008), 279-280; A. Cordewener et al., *The Clash Between European Freedoms and National Direct Tax Law: Public Interest Defences Available to the Member States*, 46 Common Market L. Rev. 1951 (2009), 1953 DOI: 10.54648/cola2009078; J. F. Nogueira (Wolters Kluwer Portugal 2010), 238; M. Poulsen, *Freedom of Establishment and the Balanced Allocation of Tax Jurisdiction*, 40(3) Intertax 200 (2012), 200 DOI: 10.54648/taxi2012023; C. Marchgraber (Kluwer Law International 2018), 136-137.

287. For instance, the CJEU has not accepted the following arguments as overriding reasons in the public interest: loss of tax revenue [*see, e.g.*, CJEU, Case C-385/00 (*De Groot*), para. 103]; administrative difficulties [*see, e.g.*, CJEU, Case C-279/93 (*Schumacker*), paras 43-45]; offsetting low taxation of another Member State [*see, e.g.*, CJEU, Case C-196/04 (*Cadbury Schweppes*), para. 49]; lack of harmonisation of direct taxation [*see, e.g.*, CJEU, Case C-204/90

certain conditions.[289] The admissible justification grounds are closely connected,[290] and sometimes, the conceptual distinction between them is unclear.[291]

(*Bachmann*), paras 10-11]; absence of reciprocity [*see, e.g.*, CJEU, Case C-270/83 (*Commission v. France – 'Avoir Fiscal'*), para. 26]; compensatory advantages [*see, e.g.*, CJEU, Case C-107/94 (*Asscher*), paras 51-54]; possibility of choosing an alternative tax regime [*see, e.g.*, CJEU, Case C-440/08 (*Gielen*), paras 49-54] or discretionary powers of tax authorities [*see, e.g.*, Case C-28/95 (*Leur-Bloem*), para. 44].

288. The CJEU has accepted the following arguments as overriding reasons in the public interest: the need to prevent tax evasion or tax avoidance, the need to preserve the balanced allocation of tax jurisdiction and the need to prevent double use of losses [*see, e.g.*, regarding all mentioned arguments, CJEU, Case C-446/03 (*Marks & Spencer*), paras 43-50]; the need for effective fiscal supervision [*see, e.g.*, CJEU, Case C-120/78 (*Rewe-Zentral – 'Cassis di Dijon'*), para. 8] and to protect the coherence of the tax systems (fiscal cohesion) [*see, e.g.*, CJEU, Case C-204/90 (*Bachmann*), paras 21-27]. Regarding the latter argument, it has limited scope and the Court has systematically refused such justification, since it cannot be used as an alternative argument to the loss of revenue. Additionally, the Court has also accepted the principle of territoriality as a valid justification [*see, e.g.*, CJEU, Case C-250/95 (*Futura Participations and Singer*), para. 22]. However, it has been pointed out that this is a principle that shapes States' taxing powers, more than a justification for unequal tax treatment. In this regard, *see* W. Schön, 68(4/5) Bull. Int'l Tax'n 271 (2015), 284; P. Wattel, *Fiscal Cohesion, Fiscal Territoriality and Preservation of the (Balanced) Allocation of Taxing Power: What Is the Difference?*, in *The Influence of European Law on Direct Taxation: Recent and Future Developments* (D. Weber ed., Kluwer Law International 2007), 140.

289. For instance, a justification based on fiscal cohesion requires the existence of a direct link between deductibility and taxation within the same tax system, in relation to one and the same person – *see, e.g.*, CJEU, Case C-80/94 (*Wielockx*), para. 24. Justifications based on the prevention of tax evasion or tax avoidance may be allowed insofar as the measure targets wholly artificial arrangements without economic reality, with a view of escaping the tax otherwise due – *see, e.g.*, CJEU, Case C-196/04 (*Cadbury Schweppes*), para. 55. And although the Member States may rely on the balanced allocation of tax jurisdiction, namely through tax treaties, to justify a measure that hinders the exercise of an EU freedom of movement, it is not admissible that such allocation of taxing rights generates, per se, the unequal tax treatment of taxpayers in comparable situations – *see, e.g.*, CJEU, Case C-385/00 (*De Groot*), paras 99-101. In this regard, *see* further: S. van Thiel, *Justifications in Community Law for Income Tax Restrictions on Free Movement: Acte Clair Rules That Can Be Readily Applied by National Courts*, in *The Acte Clair in EC Direct Tax Law* (A. P. Dourado & R. Borges eds, IBFD 2008), 89-119; S. van Thiel, *Justifications in Community Law for Income Tax Restrictions on Free Movement: Acte Clair Rules That Can Be Readily Applied by National Courts – Part 2*, 48(7) Eur. Tax'n 339 (2008); A. Cordewener et al., 46 Common Market L. Rev. 1951 (2009), 1969-1994; M. Poulsen, 40(3) Intertax 200 (2012), 202-211.

290. For instance, the risk of income shifting between the Member States, hampering the balanced allocation of tax jurisdiction, is sometimes associated to the use of artificial structures to circumvent taxation in one of the Member States. In such cases, the arguments on the need to prevent tax evasion or tax avoidance and the need to preserve the balanced allocation of tax jurisdiction work together. In this regard, *see* M. Poulsen, 40(3) Intertax 200 (2012), 204, who affirms that 'Although the risk of 'unbalanced allocation' of income seems relevant also in situations not necessarily involving tax avoidance, that is, taxpayers moving to another Member State and hereby escaping potential capital gains taxation on unrealized assets, case-law indicates that the risk of unintentional shifting of income primarily exists where taxpayers are engaged in impermissible tax avoidance.'

291. Highlighting the blurred boundaries between the territoriality principle, the need to preserve the balanced allocation of taxing rights and the need to protect fiscal cohesion through the analysis of the Court's case law, *see* further C. Marchgraber (Kluwer Law International 2018), 142-155. *See also* P. Wattel (Weber D. ed., Kluwer Law International 2007), 139-156, and P. Wattel et al. (Kluwer Law International 7th ed. 2018), 631-633 and 667-675. This author defends that all acceptable justifications grounds, including the need to prevent tax avoidance and tax evasion and the need for effective fiscal, converge, coming down to 'the need to protect

3.4.3 Proportionality Control

When overriding reasons in the public interest justify a measure hindering, in a forbidden way, the exercise of free movement, its proportionality must be ascertained.

The principle of proportionality concerns both the protection of the internal market itself and the protection of taxpayers' subjective rights arising from free movement.[292] Nevertheless, the principle of proportionality entails the balancing of conflicting pretensions.[293] In this context, the Court must balance the concrete objective pursued by a Member State underlying the overriding reason in the public interest invoked[294] against taxpayers' right to move freely within the EU as an imperative of the internal market.

---

tax base integrity'. In this regard, AG Kokott noted that the justification label of 'allocation of the power to impose taxes' is an expression of other recognised grounds of justification, such as the preservation of the coherence of a tax system and prevention of tax avoidance – Opinion of AG Kokott in Case C-48/13 (*Nordea Bank Danmark*), paras 45-46. In turn, other authors pointed out the existing differences between some of the justification grounds – A. Cordewener et al., 46 Common Market L. Rev. 1951 (2009), 1976 n. 127: '[W]e cannot accept the suggestion that coherence and balanced allocation of tax jurisdiction are the same; [...]. The first is an autonomous revenue protection argument that comes with discrimination but is acceptable only in the case of a systemic coherence in the tax system of one Member State. The second is an "agreed allocation of tax jurisdiction" argument that involves the tax systems of two Member States and that ensures that the initial discriminatory effect of the tax measure of one Member State is neutralized by the agreed action undertaken by the other Member State.' In the same line, *see* D. Weber, *An Analysis of the Past, Current and Future of the Coherence of the Tax System as Justification*, 24(1) EC Tax Rev. 43 (2015), 54 DOI: 10.54648/ecta2015005.

292. D. Freyer, *The Proportionality Principle under EU Tax Law: General and Practical Problems Caused by Its Extensive Application (Part 1)*, 57(9) Eur. Tax'n 384 (2017), 385; D. Freyer, *The Proportionality Principle under EU Tax Law: General and Practical Problems Caused by Its Extensive Application (Part 2)*, 57(10) Eur. Tax'n 428 (2017), 435.

293. The introduction of the proportionality into the judicial sphere was done by the Prussian Supreme Administrative Court, back in 1882. Today, it is considered to have a structural nature, being present in the legal order of most occidental States. Regarding the origins of the 'proportionality', *see* J. F. Nogueira (Wolters Kluwer Portugal 2010), 39-57. Regarding the incorporation of 'proportionality' within the EU legal order, *see* A. Zalasiński, *The Principle of Proportionality and (European) Tax Law*, in *Principles of Law: Function, Status and Impact in EU Tax Law* (C. Brokelind ed., IBFD 2014). Both authors discuss the configuration of 'proportionality' as a rule, a principle or as a method for rights adjudication. Departing from the same analysis, Nogueira qualifies it as a method for rights adjudication (*see* pp. 67-72), while for Zalasiński it is a legal principle (*see* pp. 305-306). Additionally, also departing from the same analysis, Englisch defends that it is a rule rather than a principle – J. Englisch, *VAT and General Principles of EU Law*, in *Traditional and Alternative Routes to European Tax Integration* (D. Weber ed., IBFD 2010), 237.

294. As explained by Nogueira, 'justification reasons' must be differentiated from 'concrete objectives'. Justification reasons are general formulations of the interests that must be protected, while the concrete objectives are the densification of those interests. The author exemplifies this with CJEU, Case C-250/95 (*Futura Participations and Singer*), in which the justification reason was the 'effectiveness of fiscal supervision' (para. 31) and the concrete objective was 'to ascertain clearly and precisely that the amount of losses to be carried forward corresponds, under the Luxembourg rules governing the calculation of income and losses applicable in the financial year in which the losses were incurred, to the amount of losses actually incurred in Luxembourg by the taxpayer' (para. 39). It is regarding the 'concrete objective' that the control of proportionality must be made. Cf. J. F. Nogueira (Wolters Kluwer Portugal 2010), 299-300.

Following the legal tradition of most Member States, the proportionality control usually entails a three-step test:[295] *(i)* the measure must be suitable, meaning that the measures must not exceed the limits of what is appropriate for attaining the legitimately objective pursued (suitability); *(ii)* it must be necessary in order to attain that objective and when there is a choice between several appropriate measures recourse must be had to the least onerous (necessity); *(iii)* the disadvantages caused must not be disproportionate to the objectives pursued (proportionality *stricto sensu*).

However, in its case law, the CJEU usually only refers to the two first steps mentioned, i.e., suitability and necessity.[296] The lack of reference to proportionality *stricto sensu* does not necessarily mean this step is unknown to the Court. Although the references to it made by the CJEU are scarce,[297] Member States have invoked it in their argumentation[298] and the Advocates General in their opinions.[299]

Several reasons have been pointed out to explain the lack of reference to the 'proportionality *stricto sensu*'. Its absence may be linked to the delicate issue of the institutional balance at the EU level[300] or the technical difficulty of its application.[301] It may also be explained by how the other steps are applied: the failure to pass one of the

295. *See, e.g.*, CJEU, Case C-331/88 (*Fedesa*), para. 13 (not regarding tax issues): 'The Court has consistently held that the principle of proportionality is one of the general principles of Community law. By virtue of that principle, the lawfulness of the prohibition of an economic activity is subject to the condition that the prohibitory measures are appropriate and necessary in order to achieve the objectives legitimately pursued by the legislation in question; when there is a choice between several appropriate measures recourse must be had to the least onerous, and the disadvantages caused must not be disproportionate to the aims pursued.'
296. *See, e.g.*, CJEU, Case C-250/95 (*Futura Participations and Singer*), para. 26: 'Consequently, the imposition of such a condition, which specifically affects companies or firms having their seat in another Member State, is in principle prohibited by Article 52 of the Treaty. It could only be otherwise if the measure pursued a legitimate aim compatible with the Treaty and were justified by pressing reasons of public interest. Even if that were so, it would still have to be of such a nature as to ensure achievement of the aim in question and not go beyond what was necessary for that purpose.' This is the very first case regarding specifically tax issues where the proportionality control was applied. For an overview of the evolution of the CJEU case law on proportionality in tax issues, *see* J. F. Nogueira (Wolters Kluwer Portugal 2010), 261-285.
297. *See* CJEU, Case C-290/04 (*Scorpio*), para. 38: '[S]ince that liability constitutes the corollary of that method of collecting income tax, it too contributes in a proportionate manner to ensuring the effectiveness of collecting the tax.'
298. CJEU, Case C-385/00 (*De Groot*), para. 64, in which the Belgian Government observes that '[...] to require the State of residence to grant all the tax advantages relating to those circumstances solely on the national share of the income would mean that that State would have to bear the entire burden of those tax advantages. That would be unfair because the State of residence is responsible for the greatest part of the public services performed for the taxpayer and the result would be disproportionate to the aim of Article 48 of the Treaty'. *See also* Case C-267/09 (*Commission v. Portugal*), para. 14.
299. Opinion of AG Kokott in Case C-231/05 (*Oy AA*), para. 32: 'A restriction on freedom of establishment is permissible only if it pursues a legitimate objective compatible with the Treaty and is justified by imperative reasons in the public interest. It is further necessary, in such a case, that its application be appropriate to ensuring the attainment of the objective thus pursued and not go beyond what is necessary to attain it. It must also be proportionate within the narrower meaning of that term.' *See also* Opinion of AG Trstenjak in C-10/10 (Commission v. Austria), para. 67; Opinion of AG Kokott in Case C-123/11 (*A Oy*), para. 61.
300. J. Englisch (D. Weber ed., IBFD 2010), 236.
301. J. F. Nogueira (Wolters Kluwer Portugal 2010), 317; C. Marchgraber (Kluwer Law International 2018), 159.

steps invalidates the remaining examination; thus, the examination of the next step depends, in part, on the analysis intensity of the previous step.[302] For instance, the analysis of 'suitability' entails pondering not only the adequacy of the measure for the aim pursued but also whether that measure exceeds what is appropriate for attaining such an aim. The analysis of 'necessity' requires considering not only the need for such a measure for achieving the purpose but also the possible less burdensome alternatives. Therefore, it may be argued that the analysis of 'proportionality *stricto sensu*' is embodied in the assessment of the other tests.[303]

Notwithstanding, examining the 'proportionality *stricto sensu*' must not be disregarded, as it makes relevant the task of pondering in each case the conflicting interests of safeguarding free movement (and, consequently, the taxpayers' legitimate expectations) and the objectives validly pursued by the Member States.[304]

As a judicial valuation that gives the CJEU an interpretative prerogative,[305] the proportionality control must follow logical and clear reasoning, where the conclusions are understandable and predictable. As Nogueira points out, one of the main problems of proportionality control is precisely the Court's lack of reasoning in its application.[306]

3.5 CONCLUDING AND SUMMARISING REMARKS

This chapter addresses the EU legal framework to clarify how EU law limits the exercise of taxing powers by the Member States.

One of the EU's main goals is to establish an internal market, implying an area without internal frontiers in which the free movement of goods, persons, services and capital is ensured. The internal market is conceived to operate, as near as possible, as a national market, where internal borders do not exist and economic activities flow.

Taxation is an internal market matter because taxes may be used as a protectionist tool to deter intra-Union cross-border trade, employment, services and investment, impelling taxpayers to stay in their home markets to avoid additional tax burdens. Therefore, the EU Treaties impose the creation of a customs union and the harmonisation of indirect taxes.

However, the EU Treaties lack specific provisions regarding direct taxes, and any attempt to promote harmonisation in this regard must be made under the general provision of Article 115 of the TFEU, with unanimity being required for the approval of Directives. Consequently, in the field of direct taxation, there are just a few Directives that cover only very particular areas of corporate taxation. Outside such particular areas, the Member States are sovereign in the design of their direct tax systems.

That does not mean that, beyond those particular areas, Member States' direct tax systems fall entirely outside the scope of EU law. The prohibitions laid down in the

302. J. F. Nogueira (Wolters Kluwer Portugal 2010), 317-318.
303. *See* further, C. Marchgraber (Kluwer Law International 2018), 157.
304. J. F. Nogueira (Wolters Kluwer Portugal 2010), 316, 326-327; C. Marchgraber (Kluwer Law International 2018), 158-159. J. Englisch (D. Weber ed., IBFD 2010), 236.
305. D. Freyer, 57(10) Eur. Tax'n 428 (2017), 435.
306. J. F. Nogueira (Wolters Kluwer Portugal 2010), 322.

provisions of the EU Treaties constrain the exercise of Member States' taxing powers, leading to a process of negative integration. As the CJEU has repeatedly affirmed, although direct taxation does not, as such, fall within the purview of the EU, the powers retained by the Member States must nevertheless be exercised consistently with EU law.

The freedoms of movement - which are set forth by primary EU law - play an essential role in limiting the Member States' exercise of taxing powers regarding direct taxation.

The EU freedoms of movement aim to protect all cross-border economic activities (i.e., employment, establishment, services and investment, as defined in light of the EU legal order) and even non-economic migration of EU citizens. Consequently, their scope of protection is determined in a comprehensive and complementary way, which sometimes leads to overlaps between the fundamental freedoms. Those overlaps do not raise concerns, except for those cases involving third States, as they only fall within the scope of protection of the free movement of capital and payments.

In order to protect cross-border activities and migration, the freedoms of movement entail a prohibition of discrimination and restrictions that cover both inbound and outbound situations. That prohibition opens the way for examining whether the Member States' direct tax provisions hinder cross-border activities unjustifiably or disproportionately. In such a case, the hindrance is deemed contrary to EU law, and the Member States are demanded to repeal those provisions.

The CJEU conducts that examination within the preliminary ruling and infringement procedures. While the infringement procedure is initiated by the European Commission or another Member State, the preliminary ruling is triggered by the national courts, which may ask the CJEU about the conformity of a domestic provision with EU law when that question is raised to them. Taxpayers have only indirect access to these procedures, as they may only challenge the compatibility of a domestic provision with EU law by filing a complaint with the European Commission - which may decide whether or not to take further action on the complaint - or by raising the issue before national courts - which are not necessarily bound to refer that question to the CJEU. Nevertheless, these are still powerful tools in taxpayers' hands, by which the laws of Member States may be challenged.

According to its case law, when assessing whether a national tax provision conflicts with EU law, the CJEU follows a step-by-step approach. After determining the freedom of movement affected by a national provision, the CJEU ascertains the obstacle created by that provision, considers the justifications for that obstacle put forward by the Member State and ponders the proportionality between them and the harm caused to the taxpayers' right to free movement.

Three categories of obstacles are likely to hinder free movement: discrimination, restrictions and disparities. According to Articles 18, 45, 49, 56 and 63 of the TFEU, EU law only forbids discrimination and restrictions, not disparities. Therefore, EU law may only limit the exercise of Member States' taxing powers when that exercise implies discrimination or restriction to the free movement.

In their pure form, the prohibition of discrimination and the prohibition of restrictions entail a different approach. While the prohibition of discrimination has a *relative* structure, requiring a *comparative assessment*, the prohibition of restrictions has an *absolute* structure linked to the *right to freedom of movement*. In this sense, the prohibition of restrictions is much more far-reaching than the prohibition of discrimination, even though restrictions may be justified by overriding reasons in the public interest, whereas discrimination may not. Nevertheless, in the field of direct taxation, the distinction between the prohibition of discrimination and restrictions has been relativised in its practical application, and the CJEU, in its decisions, never dispenses with the comparative assessment.

The comparative assessment requires establishing objective comparability between a situation where free movement is exercised and the hypothetical equivalent purely internal situation. Subsequently, it is ascertained whether those situations are offered different treatment. Although the wording of Articles 18, 45, 49 and 56 of the TFEU could suggest that the prohibitions set by EU law would only target differences in treatment on the grounds of nationality, the CJEU has made clear that those prohibitions target any national provision that by applying other differentiating criteria lead to the same result, as it is the case of residence.

Following the CJEU case law, objective comparability must be examined regarding the aim pursued by the national provisions, how the legal framework is applied to internal and cross-border situations and the factual circumstances involved.

When objective comparability is not established, the difference in treatment is not incompatible with EU law, and the Member States do not need to justify it. However, it has been discussed whether, in such cases, releasing *tout court* the Member States from further justification is the approach that better safeguards the freedoms of movement, which are the cornerstones for the proper functioning of the internal market.

Conversely, when objective comparability is established, the difference in treatment may be justified based on overriding reasons in the public interest. When the CJEU accepts the justification, it balances the concrete objective pursued by the Member State against taxpayers' right to move freely within the EU as an imperative of the internal market.

This way, the EU law limits the exercise of Member States' taxing powers when that exercise implies constraining in an unjustified or (if justified) disproportionate way the taxpayers' right to free movement by treating them worse than taxpayers in a comparable purely internal situation.

In contrast with discrimination and restrictions, the EU Treaties do not forbid disparities.

Disparities are distortions arising from the very existence of the Member States' power to tax, which allows them to define their tax jurisdiction and configure their tax systems.

In what concerns the configuration of their tax systems, the Member States are not bound by the tax policy choices of another Member State, not being obliged to mimic another Member State's tax system configuration. In other words, the Member States do not need to have the same taxes the other Member States have, do not need to apply the same tax rates the others do, nor need to assess the tax base in the same way. Consequently, any disadvantage suffered by taxpayers exercising their right to free movement that derives from: *(i)* having to bear a tax in the host State that does not exist in the State of origin; *(ii)* having to bear higher tax rates in the host State than those applicable in the State of origin; or *(iii)* having the tax assessed on a broader tax base in the host State than that used in the State of origin, is a disparity which does not fall within the EU Treaties prohibitions.

The same happens regarding the definition of tax jurisdictions. The Member States are not obliged to coordinate the definition of their tax jurisdiction because the EU Treaties do not establish anything in this regard. Therefore, if all Member States tax their residents on worldwide income and non-residents on source income, international juridical double taxation arising thereof is not, per se, incompatible with EU law, as it results from the overlap of tax jurisdictions over the same taxpayer.

Notwithstanding, despite the Member States being sovereign in the definition of their tax jurisdiction and configuration of their tax systems, the prohibition of discrimination and restriction foreseen in the EU Treaties, as said, limit the exercise of that power whenever the Member States create a unilateral disadvantage to taxpayers making use of free movement. In such cases, the CJEU becomes competent to examine Member States' provisions that set additional tax burdens to taxpayers in cross-border situations.

Ultimately, the prohibition of discrimination and restrictions laid down in the EU Treaties embody a prohibition of arbitrariness in the treatment of cross-border situations within the EU internal market. The Member States' power to tax remains intact insofar as it does not unilaterally hinder free movement.

Since this research aims to ponder whether international juridical double taxation, despite being a consequence of Member States' definition of tax jurisdiction, also entails a unilateral disadvantage for taxpayers' making use of an EU freedom of movement due to the disregard of their overall ability to pay, the relevance of individuals' ability to pay in light of EU law must be ascertained. This task is carried out in the next chapter.

CHAPTER 4

EU Law and the Consideration of Individuals' Ability to Pay Taxes

- *Examination of the ability-to-pay principle.*
- *Analysis of the CJEU's case law on cases involving (i) the consideration of expenses related to economic activity and (ii) the consideration of expenses related to personal and family circumstances.*
- *Analysis of the absolute priority given by the CJEU to the consideration of taxpayers' personal and family circumstances.*

4.1 APPROACHING THE ABILITY-TO-PAY PRINCIPLE

The dogmatic development of the ability-to-pay principle has been rough, with little consensus on its entire meaning and moments of euphoria around it, moments of denial of its relevance and moments of rehabilitation and revitalisation of its value.[307] Nevertheless, today, there is widespread acceptance of the ability to pay as a principle of justice in distributing the tax burden.

In its origin, the ability-to-pay principle emerged as the denial of the equivalence principle as a criterion for distributing the tax burden among taxpayers: while under the equivalence principle, the tax due must be in line with the benefit the taxpayer

307. For an in-depth look at the doctrinal evolution of the ability-to-pay principle, *see* C. Palao Taboada, *Apogeo y crisis del principio de capacidad contributiva*, in *Estudios jurídicos en homenaje al profesor Federico de Castro* (Tecnos 1976); C. Palao Taboada, *Nueva visita al principio de capacidad contributiva*, 124 REDF 767 (2005). These works were recently re-edited in C. Palao Taboada, *Capacidad contributiva, no confiscatoriedad y otros estudios de Derecho constitucional tributario* (Thomson Reuters Aranzadi 2018).On the ethical foundations of the ability to pay, *see* J. Englisch, *Ability to Pay*, in *Principles of Law: Function, Status and Impact in EU Tax Law* (C. Brokelind ed., IBFD 2014), 439-443.

receives from the State's public functions and services, under the ability-to-pay principle, the tax due must be in line with the taxpayer's economic strength to pay it.[308]

Yet, the dismissal of the equivalence principle by the ability-to-pay principle is not entirely unanimous among scholars.

On the one hand, it has been argued that the effectiveness of the ability to pay is restricted to taxes, not encompassing public fees.[309] Moreover, concerning taxes, the ability-to-pay principle is considered to have different intensities: while it finds its most significant effectiveness in income taxes, in consumption taxes, it has a minimal expression since consumers fall into the market anonymity.[310]

On the other hand, it has been advocated that the ability-to-pay and the equivalence principles coexist within the States' tax systems, not mutually excluding one another: the ability-to-pay principle prevails regarding direct taxation, whereas the equivalence principle assumes more relevance in indirect taxation and public fees.[311] To this effect, it has even been argued that the equivalence principle is integrated into the ability-to-pay principle by conceiving the benefit taxpayer receives as a particular manifestation of the ability to pay.[312]

The lack of consensus stems partly from the Constitutional framework each State gives to the ability-to-pay principle.

Where the ability-to-pay principle is expressly enshrined in the Constitution and covers the entire tax system, such as in Spain or Italy, the doctrine tends to be compelled to find a way of articulating the ability-to-pay principle with the equivalence principle in areas of taxation in which the principle of equivalence provides a more

308. However, under the ability-to-pay principle, the correlation between the payment of taxes and the State's public functions and public services tends to be forgotten because the public benefits received from the State are not relevant for determining the amount of tax due. In this regard, *see* L. V. Berliri, *El Impuesto justo* (F. Vicente-Arche Domingo trans., Instituto de Estudios Fiscales 1986), 42-43 n. 2, and A. Agulló Agüero, 37 REDF 23 (1983), 50 n. 75. Analysing the historical development of the equivalence principle and the ability-to-pay principle, and their interplay, *see* S. Vasques (Almedina 2008), 251-330.

309. J. Casalta Nabais, *O dever fundamental de pagar impostos* (Almedina 1998), 474-477; S. Vasques (Almedina 2008), 378-379.

310. F. Moschetti, *El principio de capacidad contributiva* (J. Calero Gallego & R. Navas Vazquez trans, Instituto de Estudios Fiscales 1980), 267; J. Casalta Nabais (Almedina 1998), 480-481.

311. Cf. A. Agulló Agüero, 37 REDF 23 (1983), 35. J. Lang, *Steuergerechtigkeit und Globalisierung*, in *Steuerzentrierte Rechtsberatung* (W. Spindler et al. eds, Verlag Dr. Otto Schmidt 2009), 52-53: the author states that a single principle of fair taxation does not monistically dominate tax law: the focus of the ability to pay is on direct taxes, while the equivalence principle dominates indirect taxes; *see also* K. Tipke & J. Lang, *Steuerrecht* (Verlag Dr. Otto Schmidt 10th ed. 2010), 91.

312. F. X. Cors Meya, *Las tasas en el marco de un sistema tributario justo*, 51 *REDF* 325 (1986), 327; J. M. Martín Delgado, *Los principios de capacidad económica e igualdad en la Constitución española de 1978*, 60 Hacienda Pública Española 61 (1979), 80; F. Sáinz de Bujanda, 7 (16/17) Rev. Fac. Derecho Universidad de Madrid 7 (1963), 100-104. Under this perspective, the ability to pay may be considered to apply to all categories of taxes and public fees, shaping both the tax system as a whole and each tax in particular. However, this point is not unanimous among scholars. Authors such as Manzoni and Moschetti defend that each tax must be ruled according to the ability to pay, whereas other authors, such as La Rosa or Hensel, argue that tax systems must be shaped by the ability-to-pay principle, without that meaning that each tax can be examined in light of that principle. Analysing further this discussion, *see* C. Palao Taboada (Tecnos 1976), 396-397.

operative answer than the ability-to-pay principle. The most illustrative example of these areas of the tax system is the public fees, which follow undeniably a commutative logic.

In turn, where the ability-to-pay principle is not expressly enshrined in the States' Constitution, being drawn from other principles, such as the equality principle, there is no need to articulate the ability-to-pay principle with the equivalence principle. In such States, it is easier to set a clear distinction between taxes, where the ability-to-pay principle applies, and public fees, where the equivalence principle operates.

Notwithstanding, even in the field of taxes, the lack of articulation between these two principles raises some difficulties. Indeed, there are taxes regarding which tailoring the amount due to the taxpayer's circumstances is challenging, as happens in the case of VAT. As advocated by Moschetti or Giardina, it may be said that the ability-to-pay principle has a more tenuous expression in such cases.[313] Even so, articulating the ability-to-pay principle with the equivalence principle by conceiving the benefit enjoyed as a concrete manifestation of the ability to pay better explains the tax phenomenon.

In any case, even if it is far-fetched to affirm that the ability to pay is the sole principle of justice for distributing the tax burden,[314] the ability to pay offers essential legal guidance and two main premises are drawn from it.

First, taxation depends on the existence of economic strength, meaning that a tax can only be imposed on a manifestation of an economic ability to pay it. This manifestation of strength must be embodied in the taxable events chosen by the legislator, which may change over time with the evolution of society.

Second, taxation must not occur where there is no manifestation of the ability to pay. The manifestation of economic strength must be relevant and express an actual ability to pay the tax, which only occurs when that economic strength is net and disposable. This way, the costs incurred to give rise to or keep the economic strength and the costs considered essential related to taxpayers' private and family sphere do not represent an ability to pay tax, being beyond the scope of taxation.

In a certain way, these premises correspond to what authors such as Giardina and Sáinz de Bujanda have designated as *absolute ability to pay* and *relative ability to*

313. F. Moschetti (Instituto de Estudios Fiscales 1980), 267; E. Giardina, *Le basi teoriche del principio della capacità contributiva* (Giuffrè 1961), 444: the author proposes the principle of most cases normality, according to which if an event typically expresses economic strength (for instance, the consumption of goods), it should constitute an indicator of ability to pay, even when in certain circumstances the economic strength could not exist. *See also* J. Casalta Nabais (Almedina 1998), 481.

314. A. Agulló Agüero, 36 REDF 555 (1982), 560; J. M. Martín Delgado, 60 Hacienda Pública Española 61 (1979), 66; M. Cortés Domínguez, *El principio de capacidad contributiva en el marco de la técnica jurídica*, 60 Revista de Derecho Financiero y Hacienda Pública 975 (1965), 1008; M. Cortés Domínguez, *Ordenamiento tributario español* (Civitas 1985), 72. Moreover, Palao Taboada highlights the tautology of identifying the ability to pay with tax justice: '*decir que es justo que tribute quien tiene la debida capacidad económica equivaldría a decir que es justo que sea sometido a imposición quien se considera justo sujetar a gravamen*' – C. Palao Taboada (Thomson Reuters Aranzadi 2018), 98.

pay.[315] The absolute ability to pay is linked to the taxpayers' abstract aptitude to contribute to public expenditure, and it is expressed in the determination of the taxable events that constitute a manifestation of economic strength. In turn, the relative ability to pay is related to each taxpayer's concrete aptitude to contribute, which must be determined by measuring and quantifying the economic strength of each taxpayer according to his/her factual situation.

Consequently, the ability to pay is the *conditio sine qua non* for taxing, and it demands knowing the person who will be taxed to graduate taxation accordingly. Or, as stressed by Manzoni, the ability to pay is the precondition of taxation and its threshold.[316]

Furthermore, the ability-to-pay and equality principles have a singular linkage. The ability to pay is regarded as the *tertium comparationis* needed to render the equality principle effective.[317] Consequently, taxpayers with the same ability to pay must be taxed the same way and taxpayers with a different ability to pay must be taxed differently.[318]

Nevertheless, the ability-to-pay principle itself cannot provide all the necessary answers to ascertain each taxpayer's fair amount of tax due. The criteria for establishing such an amount must be found in the interaction of the ability-to-pay principle with other principles and fundamental rights.[319] Thus, the ability to pay comprises a value

315. F. Sáinz de Bujanda, *Hacienda y Derecho* 3 (Instituto de Estudios Políticos 1963), 189 et seq.; F. Sáinz de Bujanda, 7 (16/17) Rev. Fac. Derecho Universidad de Madrid 7 (1963), 42 et seq.; E. Giardina (Giuffrè 1961), 53-57.
316. Nevertheless, Manzoni goes further and affirms that the ability to pay is not just the precondition and the threshold of taxation, but also its parameter, being the unitary measure of reference for determining the specific tax burden to be levied on each taxpayer – I. Manzoni, *Il Principio della capacità contributiva nell'ordinamento constituzionale italiano* (Giappichelli 1965), 14.
317. However, there is no unanimity on the nature of this connection, which is due, as explained by Palao Taboada, to the existence of different ways of understanding the equality principle. On the one hand, the equality principle may be treated as a formal and abstract principle without providing, by itself, a criterion for establishing when situations are equal or unequal. In the field of taxation, such a criterion is found in the ability-to-pay principle, which gives substance to the equality principle. On the other hand, the equality principle may be conceived as the prohibition of arbitrary discrimination, as proposed by Leibholz. The concept of arbitrariness is also indeterminable, demanding criteria that must be found in *the nature of things*, *reasonability* or *common juridical awareness*. Under this perspective, the ability to pay is conceived as independent from the equality principle and discharged from having all the answers, being just one more criterion to consider. Moreover, this perspective allows opening the door for discriminatory tax treatment whenever there is an adequate justification according to the nature of things – C. Palao Taboada (Thomson Reuters Aranzadi 2018), 162 et seq.
318. J. Lang & J. Englisch (A. Amatucci ed., Kluwer Law International 2d ed. 2012), 267. As explained by Kruse, taxation according to the ability-to-pay principle fully corresponds to the essence of distributive justice, which, under the Aristoteles' doctrine, aspires to relative equality – H. W. Kruse (P. Yebra Martul-Ortega & Izquierdo M. Macías-Picavea trans., Edersa 3d ed. 1978), 105.
319. As Moschetti observes, the ability to pay is the economic strength that should be deemed suitable to attend the public expenditure in light of the economic and social demands comprised in the constitution – F. Moschetti (Instituto de Estudios Fiscales 1980), 277; *see also* J. Casalta Nabais (Almedina 1998), 495. In the words of Tipke, despite the ability to pay being undetermined, like any other general principle, it is not undeterminable – K. Tipke, *Moral tributaria del Estado y de los contribuyentes (Besteuerungsmoral und Steuermoral)* (P. Herrera

judgment[320] on the fair amount of tax each one should pay, an amount that must be adjusted following the Constitutional purposes and taking the social development at any given time into account.

For instance, States' Constitutions may demand social and economic policies to ensure the general welfare and redistribution of wealth. The ability to pay is alien to these purposes, although it does not conflict with them. Indeed, it is assumed nowadays that the ability-to-pay principle does not demand progressive taxation, which is a tool for implementing a redistributive policy.[321]

Despite not being applied without considering other principles and fundamental rights, the ability-to-pay principle is a substantive criterion for achieving justice in distributing the tax burden among taxpayers and is regarded as constituting an authentic guarantee of taxpayers against the State.[322]

The ability to pay is embedded in the structure of most Member States' tax systems, regardless of the political choices and the concrete technical configuration employed by each State. Englisch observes that all Member States have de facto implemented important elements of the ability-to-pay principle in their tax legislation, mainly concerning personal income taxation. According to this author, there is even a

Molina trans., Marcial Pons 2002), 35. To that effect, Agulló Agüero explains that the principles guide the concrete techniques to be used to implement them, but principles cannot be identified with those concrete techniques. Furthermore, referring to the Spanish Constitutional framework, the author stresses that tax justice has to be found not only in the ability to pay, but also in equality, progressivity and prohibition of confiscation. Cf. A. Agulló Agüero, 36 REDF 555 (1982), 559-560.

320. F. Sáinz de Bujanda, 7 (16/17) Rev. Fac. Derecho Universidad de Madrid 7 (1963), 71.

321. As Englisch explains it, 'progression is not inherent to the 'objective' notion of ability-to-pay, but rather the insistence on progression is a reminiscence of the equal sacrifice theory, which has, however, been overcome for good reasons. [...] This notwithstanding, the notion of ability-to-pay is certainly flexible enough to embrace progression as a possible substantiation of its underlying social agenda, if so desired politically or required constitutionally' – J. Englisch (C. Brokelind ed., IBFD 2014), 445. *See also* K. Tipke & J. Lang (Verlag Dr. Otto Schmidt 10th ed. 2010), 89-90; J. Lang (W. Spindler et al. eds, Verlag Dr. Otto Schmidt 2009), 46; K. Tipke, *Die Steurrechtsordnung* (Verlag Dr. Otto Schmidt 2d ed. 2000), 480; K. Tipke & D. Yamashita, *Justiça fiscal e princípio da capacidade contributiva* (Malheiros 2002), 35; J. Casalta Nabais (Almedina 1998), 493; S. Vasques, 23 Fiscalidade 15 (2005), 31; G. Bizioli & E. Reimer, *Equality, Ability to Pay and Neutrality*, in *Research Handbook on European Union Taxation Law* (C. Panayi et al. eds, Elgar 2020), 64; F. Vanistendael, *Is Fiscal Justice Progressing?*, 64(10) Bull. Int'l Tax'n 526 (2010), 538-540. Conversely, linking the equal sacrifice theory with the need of progressive taxation, *see* E. Seligman, *Progressive Taxation in Theory and Practice*, 9(4) Am. Econ. Ass'n Q. 1 (1908), passim.

322. K. Tipke & J. Lang (Verlag Dr. Otto Schmidt 10th ed. 2010), 90: the authors explain that the ability to pay has developed from a redistribution policy to a legal principle, which mainly provides for the taxpayers' protection of the fundamental rights vis-à-vis the State. Conceiving the ability to pay as a fundamental right, *see* P. Herrera Molina, *Capacidad económica y Sistema fiscal: análisis del ordenamiento español a la luz del derecho alemán* (Marcial Pons 1998). Consequently, the author applies the control of proportionality to the breaches of the ability-to-pay principle. The need of controlling the breaches of the ability-to-pay principle is also present in other authors, such as Moschetti, Tipke, or in Lang and Englisch. Cf. F. Moschetti (Instituto de Estudios Fiscales 1980), 290; K. Tipke (Verlag Dr. Otto Schmidt 2d ed. 2000), 524-525; K. Tipke & D. Yamashita (Malheiros 2002), 37-42; J. Lang & J. Englisch (A. Amatucci ed., Kluwer Law International 2d ed. 2012), 268-270.

strong tendency, albeit not uniform, among the Member States regarding the constitutional relevance of the ability to pay.[323]

However, despite all Member States acknowledging the general necessity of taking into account taxpayers' situations, the specific expression of the ability to pay varies from tax to tax and from country to country, being the social and cultural diversities among the Member States of particular importance in this area. That diversity would be neglected if precise figures and requirements were established at the EU level, as Lang and Englisch stress.[324]

The next point examines how the EU law respects that diversity without undermining the prohibitions set forth by the general EU Treaty provisions that limit the exercise of Member States' taxing powers.

4.2 THE IMPACT OF EU LAW ON THE CONSIDERATION OF INDIVIDUALS' ABILITY TO PAY

Direct taxation does not, as such, fall within the competence of the EU.[325] Member States have the power to define their tax jurisdiction and configure their direct tax systems, and it is their responsibility to establish the legal principles on which the corresponding taxes should be based and define the specific techniques to be used to concretise those legal principles when framing each tax. Thus, the Member States are sovereign in determining their taxing powers and ascertaining *how* those taxing powers are *exercised*.

As already analysed in Chapter 3, the sole EU law requirement regarding direct taxation is that, when *exercising* their taxing powers, Member States must not hinder the freedom of movement by offering a worse tax treatment to cross-border situations than to comparable purely internal situations.

This way, concerning taxpayers' ability to pay, it must be noted that EU law does not impose how it should be considered – or even if it should be considered – by the

323. Following Englisch's analysis, the ability-to-pay principle is expressly mentioned as a constitutional requirement of fair taxation in eight Member States: Croatia, Cyprus, France, Greece, Italy, Spain, Bulgaria and Hungary. Elements of the ability-to-pay principle are incorporated in the Portuguese Constitution, even though the principle itself is not expressly mentioned. In Germany, Austria and Poland, the ability-to-pay principle has been derived from other constitutional guarantees, such as equality and solidarity. It has attained the status of a constitutionally enforceable right due to the judicial activism of the respective constitutional court. This is also the prevailing opinion among scholars in the Netherlands and Estonia, although it is not yet settled case law of the respective constitutional court. In Romania, Finland, Sweden, Luxembourg and Denmark, the ability to pay is considered an important guiding principle for tax law design, but without constitutional rank. In Belgium, Ireland, Malta and the Czech Republic, the ability to pay is not a particular relevant criterion in tax policy debates. Finally, the position of the remaining four Member States (Latvia, Lithuania, Slovakia and Slovenia) is yet unknown to the author – J. Englisch (C. Brokelind ed., IBFD 2014), 447-448. However, only the systematic interpretation of Member States' infra-constitutional law reveals the concrete implementation of the ability-to-pay principle, which varies according to the configuration and technics each State considers the most appropriate to tax fairly.

324. J. Lang & J. Englisch (A. Amatucci ed., Kluwer Law International 2d ed. 2012), 267.

325. *See* further Chapter 3.

Member States.[326] That choice, as said, belongs exclusively to the Member States, which do not have to mimic the other Member States' choices. Hence, each Member State may consider (or not) taxpayers' ability to pay on its terms, leading to completely different approaches among the Member States.

However, EU law acknowledges how each Member State configures its taxes and decides to assess taxpayers' ability to pay regarding internal situations, forbidding a different assessment in a comparable situation just because freedom of movement was exercised.[327] As Vanistendael explains it, '[t]he question is not so much whether there are specific EU positions with respect to the ability to pay, but rather whether the national concepts of the ability to pay, which apply in the internal situations of the Member States, are also applied without distinction on cross-border transactions or cross-border flows of income'.[328] In other words, EU law demands each Member State to apply the same criteria that it applies in purely internal situations to cross-border situations where these situations are comparable, and there are no overriding reasons in the public interest that justify otherwise.

326. P. Herrera Molina, *The Restrictive Impact of the Principles of EU Law on Tax Sovereignty and the Concept of Tax in the EU Member States*, in *The Concept of Tax: 2005 EATLP Congress* (B. Peeters et al. eds, IBFD 2005), 211, who affirms that: 'It should be understood that at an EU level there is no ability to pay principle regarding aspects such as: a) tax rates; b) personal deductions; c) basic tax-free allowances; d) progression in tax rates; and e) the appropriateness of taking into consideration family and personal matters. Each Member State has complete autonomy in all these matters.' However, the legal value of the ability-to-pay principle at the EU level is not unanimous among scholars. Englisch advocates that the ability-to-pay principle can be derived from the fundamental rights and general principles of the EU as their special manifestation or corollary in the field of taxation. Moreover, this author defends that 'there is strong support in the 'common' constitutional traditions of Member States for characterizing ability-to-pay as a constitutionally relevant reflection of the above mentioned fundamental rights and general principles of Union law' – J. Englisch (C. Brokelind ed., IBFD 2014), 446-455. García Prats argues that the CJEU 'should make the proposition of incorporating the ability to pay principle in the *acquis communautaire* as a supranational EU law principle', affirming that the ECJ has already taken an approach based on the ability to pay – A. García Prats, *Revisiting 'Schumacker': Source, Residence and Citizenship in the ECJ Case-Law on Direct Taxation*, in *Allocating Taxing Powers Within The European Union* (I. Richelle et al. eds, Springer 2013), 24. Bardini, although stressing that ability to pay does not form part of the common constitutional traditions of Member States, sustains that 'its existence in EU law, in the light of the ECJ decisions delivered to date, is not denied' – C. Bardini, *Ability to Pay in the European Market: An Impossible Sudoku for the ECJ*, 38(1) Intertax 2 (2010), 18 DOI: 10.54648/taxi2010001. In turn, Cerioni submits that the CJEU could develop a new EU ability-to-pay principle based on a teleological reading of the EU Treaties and the EU equality principle – L. Cerioni, *The Never-Ending Issue of Cross-Border Loss Compensation Within the EU: Reconciling Balanced Allocation of Taxing Rights and Cross-Border Ability-to-Pay*, 24 EC Tax Rev. 268 (2015), 274-277 DOI: 10.54648/ecta2015027.

327. According to García Prats, the requirements deriving from the ability-to-pay principle are incorporated into the European legal order as a logical consequence of the comparability benchmark between taxpayers who exercise free movement and those who do not – cf. A. García Prats, *La jurisprudencia del TJCE y el artículo 33 de la Ley del Impuesto de la Renta de no Residentes (De la asunción del principio de capacidad económica como principio del ordenamiento comunitario)*, 117 REDF 61 (2003), 76.

328. F. Vanistendael, *Ability to Pay in European Community Law*, 23(3) EC Tax Rev. 121 (2014), 122 DOI: 10.54648/ecta2014013. Moreover, according to Bizioli and Reimer, 'the reference to the ability to pay principle [in the CJEU's case law] does not develop an autonomous EU concept of that principle, but the domestic legal requirements for the calculation of the ability to pay become part of the judicial reasoning for assessing the nondiscrimination test' – G. Bizioli & E. Reimer (C. Panayi et al. eds, Elgar 2020), 69.

This demand for non-discrimination is made broadly: it covers all the relevant elements for determining the amount of tax due since all those elements are linked with taxpayers' ability to pay, seeking to perceive and quantify the taxpayers' economic strength.[329]

The importance the Court gives to the respect for the principle of ability to pay, just as enshrined by each Member State, is particularly noteworthy regarding two elements for determining the amount of tax due: *(i)* the consideration of expenses related to economic activity; and *(ii)* the consideration of expenses related to taxpayers' personal and family circumstances. These elements, which could be deemed to be what some authors designate as *objective net income* and *subjective net income*, respectively,[330] are analysed below.

---

329. For instance, determining what should be deemed as income, how it should be assessed and which tax rate should be applied are clear manifestations of measuring the economic strength of taxpayers and, therefore, their ability to pay. It is settled case law that the tax must not be assessed according to different criteria just because an EU freedom of movement is exercised. An example of the prohibition of setting different criteria for determining the income subject to tax regarding residents and non-residents is the CJEU, Case C-383/05 (*Talotta*). In this case, Mr Talotta, a non-resident pursuing a business activity in Belgium, did not submit his tax return in time. Consequently, his turnover was determined by applying the minimum tax bases, a method not used in the case of resident taxpayers who did not submit their tax returns. The Court considered that 'even on the assumption that the Belgian tax system is more often favourable to non–resident taxpayers, the fact remains that where that system proves disadvantageous for non-resident taxpayers, it results in unequal treatment by comparison with resident taxpayers and thus creates a hindrance to the freedom of establishment' (para. 31). Other examples of the discriminatory tax treatment of non-residents regarding the assessment of income are found in the *Hollmann* case and the *MK v. Autoridade Tributária e Aduaneira* case. In these cases, the basis for assessing tax on capital gains resulting from the transfer of immovable property was not the same for residents and non-residents. Non-resident taxpayers were taxed on the total amount of the capital gains realised, at a rate of 28%, while resident taxpayers were taxed on half of that amount at progressive tax rates. Cf. Case C-443/06 (*Hollmann*); Case C–388/19 (*MK v. Autoridade Tributária e Aduaneira*). In this latter case, the Court considered that the fact that non-residents had the option of being taxed as residents did not validate the discriminatory tax treatment, as already observed in the Case C–440/08 (*Gielen*). In turn, in the Case C-265/04 (*Bouanich*), the same item of income was classified as capital gains when obtained by resident taxpayers or as a dividend when obtained by non-resident taxpayers, with significant consequences on the deductibility of costs. Furthermore, there are also cases in which it is discussed whether applying heavier tax rates to non-residents than those applied to residents constitutes a discriminatory tax treatment: *see, e.g.*, Case C-107/94 (*Asscher*); Case C-234/01 (*Gerritse*); Case C-520/04 (*Turpeinen*); Case C-632/13 (*Hirvonen*). It is clear that non-residents' tax burden must not exceed residents' tax burden on the same net income amount. However, the difficulty of these cases is determining the suitable base of comparability. On the one hand, in the case of non-residents, to ease their taxation, flat tax rates are often applied instead of progressive tax rates, as in the case of residents, and, on the other hand, the tax-free allowance granted to resident taxpayers must be disregarded because non-resident taxpayers are not, as a rule, entitled to it. For an analysis of the cases in which the CJEU dealt with the structure of the scale rate in personal income, *see* F. Vanistendael, 23(3) EC Tax Rev. 121 (2014), 126-128.
330. K. Tipke & J. Lang (Verlag Dr. Otto Schmidt 10th ed. 2010), 242; J. Lang, *Tributación familiar*, 94 Hacienda Pública Española 407 (1985), 410-412. Following the same terminology, *see, e.g.*, P. Herrera Molina (Marcial Pons 1998), 117 and 120; J. Casalta Nabais (Almedina 1998), 520-524; A. Steichen, *La Justice dans l'impôt* (Centre Universitaire de Luxembourg 1994), 325, 419; C. Bardini, 38(1) Intertax 2 (2010), 3-4; J. Lang & J. Englisch (A. Amatucci ed., Kluwer Law

4.2.1 The Consideration of Expenses Related to Economic Activity

It is widely accepted today that the income perceived by taxpayers must be taxed on its net amount. That is to say, the costs of obtaining the income must be considered and deducted from the gross income amount. Otherwise, if taxpayers were taxed on their gross income without considering the relevant expenses incurred to derive such income, the tax burden would fall on an artificial economic strength that would not reflect an actual ability to pay the tax.[331]

Taxing gross income, on the one hand, amounts to taxing the economic strength of others for the monies that are owed to them instead of taxing the taxpayer's own economic strength, and, on the other hand, leads to inequality in taxation, as taxpayers with a similar ability to pay would be subject to a different level of taxation according to the costs incurred by them.[332]

As Moschetti affirms, although there is no doubt that any manifestation of the ability to pay must be taxed on the net amount perceived, difficulties arise when converting this general principle into a concrete norm.[333] Proof of that is the non-existence of standard criteria for ascertaining the net income.

Indeed, Alarcón identifies three groups of criteria used to determine net income. The first group consider the expenses linked to the activity generating the income; the second considers the expenses linked with the income perceived; and the third resorts to presumptive tax bases determined by indicators and coefficients. Regarding the first and second groups, finding the causal nexus between the two elements (i.e., the expenses and the activity/income) is necessary. As noted by the author, this causal nexus may be conceived as a *conditio sine qua non* – i.e., the expenses generated by the activity/the obtention of income – or as a *causa finalis* – i.e., the costs generated by the activity with the intention of obtaining taxable income.[334]

In this regard, the Member States may freely define the criteria and techniques to ascertain the net income, establishing the costs whose deductibility is accepted. As a result, the deductible expenses vary significantly from one Member State to another.

Because the definition of deductible expenses forms part of the Member States' power to configure their tax systems, the CJEU does not – it cannot – interfere with that definition and does not seek to set any uniform criteria in this regard.

As already noted, the problem for EU law arises only when the Member States establish distinct criteria for the deductibility of costs depending on whether taxpayers

International 2d ed. 2012), 267; E. Traversa, *Objective Ability to Pay: The Gerritse Case*, in *Landmark Decisions of the ECJ in Direct Taxation* (W. Haslehner et al. eds, Kluwer Law International 2015), 5-6.

331. *See, e.g.*, B. Griziotti (E. Mata trans., Editorial Reus 2d ed. 1958), 147-148; E. Giardina (Giuffrè 1961), 208; F. Sáinz de Bujanda, 7 (16/17) Rev. Fac. Derecho Universidad de Madrid 7 (1963), 53-54; F. Moschetti (Instituto de Estudios Fiscales 1980), 404-405; J. Casalta Nabais (Almedina 1998), 520-521; S. Vasques, 23 Fiscalidade 15 (2005), 25.
332. E. Giardina (Giuffrè 1961), 208-209; F. Moschetti (Instituto de Estudios Fiscales 1980), 405.
333. F. Moschetti (Instituto de Estudios Fiscales 1980), 405.
334. G. Alarcón García, *La determinación de los rendimientos netos en el ordenamiento alemán: relevancia para España y utilidad como modelo de armonización fiscal en la Unión Europea*, 1 Impuestos 1158 (1997).

carry out an activity domestically or cross-borders when those activities are comparable.[335] In such a case, the existence of Member States' power to configure the tax system is not at stake, but the *exercise* of that power in a way that creates a unilateral disadvantage to taxpayers benefiting from free movement.

4.2.1.1 The Concept of Expenses Directly Linked and Its Purpose

The CJEU uses the expression 'expenses directly linked' to refer to the deductible costs and has already enlightened what should be understood by that expression.

Accordingly, *expenses directly linked* are those expenses that have a direct economic connection to the activity giving rise to taxable income in a Member State and, therefore, are inextricably linked to that activity,[336] which does not mean that it is sufficient a mere correlation, of whatever kind, between the amounts of the expenditure and the taxable income.[337] Furthermore, such expenses must be necessary,[338] which does not mean that those expenses must be unavoidable.[339]

Interestingly, when referring to the 'direct link', the Court does so in an oscillatory manner, sometimes referring to the direct link between expenses and activity generating the taxable income,[340] sometimes referring to the direct link between expenses and taxable income.[341] This duality of references sometimes even occurs within the same decision.[342]

---

335. As explained by Traversa, 'taxation on a net basis is not a principle of European Union law. However, as it is often the case when applying EU fundamental freedoms, the Court requires Member States to be coherent in the tax treatment of expenses between domestic and cross-border situations. [...] when recognized at the domestic level, objective ability to pay also has to be extended without territorial limitation in two- or more country situations' – E. Traversa (W. Haslehner et al. eds, Kluwer Law International 2015), 14.
336. CJEU, Case C–345/04 (*Centro Equestre da Lezíria Grande*), para. 25: 'Operating expenses directly connected to the income received in the Member State in which the activity is pursued must be understood as being expenses which have a direct economic connection to the provision of services which gave rise to taxation in that State and which are therefore inextricably linked to those services, such as travel and accommodation costs. In that context, the place and time at which the costs were incurred are immaterial.'
337. CJEU, Case C-450/09 (*Schröder*), para. 43: '[T]he fact remains that the existence of a direct link within the meaning of the case-law cited in paragraph 40 of the present judgment results, not from a correlation, of whatever kind, between the amount of the expenditure in question and that of the taxable income, but from the fact that that expenditure is inextricably linked to the activity which gives rise to that income.'
338. CJEU, Case C-559/13 (*Grünewald*), para. 30: 'Thus, expenses occasioned by the activity in question are directly linked to that activity and are accordingly necessary in order to carry out that activity.' *See also* Case C-480/17 (*Montag*), para. 37.
339. CJEU, Case C-480/17 (*Montag*), para. 41: '[T]he fact that the applicant in the main proceedings may have been able to avoid such expenses cannot alter their characterisation. The existence of a direct link, within the meaning of the case-law set out in paragraph 33 above, does not mean that an expense must be unavoidable.'
340. For example, Case C-234/01 (*Gerritse*), para. 27.
341. For example, Case C–345/04 (*Centro Equestre da Lezíria Grande*), para. 25.
342. For example, CJEU, Case C-346/04 (*Conijn*), paras 20 and 22 (emphasis added): '20. In relation to *expenditure linked directly to the income* of a person with restricted tax liability, the Court has held that, for *expenditure such as business expenses linked with an activity* in another Member State, a person with restricted tax liability must be treated in the same way as a person with

However, determining the deductibility of costs based on the direct link between expenses and activity does not lead exactly to the same result as determining such deductibility based on the direct link between expenses and taxable income. The first scenario (i.e., the direct link between expenses and activity) could lead to broader deductibility of expenses than the second scenario (i.e., the direct link between expenses and income) since the expenses directly related to the activity may not be directly connected to the obtainment of income.

Despite the variation of the terms used by the Court, the clarification provided by the CJEU on the meaning of 'direct link' shows that the Court has an unambiguous stance and adopts a comprehensive approach, which necessarily involves choosing the *direct link between expenses and activity* as the relevant connection for determining the deductibility of expenses.

This approach is particularly noticeable in its case law involving the deduction of expenses by individual taxpayers.[343]

In the *Conijn* case,[344] costs incurred in obtaining tax advice to prepare the tax return were qualified as a special expense under national law and could only be deducted by resident taxpayers. The Court found that this expense affected in the same way the income received by all taxpayers, whether residents or non-residents. When referring to the 'expenses directly linked' in its reasoning, the Court mentioned the connection to both the *activity* and *taxable income*. Although there is a correlation

---

unrestricted tax liability. [...] 22. [...] *Costs incurred in obtaining tax advice are therefore linked directly to the income taxed* in that Member State, with the result that they affect in the same way the income received by all taxable persons whether resident or non-resident.'

343. There are also examples involving undertakings. A very illustrative example is the *Brisal and KBC Finance Ireland* case. In this case, the Court addressed what could be considered, on the one hand, expenses directly linked to income and, on the other hand, expenses directly linked to the activity generating income. The CJEU concluded that both kinds of expenses could be deducted by non-resident taxpayers. In this case, the income-related expenses were the direct costs connected with the granting of a loan, while the activity-related expenses were the overheads regarded as necessary to carry out that activity, but regarding which it is more challenging to establish a direct link with a concrete loan or the actual amount involved. Cf. CJEU, Case C–18/15 (*Brisal and KBC Finance Ireland*), paras. 47-50. Notwithstanding, in the *Miljoen* case, the Court had followed a more restrictive approach, holding that an undertaking could not deduct from the dividends received the financing costs incurred to acquire the respective shares. The Court considered that the financing costs concerned ownership of the shares per se, not being directly linked to the actual payment of dividends deriving from those shares. Cf. CJEU, Case C-10/14 (*Miljoen*), para. 60. The Opinion of the AG sheds light on why the Court adopted a more restrictive approach in this case. The Member State in question had taxing rights regarding the dividends received by non-residents from holding shares in that State's companies, but it did not have taxing rights on the capital gains derived by non-residents that the sale of those shares could originate. That difference in the taxing rights – that did not exist in purely internal situations – led to the need to distinguish between expenses directly linked to receipt of dividends and those linked to the transaction as a whole. *See* Opinion of the AG Jääskinen in Case C-10/14 (*Miljoen*), paras. 94-95. *See also* CFE ECJ Task Force, *Opinion Statement ECJ-TF 1/2016 on the Decision of the European Court of Justice in Joined Cases Miljoen (Case C-10/14), X (Case C-14/14) and Société Générale (Case C-17/14) on the Netherlands Dividend Withholding Tax*, 56 Eur. Tax'n 255 (2016). Taking a critical view of the decision on the *Miljoen* case, *see* P. Wattel et al. (Kluwer Law International 7th ed. 2018), 856-857. On general business expenditures, *see also* W. Schön, 68(4/5) Bull. Int'l Tax'n 271 (2015), 286.

344. CJEU, Case C-346/04 (*Conijn*).

between the income received and the need to present a tax return, the costs related to the tax return do not generate any taxable income; on the contrary, those costs result from obtaining taxable income. This way, the CJEU's stance, in this case, indicates that the relevant link must be established between expenses and activity generating the taxable income, as this link allows for broader results.

This stance of the Court was confirmed in the *Schröder* case[345] and the *Grünewald* case.[346] In these cases, the Court clearly stated that the relevant link results from the connection between expenses and activity. In the *Schröder* case, the Court held that a non-resident could deduct the annuities paid to a relative in the context of an anticipated succession of immovable property from the rental income derived from that property because it was an expenditure directly linked to the activity in letting the immovable property. The *Grünewald* case deals with a similar issue and reaches the same conclusion. The case concerned the deductibility of annuities paid in the context of an anticipated succession of shares in a business from the commercial income generated by those shares.

Furthermore, in the *Montag* case,[347] contributions to an occupational pension scheme were found by the Court as directly linked to professional income obtained by the taxpayer since the payment of the contributions to the lawyers' provident institution was necessary on account of membership of the bar association, which was itself necessary in order to carry out the activity which generated the taxable income.[348]

It must be noted that the concept of 'direct link' introduced by the CJEU does not oblige the Member States to consider all expenses inextricably linked to economic activity. As observed, the Member States remain sovereign in this regard: they may follow the criteria and techniques they wish to determine the net income and accept the deductibility of the costs they deem most appropriate.

The concept of 'direct link' provided by the CJEU serves another purpose: it aims to set the base for differentiation between expenses related to economic activity and expenses related to personal and family circumstances.

Regarding the expenses related to economic activity (i.e., *expenses directly linked to the activity generating the taxable income*), the CJEU is emphatic in affirming that

345. CJEU, Case C-450/09 (*Schröder*).
346. CJEU, Case C-559/13 (*Grünewald*).
347. CJEU, Case C-480/17 (*Montag*).
348. Another case concerning the deduction of compulsory expenses is the CJEU, Case C–314/08 (*Filipiak*). At issue were compulsory social security contributions and compulsory health insurance contributions paid in the source Member State. The taxpayer intended to deduct such contributions in his Member State of residence, which did not accept it because those expenses were incurred abroad. However, in this case, it is not clear whether the CJEU considered these expenses as expenses related to economic activity - because necessary for pursuing the economic activity - or as expenses related to personal and family circumstances. Assuming that those expenses had not been deducted in the source Member State, the Court merely concluded that the Member State of residence would have to consider them. With a different opinion, Rust considers that the Court treated the compulsory social security contributions as private expenses rather than income-related expenses - A. Rust, *Germany II: Case C-20/16 (Bechtel & Bechtel)*, in *CJEU – Recent Developments in Direct Taxation 2016* (M. Lang et al. eds, Linde Verlag 2017), 83.

there is no objective difference between resident and non-resident taxpayers,[349] as they are in a comparable situation.

The comparability of their situation lies in the fact that, in both cases (i.e., in the case of residents and non-residents), taxing a gross income amounts to taxing an artificial economic strength that does not represent an actual ability to pay.

Consequently, the Member States cannot, without breaching EU law, adopt different and more burdensome criteria and techniques for determining the net income of non-resident taxpayers than those for determining the net income of resident taxpayers. For example, Member States cannot allow the deductibility of expenses by residents and forbid it for non-residents.

Moreover, the prohibition of non-discrimination regarding expenses related to economic activity must be understood broadly, covering not only non-resident taxpayers but also resident taxpayers who exercise free movement by carrying out cross-border activities.[350]

In contrast, regarding expenses related to personal and family circumstances, residents and non-residents are not, as a rule, in a comparable situation, as addressed further in the next section.

Given the significant consequence of characterising expenses as related to economic activity or personal and family circumstances, the CJEU has set this autonomous concept of *expenses directly linked to the activity generating the taxable income*, which is independent of the Member States' legal classification of expenses.[351]

The need for such an autonomous concept is explained by the fact that *(i)* it is not always easy to determine in the Member States' tax law which deductible expenses are characterised as economic activity expenses or as personal and family expenses; *(ii)* that characterisation may vary from one Member States to another; and *(iii)* that characterisation may be carried out artificially by the Member States in order to differentiate situations whose different treatment would not be admissible otherwise.

Therefore, the autonomous concept of *expenses directly linked to the activity generating the taxable income* adopted by the CJEU is a tool for the national courts to

349. CJEU, Case C-234/01 (*Gerritse*), para. 27: 'It is to be noted at this stage that the business expenses in question are directly linked to the activity that generated the taxable income in Germany, so that residents and non-residents are placed in a comparable situation in that respect.' *See also* Case C-265/04 (*Bouanich*), para. 40; Case C-346/04 (*Conijn*), para. 20; Case C–345/04 (*Centro Equestre da Lezíria Grande*), paras 23-24; Case C-440/08 (*Gielen*), paras 45-47; Case C-450/09 (*Schröder*), paras 40-41; Case C-559/13 (*Grünewald*), para. 29; Case C-10/14 (*Miljoen*), para. 57; Case C-480/17 (*Montag*), para. 30.

350. As Van Raad notes, 'it should be equally obvious that in respect of foreign-source income resident taxpayers should be entitled to the same business deductions as in respect of domestic-source income' – K. Van Raad, *Non-residents – Personal Allowances, Deduction of Personal Expenses and Tax Rates*, 2(2) World Tax J. 154 (2010), 155 DOI: 10.59403/mz4c1s.

351. In this regard, *see* A. Rust (M. Lang et al. eds, Linde Verlag 2017), 83, who affirms that, 'In order for an expense to qualify as an income related expense or as a private expense, the characterization in domestic law is not decisive.'

uniformly draw the line between expenses related to economic activity and expenses related to personal and family circumstances.[352]

4.2.2 The Consideration of Expenses Related to Personal and Family Circumstances

Today, it is commonly accepted that taxation should not deprive individuals of what is necessary to support themselves and their families. In other words, taxes should be levied on individuals' disposable economic strength, i.e., on the remaining income once their basic livelihood needs and that of their families have been ensured.[353]

There is, thus, an intangible economic strength aimed at satisfying existential needs, which does not express the ability to pay taxes.[354] In this respect, several justifications for exempting a portion of individuals' income have been presented.

It has been observed that respect for human needs corresponds to a political and social imperative,[355] reflecting a norm of solidarity,[356] the violation of which would undeniably lead to a feeling of injustice[357] and would undermine human dignity as the structural principle of States based on the rule of law.

The exemption of a portion of individuals' income has also been explained by the theory of human capital reintegration, which regards the minimum income as a production expense intended to reintegrate the working energy consumed by those who obtain income from their labour. Moreover, the extension of that minimum to handle family burdens is regarded as an expense for raising and educating new human capital to continue the labour source.[358] However, subjective considerations, such as the intensity and urgency in satisfying essential needs, must complement this theory; otherwise, this theory would be incapable of justifying the minimum income exemption in the case of unemployed or retired persons.[359]

Finally, administrative considerations have also been pointed out in this regard. Accordingly, it would be uneconomical to levy taxes on a minimum income, the collection costs of which would be higher than the revenue obtained.[360] Still, such considerations alone could lead to a hasty conclusion on whether the exemption of a

352. *See, e.g.*, CJEU, Case C-559/13 (*Grünewald*), paras 31-32, where the Court clarifies that despite its guidance, ultimately, it is for the national courts to ascertain whether a given expense is an activity expense or an expense connected to the taxpayer's personal situation.
353. B. Griziotti (E. Mata trans., Editorial Reus 2d ed. 1958), 153-154. E. Giardina (Giuffrè 1961), 212; F. Sáinz de Bujanda (Instituto de Estudios Políticos 1963), 240; I. Manzoni, (Giappichelli 1965), 74-75; F. Moschetti (Instituto de Estudios Fiscales 1980), 267; J. Lang, 94 Hacienda Pública Española 407 (1985), 410; L. V. Berliri (F. Vicente-Arche Domingo trans., Instituto de Estudios Fiscales 1986), 252-253; J. Casalta Nabais (Almedina 1998), 522-523.
354. To the same effect, *see* K. Tipke (P. Herrera Molina trans., Marcial Pons 2002), 35.
355. B. Griziotti (E. Mata trans., Editorial Reus 2d ed. 1958), 153.
356. F. Moschetti (Instituto de Estudios Fiscales 1980), 269.
357. L. V. Berliri (F. Vicente-Arche Domingo trans., Instituto de Estudios Fiscales 1986), 252.
358. Explaining it further and presenting the criticism regarding this theory, E. Giardina (Giuffrè 1961), 213-219.
359. E. Giardina (Giuffrè 1961), 215-216.
360. B. Griziotti (E. Mata trans., Editorial Reus 2d ed. 1958), 154. L. V. Berliri (F. Vicente-Arche Domingo trans., Instituto de Estudios Fiscales 1986), 249.

portion of income should apply to all taxpayers without exception or cover only low-income taxpayers.[361]

Furthermore, as Griziotti notes, the minimum income exempted varies with the development of society.[362] Today, it is not understood *stricto sensu* as implying only a tax-free allowance, but as related to all taxpayers' personal and family circumstances that States consider as being evidence of economic strength loss. It is, thus, a means of tailoring the tax to the individuals' idiosyncrasies, ensuring that all individuals pay taxes according to their own ability.

There are numerous ways of considering the taxpayers' personal and family circumstances, and the States have the power to decide how to take them into account. The States may implement such consideration by allowing personal and family tax deductions or granting tax-free allowances. Moreover, the States may also ensure the basic needs of individuals and their families through government subsidies or by providing public services free of charge. States tend to build systems that combine these multiple options.

Therefore, as far as the EU is concerned, the Member States are sovereign to decide whether personal and family circumstances should be taken into account at a tax level. In that case, the Member States must define how taxpayers' personal and family circumstances are to be protected: *(i)* whether through tax deductions, tax-free allowances, or a combination of both; *(ii)* what are the relevant tax deductions and tax-free allowances; and *(iii)* what should be the ideal measure of these tax deductions and tax-free allowances. Consequently, there is a multiplicity of different approaches among the Member States.

All tax advantages granted by the Member States to taxpayers, which are not linked to a taxable activity, are considered to be how those Member States take into account personal and family circumstances. Such tax advantages may be connected to taxpayers' family situation – *inter alia*, joint taxation,[363] tax-free income allowance for dependent children,[364] maintenance payments[365] – and to taxpayers' private situation – *inter alia*, tax-free allowances,[366] pension, life, and health insurance contributions,[367] negative income related to a dwelling or a property,[368] and other living expenses[369]

361. On this question, *see* further E. Giardina (Giuffrè 1961), 219-223.
362. B. Griziotti (E. Mata trans., Editorial Reus 2d ed. 1958), 154.
363. CJEU, Case C-279/93 (*Schumacker*); Case C-391/97 (*Gschwind*); Case C-87/99 (*Zurstrassen*); Case C-329/05 (*Meindl*); Case C-425/11 (*Ettwein*).
364. CJEU, Case C-303/12 (*Imfeld and Garcet*).
365. CJEU, Case C-385/00 (*De Groot*); Case C–403/03 (*Schempp*).
366. CJEU, Case C-385/99 (*De Groot*); Case C-234/01 (*Gerritse*); Case C-169/03 (*Wallentin*); Case C-174/18 (*Jacob and Lennertz*). However, not all tax-free allowances are to be regarded as based on personal circumstances – *see, e.g.*, Case C-10/14 (*Miljoen*) and Case C-181/12 (*Welte*).
367. CJEU, Case C-204/90 (*Bachmann*); Case C-80/94 (*Wielockx*); Case C–314/08 (*Filipiak*); Case C-20/16 (*Bechtel*).
368. CJEU, Case C-152/03 (*Ritter-Coulais*); Case C-182/06 (*Lakebrink and Peters-Lakebrink*); Case C-527/06 (*Renneberg*); Case C-9/14 (*Kieback*); Case C-632/13 (*Hirvonen*); Case C-283/15 (*X*). According to the Opinion of AG Léger in the *Ritter-Coulais* case and of AG Mengozzi in the *Lakebrink and Peters-Lakebrink* case, the consideration of negative income related to property was a tax benefit unconnected with taxpayers' personal and family circumstances. However, the principle of non-discrimination, which implies the national treatment of non-residents in a

stipulated by the Member States. According to the Court, it is not necessary for the tax advantages granted to have a social purpose.[370] Even tax benefits designed mainly to encourage taxpayers to spend and make investments are considered linked to their personal and family situation insofar as they impact their ability to pay taxes.[371]

The notion of 'personal and family circumstances' adopted by the Court, therefore, has a broad meaning, and its concretion depends on each Member State's domestic law.[372]

Since the decision to protect taxpayers' personal and family circumstances at a tax level falls within the Member States' power to configure their tax systems, the CJEU accepts all Member States' measures in this regard, and EU law does not require any further measure. The sole EU law requirement imposed on the Member States derives from the fundamental freedoms' provisions: taxpayers who exercise an EU freedom of movement must not be treated worse than those who do not exercise it, as far as their situation is comparable.[373]

---

comparable situation, should encompass all aspects of overall ability to pay [Opinion of AG Léger in Case C-152/03 (*Ritter-Coulais*), paras 98-102; Opinion of AG Mengozzi in Case C-182/06 (*Lakebrink and Peters-Lakebrink*), paras 34, 36]. The Court, in the *Lakebrink and Peters-Lakebrink* case, states that the *Schumacker* doctrine concerns 'all the tax advantages connected with the non-resident's ability to pay tax which are not taken into account either in the State of residence or in the State of employment (...), since the ability to pay tax may indeed be regarded as forming part of the personal situation of the non-resident within the meaning of the judgment in *Schumacker*' [CJEU, Case C-182/06 (*Lakebrink and Peters-Lakebrink*), para. 34]. It seems, therefore, that the Court considers that all tax advantages connected with taxpayers' ability to pay form part of taxpayers' personal situation. It is interesting to note the reservation presented by AG Mengozzi about the fact that in the *Lakebrink and Peters-Lakebrink case, the ability to pay was regarded as part of the taxpayer's personal circumstances. According to the AG, such assimilation could be risky and should be understood as an obiter dictum [Opinion of AG Mengozzi in Case C-527/06 (Renneberg), paras 54-57]. Indeed, identifying the ability to pay with taxpayers' personal and family circumstances, if read out of the Court's statement context, can be misleading, as taxpayers' ability to pay is formed by their aggregate income, minus activity expenses and personal and family circumstances, and it is measured according to a tax rate. Nevertheless, the Court's statement was never misread in the sense feared by the AG.*

369. For instance, in the *Jacob and Lennertz* case, at issue were tax reductions in respect of long-term savings, services paid with service vouchers, costs incurred in saving energy in the home, costs incurred in protecting the home against theft or fire and charitable donations – *see* CJEU, Case C-174/18 (*Jacob and Lennertz*); *see also* CJEU, Case C–241/20 (*BJ v. État belge*).
370. CJEU, Case C-174/18 (*Jacob and Lennertz*), para. 38: 'By taking into account such negative rental income the Court opted for a broad meaning of the notion of 'personal and family situation' without reference to any social purpose.'
371. *Ibid.*, paras 40-41: '40. In that regard, it must be considered that tax reductions such as those at issue in the main proceedings [...] are designed, principally, to encourage taxpayers to spend and make investments which necessarily have an impact on their ability to pay taxes. 41. As a result, such tax reductions may be considered to be linked to the personal and family situation of the applicants in the main proceedings, in the same way as the tax reductions in respect of the tax-free allowance.'
372. A. García Prats (I. Richelle et al. eds, Springer 2013), 18.
373. CJEU, Case C-385/00 (*De Groot*), para. 114: 'Community law lays down no specific requirement with regard to the way in which the State of residence must take account of the personal and family circumstances of a worker who, during a particular tax year, received income in that State and in another Member State. However, [...] the conditions governing the way in which the State of residence takes into account such a taxpayer's personal and family circumstances

Indeed, although the Member States have the power to configure their tax systems, they must not create unilateral disadvantages to taxpayers making use of an EU freedom of movement. Therefore, if the Member States decide to consider taxpayers' personal and family circumstances, they must consider them regarding all taxpayers, regardless of whether they have made use of an EU freedom of movement. Any difference in treatment will only be compatible with EU law if the situation of taxpayers exercising an EU freedom of movement is not objectively comparable to that of taxpayers not exercising it, or when their situation is objectively comparable, the CJEU finds that difference in treatment justified and proportional, as studied in more detail in Chapter 3.

4.2.2.1 *Comparability Between Taxpayers and the Absolute Need to Consider Their Personal and Family Circumstances*

As acknowledged by the CJEU, there is a correlation between being subject in a Member State to taxation on the worldwide income and having personal and family circumstances considered in that State.[374]

Taxpayers are subject to worldwide taxation in the State with which they have a personal attachment. As a rule, personal attachment is found in residence among the Member States. The primary justification for worldwide taxation in the State of residence derives from the fact that this is the State where taxpayers use most public infrastructures and services (e.g., water services, waste management, health, education, social care, transport) and fully enjoy the State's public functions (e.g., public security, justice, diplomacy).[375] Consequently, taxpayers' main tax contributions should be made there.

Due to the worldwide taxation taxpayers are subject to in their residence State, it is also in this State where it is easier to consider their overall ability to pay because worldwide taxation implies further report obligations, such as a tax return containing all the taxpayers' aggregate income and their personal and family situation.

In contrast, regarding non-residents, States usually only tax them on the activities performed or carried out within their territory, ignoring income derived from other sources. Non-residents are typically taxed through withholding taxes at flat rates due to the lack of a permanent physical presence in a State. This way, in general, those States do not have information regarding non-residents' aggregate income or personal and family situation.

Since States, in general, have at their disposal much information on residents and little on non-residents, the CJEU concludes that, as a rule, considering taxpayers'

must not constitute discrimination, either direct or indirect, on grounds of nationality, or an obstacle to the exercise of a fundamental freedom guaranteed by the Treaty.'

374. *Ibid.*, para. 99, where the Court points out the 'correlation between the total income of residents and residents' general personal and family circumstances to be taken into account by the State of residence'.

375. *See supra* section 1.2.1.

personal and family circumstances is a matter of the residence State because this State is best placed to assess the taxpayer's ability to pay tax.[376]

From this conclusion, the CJEU draws that, regarding personal and family circumstances, the Member States must treat their residents alike, regardless of whether they have exercised an EU freedom of movement, but they do not have to treat non-residents and residents in the same way. This finding is in line with Article 24(3) of the OECD MC, which confirms the international practice of restricting personal deductions to residents and denying them to non-residents.[377]

It must be noted that the CJEU does not explain why, regarding the consideration of personal and family circumstances, residents who exercise free movement are comparable to residents who do not. Indeed, there is a significant difference between them: residents who carry out purely internal activities obtain only domestic income, while residents who carry out cross-border activities also obtain income from abroad.

It may be assumed that the comparability between them stems from factual circumstances. Due to the worldwide taxation residents are usually subject to in their residence State, this State is able to know their personal and family situation, as well as all the income they obtained, regardless of its source. Thus, the fact that residents obtain income from abroad does not prevent, in general, the residence State from being best placed to assess their overall ability to pay.

Since residents are comparable to each other, the residence Member State must fully consider all residents' personal and family circumstances. Consequently, in practical terms, the residence Member State must allocate the total amount of personal and family circumstances to residents' domestic income, even when not all their income is derived domestically and that Member State refrains from taxing their foreign income,[378] as illustrated *infra* in section 6.1.

---

376. CJEU, Case C–241/20 (*BJ v. État belge*), para. 25: 'Moreover, it is, in principle, a matter for the Member State of residence to grant the taxpayer all the tax advantages relating to his or her personal and family circumstances, because that State is, as a rule, best placed to assess the taxpayer's personal ability to pay tax, determined by reference to his or her aggregate income and his or her personal and family circumstances, since that is where his or her personal and financial interests are centred.' *See also*: CJEU, Case C-279/93 (*Schumacker*), para. 32; Case C-391/97 (*Gschwind*), para. 22; Case C-87/99 (*Zurstrassen*), para. 21; Case C-385/00 (*De Groot*), para. 90; Case C-234/01 (*Gerritse*), para. 43; Case C-169/03 (*Wallentin*), para. 15; Case C-520/04 (*Turpeinen*), para. 27; Case C-329/05 (*Meindl*), para. 23; Case C-425/11 (*Ettwein*), para. 45; Case C-168/11 (*Beker*), para. 43; Case C-303/12 (*Imfeld and Garcet*), para. 43; Case C-9/14 (*Kieback*), para. 22; Case C-632/13 (*Hirvonen*), para. 31; Case C-283/15 (*X*), para. 30; Case C-20/16 (*Bechtel*), para. 55; Case C-174/18 (*Jacob and Lennertz*), para. 26.
377. As noted by K. Van Raad, 2(2) World Tax J. 154 (2010), 155-156, 'The permanent establishment non-discrimination provision of Art. 24(3) of the OECD Model, which in its first sentence grants to non-resident taxpayers the right to be taxed on their business income earned through a permanent establishment in the source country not less favourably than resident taxpayers, confirms this practice by denying in its second sentence expressly these non-resident taxpayers the right to the personal expense deductions that resident taxpayers have.' According to this author, the States do not provide non-residents such personal benefits because 'an extension of these benefits to them by the source country is assumed to give them double benefits and thereby an advantage over the source country's resident taxpayers'. The OECD MC, Commentary on Art. 24, para. 36, confirms this view.
378. H. Niesten, *Growing Impetus for Harmonisation of Personal and Family Allowances: Current State of Affairs of the Schumaker-Doctrine after Imfeld and Garcet*, 24(4) EC Tax Rev. 185 (2015), 192

In turn, the Member States do not have to treat residents and non-residents alike regarding their personal and family circumstances since there is, as a rule, an objective difference between their situations: resident taxpayers, as said, are subject to worldwide taxation, while non-residents are subject to source taxation. The personal and family circumstances of those non-residents are to be taken into account in their residence State, which is best placed to consider them. Moreover, granting those taxpayers personal and family tax benefits in their residence State is, in principle, enough to ensure that their intangible economic strength remains untouchable. Hence, as a rule, the Member States do not discriminate against non-residents when they do not take into account their personal and family circumstances.[379]

However, exceptions exist in this regard: when non-residents derive almost all their income from the source Member State,[380] having no significant income in their residence Member State, their situation becomes very similar to those residing in the source State. In such a case, the economic relationship of those non-resident taxpayers with the source Member State is identical to the economic relationship between that State and its own residents. Although those non-resident taxpayers are not formally subject to worldwide taxation in the source Member State, such worldwide taxation happens in practice, all their income being subject to taxation in the source State. In the words of García Prats, 'limited taxation may be de facto unlimited taxation of all the income attributable to a certain taxpayer'.[381]

DOI: 10.54648/ecta2015019. *See, e.g.*, the CJEU, Case C–241/20 (*BJ v. État belge*). In this case, the taxpayer did not receive significant income in the Member State of residence. Nevertheless, the CJEU pointed out that, according to the order for reference, the taxpayer received sufficient income in his residence State for his personal and family circumstances to be taken into account in that State. In this regard, the Court stressed that '[w]hat remains the decisive criterion is whether it is impossible for a Member State to take into account, for the calculation of tax, the personal and family circumstances of a taxpayer in the absence of sufficient taxable income, although such circumstances can otherwise be taken into account when there is sufficient income' (para. 39).

379. CJEU, Case C-283/15 (*X*), para. 31: '[T]he fact that a Member State does not grant to a non-resident certain tax benefits which it grants to a resident is not, as a rule, discriminatory, having regard to the objective differences between the situations of residents and of non-residents, both from the point of view of the source of their income and their personal ability to pay tax or their personal and family circumstances.' *See also*: CJEU, Case C-279/93 (*Schumacker*), para. 34; Case C-80/94 (*Wielockx*), para. 18; Case C-107/94 (*Asscher*), para. 41; Case C-391/97 (*Gschwind*), para. 23; Case C-234/01 (*Gerritse*), para. 44; Case C-169/03 (*Wallentin*), paras 15-16; Case C-520/04 (*Turpeinen*), paras 26-27; Case C-329/05 (*Meindl*), para. 23; Case C-383/05 (*Talotta*), para. 19; Case C-182/06 (*Lakebrink and Peters-Lakebrink*), paras 28-29; Case C-527/06 (*Renneberg*), para. 59; Case C–39/10 (*Commission v. Estonia*), para. 49; Case C-425/11 (*Ettwein*), paras 45-46; Case C-9/14 (*Kieback*), para. 22; Case C-632/13 (*Hirvonen*), paras 31-32.

380. By 'almost all income' is meant at least 75% of a person's total taxable income during the tax year, according to the Commission Recommendation 94/79/EC, of 21 December 1993, on the taxation of certain items of income received by non-residents in a Member State other than that in which they are resident. However, the CJEU has accepted the Member States interpretation of 'almost all income' as meaning 90% of the household's aggregated taxable income – *see* CJEU, Case C-279/93 (*Schumacker*); Case C-391/97 (*Gschwind*).

381. A. García Prats (I. Richelle et al. eds, Springer 2013), 7.

In such cases, the source Member State is requested to consider those non-resident taxpayers' personal and family circumstances when taxing them in the same terms it does regarding its resident taxpayers.

The Court introduced this exception in the *Schumacker* case, marking the path for the case law on taxpayers' personal and family circumstances,[382] which is analysed *infra* in section 6.2.1.d).

Notwithstanding, the evolution of the Court's decisions allows understanding that the exception introduced with the *Schumacker* case is not absolute. What is absolute is the need to consider taxpayers' personal and family circumstances somewhere, even though taxpayers are not de jure or de facto subject to worldwide taxation anywhere.[383]

Precisely, in the *X* case,[384] the Court introduced a specification to the Schumacker exception, aiming to cover its grey area: the case of taxpayers who, despite not earning (almost) any income in the residence State, do not derive (almost) all their income from a single source State.

In such a case, what is relevant is no longer the fact that the non-resident is subject to taxation in the source State in a similar way to a resident there, i.e., subject to (de facto) worldwide taxation. Instead, what becomes relevant is the fact that the residence Member State cannot take that taxpayer's circumstances into account due to the lack of taxable base, while there are two (or more) source States where the taxpayer has enough taxable base for his personal and family circumstances to be considered.[385,386] According to the Court, 'discrimination arises from the fact that the personal and family circumstances of a non-resident who receives the major part of his income and almost all his family income in a Member State other than that of his

382. CJEU, Case C-279/93 (*Schumacker*); Case C-80/94 (*Wielockx*); Case C-87/99 (*Zurstrassen*); Case C-169/03 (*Wallentin*); Case C-520/04 (*Turpeinen*); Case C-152/03 (*Ritter-Coulais*); Case C-182/06 (*Lakebrink and Peters-Lakebrink*); Case C-527/06 (*Renneberg*); Case C–39/10 (*Commission v. Estonia*); Case C-425/11 (*Ettwein*), Case C-283/15 (*X*).

383. In this regard, AG Wathelet, in his Opinion in Case C–283/15 (*X*), stresses that: 'Would it not be paradoxical if a citizen who exercises one of the fundamental freedoms guaranteed by the Treaties in two Member States did not benefit from the Schumacker exception, when a citizen who has exercised that freedom in only one would benefit from it?' (para. 54). As noted by García Prats, the Court aims to ensure that the taxpayers exercising their right to free movement also enjoy their right to the personalisation of taxation as a consequence of the ability-to-pay principle in its subjective dimension – cf. A. García Prats, 117 REDF 61 (2003), 79.

384. CJEU, Case C-283/15 (*X*). The case concerned a taxpayer resident in Spain, who derived all his taxable income from the Netherlands (60%) and Switzerland (40%). In his residence State, his personal and family situation was not considered as he did not have any taxable income there. In the source States, it was not considered either because he was a non-resident, not obtaining almost all his taxable income from any of those States alone. For a critical analysis of the *X* case, *see* A. García Prats, *El 'prorrateo' de las ventajas fiscales personales y familiares, según el TJUE*, 1-2 Quincena Fiscal 103 (2018).

385. *Ibid.*, para. 42: '[W]hat remains the decisive criterion is whether it is impossible for a Member State to take into account, for the calculation of tax, the personal and family circumstances of a taxpayer in the absence of sufficient taxable income, although such circumstances can otherwise be taken into account when there is sufficient income.'

386. As García Prats observed, the CJEU is no longer concerned with assessing the objective comparability between residents and non-residents but with protecting taxpayers when their residence Member State cannot consider their personal and family situation – cf. A. García Prats, 1-2 Quincena Fiscal 103 (2018), 114.

residence are taken into account neither in the Member State of residence nor in the Member State[s] of employment'.[387]

Therefore, in this case, as the residence State could not grant the taxpayer benefits regarding his personal and family circumstances for lack of taxable income, the source Member States had to grant these in proportion to the income derived from their territory.[388]

This case clearly illustrates the Court's absolute priority of having taxpayers' personal and family circumstances taken into account.

Nevertheless, the prioritisation of taxpayers' personal and family circumstances did not come as a surprise after the *Commission v. Estonia* case.[389] At issue was the situation of a taxpayer that received two low retirement pensions of almost the same amount, one from his residence Member State (Finland) and another from another Member State (Estonia). In Finland, the aggregate amount of the two pensions did not exceed the personal tax allowance threshold, so no tax was due by the taxpayer. The pension income from Estonia was subject to tax there, and the taxpayer was not entitled to tax allowances since he was a non-resident not earning almost all his income from that State. However, the two pensions' aggregate amount would only slightly exceed the exemption threshold for pensioners residing in Estonia.

This way, on the one hand, the taxpayer only derived 50 % of his income from the source Member State and, on the other hand, the residence Member State had indeed considered the taxpayer's personal and family circumstances by granting him a personal tax allowance, which is why the taxpayer did not have to pay any tax there.

As one can observe, the *Commission v. Estonia* case does not cover a taxpayer's situation falling into the Schumacker exception (taxpayer earning almost all income from the source State, i.e., de facto worldwide taxation) nor in the *X* case specification (impossibility of the residence Member State to take into account taxpayers' personal and family circumstances due to the lack of taxable income there).

Yet, the Court considered this situation inadmissible: if the taxpayer had earned all income just in a Member State (either Finland or Estonia), he would not have to pay any tax, or only a minor amount, due to the tax allowance that would be granted to him in any of the States.

In order to prioritise the taxpayer's personal and family circumstances, the Court disregarded the personal tax allowance the residence State granted him, demanding the source State to take into account his personal and family situation and denying the accumulation of tax advantages in such a case.[390]

---

387. CJEU, Case C-283/15 (*X*), para. 34.
388. *Ibid.*, para. 49.
389. CJEU, Case C–39/10 (*Commission v. Estonia*).
390. *Ibid.*, paras 55-57: '55 However, in a case such as that of the complainant, who because of the modest amount of worldwide income is not taxable in the Member State of residence, under that State's tax legislation, that State is not in a position to take into account the ability to pay tax and the personal and family circumstances of the person concerned, in particular the consequences for that person of taxation of the income received in another Member State. 56 In those circumstances, the refusal of the Member State in which the income in question is received to grant an allowance provided for under its tax legislation penalises non-resident taxpayers such as the complainant simply because they have exercised the freedoms of

If the *X* case has set the framework to be followed in the Schumacker exception grey area cases, the *Commission v. Estonia* case has established the framework to be followed in the borderline cases. Such are the cases where taxpayers' aggregate income is so low that those taxpayers would be (nearly) taxed neither in the residence State nor in the source State (if they were subject to worldwide taxation there) since the tax benefits for personal and family circumstances granted by each State are higher than their taxable income. In these borderline cases, the source State must also consider the non-residents' personal and family circumstances in the same way it does regarding resident taxpayers.

Otherwise, if the source State could tax without taking into account the personal and family circumstances of taxpayers in such a borderline situation, the amount defined by it as the intangible economic strength aimed at satisfying personal and family existential needs would be breached. The Court could not tolerate that taxpayers' intangible economic strength could be disregarded just because they have exercised an EU freedom of movement.[391] Ultimately, it would mean the freedoms of movement ensured within the EU internal market could jeopardise taxpayers' human dignity, one of the fundamental values of the EU,[392] which seems inadmissible.

In brief, the Court's position regarding the consideration of taxpayers' personal and family circumstances may be summarised as follows:

(i) *The rule:* A Member State must attribute 100% of the tax benefits for personal and family circumstances foreseen in its legislation to resident taxpayers who have exercised an EU freedom of movement, regardless of the domestic income earned; in turn, it does not have to grant non-residents those tax benefits because they are not in an objectively comparable situation.

(ii) *The exception:* A Member State must attribute non-residents all the tax benefits for personal and family circumstances foreseen in its legislation whenever non-residents derive (almost) all their income from its territory, not earning enough income in their residence State for their personal and family situation to be considered there for tax purposes.

(iii) *Grey area cases:* A Member State must attribute non-residents the tax benefits for personal and family circumstances foreseen in its legislation in the

movement guaranteed by the FEU Treaty. 57 The difference of treatment resulting from such legislation could be justified only if it were based on objective considerations proportionate to the legitimate aim of the national provisions (...). In this respect, although the Republic of Estonia has argued that the condition in question is intended to avoid non-resident taxpayers accumulating allowances in both the Member States concerned, it must be stated that, in a case such as that of the complainant, there cannot be any unjustified accumulation of advantages.'

391. In this regard, García Prats notes that 'Income taxes should not be imposed below a minimum level of subsistence on individuals. Ability to pay should require that EU Member States would not be legitimized under EU law requirements not to take into account the personal and familiar situation of EU resident/citizen taxpayers anywhere in the EU' – A. García Prats (I. Richelle et al. eds, Springer 2013), 25.

392. Article 2 TEU: 'The Union is founded on the values of respect for human dignity, freedom, democracy, equality, the rule of law and respect for human rights, including the rights of persons belonging to minorities. These values are common to the Member States in a society in which pluralism, non-discrimination, tolerance, justice, solidarity and equality between women and men prevail.'

proportion of the income earned in its territory whenever non-residents derive (almost) all their income from the said State and other States, none being their residence State, the residence State being precluded from taking into account their personal and family situation for tax purposes.

(iv) *Borderline cases*: A Member State must attribute non-residents all the tax benefits for personal and family circumstances foreseen in its legislation, in similar terms it does regarding residents, whenever non-residents' aggregate income is so low that they are barely taxed neither in the residence State nor in that State, due to the fact the tax benefits for personal and family circumstances granted by each State are higher than their taxable income.

4.2.2.2 ***Personal and Family Circumstances Considered* at Least *Once and* Preferably *Not More than Once: The Existence of Disparities***

Despite the correlation between taxpayers' worldwide taxation and the consideration of their personal and family circumstances, the Member States may agree by way of a bilateral or multilateral convention on the obligation to consider personal and family circumstances. Even in the absence of such agreement, Member States may be released from the obligation of granting taxpayers benefits for personal and family circumstances if the other Member State is already granting those taxpayers such benefits,[393] provided those taxpayers' situation falls outside the borderline cases.

That is to say, under the Court approach, taxpayers' personal and family circumstances must be fully considered within the EU context at least once, and *preferably*, not more than once.[394]

393. CJEU, Case C-385/00 (*De Groot*), paras 99 and 100: '99. [...] The State of residence can therefore be released by way of an international agreement from its obligation to take into account in full the personal and family situation of taxpayers residing in its territory who work partially abroad. 100. The State of residence may also be released from that obligation if it finds that, even in the absence of a convention, one or more of the States of employment, with respect to the income taxed by them, grant advantages based on the personal and family circumstances of taxpayers who do not reside in the territory of those States but receive taxable income there.' *See also* CJEU, Case C-168/11 (*Beker*), para. 56; Case C-303/12 (*Imfeld and Garcet*), para. 61; Case C–241/20 (*BJ v. État belge*), paras 44-45.

394. The CJEU in the *X* case states that 'the freedom of the Member States [...] to allocate among themselves their powers to impose taxes, in particular to avoid the accumulation of tax advantages, *must be reconciled* with the necessity that taxpayers of the Member States concerned are assured that, ultimately, all their personal and family circumstances will be duly taken into account, irrespective of how the Member States concerned have allocated that obligation amongst themselves' (emphasis added), [CJEU, Case C-283/15 (*X*), para. 47]. As Cerioni explains it, the idea of reconciliation put forward by the Court appears to mean that two objectives must be simultaneously achieved: on the one hand, ensuring that taxpayers are granted 100% of the tax advantages regarding their personal and family situation; on the other hand, ensuring that those tax advantages are not duplicated, and the taxpayers are not granted in two or more jurisdictions more than 100% of those tax advantages. *See* L. Cerioni, *Case Note: X v Staatssecretaris van Financiën: A Step Forward in a Proper Application of the Ability-to-Pay Principle in Cross-Border Situations?*, 2 Brit. Tax Rev. 162 (2017), 165.

It is stated *preferably* because the attribution of personal and family benefits in the source Member State does not always prevent the CJEU from finding an unjustifiable restrictive tax treatment in the residence Member State due to the lack of consideration of those taxpayers' personal and family circumstances.

Indeed, in the *Imfeld and Garcet* case,[395] the Court did not accept the argument presented by the residence Member State, which justified the refusal to grant a tax allowance for dependent children based on the fact that an equivalent benefit had been granted in the source Member State. The Court noted that the applicants failed to benefit from the tax allowance in the residence State, not because they benefited from an equivalent advantage in the source Member State, but because it was inevitably nullified by the residence Member State's tax rules.[396] This way, the rejection of the justification is explained by the fact that the residence Member State's tax regime lays down a rule that *automatically* excludes the appellants from having their personal and family circumstances considered, regardless of whether or not they have enjoyed equivalent benefits in other Member State.[397] Even if the justification presented by the residence Member State is suitable for avoiding double dips, it goes further than what is necessary for preventing double advantages, running the risk of depriving taxpayers exercising an EU freedom of movement from any tax advantage for their personal and family circumstances.[398] Although the Court did not mention the proportionality control when disallowing the justification presented, it seems implicit in the Court's reasoning.

That is to say that the unilateral granting by the source Member State of tax advantages based on the personal and family circumstances to non-residents deriving taxable income from its territory is not enough to justify the lack of consideration of those taxpayers' personal and family circumstances in their residence Member State. Such a lack of attribution of personal and family benefits in the residence State *must be*

395. CJEU, Case C-303/12 (*Imfeld and Garcet*).
396. *Ibid.*, para. 73. *See also* CJEU, Case C-241/20 (*BJ v. État belge*), para. 49: 'The tax legislation at issue in the main proceedings does not establish any correlation between the tax advantages it grants to taxpayers residing in the Member State concerned and the tax advantages for which they may qualify in connection with their taxation in another Member State [...], since the partial loss of the former advantages is not the result of qualifying for equivalent tax advantages in Luxembourg, but is the automatic consequence of receiving income exempted under international conventions for the avoidance of double taxation.' *See infra* section 6.1.1.2.1.d).
397. To the same effect, *see* B. Peeters, *Mobility of EU Citizens and Family Taxation: A Hard to Reconcile Combination*, 23(3) EC Tax Rev. 118 (2014), 119 DOI: 10.54648/ecta2014012; A. García Prats, *Subjective Ability to Pay: Schumacker*, in *Landmark Decisions of the ECJ in Direct Taxation* (W. Haslehner et al. eds, Kluwer Law International 2015), 27.
398. This way, we do not agree with Niesten, who criticises this decision, stating that 'the CJEU in Imfeld and Garcet missed an interesting opportunity to analyse the effects of double advantages on the EU internal market, i.e., fostering cross-border movement. The CJEU gave an incoherent application to the overall-approach – i.e., the possibility of double personal and family allowances – that gives the impression that the CJEU either underestimates the effect of double allowances or does not consider them to violate the principle of equality' – H. Niesten, 24(4) EC Tax Rev. 185 (2015), 194; H. Niesten, *Personal and Family Tax Benefits in the EU Internal Market: From Schumacker to Fractional Tax Treatment*, 55(3) Common Market L. Rev. 819 (2018), 825 DOI: 10.54648/cola2018071. *See also* L. Cerioni, *Guido Imfeld and Nathalie Garcet v. Belgian State: A Continuation of the Schumacker Doctrine?*, 2 Brit. Tax Rev. 128 (2014), 133-135.

due to the unilateral granting of equivalent benefits in the other State, not merely *fortuitous*. There must exist, in the residence Member State's tax legislation, a correlation between the refusal of granting personal and family tax advantages that residents are, as a rule, entitled to and the granting of such tax benefits to those taxpayers in another Member State.

In the *BJ v. État belge* case, the Court had the opportunity to reaffirm its position in this regard. The CJEU stressed that 'irrespective of the tax treatment accorded to that taxpayer in that other Member State, it is the automatic nature of that loss which is contrary to the freedom of movement'.[399]

Once again, this stance of the Court illustrates the absolute priority given to taxpayers' personal and family circumstances. The granting of personal and family benefits to taxpayers exercising an EU freedom of movement cannot be left to chance, hoping that the exercise in parallel of Member States' tax sovereignty results in taxpayers' personal and family circumstances being taken into account in *some* Member States.

Yet, as already mentioned, it does not mean that EU law obliges the Member States to grant taxpayers benefits regarding their personal and family circumstances. The States may or may not grant personal and family-related benefits. However, if they foresee such tax advantages in their tax legislation, they must attribute them to resident taxpayers regardless of whether they have exercised an EU freedom of movement.[400]

This way, the absolute priority given to taxpayers' personal and family circumstances does not invalidate the existence of disparities in this regard.

For instance, suppose the extreme case of a Member State that does not grant, under its tax law, any personal and family benefits to resident taxpayers. This would not mean such taxpayers were entitled to benefit from equivalent tax advantages in another Member State where they also earn income. In such a case, the absence of granting personal and family benefits to resident taxpayers does not result from the residence Member State's impossibility to take them into account due to the lack of taxable income there but rather from the fact that State does not foresee in its tax law any tax benefits in this regard. In such a situation, the resident taxpayers would only be entitled to personal and family benefits in the other Member State from where they also derive income: *(i)* if they receive (almost) all their income from there, being comparable to resident taxpayers in the source State or *(ii)* if that State grants unilaterally tax benefits to non-residents.

Such a scenario amounts to a certain extent to the *D* case, which concerns wealth taxes.[401] In this case, the taxpayer, who held 90% of his wealth in his residence Member State, was not entitled to a free tax allowance because any wealth tax was imposed there, and consequently, the personal and family circumstances of resident taxpayers were irrelevant. In the other Member State where he held part of his wealth (the remaining 10%), he was also not entitled to the free tax allowance foreseen for

399. CJEU, Case C-241/20 (*BJ v. État belge*), para. 55.
400. To the same effect, *see* N. Bammens, *Free Movement of Citizens and Family Taxation*, in *Research Handbook on European Union Taxation Law* (C. Panayi et al. eds Elgar 2020), 175.
401. CJEU, Case C-376/03 (*D*).

resident taxpayers, as he did not hold almost all his wealth (the threshold being 90%) in that State. The Court ruled that the other Member State was not required to grant him the benefits it grants to its own residents, as they were not in a comparable situation.[402]

The *Gschwind* case[403] is another example that illustrates the disparities that may exist regarding personal and family circumstances. The disparity, in this case, derived from different tax benefits granted by the residence Member State and the source Member State. While married taxpayers are subject to individual assessment in the residence State, married taxpayers are subject to joint assessment in the source State. When a non-resident couple earns only a part of their household income from the source State, they are not entitled to joint assessment there, as they are not comparable to resident couples. The fact that they can benefit from joint taxation neither in their residence Member State (which does not foresee that tax advantage) nor in the source Member State (which only provides that tax advantage for resident couples) is just the result of a disparity between Member States' tax law, which is not forbidden under the EU Treaties.

4.2.2.3 Scholars' Concerns and the Alternative Routes Suggested

Despite our reading of the Court's case law on personal and family circumstances as reflecting an absolute prioritisation of taxpayers' ability to pay,[404] this line of case law is not entirely devoid of doubts, having been widely criticised among scholars over time.[405]

402. *Ibid.*, para. 41: 'The different treatment of residents and non-residents by the Member State in which the person concerned holds only 10% of his wealth and the lack of an allowance in that case can be explained by the fact that the person concerned holds only a minor part of his wealth in that State and that he is accordingly not in a situation comparable to that of residents. The circumstance that that person's State of residence has abolished wealth tax has no bearing on this factual situation. Since he holds the major part of his wealth in the State where he is resident, the Member State in which he holds only a proportion of his wealth is not required to grant him the benefits which it grants to its own residents.' Notwithstanding, attention has been drawn to the fact that the Court differentiates between the D case and the Case C-169/03 (*Wallentin*) in somewhat confusing terms. Cf. A. Cordewener, *Personal Income Taxation of Non-residents and the Increasing Impact of the EC Treaty Freedoms*, in *The Influence of European Law on Direct Taxation: Recent and Future Developments* (D. Weber ed., Kluwer Law International 2007), 63-64; M. Lang, 18(3) EC Tax Rev. 98 (2009), 102; G. Kofler & C. P. Schindler, *'Dancing with Mr D': The ECJ's Denial of Most-Favoured-Nation Treatment in the 'D' Case*, 45(12) Eur. Tax'n 530 (2005), 536. In the *Wallentin* case, the CJEU held that the income received by the taxpayer in the residence Member State did not by its nature constitute taxable income, assimilating the taxpayer to a resident in the source Member State, while in the *D* case, such assimilation did not occur despite the fact there was no tax base in the residence Member State.
403. CJEU, Case C-391/97 (*Gschwind*).
404. In turn, Kemmeren reads this line of case law as reflecting *an internal market approach*. Cf. E. Kemmeren (L. Hinnekens & P. Hinnekens eds, Kluwer Law International 2008), 568.
405. *See, e.g.*, P. Wattel, *Progressive Taxation of Non-residents and Intra-EC Allocation of Personal Tax Allowances: Why Schumacker, Asscher, Gilly and Gschwind Do Not Suffice*, 60(6) Eur. Tax'n 210 (2000); J. Avery Jones, *A Comment on 'Progressive Taxation of Non-residents and Intra-EC Allocation of Personal Tax Allowances'*, 40(8) Eur. Tax'n 375 (2000); N. Mattsson, *Does the European Court of Justice Understand the Policy Behind Tax Benefits Based on Personal and Family Circumstances?*, 43(6) Eur. Tax'n 186 (2003); A. Cordewener (D. Weber ed.,

The *X* case - applicable to the grey area cases - has already shed some light on certain concerns raised in the academic literature. In this regard, it was argued that the Schumacker exception was arbitrary when establishing a 90% threshold, remaining doubtful *(i)* whether taxpayers earning 89% of their income would be entitled to benefits regarding their personal and family circumstances in the source Member State, and *(ii)* and what would occur in cases where there was more than one source Member State.[406]

Since the Court nuanced the Schumacker exception, the answer for these cases rests on knowing whether or not there is enough taxable base in the residence Member State to grant resident taxpayers all benefits regarding their personal and family circumstances. If the answer is affirmative, the residence Member State should fully take into account taxpayers' personal and family circumstances. In contrast, if the answer is negative, the source Member State(s) should take into account those taxpayers' personal and family circumstances even when they do not derive 90% of their income from its territory. The fractional granting of personal and family circumstances by source States only occurs when non-residents cannot be equated with residents anywhere.

Other concerns have to do with the fact that the Member States may consider personal and family circumstances by means other than taxation, for instance, through government subsidies. Indeed, personal and family circumstances may also be a social law affair, and the attribution of the respective benefits may be governed by criteria other than residence in a Member State. From the CJEU's case law, it is not clear whether the granting of social benefits similar to tax benefits must be regarded when analysing the (im)possibility of the residence Member State considering taxpayers' personal and family circumstances.[407]

Attention has also been drawn to the fact that, according to the Court's case, personal and family circumstances must be taken into account *somewhere* within the EU, while the Member States are not obliged to eliminate international juridical double taxation.[408] Ultimately, international juridical double taxation represents an additional burden that undermines the overall ability to pay, which does not need to be taken into account *anywhere*.

Moreover, if the Member States decide to eliminate international juridical double taxation, the concrete method chosen to do so may impact significantly which Member

Kluwer Law International 2007), 35-73; M. Lang, 18(3) EC Tax Rev. 98 (2009), 98-113; N. Bammens (IBFD 2012), 606-607; B. Peeters, 23(3) EC Tax Rev. 118 (2014), 118-120; W. Schön, 68(4/5) Bull. Int'l Tax'n 271 (2015), 271-293; H. Niesten, 24(4) EC Tax Rev. 185 (2015), 185-201; H. Niesten, 55(3) Common Market L. Rev. 819 (2018).

406. M. Lang, 18(3) EC Tax Rev. 98 (2009), 101-102; P. Wattel, 60(6) Eur. Tax'n 210 (2000), 216-217; P. Wattel, *Red Herrings in Direct Tax Cases Before the ECJ*, 31(2) Legal Issues Econ. Integration 81 (2004), 85 DOI: 10.54648/leie2004009; B. Peeters, 23(3) EC Tax Rev. 118 (2014), 119; A. Cordewener (D. Weber ed., Kluwer Law International 2007), 62-63.

407. N. Mattsson, 43(6) Eur. Tax'n 186 (2003), 189; A. Cordewener (D. Weber ed., Kluwer Law International 2007), 61; M. Lang, 18(3) EC Tax Rev. 98 (2009), 102; B. Peeters, 23(3) EC Tax Rev. 118 (2014), 119-120; W. Schön, 68(4/5) Bull. Int'l Tax'n 271 (2015), 291; H. Niesten, 55(3) Common Market L. Rev. 819 (2018), 830-831.

408. W. Schön, 68(4/5) Bull. Int'l Tax'n 271 (2015), 291; A. Cordewener (D. Weber ed., Kluwer Law International 2007), 66-67; P. Wattel, 31(2) Legal Issues Econ. Integration 81 (2004), 87-88.

State will bear the obligation of taking taxpayers' personal and family circumstances into account.[409]

These two issues are dealt with in the following chapters.

Alongside the criticism, Van Raad and Wattel, among other scholars, have pointed out an alternative route for considering personal and family circumstances within the EU: fractional taxation.[410] Accordingly, non-residents should be offered national treatment in source Member States in the proportion of the income derived from their territory. In other words, non-residents would be taxed as if they were residents in the source States, which implies progressive taxation determined based on their worldwide income and attribution of all tax benefits related to their personal and family circumstances. However, effective taxation in such terms would only occur on a pro rata basis. The same fractional taxation system would also be applied in the residence Member State of those taxpayers. Therefore, in the residence State, the tax due would be calculated on a worldwide basis, applying progressive taxation and benefits for personal and family circumstances fully, but effective taxation would only occur in the proportion of the income derived domestically.

This system amounts to *(i)* a pro rata allocation of personal and family tax advantages to income derived in each Member State, and *(ii)* fractional taxation of the income derived in each Member State. The progression benefit – i.e., the advantage of not being subject to progressive taxation in the source State – would be neutralised, as taxpayers would be subject to progressive taxation in all Member States from where they derive income.

Nevertheless, each Member State's tax system has its internal coherence: personal and family tax advantages are specifically designed to achieve a purpose and are thought of as a whole within a tax. Therefore, one may wonder if the fractional consideration of personal and family circumstances in more than one Member State is equivalent to their consideration in just one Member State.[411]

---

409. J. Avery Jones, *Carry on Discriminating*, 36(2) Eur. Tax'n 46 (1996); J. Avery Jones, 40(8) Eur. Tax'n 375 (2000), 375; F. Vanistendael, 23(3) EC Tax Rev. 121 (2014), 132-133.

410. K. Van Raad, *Fractional Taxation of Multistate Income of EU Resident Individuals – A Proposal*, in *Liber Amicorum Sven- Olof Lodin* (K. Andersson et al. eds, Kluwer Law International 2001), 220-221; K. Van Raad, 2(2) World Tax J. 154 (2010), 154-161; P. Wattel, 60(6) Eur. Tax'n 210 (2000), 214-223; F. Vanistendael, 23(3) EC Tax Rev. 121 (2014), 134; A. Cordewener (D. Weber ed., Kluwer Law International 2007), 67-68; H. Niesten, 24(4) EC Tax Rev. 185 (2015), 198-199; H. Niesten, 55(3) Common Market L. Rev. 819 (2018), 847-854; W. Schön, 68(4/5) Bull. Int'l Tax'n 271 (2015), 291-292; N. Bammens (IBFD 2012), 666-667; N. Bammens (C. Panayi et al. eds, Elgar 2020), 173.

411. As observed by Schön, 'The underlying concept of a full and comprehensive recognition of income in a synthetic manner, including certain limited deductions for personal expenditure and the application of a progressive tax rate, implicitly presupposes the existence of a single tax authority assessing and taxing the whole income of the taxpayer, taking into account all relevant income-generating activities and personal circumstances. Only in a single-country situation this technique works without constraints' – W. Schön, *International Tax Coordination for a Second-Best World (Part I)*, 1(1) World Tax J. 67 (2009), 72 DOI: 10.59403/2c2zh72. With a different view, Wattel affirms that '(fractional taxation) leads to just one cake. It may not be a very coherent cake because it will be made up of wedges from different national bakeries, but together, the national wedges will make up one, round EU cake, not half a cake or no cake at all, and not one-and-a-half, or even two or three different cakes (if there is more than one host State)' – quoted in J. Avery Jones, 40(8) Eur. Tax'n 375 (2000), 377.In this

Furthermore, implementing a fractional taxation system through negative integration seems too ambitious when eliminating international juridical double taxation is not even mandatory within the EU.[412] Fractional taxation implies that all Member States must eliminate juridical double taxation through the exemption with progression, the modified exemption or the ordinary credit methods.

4.3 CONCLUDING AND SUMMARISING REMARKS

This chapter addresses the relevance of individuals' ability to pay in light of EU law.

In its origin, the ability-to-pay principle emerged as the denial of the equivalence principle. However, these two principles may coexist in States' legal order, as each offers a more operative answer in certain areas of taxation than the other. The concrete terms of their articulation depend mainly on States' constitutional framework.

Under the ability-to-pay principle, it is not enough that the taxable events chosen by the legislator reflect a manifestation of taxpayers' economic strength; it is also necessary that that manifestation of economic strength be relevant and express an actual ability to pay, meaning it must be net and disposable. Hence, the costs incurred to give rise to or keep the economic strength and the costs considered essential related to private and family spheres do not represent an ability to pay, being beyond the scope of taxation. Therefore, the ability to pay is the *conditio sine qua non* for taxing, and it demands knowing the person who will be taxed to tailor taxation accordingly. It constitutes an authentic guarantee of taxpayers against the State.

The ability to pay is also regarded as the *tertium comparationis* needed to render the equality principle effective, reaching the axiom that taxpayers with the same ability to pay must be taxed the same way, and taxpayers with a different ability to pay must be taxed differently.

Although the ability to pay offers essential guidance in achieving justice in distributing the tax burden among taxpayers, the criteria for establishing the fair amount each one must pay can only be found in the interaction of the ability-to-pay principle with other principles and fundamental rights, taking the constitutional purposes and the social development at any given time into account.

It is observed that the ability to pay is embedded in the structure of most Member States' tax systems, regardless of the political choices and the concrete technical configuration employed by each State.

However, adopting and implementing the ability-to-pay principle is not an EU law imperative. EU law only demands the Member States observe the prohibition of discrimination and restrictions laid down in the EU Treaties.

---

regard, the CJEU, in the Case C-241/20 (*BJ v. État belge*), para. 58, has already stated that 'it cannot be inferred from the fact that, [in the source Member State, the taxpayer] obtained a tax reduction in an amount at least equivalent to that of the tax advantages which he lost in [his residence Member State] that his personal and family circumstances were taken into account in full, especially since it is apparent that those circumstances are taken into account only in part, since that tax reduction does not include some of the tax advantages to which he is in principle entitled in [his residence Member State]'.

412. *See* further Chapter 5.

That demand is particularly noteworthy in the CJEU's case law on cases involving *(i)* the consideration of expenses related to economic activity and *(ii)* the consideration of expenses related to personal and family circumstances.

Today, it is widely accepted that the expenses incurred to derive income must be considered in order to avoid the tax burden falling on an artificial economic strength that does not reflect an actual ability to pay the tax.

Since the definition of the costs whose deductibility is accepted forms part of Member States' power to configure their tax systems, EU law does not interfere with that definition and does not aim to set any uniform criteria. However, EU law prevents the Member States from establishing more burdensome criteria for the consideration of costs incurred by taxpayers carrying out a cross-border activity than those established for taxpayers carrying out a domestic activity whenever those taxpayers are in a comparable situation, and the difference in treatment is not justified and proportional.

In its case law, the CJEU uses the expression 'expenses directly linked' to refer to the deductible costs. Accordingly, 'expenses directly linked' are those that have a direct economic connection to the activity giving rise to taxable income in a Member State and, therefore, are inextricably linked to that activity, which does not mean that it is sufficient a mere correlation, of whatever kind, between the amounts of the expenditure and the taxable income. Furthermore, such expenses must be necessary, which does not mean that those expenses must be unavoidable. From this clarification provided by the CJEU on the meaning of 'direct link' and from its case law, it is evident that the relevant connection for determining the deductibility of costs is the direct link between expenses and economic activity, even if sometimes the CJEU refers to the direct link between expenses and taxable income.

The concept of 'expenses directly link' provided by the CJEU is independent of the Member States' legal classification of expenses and seeks to set the base for differentiation between expenses related to economic activity and expenses related to personal and family circumstances. That differentiation is necessary because the Member States do not classify expenses similarly, and there is a significant consequence in light of EU law of characterising expenses as related to economic activity or personal and family circumstances.

Regarding expenses related to economic activity, the CJEU has stressed that there is no objective difference between taxpayers exercising an EU freedom of movement and those not exercising it. That is to say, resident and non-resident taxpayers are in a comparable situation, as well as resident taxpayers pursuing a domestic activity and resident taxpayers pursuing that activity cross-borders. The comparability of their situation lies in the fact that, in any case, taxing a gross income amounts to taxing an artificial economic strength that does not represent an actual ability to pay. Consequently, under the EU Treaties, the Member States are forbidden from adopting different and more burdensome criteria and techniques for determining the objective net income of taxpayers exercising an EU freedom of movement than those for determining the objective net income of taxpayers not exercising it.

In contrast, regarding expenses related to personal and family circumstances, the comparability between taxpayers exercising an EU freedom of movement and those not exercising it cannot always be established.

The consideration of personal and family circumstances is justified by the fact that taxation must not deprive individuals of what is necessary to support themselves and their families. There is, thus, an intangible economic strength aimed at satisfying existential needs, which is considered not to express an ability to pay taxes.

The notion of 'personal and family circumstances' adopted by the CJEU covers all tax advantages granted by the Member States to taxpayers that are not linked to economic activity. Such tax advantages may be connected to taxpayers' family situation (e.g., joint taxation, tax-free income allowance for dependent children, maintenance payments) and taxpayers' personal situation (e.g., tax-free allowances, pension, life, and health insurance contributions, negative income related to a dwelling/property, and other living expenses stipulated by States). According to the Court, it is not necessary for the tax advantages granted to have a social purpose. Even tax benefits designed mainly to encourage taxpayers to spend and make investments are considered linked to their personal and family situation insofar as those expenses impact their ability to pay.

The decision to protect taxpayers' personal and family circumstances at a tax level falls within the Member States' power to configure their tax systems. Hence, the sole EU law requirement imposed on the Member States derives from the fundamental freedoms' provisions: taxpayers who exercise them must not be treated worse than those who do not exercise them, as far as their situation is comparable.

In this regard, comparability between taxpayers exercising an EU freedom of movement and taxpayers not exercising it is assessed based on factual circumstances.

As acknowledged by the CJEU, there is a correlation between being subject in a Member State to taxation on the worldwide income and having personal and family circumstances considered in that State. Due to the worldwide taxation taxpayers are subject to in the residence State, it is in this State where, in principle, it is easier to consider their overall ability to pay because worldwide taxation implies further report obligations, such as a tax return containing all the taxpayers' aggregate income and their personal and family situation.

This way, residents engaged in cross-border activities and residents engaged in purely internal activities are in a comparable situation. All of them are subject to worldwide taxation in the residence State, this State being able to know their personal and family situation, as well as all the income they obtained, regardless of its source. Therefore, the fact that residents obtain income from abroad does not prevent the residence Member State from being best placed to assess their overall ability to pay.

As residents are in a comparable situation regarding expenses related to personal and family circumstances, the residence State must fully consider their personal and family circumstances, even when not all their income is derived domestically, and the State refrains from taxing foreign income.

Conversely, as a rule, resident taxpayers – subject to worldwide taxation – and non-residents – subject to source taxation – are not in a comparable situation since the Member States, as a rule, have limited information on non-residents' aggregate income or personal and family situation. Due to their lack of comparability, the Member States do not breach EU law when they consider residents' personal and family circumstances but do consider those of non-residents.

However, the incomparability between residents and non-residents is not absolute. It gives in whenever taxpayers' personal and family circumstances are not duly considered in any Member State because taxpayers have exercised an EU freedom of movement.

After all, expenses related to personal and family circumstances represent what each Member State defines as taxpayers' intangible economic strength aimed at satisfying existential needs, and it seems inadmissible that the freedoms of movement ensured within the internal market could jeopardise taxpayers' human dignity, which is one of the fundamental values of the EU.

This way, in the Court's case law, absolute priority is given to the consideration of taxpayers' personal and family circumstances. That priority emerged with the exception introduced in the *Schumacker* case, and it was further enhanced with the *X* case and the *Commission v. Estonia* case, which set the path to be followed in the grey area and borderline cases.

In its case law, the CJEU aims to ensure that taxpayers' personal and family circumstances are fully considered within the EU context *at least* once and, *preferably*, not more than once. It is stated preferably because the Member States may be released from the obligation of granting benefits for personal and family circumstances to some taxpayers if another Member State already grants them such benefits. However, in such a case, the lack of attribution of personal and family tax benefits in the residence State to some taxpayers cannot be merely fortuitous; that is to say, it must be due to the fact that the personal and family circumstances of those taxpayers were already considered in the other State.

Despite the absolute priority given to the consideration of taxpayers' personal and family circumstances, disparities may still exist in this regard, and taxpayers may be prevented from benefiting from such benefits. In those cases, the CJEU cannot interfere because the lack of consideration of personal and family circumstances does not derive from a unilateral disadvantage created by a Member State.

The Court's case law on personal and family circumstances is not entirely devoid of doubts.

For instance, under the Court's case law, the Member States are not obliged to eliminate international juridical double taxation, which represents an additional burden that undermines taxpayers' overall ability to pay. Thus, while personal and family circumstances must be taken into account *somewhere* within the EU, international juridical double taxation does not need to be taken into account *anywhere*. This issue is further analysed in Chapter 5.

Moreover, if the Member States decide to eliminate international juridical double taxation, *(i)* whether or not taxpayers obtain income in their Member State of residence and *(ii)* the particular method applied by this State to avoid double taxation may have a significant impact on which Member State must assume the obligation to consider those taxpayers' personal and family circumstances. This issue is further addressed in Chapter 6.

In the last place, it is observed that fractional taxation has been proposed as an alternative route for considering personal and family circumstances within the EU. However, it seems too ambitious to implement a fractional taxation system through negative integration when, within the EU, the elimination of international juridical double taxation is not mandatory, and this system, to work properly, implies such elimination.

On balance, although EU law does not adopt the ability to pay as a principle of justice for distributing the tax burden, it protects this principle as long as it is common to the Member States involved in a given case. Indeed, the Court's case law on the consideration of expenses related to economic activity and personal and family circumstances shows that the Court seeks to ensure that individuals are taxed on their *net income* within the EU, provided that internal situations are taxed in the same way. Nevertheless, this approach does not prevent disparities because it is based on prohibiting discrimination and restrictions, which aim to ensure free movement and not justice in distributing the tax burden among taxpayers.

CHAPTER 5
Unrelieved International Juridical Double Taxation: Compatibility with EU Law

– Analysis of CJEU's case law and the academic literature about the compatibility of international juridical double taxation with EU law.

– International juridical double taxation as not being forbidden under EU law since it is a consequence of the definition of Member States' tax jurisdiction.

– Analysis of the critics formulated regarding the CJEU approach to international juridical double taxation and the concrete suggestions made on how the Court should tackle this issue.

5.1 THE COURT'S APPROACH TO THE LACK OF ELIMINATION OF INTERNATIONAL JURIDICAL DOUBLE TAXATION

Given the absolute priority that the Court concedes to the consideration of taxpayers' personal and family circumstances, it could be expected that the CJEU would be fierce against international juridical double taxation of individuals.

As AG Léger explains in his Opinion in the *Schumacker* case, the refusal by the residence Member State and the source Member State to consider taxpayers' personal and family circumstances leads to overtaxing non-residents.[413]

Similarly, international juridical double taxation implies the overtaxation of taxpayers engaged in a cross-border situation due to disregarding the tax borne in the other State.

As Monsenego observes, 'it is unclear why the ECJ believes double nondeduction breaches EC law, while juridical double taxation is acceptable. Double taxation and

413. Opinion of AG Léger in Case C-279/93 (Schumacker), para. 67: 'This sort of 'negative conflict' of jurisdiction between the State of employment and the State of residence (which both refuse to grant tax relief in respect of personal and family responsibilities) leads to 'overtaxation' of non-residents.'

double nondeduction have a similar result for the taxpayer: overtaxation. The ECJ's holdings on those matters should not differ to such a great extent'.[414] Despite not reaching the same conclusion, Lang also noted that 'not allowing deductions in either state and taxing income in both states are two sides of the same coin'.[415]

Notwithstanding, the CJEU's approach to international juridical double taxation differs significantly from its stance on taxpayers' personal and family circumstances.

So far, in what concerns individuals and international juridical double taxation, the Court has dealt with three fundamental issues: *(i)* overtaxation due to the non-existence of a bilateral tax treaty and the ineffectiveness of unilateral measures to avoid double taxation; *(ii)* overtaxation due to the override of an existing bilateral tax treaty; and *(iii)* overtaxation despite the application of a bilateral tax treaty. These issues are analysed further below.[416]

5.1.1 Overtaxation Due to the Non-existence of a Treaty and Ineffectiveness of Unilateral Measures to Avoid Double Taxation

The Court dealt with the non-existence of a bilateral tax treaty and the ineffectiveness of unilateral measures to avoid double taxation in the *Block* case.[417]

This case concerned a resident in Germany who inherited capital assets invested in Germany and Spain. There was no inheritance tax treaty in place between these Member States.

According to German law, the inheritance tax was levied on worldwide inheritance if, at the time of the death, the deceased or the heir was resident in Germany. In order to eliminate double taxation, foreign inheritance taxes paid abroad could be credited against the German inheritance tax due up to the amount of that tax. However, the tax credit was denied in the case because the assets invested in Spain were not deemed foreign under German tax law. In that regard, the relevant criterion was the creditor's residence - i.e., the residence of the deceased or the heir - which in this case was Germany.

414. J. Monsenego, *Double Taxation in the EU: The Future after Block*, 54(3) Tax Notes Int'l 215 (2009), 216.
415. M. Lang, *Double Taxation and EC Law*, in *Comparative Fiscal Federalism: Comparing the European Court of Justice and the US Supreme Court's Tax Jurisprudence* (R. Avi-Yonah et al. eds, Kluwer Law International 2007), 16: 'The Advocate General's Opinion and the ECJ's judgment [in the *Schumacker* case] are very interesting because not allowing deductions in either state and taxing income in both states are two sides of the same coin. The Advocate General has expressed this idea by describing a situation in which allowances are nowhere taken into account as "overtaxation". Therefore, one could infer from this decision that the freedoms require avoidance of "overtaxation" by allocation of the taxing rights for every type of income to one of the Member States. This would mean that the freedoms require the Member States to avoid double taxation.' However, the author stresses that it is necessary 'to be very careful about deriving such far-reaching conclusions' because the CJEU 'only requires the avoidance of "overtaxation" in this area, but not in general'.
416. The Court's approach to international juridical double taxation is the same in cases involving legal persons. *See, e.g.*, CJEU, Case C-194/06 (*Orange European Smallcap Fund*), para. 42; Case C-96/08 (*CIBA*), paras 28-29; Joined Cases C-436/08 and C-437/08 (*Haribo Lakritzen Hans Riegel*), paras 171-172; Case C-403/19 (*Société Générale*), para. 29.
417. CJEU, Case C-67/08 (*Block*).

In contrast, under Spanish domestic law, the relevant criterion for taxing inherited capital assets was the debtor's residence - i.e., the residence of the financial institution - which in this case was Spain.

The asymmetry between those Member States' domestic tax laws and the lack of a bilateral tax treaty led to Ms Block being double taxed without any relief from such an international juridical double taxation being granted.

Ms Block challenged the denial of the tax credit, arguing that it constituted an obstacle to the free movement of capital because the inheritance of capital claims against a financial institution established abroad would bear a higher tax burden than claims against a financial institution established in Germany. The risk of double taxation would deter investors and their heirs from investing in the other Member States.

The case was brought before the CJEU for a preliminary ruling. Despite recognising the existence of the said tax disadvantage, the Court affirmed that it is the result of the exercise in parallel by the Member States concerned of their fiscal sovereignty. That exercise in parallel of fiscal sovereignty is demonstrated by the different criteria adopted by each Member State to define their tax jurisdiction.[418]

The Court stressed that in the current stage of the development of EU law, there are no general criteria for the attribution of areas of competence between the Member States regarding the elimination of double taxation within the EU.[419] Consequently, the Member States are not obliged to eliminate juridical double taxation arising from the parallel exercise of their fiscal sovereignty, provided that they comply with EU law.[420]

EU law prevents the Member States from constraining free movement through discriminatory or restrictive tax measures. Therefore, although the overtaxation derived from international juridical double taxation may deter taxpayers from investing abroad, the Member States involved do not breach EU law if they do not treat taxpayers exercising an EU freedom of movement worse than those not exercising it. From the perspective of the residence Member State, that is the case where residents engaged in cross-border activities are subject to the same tax rates on the same tax base as residents performing the same domestic activities. From the perspective of the source

418. *Ibid.*, para. 28: '[T]hat fiscal disadvantage is the result of the exercise in parallel by the two Member States concerned of their fiscal sovereignty, which is demonstrated by the fact that one State, the Federal Republic of Germany, has decided to make capital claims subject to German inheritance tax where the creditor is resident in Germany, while the other, the Kingdom of Spain, has decided to make such claims subject to Spanish inheritance tax where the debtor is established in Spain.'
419. *Ibid.*, para. 30: 'Community law, in the current stage of its development and in a situation such as that in the main proceedings, does not lay down any general criteria for the attribution of areas of competence between the Member States in relation to the elimination of double taxation within the European Community.'
420. *Ibid.*, para. 31: '[I]n the current stage of the development of Community law, the Member States enjoy a certain autonomy in this area provided they comply with Community law, and are not obliged therefore to adapt their own tax systems to the different systems of tax of the other Member States in order, *inter alia,* to eliminate the double taxation arising from the exercise in parallel by those Member States of their fiscal sovereignty and, in consequence thereof, to allow the inheritance tax paid in a Member State other than that in which the heir is resident to be deducted in a case such as that of the main proceedings.'

Member State, that is the case where non-residents are subject to the same tax rates on the same tax base as residents performing the same activities.

The overtaxation derived from international juridical double taxation is, thus, a disadvantage suffered by taxpayers engaged in cross-border activities that stems from the cumulative effect of being taxed in two Member States on the same item of income. Because that disadvantage is not the direct result of discriminatory or restrictive tax treatment, it is not forbidden in light of EU law.

As international juridical double taxation is not forbidden, EU law does not require the Member States to eliminate it, meaning the Member States are not obliged to conclude tax treaties with each other or adopt unilateral measures to avoid international juridical double taxation. Consequently, EU law does not limit the Member States' tax jurisdiction, the Member States being sovereign to decide *to what extent* they are willing to exercise their taxing powers. Thus, the Member States have the power to define their tax jurisdiction, and if they wish, they can restrain it through agreements or unilateral measures to avoid double taxation in any event or only in limited cases.

In brief, the Court found that the double taxation suffered by Ms Block did not constitute an obstacle to the EU freedoms of movement because it was a consequence of the exercise in parallel of Member States' tax sovereignty and did not entail a discriminatory or restrictive tax treatment.

5.1.2 Overtaxation Due to the Override of an Existing Tax Treaty

The OECD Report on Tax Treaty Override defines treaty override as 'the enactment of domestic legislation intended by the legislature to have effects in clear contradiction to international treaty obligations'.[421] Treaty override is thus a violation of a treaty under international law caused by the unilateral action of a Contracting State, which enacts new domestic law intended to be contrary to an existing treaty.[422]

In the *Kerckhaert and Morres*,[423] *Damseaux*,[424] and *Levy and Sebbag*[425] cases, the CJEU dealt with international juridical double taxation resulting from the override of a tax treaty by a Member State.

The facts are essentially the same in these three cases: individual taxpayers, residents in Belgium and subject to worldwide taxation there, received dividends from undertakings established in France. In Belgium, the dividends were subject to a tax of 25%.[426] Under the Belgium–France tax treaty, France imposed a withholding tax of 15% on the dividends. According to the said tax treaty, individual taxpayers were

421. Report on Tax Treaty Override, adopted by the OECD Council on 2 October 1989 (OECD Publishing 1989), para. 5.
422. E. Reimer & A. Rust eds, *Klaus Vogel on Double Taxation Conventions* (Kluwer Law International 4th ed. 2015), 'Introduction', m.no. 155; P. Ribeiro de Sousa, *Tax Treaty Override*, in *Fundamental Issues and Practical Problems in Tax Treaty Interpretation* (M. Schilcher & P. Wenignger eds, Linde Verlag 2008), 252.
423. CJEU, Case C-513/04 (*Kerckhaert and Morres*).
424. CJEU, Case C-128/08 (*Damseaux*).
425. CJEU, Case C-540/11 (*Levy and Sebbag*).
426. In the *Damseaux* case, the Belgian tax imposed was 15%. Cf. CJEU, Case C-128/08 (*Damseaux*), para. 8.

entitled to a tax credit granted by Belgium regarding the tax paid in France, and the conditions for that tax credit ought to be regulated in Belgian domestic law. However, following legislative amendments to the Belgian domestic law, the tax credit was unilaterally withdrawn, leading to a treaty override situation.[427]

The appellants in each case challenged the denial of the tax credit before Belgian national courts, exploring different angles upon which the issue could be perceived under EU law. Consequently, the cases were brought before the CJEU for a preliminary ruling pondering different approaches to the same problem.

In the *Kerckhaert and Morres* case, the Belgium-France tax treaty was not at issue. The question raised addressed the Belgian national law, which established a uniform tax rate for dividends received domestically and abroad, without, in the latter case, providing for a tax credit for the tax paid in another Member State. The lack of a tax credit implied that Belgian residents receiving French dividends were subject to a heavier tax burden than Belgian residents receiving domestic dividends, penalising those who had invested abroad.

The CJEU highlighted that the Belgian tax law did not distinguish between dividends received domestically or cross-borders. The tax rate applicable to all dividends was the same, regardless of their source, and therefore, no worse treatment was offered to foreign dividends.[428] Accordingly, the overtaxation borne by the taxpayers resulted from France also taxing those dividends.

Hence, the Court held that the adverse consequences suffered by the taxpayers derived from the exercise in parallel by two Member States of their fiscal sovereignty.[429] Furthermore, the CJEU stressed that preventing international juridical double taxation is a matter for the Member States since EU law does not lay down any general criteria for allocating taxing rights among the Member States.[430]

427. Some authors and the Belgian courts do not consider those cases to constitute a tax treaty override because Belgium did not deviate from the Belgium-France tax treaty provisions. After all, the allocation rules were followed and the double taxation relief rules remitted to Belgian domestic law, which would detail how the relief would be granted. However, at the time of the cases, the Belgian domestic law did not foresee any measure to relieve double taxation regarding individuals. Double taxation relief was not granted not because the tax treaty was being misapplied but because the domestic rule to which the tax treaty remitted was missing. In other words, there was not a misapplication of the treaty but rather a jeopardising of its aims - *see* P. Smet & H. Laloo, *ECJ to Rule on Taxation of Inbound Dividends in Belgium*, 45(4) Eur. Tax'n 158 (2005), 159; K. Daxkobler & E. Huisman, *Levy & Sebbag: The ECJ Has Once Again Been Asked to Deliver Its Opinion on Juridical Double Taxation in the Internal Market*, 53(8) Eur. Tax'n 400 (2013), 402; C. Marchgraber (Kluwer Law International 2018), 256-259. In contrast, other authors do consider the lack of Belgian domestic provisions aimed at avoiding double taxation as a treaty override because such an absence was contrary to the wording of the treaty - *see* A. Rust, *How European Law Could Solve Double Taxation*, in *Double Taxation Within the European Union* (A. Rust ed., Kluwer Law International 2011), 151; C. De Pietro, *Tax Treaty Override and the Need for Coordination Between Legal Systems: Safeguarding the Effectiveness of International Law*, 7(1) World Tax J. 73 (2015), 90.
428. CJEU, Case C-513/04 (*Kerckhaert and Morres*), paras 17-18.
429. *Ibid.*, para. 20.
430. *Ibid.*, paras 22-23: '22. Community law, in its current state and in a situation such as that in the main proceedings, does not lay down any general criteria for the attribution of areas of competence between the Member States in relation to the elimination of double taxation within the Community. [...] 23. Consequently, it is for the Member States to take the measures

In the *Damseaux* case, the questions raised concerned the France–Belgium tax treaty and its compatibility with the EU freedoms of movement when juridical double taxation subsists.

The CJEU noted its lack of jurisdiction to interpret the France–Belgium tax treaty, either to establish the obligations which arise under it or to rule on a possible infringement by a contracting Member State, such issues being outside the scope of the interpretation of EU law.[431] The Court then stressed that juridical double taxation is not contrary to EU law as long as it results from the parallel (non-discriminatory) exercise of tax competences by the different Member States.[432]

Since no unifying or harmonising measure designed to eliminate double taxation has been adopted at the EU-law level, the Member States retain the power to define their tax jurisdiction. Restraining their taxing powers to eliminate juridical double taxation is a choice to be made by the Member States unilaterally or through agreements between them.[433] Moreover, due to the lack of general criteria in EU law for the attribution of areas of competence between the Member States concerning the elimination of double taxation, EU law is unable to oblige the residence Member State to avoid it, even when such obligation is foreseen in a bilateral tax treaty.[434]

necessary to prevent situations such as that at issue in the main proceedings by applying, in particular, the apportionment criteria followed in international tax practice. [...].' AG Geelhoed, in his opinion in Case C-513/04 (*Kerckhaert and Morres*), qualified the adverse consequences suffered by the taxpayers as a distortion resulting from the coexistence of discrete tax systems – a 'quasi restriction'. As affirmed by the AG, the power to choose the criteria to define and allocate tax jurisdiction lies purely with the Member States, international and juridical double taxation being a consequence of those choices. The free movement provisions of the Treaty cannot oblige home States to relieve juridical double taxation resulting from the dislocation of tax base between two Member States, as there are no alternative criteria to be found in EU law (cf. paras 30, 31 and 38). *See also* Opinion of AG Geelhoed in Case C-374/04 (*Test Claimants in Class IV of the ACT Group Litigation*), paras 38-39.

431. CJEU, Case C-128/08 (*Damseaux*), paras 20 and 22.
432. *Ibid.*, paras 26 and 27.
433. *Ibid.*, paras 29 and 30: '29 [N]o unifying or harmonising measure designed to eliminate cases of double taxation has as yet been adopted at Community-law level [...]. 30 In the absence of any unifying or harmonising Community measures, Member States retain the power to define, by treaty or unilaterally, the criteria for allocating their powers of taxation, particularly with a view to eliminating double taxation [...]. It is for the Member States to take the measures necessary to prevent situations of double taxation by applying, in particular, the criteria followed in international tax practice.'
434. *Ibid.*, paras 33-34: '33 Even though such an attribution of powers complied, in particular, with the rules of international legal practice as reflected in the model tax convention on income and on capital drawn up by the Organisation for Economic Cooperation and Development (OECD), in particular Article 23B thereof, it is not in dispute that Community law, in its current state and in a situation such as that at issue in the main proceedings, does not lay down any general criteria for the attribution of areas of competence between the Member States in relation to the elimination of double taxation within the Community [...]. 34 Consequently, if a Member State cannot rely on a bilateral convention in order to avoid the obligations imposed on it by the [EU] Treaty [...], the fact that both the Member State in which the dividends are paid and the Member State in which the shareholder resides are liable to tax those dividends does not mean that the Member State of residence is obliged, under Community law, to prevent the disadvantages which could arise from the exercise of competence thus attributed by the two Member States.'

In the *Levy and Sebbag* case, the question raised concerned the compatibility with EU law of the amendment to the Belgian domestic law made after the conclusion of the Belgium–France tax treaty, which provided for the mechanism to avoid double taxation referred to in that treaty. The national court asked the CJEU whether the provision on the free movement of capital read in light of the principle of loyal cooperation – now enshrined in Article 4(3) of the TEU – was not being disregarded.

The Court explained that the principle of loyal cooperation lays down a general obligation for the Member States. The specific content of such obligation depends on the provisions of the EU Treaties.[435] Therefore, this principle cannot be interpreted alone as giving rise to independent obligations.

Moreover, the principle of loyal cooperation could not be read together with the former Article 293 of the Treaty establishing the European Community (hereinafter 'EC Treaty').

Former Article 293 of the EC Treaty established the Member States' obligation, so far as necessary, to enter into negotiations to conclude tax agreements to eliminate double taxation within the EU.[436] However, that article lacked direct effect, not containing a precise, clear and unconditional obligation that should be observed. It did not lay down an operative rule but merely outlined the framework for negotiations that the Member States could enter into with each other as needed.[437] Consequently, the former Article 293 neither conferred taxpayers a right that could be invoked before national courts nor created an independent obligation for the Member States under the principle of loyal cooperation.[438]

The cases analysed revealed that the CJEU considered international juridical double taxation resulting from treaty override as a non-issue for EU law because the Member States are sovereign to define their tax jurisdiction and to restrain it if they wish. Therefore, if the Member States are willing to restrain their tax jurisdiction, they may do it unilaterally or by agreeing on allocating taxing powers between them. In case of treaty override, EU law is of no help, as it does not lay down any general criteria for allocating taxing powers among the Member States.

However, despite EU law not requiring the elimination of international juridical double taxation, tax treaties between the Member States have an *effet utile* for the proper functioning of the EU internal market by avoiding overtaxation of cross-border activities resulting from such double taxation. Therefore, tax treaties concluded between the Member States create obligations relevant to the EU internal market that should not be neglected in light of the principle of loyal cooperation.[439]

435. CJEU, Case C-540/11 (*Levy and Sebbag*), para. 26.
436. Article 293 EC Treaty, second indent: 'Member States shall, so far as is necessary, enter into negotiations with each other with a view to securing for the benefit of their nationals: [...] – the abolition of double taxation within the Community.'
437. CJEU, Case C-336/96 (*Gilly*), para. 15. The lack of practical effect of such a provision led to the assumption that Art. 293 was a policy statement rather than a substantive norm: double taxation should be eliminated because it goes counter to the internal market – E. Reimer, *The Abolition of Article 293 EC: Comments on Hofmann's Analysis*, in *Double Taxation Within the European Union* (A. Rust ed., Kluwer Law International 2011), 88.
438. Cf. CJEU, Case C-540/11 (*Levy and Sebbag*), paras 27 and 28; Case C-336/96 (*Gilly*), para. 16.
439. R. Offermanns, *Restrictions on Treaty Override Resulting from EU Law*, 53(9) Eur. Tax'n 430 (2013), 434-435.

From this perspective, it has been argued that in the cases at hand, it was unnecessary to establish under the EU law rules on the allocation of taxing powers between France and Belgium because those Member States had already established such rules in the tax agreement concluded by them. Given the *effet utile* of tax treaties on the proper functioning of the EU internal market, it would not be unreasonable to demand *pacta sunt servanda*[440] of those existing bilateral tax treaties.[441]

After all, the existing tax treaties within the EU result from the Member States' tax sovereignty and their willingness to eliminate international juridical double taxation. Demanding compliance with bilateral tax treaties does not make the Member States prisoners of their choices: they are sovereign to renegotiate[442] or terminate such treaties,[443] but they should not be allowed to override them.[444,445]

Yet, the CJEU did not follow such an approach to the problem, holding the issue to fall outside the scope of EU law and noting that it lacked jurisdiction to interpret the France-Belgium tax treaty.[446]

440. *Pacta sunt servanda* is foreseen in Art. 26 of the Vienna Convention on the Law of Treaties (VCLT), according to which: 'Every treaty in force is binding upon the parties to it and must be performed by them in good faith.'

441. In this regard, Kemmeren, alluding to the CJEU, Case C-265/04 (*Bouanich*), has defended that 'the relevant DTC 'must be taken into account' for the interpretation of Community law. This can only be done adequately if the Member State concerned is obliged to apply the DTC, i.e., to fulfil its obligations under the relevant DTC'. And the author stresses that this reasoning implies 'that a Member State must grant relief of double taxation if a DTC requires the Member State to do so; not granting relief is inconsistent with, *inter alia*, Community loyalty' – E. Kemmeren, *Non-application of DTCs: Inconsistent with Community and EEA Loyalty*, in *The EU and Third Countries: Direct Taxation* (M. Lang & P. Pistone eds, Kluwer Law International 2007), 63. To the same effect, De Broe affirms that 'A Member State should not be allowed to erode the effet utile of Community law achieved by a DTC which for many years effectively eliminates double taxation, by subsequently enacting rules in domestic tax law that lead to the contrary result. This would be at odds with the principle of good faith that governs the application and interpretation of all international treaties (Articles 26 and 31 Vienna Convention on the Laws of Treaties) and which is, of course, also applicable in Union law as recognised by the ECJ' – L. De Broe, *Relief of Double Taxation of Cross-Border Dividends Within the Union and the Principle of Loyal Cooperation*, 21(4) EC Tax Rev. 180 (2012), 181 DOI: 10.54648/ecta 2012017; *see also* A. Rust (A. Rust ed., Kluwer Law International 2011), 150-151; R. Offermanns, 53(9) Eur. Tax'n 430 (2013), 434-435.

442. Article 39 VCLT: 'A treaty may be amended by agreement between the parties.'

443. Article 42(2) VCLT: 'The termination of a treaty, its denunciation or the withdrawal of a party, may take place only as a result of the application of the provisions of the treaty or of the present Convention. The same rule applies to suspension of the operation of a treaty.'

444. Article 27 VCLT: 'A party may not invoke the provisions of its internal law as justification for its failure to perform a treaty.'

445. With a different view, Wattel argues that 'the Member State allegedly overriding the treaty is competent to terminate the treaty altogether, and is also competent not to enter into it in the first place. Hence, it cannot be bound by a rule it has rejected' – P. Wattel, *Passing the Buck Around: Who Is Responsible for Double Taxation?: Comments on Profs. Kofler and Rust's Analysis*, in *Double Taxation Within the European Union* (A. Rust ed., Kluwer Law International 2011), 164.

446. CJEU, Case C-128/08 (*Damseaux*), para. 22. *See also* Case C-298/05 (*Columbus Container Services*), para. 47. In this case the Court followed the Opinion of AG Mengozzi in Case C-298/05 (*Columbus Container Services*), para. 75, who argued that 'a (possible) conflict between rules of domestic law and rules of international law (…) has nothing to do with Community law', and 'it does not fall to the Court to resolve such a conflict of rules'.

Supposing these cases had occurred today, the main question would be whether EU law already provides mechanisms for avoiding international juridical double taxation resulting from tax treaty override. For instance, would the Directive on tax dispute resolution mechanisms be applicable in cases like these?

The Directive on tax dispute resolution mechanisms is designed to resolve disputes between the Member States when those disputes arise from the interpretation and application of agreements or conventions that provide for the elimination of double taxation.

It is doubtful whether the situations of tax treaty override fall within this Directive's scope of application.

On the one hand, it is questionable whether tax treaty override is an issue arising from applying or interpreting a tax treaty per se. Tax treaty override results from the fact that the domestic law of a Contracting State frustrates the aim of the tax treaty. However, it does not necessarily mean that the tax treaty is not being observed as such. The main difficulty is knowing whether the jeopardising of a tax treaty aim may be considered a form of misapplication or misinterpretation.

On the other hand, there is a critical concern regarding the relationship between the legislative and executive powers of the Member States that must be pondered. The mutual agreement procedure foreseen in the Directive on tax dispute resolution mechanisms is based on the dialogue between the concerned Member States' tax authorities. Do they have such power to counter an intentional act of the legislator who has decided to override a tax treaty? The same doubt is even more compelling when the Advisory Commission must resolve the dispute resolution, as independent persons of standing also have a seat at the table.

It is hard to believe that the Directive on tax dispute resolution mechanisms provides the proper means to resolve a unilateral intended infringement introduced by a Member State's law. After all, accepting that tax treaty override may be overcome by the action of tax authorities and independent persons of standing, countering a Member State's legislative power, leads to a severe breach in that State's rule of law.

Notwithstanding, excluding cases of tax treaty override from the scope of the Directive on tax dispute resolution mechanisms seriously mitigates its aim, making it impossible to resolve double taxation in an essential range of cases.

5.1.3 Overtaxation Despite the Application of a Tax Treaty

The *Gilly* case[447] regards a situation of overtaxation despite a tax treaty being in force and correctly applied.

This case concerns Mr and Mrs Gilly, who resided in France. Mrs Gilly, with French and German nationality, worked in a State school in Germany. Under the Germany–France tax treaty, the public remuneration received by Mrs Gilly in Germany

447. CJEU, Case C-336/96 (*Gilly*).

was taxed both in Germany and in France. To avoid double taxation, France granted a tax credit, which was lower than the tax paid in Germany.[448]

The appellants challenged the tax credit granted, claiming that it penalised those who had exercised an EU freedom of movement, as French residents deriving income from another Member State were taxed more heavily than French residents earning the same income domestically. According to the applicants, juridical double taxation could not be entirely avoided by an ordinary tax credit but by a full credit, i.e., a tax credit equal to the amount of tax charged in Germany.[449]

The Court observed that the tax treaty at issue seeks to avoid juridical double taxation of French residents deriving income from Germany when such income is also taxed in Germany, but it does not guarantee that the tax due in one State is no higher than the tax due in the other State.[450] That unfavourable consequence suffered by the taxpayer results from the difference between Member States' tax rates, which EU law cannot resolve in the absence of harmonisation rules in the field of direct taxes.[451] Moreover, granting a full credit would imply that the taxes of another State were paid by the public treasury of the residence State, which would entail a loss of tax revenue for that State, encroaching on its sovereignty in matters of direct taxation.[452]

While in the *Block*, *Kerckhaert and Morres*, *Damseaux*, and *Levy and Sebbag* cases, the Court found that the overtaxation suffered by taxpayers resulted from the

448. Under Art. 20(2)(a)(cc) of the Germany–France tax treaty, 'double taxation of persons resident in France shall be avoided in the following manner: [...] Profits and other positive income arising in the Federal Republic and taxable there under the provisions of this Convention shall also be taxable in France where they accrue to a person resident in France. *The German tax shall not be deductible for calculation of the taxable income in France*. However, the recipient shall be entitled to a tax credit to be set against the French tax charged on the taxable amount which includes that income. That tax credit shall be equal: [...] *to the amount of the French tax on the relevant income*' (emphasis added) – *see* CJEU, Case C-336/96 (*Gilly*), para. 8. Although, in this case, the method for eliminating double taxation is referred to as credit, in reality, the use of a modified exemption seems to be at issue. Indeed, the tax paid in Germany is never credited, irrespective of whether it is higher than the tax that would be due in France on income derived from Germany. On the contrary, it is the amount of tax due in France on German-source income that is, in any case, deducted from the total tax, even if that amount is higher than the tax effectively paid in Germany. On the differences between the methods for eliminating juridical double taxation, *see* further *supra* section 2.2.
449. CJEU, Case C-336/96 (*Gilly*), para. 45.
450. *Ibid.*, para. 46: 'The object of a convention such as that in issue is simply to prevent the same income from being taxed in each of the two States. It is not to ensure that the tax to which the taxpayer is subject in one State is no higher than that to which he or she would be subject in the other.'
451. *Ibid.*, para. 47: 'However, it is common ground that any unfavourable consequences entailed in the present case by the tax credit mechanism set up by the bilateral convention, as implemented in the context of the tax system of the State of residence, are the result in the first place of the differences between the tax scales of the Member States concerned, and, in the absence of any Community legislation in the field, the determination of those scales is a matter for the Member States.'
452. *Ibid.*, para. 48: '[I]f the State of residence were required to accord a tax credit greater than the fraction of its national tax corresponding to the income from abroad, it would have to reduce its tax in respect of the remaining income, which would entail a loss of tax revenue for it and would thus be such as to encroach on its sovereignty in matters of direct taxation.'

exercise in parallel by two Member States of their fiscal sovereignty;[453] in the *Gilly* case, the CJEU held that the higher taxation suffered by the taxpayer resulted from a *disparity* between the tax rates of the two Member States.[454] Although the difference in the terminology used represents only a slight nuance,[455] it shows that the underlying problem in these cases is not the same.

In the *Block, Kerckhaert and Morres, Damseaux,* and *Levy and Sebbag* cases, the issue was the compatibility with the EU law of international juridical double taxation, which entails a disadvantage resulting from the definition of Member States' tax jurisdiction.

In contrast, in the *Gilly* case, the issue was the compatibility with the EU law of the ordinary credit employed to eliminate international juridical double taxation. An immediate consequence of the credit method is that taxpayers always bear the highest tax rate in play: their residence State's tax rate or the other State's tax rate. The disadvantage suffered by the taxpayer stemmed from the different configurations of the Member States' tax system, specifically regarding tax rates.

Therefore, despite all these cases concern an overtaxation related to international juridical double taxation, in the *Gilly* case, international juridical double taxation was eliminated; thus, the overtaxation suffered by the taxpayer is not caused directly by international juridical double taxation, as framed by the appellants.

The Court treated the disadvantage suffered in the *Gilly* case as a disparity resulting from the difference between Member States' tax rates, which does not fall within the EU Treaties prohibitions. Nevertheless, it has been argued that the Court could have reached another conclusion if the case had been framed differently,[456] as it is unclear whether the higher tax burden suffered by the taxpayer derived *exclusively* from the source Member State having higher tax rates than her residence State.[457]

It has been pointed out that the consideration of personal and family circumstances by the residence State reduced the tax due in that State, which led to a minor tax credit being conceded for the tax paid in the other State than the tax credit that would be conceded if those circumstances were not taken into account.[458] In such a case,

453. CJEU, Case C-67/08 (*Block*), para. 28; Case C-513/04 (*Kerckhaert and Morres*), para. 20; Case C-128/08 (*Damseaux*), para. 27; Case C-540/11 (*Levy and Sebbag*), para. 18.
454. CJEU, Case C-336/96 (*Gilly*), para. 49.
455. As noted *supra* in section 3.4.1.2., disparities may arise from the configuration of Member States' tax system and the definition of Member States' tax jurisdiction. Although the Court uses the expression 'exercise in parallel by two Member States of their fiscal sovereignty' to refer to disadvantages resulting from the definition of Member States' tax jurisdiction, the CJEU does not treat them as a separate or autonomous category of disparities.
456. J. Avery Jones, 39(1) Eur. Tax'n 2 (1999), 3; K. Vogel, *Some Observations Regarding Gilly*, 7(3) EC Tax Rev. 150 (1998), 150 DOI: 10.54648/ecta1998024; F. Vanistendael, *Case C-336/96, Mr and Mrs Robert Gilly v. Directeur des Services Fiscaux du Bas Rhin*, 37(1) Common Market L. Rev. 167 (2000), 176-178 DOI: 10.54648/256124.
457. F. Vanistendael, 37(1) Common Market L. Rev. 167 (2000), 176-177; P. Wattel, 60(6) Eur. Tax'n 210 (2000), 220-222.
458. K. Vogel, 7(3) EC Tax Rev. 150 (1998), 150. To the same effect, Wattel refers that, aside from the difference in the tax rates, there is in the *Gilly* case a second disadvantage, which is 'caused by the fact that the home State (France) does not completely take Mrs Gilly's personal circumstances into account, and by the fact that she does not receive any allowances and deductions in the host State, either' – P. Wattel, 60(6) Eur. Tax'n 210 (2000), 220; *see also* N.

despite being formally considered, the taxpayer's personal and family circumstances are consumed by the tax credit mechanism, as analysed further below in section 6.2.2.

Therefore, if the issue raised had been on the substantial loss of the taxpayers' personal and family tax benefits instead of the ordinary credit mechanism per se, the case outcome could have been different.

5.2 THE OPEN DEBATE

The Court's stance on international juridical double taxation was clearly expressed in the case law analysed. International juridical double taxation resulting from the (non-discriminatory) exercise in parallel by two Member States of their fiscal sovereignty is not contrary to EU law, even if it entails a disadvantage to taxpayers making use of an EU freedom of movement.

Notwithstanding, the Court's approach was not without criticism, triggering an intense debate in the academic literature on the issue.

The discussion usually has two layers. First, it is discussed whether or not EU law supports the elimination of international juridical double taxation. Then, if the answer is affirmative, the discussion evolves into determining how to ensure its elimination.

Naturally, the discussion revolves around the cases of unrelieved double taxation, whether because there are no legal means to avoid double taxation in force (i.e., unilateral, bilateral or unilateral measures) or because the existing means fail to be applied.

5.2.1 Does EU Law Support the Elimination of International Juridical Double Taxation?

Before the Treaty of Lisbon, EU law expressly mentioned the need to eliminate double taxation within the EU. The former Article 293 of the EC Treaty foresaw the Member States' obligation to enter into negotiations, so far as is necessary, to conclude tax agreements to eliminate double taxation within the EU.[459]

According to the Court, it was clear that the elimination of international juridical double taxation was included among the EU objectives.[460]

When the Treaty of Lisbon repealed Article 293 of the EC Treaty without any reason being stated,[461] an essential question was left to be answered: is the elimination of double taxation no longer among the EU's objectives?

Bammens (IBFD 2012), 617-618. In turn, Vanistendael advocates that the higher tax burden borne by the taxpayers in the *Gilly* case had to do with the fact that the employment State (Germany) treated Mrs Gilly as a single person rather than a married person. Cf. F. Vanistendael, 37(1) Common Market L. Rev. 167 (2000), 177.

459. Article 293 EC Treaty, second indent: 'Member States shall, so far as is necessary, enter into negotiations with each other with a view to securing for the benefit of their nationals: [...] – the abolition of double taxation within the Community.'

460. CJEU, Case C-336/96 (*Gilly*), para. 16: 'Although the abolition of double taxation within the Community is thus included among the objectives of the Treaty [...].' *See also* Case C-128/08 (*Damseaux*), para. 28; Case C-540/11 (*Levy and Sebbag*), para. 27.

461. Article 2(280) of the Treaty of Lisbon amending the Treaty on European Union and the Treaty establishing the European Community (2007/C 306/01).

Such repeal has been seen in different ways.

While the belief that the elimination of double taxation was no longer an EU objective was minimal,[462] the voices that advocated its continuity among the EU aims were not unanimous regarding the meaning to be given to the repeal of Article 293.

On the one hand, the removal of Article 293 of the EC Treaty has been explained by the willingness to simplify the EU Treaties, not having any other substantive or political reason.[463]

On the other hand, it has also been seen as allowing a paradigm shift. Accordingly, the obligation to eliminate double taxation may be applied more widely under the EU Treaties than under the EC Treaty,[464] and double taxation is no longer an issue to be dealt with exclusively by the Member States.[465]

The common ground is that the legal basis for the need to eliminate double taxation within the EU may still be found in the general provisions of the EU Treaties.

According to Article 3(3) of the TEU, one of the goals of the EU is the establishment of an internal market, which - under Article 26(2) of the TFEU - should encompass an area without internal frontiers where the EU freedoms of movement are ensured in accordance with the provisions of the Treaties.

International juridical double taxation entails an additional burden to taxpayers exercising an EU freedom of movement, hindering cross-border activities within the EU, and this obstacle undeniably constrains the proper functioning of the internal market.

In this regard, AG Ruiz-Jarabo Colomer has stressed that 'the fact that a taxable event might be taxed twice is the most serious obstacle there can be to people and their capital crossing internal borders'.[466]

The European Commission has noted that 'it is not appropriate in a single market that problems such as double taxation [...] should deter individuals from engaging in

462. T. O'Shea, *European Tax Controversies: A British-Dutch Debate: Back to Basics and Is the ECJ Consistent?*, 5(1) World Tax J. 100 (2013), 105 DOI: 10.59403/1df756z.
463. P. Wattel et al. (Kluwer Law International 7th ed. 2018), 19-20.
464. E. Kemmeren, *After Repeal of Article 293 EC Treaty under the Lisbon Treaty: The EU Objective of Eliminating Double Taxation Can Be Applied More Widely*, 17(4) EC Tax Rev. 156 (2008), 158 DOI: 10.54648/ecta2008068; E. Kemmeren, 21(3) EC Tax Rev. 156 (2012), 161; J. Monsenego (IBFD 2012), 268-269; J. Monsenego, *Réflexions sur les conséquences de l'abrogation de l'article 293, alinéa 2 du Traité CE*, 9 Revue de Droit Fiscal 15 (2011), 17; R. Offermanns, 53(9) Eur. Tax'n 430 (2013), 431; L. Cerioni, *Double Taxation and the EC Internal Market: Reflections on the ECJ's Decisions in Block and Damseaux and the Potential Implications*, 63(11) Bull. Int'l Tax'n 543 (2009), 556; H. Hofmann, *Double Tax Agreements: Between EU Law and Public International Law*, in *Double Taxation Within the European Union* (A. Rust ed., Kluwer Law International 2011), 84-85; S. van Thiel (A. Rust ed., Kluwer Law International 2011), 178.
465. E. Reimer (A. Rust ed., Kluwer Law International 2011), 93-95; L. Hinnekens, *The Uneasy Case and Fate of Article 293 Second Indent EC*, 37(11) Intertax 602 (2009), 607 DOI: 10.54648/taxi 2009061; with the opposite view, Lang argued that even with Art. 293 of the EC Treaty in place, taking measures to avoid double taxation was not reserved to the Member States - M. Lang (R. Avi-Yonah et al. eds, Kluwer Law International 2007), 15.
466. Opinion of AG Ruiz-Jarabo Colomer in Case C-376/03 (*D.*), para. 85.

cross-border activity or penalise them when they do'.[467] Somewhere else, the European Commission has also observed that 'double taxation in a cross-border context as a result of inconsistent interaction of different domestic tax systems, is a major impediment and a real challenge for the internal market'.[468]

AG Mengozzi has highlighted that 'the elimination or avoidance of double taxation by convention will ultimately assist the realisation of the internal market and the exercise of the freedoms of movement', a finding that, in the view of the AG, remains valid even after the repeal of Article 293 of the EC Treaty.[469]

Moreover, under Article 4(3) of the TEU,[470] the Member States shall facilitate the achievement of the Union's tasks and refrain from any measure which could jeopardise the attainment of the EU's objectives.

This way, the need to eliminate international juridical double taxation within the EU is an immediate consequence of one of the EU's central goals: establishing the internal market.[471]

5.2.2 How to Ensure the Elimination of International Juridical Double Taxation Within the EU?

Assuming that the legal basis for the need to eliminate double taxation within the EU may be found in the general provisions of the EU Treaties, the second layer of debate entails dealing with a critical question: how to ensure its elimination?

467. *See* Communication from the Commission to the Council, the European Parliament and the European Economic and Social Committee, *Removing cross-border tax obstacles for EU citizens*, COM(2010) 769 final, p. 4.
468. Communication from the Commission to the European Parliament, the Council and the European Economic and Social Committee, *Double Taxation in the Single Market*, COM(2011)712 final, p. 3.
469. Opinion of AG Mengozzi in Case C-648/15 (*Austria v. Germany*), paras 51-52.
470. Under Art. 4(3) TEU: 'Pursuant to the principle of sincere cooperation, the Union and the Member States shall, in full mutual respect, assist each other in carrying out tasks which flow from the Treaties.

    The Member States shall take any appropriate measure, general or particular, to ensure fulfilment of the obligations arising out of the Treaties or resulting from the acts of the institutions of the Union.

    The Member States shall facilitate the achievement of the Union's tasks and refrain from any measure which could jeopardise the attainment of the Union's objectives.'
471. P. Wattel, 60(6) Eur. Tax'n 210 (2000), 213; G. Fibbe & A. De Graaf, *Is Double Taxation Arising from Autonomous Tax Classification of Foreign Entities Incompatible with EC Law?*, in *A Tax Globalist – Essays in Honour of Maarten J. Ellis* (H. Van Arendonk et al. eds, IBFD 2005), 255; M. Hofstätter, *Who Is Competent to Issue Measures for the Elimination of Double Taxation Within the Community?*, in *Tax Treaty Law and EC Law* (M. Lang et al. eds, Kluwer Law International 2007), 27-28; G. Kofler & R. Mason, 14 Colum. J. Eur. L. 63 (2007), 65; M. Lehner, *Avoidance of Double Taxation Within the European Union: Is There an Obligation under EC Law?*, in *Tax Treaty Law and EC Law* (M. Lang et al. eds, Kluwer Law International 2007), 13-15; J. Malherbe et al., *Direct Taxation in the Case-Law of the European Court of Justice* (Larcier 2008), 131; F. Vanistendael, *Does the ECJ Have the Power of Interpretation to Build a Tax System Compatible with the Fundamental Freedoms?*, 17(2) EC Tax Rev. 52 (2008), 59 DOI: 10.54648/ecta2008054; L. Cerioni, 63(11) Bull. Int'l Tax'n 543 (2009), 553; J. Monsenego, 9 Revue de Droit Fiscal 15 (2011), 17; D. Gutmann (I. Richelle et al. eds, Springer 2013), 67; M. Helminen (C. Brokelind ed., IBFD 2014), 392 and 395.

Little consensus exists on the issue, and the divergence among scholars starts with categorising double taxation as an obstacle to the proper functioning of the EU internal market.

It is common ground that international juridical double taxation results from the juxtaposition of tax jurisdictions. Such an overlap gives rise to additional tax burdens (double burdens) in cross-border situations, and it occurs even when the Member States use the same connecting factors to define their tax jurisdiction: tax residents on their worldwide income and non-residents on their source income.

Some authors follow the Court's categorisation, affirming that double taxation is a mere disparity derived from the exercise in parallel by two Member States of their fiscal sovereignty. These scholars support the Court's approach in the *Block, Kerckhaert and Morres, Damseaux*, and *Levy and Sebbag* cases. For them, the only way to overcome double taxation is through positive integration.[472]

Accordingly, because the lack of EU measures establishing criteria for allocating taxing powers between the Member States renders it impossible to decide which State has the better right to tax, the Court was correct in refusing to intervene in these cases.[473] It is up to the EU legislator to assume such responsibility.[474] Meanwhile, the Member States may decide whether or not to eliminate double taxation.

In turn, some other authors categorise double taxation as a clear obstacle to the EU freedoms of movement.[475] Others stress that this tax disadvantage is relevant in light of

472. M. Lang, 18(3) EC Tax Rev. 98 (2009), 110; P. Wattel (A. Rust ed., Kluwer Law International 2011), 166; D. Weber, 34(12) Intertax 585 (2006), 594; S. Douma, *The Three Ds of Direct Tax Jurisdiction: Disparity, Discrimination and Double Taxation*, 46(11) Eur. Tax'n 522 (2006), 531-532; K. Lenaerts, *'United in Diversity' – Also in Fiscalibus?*, in *A Vision of Taxes Within and Beyond European Borders* (L. Hinnekens & P. Hinnekens eds, Kluwer Law International 2008), 628-629; M. Gammie, *Double Taxation, Bilateral Treaties and the Fundamental Freedoms of the EC Treaty*, in *A Tax Globalist – Essays in Honour of Maarten J. Ellis* (H. Van Arendonk et al. eds, IBFD 2005), 276-277; M. Gammie, *Non-discrimination and the Taxation of Cross-Border Dividends*, 2(2) World Tax J. 162 (2010), 172-173 DOI: 10.59403/dw8mnv; T. O'Shea, 5(1) World Tax J. 100 (2013), 105-107; W. Schön, 68(4/5) Bull. Int'l Tax'n 271 (2015), 274-277; D. Smit, *International Income Allocation under EU Tax Law: Tinker, Tailor, Soldier, Sailor*, 26(2) EC Tax Rev. 67 (2017), 70 DOI: 10.54648/ecta2017008; M. Lang, *Double Taxation Conventions in the Case Law of the CJEU*, 46(3) Intertax 181 (2018), 181-182 DOI: 10.54648/taxi2018021.

473. The CJEU justified itself for not taking action on the fact that EU law 'does not lay down any general criteria for the attribution of areas of competence between the Member States in relation to the elimination of double taxation within the EU'. Cf. CJEU, Case C-513/04 (*Kerckhaert and Morres*), para. 22; CJEU, Case C-67/08 (*Block*), para. 30; Case C-128/08 (*Damseaux*), para. 33; Case C-540/11 (*Levy and Sebbag*), para. 22. Case C-298/05 (*Columbus Container Services*), para. 45; Case C-96/08 (*CIBA*), para. 27; Joined Cases C-436/08 and C-437/08 (*Haribo Lakritzen Hans Riegel*), para. 170; Case C-35/11 (*Test Claimants in the FII Group Litigation*), para. 40; Case C-403/19 (*Société Générale*), para. 29.

474. In this regard, efforts have indeed been made to identify possible legislative solutions at the EU level to overcome double taxation. *See* European Commission expert group, *Ways to tackle cross-border tax obstacles facing individuals within the EU*, Directorate-General for Taxation and Customs Union (2015), and European Commission expert group, *Ways to tackle inheritance cross-border tax obstacles facing individuals within the EU*, Directorate-General for Taxation and Customs Union (2015).

475. F. Vanistendael, 17(2) EC Tax Rev. 52 (2008), 61; F. Vanistendael, *In Defence of the European Court of Justice*, 62(3) Bull. Int'l Tax'n 90 (2008), 97; E. Kemmeren, 17(4) EC Tax Rev. 156 (2008), 169; P. Herrera Molina, *STJCE 4.11.2006, Kerckhaert-Morres, As. C-513/04: ¿es discriminatoria la doble imposición jurídica internacional?*, 148 Crónica tributaria 248 (2013), 249; M.

the internal market, although admitting that the concept of discrimination/restriction is ineffective in the case of international juridical double taxation since the tax disadvantage is not created by one single Member State.[476]

These scholars tend to agree that the Court could have done more (and still can) within its competence to deter a crucial hindrance to the proper functioning of the internal market whilst an EU legislative solution is not adopted.

The most frequent criticism in this regard concerns the fact that the CJEU managed to establish priority rules between the Member States in fields such as VAT, social security or mutual recognition of regulatory competences, refusing to do the same in cases of international juridical double taxation.[477] Even regarding direct taxation, it is noted that the Court has already set priority rules through the interpretation of EU law, indicating which Member State is responsible for taking away the tax disadvantage created by the interaction of two Member States' tax systems.[478] As examples of such priority rules, the cases of personal and family circumstances[479] and undertakings' final losses[480] are often pointed out.

In terms of concrete suggestions on how the Court should tackle international juridical double taxation, it has been noted that EU law offers enough clues, and guidelines from other tax systems may also be drawn and used within the EU. The proposals put forward are usually centred on establishing criteria for dividing tax jurisdictions and allocating taxing powers among the Member States.[481]

Two situations are often distinguished: the cases where there is a bilateral tax treaty and those where there is not.

In cases where double taxation is not eliminated despite a bilateral tax treaty being in force, it has been suggested that priority rules do not have to be created

---

Wathelet (L. Hinnekens & P. Hinnekens eds, Kluwer Law International 2008), 916; V. Heydt, *Juridical Double Taxation: Kerckhaert and Morres*, in *Landmark Decisions of the ECJ in Direct Taxation* (W. Haslehner et al. eds, Kluwer Law International 2015), 187-189.

476. G. Kofler (A. Rust ed., Kluwer Law International 2011), 101; D. Gutmann (I. Richelle et al. eds, Springer 2013), 67; L. Cerioni, 63(11) Bull. Int'l Tax'n 543 (2009), 553; M. Lehner (M. Lang et al. eds, Kluwer Law International 2007), 15-16; S. van Thiel (R. Avi Yonah and M. Lang eds, Kluwer Law International 2016), 122.
477. F. Vanistendael, 46(9) Eur. Tax'n 413 (2006), 418; G. Kofler & R. Mason, 14 Colum. J. Eur. L. 63 (2007), 69-72; G. Kofler (A. Rust ed., Kluwer Law International 2011), 123-128; A. Rust (A. Rust ed., Kluwer Law International 2011), 140; J. Malherbe et al. (Larcier 2008), 130-131; S. van Thiel, *Why the European Court of Justice Should Interpret Directly Applicable Community Law as a Right to Most-Favoured-Nation Treatment and a Prohibition of Double Taxation*, in *The Influence of European Law on Direct Taxation: Recent and Future Developments* (D. Weber ed., Kluwer Law International 2007), 110-118;S. van Thiel (A. Rust ed., Kluwer Law International 2011), 171-175; S. van Thiel (R. Avi Yonah and M. Lang eds, Kluwer Law International 2016), 105-115.
478. G. Kofler & R. Mason, 14 Colum. J. Eur. L. 63 (2007), 80; G. Kofler (A. Rust ed., Kluwer Law International 2011), 130-132.; J. Snell, 56(2) Int'l & Compar. L.Q. 339 (2007), 361-362; A. Rust (A. Rust ed., Kluwer Law International 2011), 140-141;S. van Thiel (Weber D. ed., Kluwer Law International 2007), 124-125;S. van Thiel (A. Rust ed., Kluwer Law International 2011), 175-176; S. van Thiel (R. Avi Yonah and M. Lang eds, Kluwer Law International 2016), 116.
479. As symptomatic examples: CJEU, Case C-279/93 (*Schumacker*) and Case C-385/00 (*De Groot*).
480. As symptomatic example: CJEU, Case C-446/03 (*Marks & Spencer*).
481. For an overview of the alternative routes suggested in the tax literature for dealing with double taxation and their critical analysis, *see* C. Marchgraber (Kluwer Law International 2018), 238-250.

because they already exist. Therefore, the Court must demand that the Member States apply the bilateral agreement to ensure the proper functioning of the internal market.[482]

In turn, where there is no bilateral tax treaty in force, it has been advocated that allocation rules may be drawn from other instruments. In this regard, it has been suggested to follow: *(i)* the OECD MC as a neutral regulatory framework,[483] *(ii)* the few Directives in the field of direct taxation, which provide some guidance when deciding on the Member State responsible for avoiding double taxation,[484] as well as *(iii)* the almost unanimous policy choices of the Member States regarding the allocation of taxing rights.[485]

In the cases where no tax treaty is in place, it has also been defended that the Member States involved should be jointly and severally liable for avoiding double taxation. In this regard, it is argued that unrelieved double taxation results from both States acting contrary to their obligations under EU law, and therefore, they must sort

482. J. Englisch, 33(8/9) Intertax 310 (2005), 324; G. Kofler & R. Mason, 14 Colum. J. Eur. L. 63 (2007), 82; J. Lang & J. Englisch (A. Amatucci ed., Kluwer Law International 2d ed. 2012), 291; L. De Broe, 21(4) EC Tax Rev. 180 (2012), 181-182; D. Gutmann (I. Richelle et al. eds, Springer 2013), 69-70; A. Rust (A. Rust ed., Kluwer Law International 2011), 150-151; G. Kofler (A. Rust ed., Kluwer Law International 2011), 132 n. 203, noting, however, that '[a]s the ECJ is not competent to interpret DTCs, it would be for the referring national court and the parties in the proceedings to demonstrate the obligations of the respective Member State under a DTC'. *See also* P. Pistone (A. Rust ed., Kluwer Law International 2011), 192-194.

483. In its case law the CJEU considers the OECD MC a reflection of the international legal practice and states that 'in the allocation of fiscal jurisdiction, it [is not] unreasonable for the Member States to base their agreements on international practice and the model convention drawn up by the OECD' - CJEU, Case C-336/96 (*Gilly*); Case C-414/06 (*Lidl Belgium*), para. 22; Case C-513/03 (*van Hilten van der Heijden*), para. 48; Case C-234/01 (*Gerritse*), para. 45; Case C-107/94 (*Asscher*), para. 47. In this regard, Hofmann argues that a Member State complying with the OECD MC should be given the benefit of the doubt as being compliant with the principle of proportionality - H. Hofmann (A. Rust ed., Kluwer Law International 2011), 85-86; *see also* E. Kemmeren, 21(3) EC Tax Rev. 156 (2012), 169-170; G. Kofler & R. Mason, 14 Colum. J. Eur. L. 63 (2007), 81. In contrast, Schön affirms that the fact that a provision follows the OECD MC 'cannot pre-empt the judgement on its compatibility with the Internal Market' - W. Schön, 68(4/5) Bull. Int'l Tax'n 271 (2015), 275. Rust observes that the rules of the OECD MC cannot offer clear guidance for the allocation of taxing rights because such rules are not unconditional and change over time. Moreover, not all Member States are members of the OECD - cf. A. Rust (A. Rust ed., Kluwer Law International 2011), 149-150.

484. F. Vanistendael, 17(2) EC Tax Rev. 52 (2008), 59, who observes, however, that not all cases can be resolved this way. In this regard, A. Rust (A. Rust ed., Kluwer Law International 2011), 144-148, notes that the analogous application of the directives is of limited help, as they do not follow a consistent pattern.

485. Vanistendael mentions that there is *almost unanimous agreement* at the international level to tax real estate income in the State where it is located. However, this author also notes that there is not always a broad consensus among the Member States and therefore their policy choices cannot offer clear guidelines. Cf. F. Vanistendael, 17(2) EC Tax Rev. 52 (2008), 60, 66; F. Vanistendael, 62(3) Bull. Int'l Tax'n 90 (2008), 98. In turn, Joachim Lang and Joachim Englisch allude to a *silent consensus* within the EU regarding the responsibility to avoid double taxation, which belongs to the home State rather than the host State. The authors deduct such a responsibility from the fact that the Member States only grant unilateral relief from juridical double taxation to their residents and not to non-residents. Cf. J. Lang & J. Englisch (A. Amatucci ed., Kluwer Law International 2d ed. 2012), 291; J. Englisch, 33(8/9) Intertax 310 (2005), 325.

out the problem caused.[486] Another alternative is to make just one State responsible for avoiding double taxation, and that would be the taxpayers' residence State as a counterpart for taxing their worldwide income.[487]

Furthermore, attention has been drawn to the experience of other multi-state tax systems in which juridical double taxation has been overcome through judicial activism, as is the case in the US and Switzerland.

In the US, there is no constitutional requirement to eliminate interstate double taxation. Nevertheless, the US Supreme Court has interpreted the Commerce Clause as entailing a dormant prohibition for the states to discriminate against interstate commerce, which led to the ban of interstate double taxation in certain circumstances. This prohibition only targets structural, rather than factual, juridical double taxation. The US Supreme Court applies the 'internal consistency test' to identify the cases of structural juridical double taxation. This test examines whether or not the hypothetical application by all US states of the challenged tax scheme would inevitably lead to more burdensome taxation of interstate activities than purely domestic activities.[488]

In Switzerland, although the prohibition of inter-cantonal double taxation is enshrined in the Constitution, the legislator did not introduce binding allocation rules. To comply with the constitutional imperative, the Tribunal Fédéral developed detailed rules to allocate taxable objects among cantons based on the territory principle. Accordingly, an item of income may be taxed by the canton that has the strongest connection with it.[489]

486. In this regard, Van Thiel explains that: 'In so far as a home Member State taxes residents on worldwide income without securing the avoidance of double taxation on the foreign source income of its residents, it maintains an exit restriction contrary to Union law, and affected residents should be able to go to national courts in order to obtain full relief from double taxation. Likewise, a host Member State that taxes domestic source income of a non-resident by means of a withholding tax, would, if it ignored the (costs and the) tax imposed on that income by the home state of the economic operator, in effect maintain a nondiscriminatory access restriction' – S. van Thiel (R. Avi Yonah and M. Lang eds, Kluwer Law International 2016), 118. *See also* P. Farmer (A. Arnull & D. Chalmers eds, Oxford 2015), 815; G. Kofler (A. Rust ed., Kluwer Law International 2011), 129; G. Kofler & R. Mason, 14 Colum. J. Eur. L. 63 (2007), 81; P. Herrera Molina (Instituto de Estudios Fiscales 2009), 304-305; P. Herrera Molina, 148 Crónica tributaria 248 (2013), 250; V. Heydt (W. Haslehner et al. eds, Kluwer Law International 2015), 189-190.

487. H. Schaumburg, *Das Leistungsfähigkeitsprinzip im internationalen Steuerrecht*, in *Die Steuerrechtsordnung in der Diskussion: Festschrift für Klaus Tipke* (J. Lang ed., Verlag Dr. Otto Schmidt 1995), 145. *See also* H. Kube, *Double Burdens Within the European Union: Solutions in Other Areas of Law: Constitutional Law*, in *Double Taxation Within the European Union* (A. Rust ed., Kluwer Law International 2011), 66.

488. *See* further G. Kofler & R. Mason, 14 Colum. J. Eur. L. 63 (2007), 83-91; R. Mason, 49 Bost. Coll. L. Rev. 1277 (2008), 1277-1326; J. Snell, 56(2) Int'l & Compar. L.Q. 339 (2007), 360-361; R. Mason & M. Knoll, *What Is Tax Discrimination?*, 121(5) Yale L.J. 1017 (2011), 1113-1114; M. S. Knoll & R. Mason, *Wynne: It's Not About Double Taxation*, 75 ST. Tax Notes 413 (2015), 420; A. Van de Vijver, *International Double Taxation in the European Union: Comparative Guidelines from Switzerland and the United States*, 26(1) EC Tax Rev. 10 (2017), 13-15 DOI: 10.54648/ecta2017002.

489. *See* further A. Van de Vijver, 26(1) EC Tax Rev. 10 (2017), 12-13; M. Simonek, *Tax Coordination Between Cantons in Switzerland – Role of the Courts*, in *Horizontal Tax Coordination* (M. Lang et al. eds, IBFD 2012), 225-229.

It has been suggested that the CJEU may take these courts' experiences as an example.

On the one hand, the CJEU could apply an internal consistency approach, demanding the Member States to be internally coherent: if a Member State, in the source State position, considers itself competent to tax a given item of income, it must conversely refrain from taxing the same item of income when it is in the residence State position. In other words, the residence Member State would only be obliged to grant relief from double taxation when it would have taxed that item of income if it were in the position of the source State.[490] Nevertheless, as international juridical double taxation cases always involve at least two States, one could reach the conclusion that both Member States' tax systems are internally incoherent without having any clue on which State would be responsible for dropping its tax claim or granting relief from double taxation.

On the other hand, the CJEU could use the territory principle as a guideline to establish allocation rules among the Member States.[491] However, this approach amounts to establishing criteria for allocating taxing powers among the Member States, which the CJEU is unwilling to do.

Last but not least, it has also been submitted that unrelieved double taxation within the EU, in certain circumstances, could breach the right to property enshrined in Article 17 of the Charter of Fundamental Rights of the EU.[492]

Yet, despite scholars' efforts to find ways to overcome international juridical double taxation within the EU through the action of the CJEU, the Court has refused to take that path.

5.3 THE IRRELEVANCE OF INDIVIDUALS' ABILITY TO PAY TAXES

As analysed in more detail in Chapter 3, in the direct tax field, the Member States' power to tax is virtually unlimited under EU law, except for a few Directives in particular areas. For instance, EU law does not lay down any general criteria for allocating taxing powers among the Member States.[493] The exercise of Member States'

490. A. Van de Vijver, 26(1) EC Tax Rev. 10 (2017), 21; G. Kofler & R. Mason, 14 Colum. J. Eur. L. 63 (2007), 91-94; R. Mason, 49 Bost. Coll. L. Rev. 1277 (2008), 1277 et seq.; J. Snell, 56(2) Int'l & Compar. L.Q. 339 (2007), 364; A. Rust (A. Rust ed., Kluwer Law International 2011), 153-154. For a critical view of this approach, *see* W. Schön, 68(4/5) Bull. Int'l Tax'n 271 (2015), 275 n. 41; P. Wattel (A. Rust ed., Kluwer Law International 2011), 166; C. Marchgraber (Kluwer Law International 2018), 243-246.
491. A. Van de Vijver, 26(1) EC Tax Rev. 10 (2017), 19-20.
492. G. Kofler (A. Rust ed., Kluwer Law International 2011), 134; A. Van de Vijver, 26(1) EC Tax Rev. 10 (2017), 18-19. *See also* F. Debelva (IBFD 2019), 413-464, whose findings are also relevant for the interpretation and application by the CJEU of the right to property as included in Charter of Fundamental Rights of the EU. In turn, Monsenego considers, based on the case law, that the right to property is a rather weak argument to challenge international double taxation, admitting, however, that that case law could change in the future – cf. J. Monsenego (IBFD 2012), 276-280.
493. Cf. CJEU, Case C-513/04 (*Kerckhaert and Morres*), para. 22; Case C-67/08 (*Block*), para. 30; Case C-128/08 (*Damseaux*), para. 33; Case C-540/11 (*Levy and Sebbag*), para. 22; Case C-298/05 (*Columbus Container Services*), para. 45; Case C-96/08 (*CIBA*), para. 27; Joined Cases

taxing powers is only limited by the general EU Treaty provisions that forbid discrimination or restrictions on free movement.

The definition of Member States' tax jurisdiction does not restrict free movement or discriminate against taxpayers making use of an EU freedom of movement since such definition only defines to what extent the Member States may exercise their taxing power over taxpayers. It says nothing about how those taxing powers will be exercised.

Therefore, international juridical double taxation, as a consequence of the definition of Member States' tax jurisdiction that leads to situations of overlapping, does not breach EU law because the disadvantage suffered by taxpayers in such cases stems from the cumulative effect of being subject to tax in a non-discriminatory way in two Member States on the same item of income.

The reasoning followed by the CJEU in its case law is, therefore, based on a jurisdictional perspective of the problem. International juridical double taxation is not contrary to EU law because it is a consequence of the overlap of tax jurisdictions, and those tax jurisdictions were not defined in a restrictive or discriminatory way against taxpayers making use of an EU freedom of movement.

Most of the scholars' proposals for overcoming international juridical double taxation within the EU also follow a jurisdictional perspective, focusing on identifying or creating rules on allocating taxing powers between the Member States.

International juridical double taxation is undeniably a problem resulting from the definition of tax jurisdictions, and setting rules for limiting and allocating taxing powers between the Member States is a suitable way to overcome it.

Notwithstanding, international juridical double taxation may also be regarded through an ability-to-pay perspective.

Taxpayers carrying out an activity cross-borders have the same economic strength as taxpayers deriving the same income by carrying out the same activity domestically. In cases where international juridical double taxation is not avoided, taxpayers pursuing an activity cross-borders will bear two tax burdens, while taxpayers carrying out the same domestic activity will bear a tax burden just once despite having the same economic strength.

When taxing, the Member States involved ignore the tax that is also due in the other Member State by taxpayers in the cross-border situation; that is to say, none of them considers the decrease in taxpayers' economic strength caused by the tax liability in the other Member State. Thus, the Member States tax an artificial economic strength that does not represent those taxpayers' overall ability to pay.

Consequently, while taxpayers in the domestic situation bear a total tax according to their overall ability to pay, based on their actual economic strength, the taxpayers in the cross-border situation bear a total tax that disregards their overall ability to pay, as the decrease in their economic strength was not considered in any of the Member States involved.

As analysed in Chapter 4, the CJEU's case law on the consideration of expenses related to economic activity and personal and family circumstances shows that the

C-436/08 and C-437/08 (*Haribo Lakritzen Hans Riegel*), para. 170; Case C-35/11 (*Test Claimants in the FII Group Litigation*), para. 40; Case C-403/19 (*Société Générale*), para. 29.

Court seeks to ensure that individuals are taxed on their net income within the EU, provided that internal situations are taxed in the same way.

Therefore, it is not unreasonable to examine whether the difference in treatment regarding the consideration of taxpayers' overall ability to pay constitutes discrimination or a restriction on the free movement unilaterally caused by one Member State.

Before examining whether there is room for considering a Member State responsible for taking into account taxpayers' overall ability to pay in cases where international juridical double taxation was not avoided, it is worth looking into the CJEU's decisions on cases where taxpayers' ability to pay was undermined in the process of eliminating international juridical double taxation. This analysis is carried out in Chapter 6.

5.4 CONCLUDING AND SUMMARISING REMARKS

This chapter addresses the compatibility of international juridical double taxation with EU law, analysing the CJEU's case law and the academic literature in this regard.

As derived from Chapter 4, the CJEU gives absolute priority to the consideration of taxpayers' personal and family circumstances. The lack of consideration of taxpayers' personal and family circumstances leads to overtaxing those taxpayers. Likewise, international juridical double taxation implies the overtaxation of taxpayers engaged in a cross-border situation due to disregarding the tax borne in the other State. However, the CJEU does not regard those situations as analogous. Thus, the CJEU's approach to international juridical double taxation differs significantly from its stance on taxpayers' personal and family circumstances.

So far, the CJEU has dealt with three fundamental issues regarding individuals and international juridical double taxation: *(i)* overtaxation due to the non-existence of a bilateral tax treaty and the ineffectiveness of unilateral measures to avoid double taxation; *(ii)* overtaxation due to the override of an existing bilateral tax treaty; and *(iii)* overtaxation despite the application of a bilateral tax treaty.

Regarding the first issue, the Court found that although the overtaxation derived from international juridical double taxation may deter taxpayers from investing abroad, that disadvantage does not constitute a forbidden obstacle to free movement because it is a consequence of the exercise in parallel of Member States' tax sovereignty and it does not entail a discriminatory or restrictive tax treatment. As double taxation is not forbidden under EU law, the Member States are not required to eliminate it. In other words, the Member States are not obliged to conclude tax treaties with each other or adopt unilateral measures to avoid international juridical double taxation.

In the second place, the CJEU dealt with international juridical double taxation arising from the override of a tax treaty. In such cases, a tax treaty is in place, but it fails its purposes due to a Contracting State's unilateral action, which enacts new domestic law that breaches that treaty. Again, the CJEU held that the overtaxation borne by taxpayers derived from the exercise in parallel by two Member States of their fiscal sovereignty. The CJEU observed that it lacked jurisdiction to interpret tax treaties. Since EU law does not lay down any general criteria for allocating taxing rights among the Member States, it cannot oblige one of the States to eliminate double taxation, even when such obligation is foreseen in a bilateral tax treaty. Moreover, the Court concluded that the principle of loyal cooperation, now enshrined in Article 4(3) of the TEU, does not give rise to independent obligations in this regard.

Notwithstanding, we sustain that tax treaties contribute to the proper functioning of the internal market, and it is not unreasonable to demand *pacta sunt servanda* of those existing tax treaties. Demanding compliance with tax treaties does not make the Member States prisoners of their choices: they are sovereign to renegotiate or terminate such treaties, but they should not be allowed to override them to the detriment of the internal market.

Furthermore, we pondered whether the Directive on tax dispute resolution mechanisms is of any help in situations of tax treaty override. On the one hand, it is unclear whether jeopardising a tax treaty's aims may be considered a form of misapplication or misinterpretation of that tax treaty. On the other hand, accepting that tax treaty override may be overcome by the action of tax authorities and independent persons of standing, countering a Member State's legislative power may lead to a severe breach in that State's rule of law.

In third place, the CJEU has also addressed the case of overtaxation despite the correct tax treaty application. In this case, the taxpayer claimed that an ordinary tax credit could not entirely avoid international juridical double taxation. The CJEU concluded that the overtaxation suffered resulted from the difference between Member States' tax rates, which EU law cannot resolve in the absence of harmonisation rules in the field of direct taxation. We have noted that if the issue raised had been on the substantial loss of personal and family tax benefits instead of the ordinary credit mechanism per se (as framed by the appellants), the case outcome could have been different.

The case law analysed shows that the CJEU has firm handling in what concerns international juridical double taxation: if it results from the non-discriminatory exercise in parallel by two Member States of their fiscal sovereignty, it is not contrary to EU law, even if it entails a disadvantage to taxpayers making use of free movement.

Nevertheless, the Court's approach to double taxation was not without criticism.

Although after the repeal of Article 293 of the EC Treaty, the EU Treaties lack any reference to the elimination of double taxation, it has been argued that the legal basis for the need to eliminate it within the EU may still be found in the general provisions of the EU Treaties.

Among scholars, little consensus exists on how international juridical double taxation could be avoided under the EU law framework. Some authors sustain that it may only be overcome through positive integration. Others argue that it can be overcome through the action of the CJEU whilst an EU legislative solution is not adopted, as the Court has already managed to establish priority rules between the Member States through the interpretation of EU law, even regarding tax matters.

Some concrete suggestions on how the Court should tackle international juridical double taxation have been pointed out. Most of those suggestions involve establishing criteria for dividing tax jurisdictions and allocating taxing powers among the Member States. Yet, the Court has refused to take that path.

We argue that the CJEU's approach to international juridical double taxation is based on a jurisdictional perspective of the problem. Double taxation is a consequence of the definition of Member States' tax jurisdiction that leads to situations of overlapping. The definition of Member States' tax jurisdiction does not restrict free movement or discriminate against taxpayers making use of free movement since such definition only sets *to what extent* the Member States may exercise their taxing power over taxpayers. The disadvantage taxpayers suffer in such cases derives from the cumulative effect of being subject to tax in two Member States on the same item of income.

However, international juridical double taxation may also be regarded from an ability-to-pay perspective. The cumulative taxation suffered by taxpayers engaged in cross-border activities when double taxation is not avoided decreases their economic strength, affecting their overall ability to pay. That overall ability to pay is not considered in any of the Member States involved because each of them ignores the tax also due in the other. This way, each of these States taxes those taxpayers on an *artificial* economic strength that does not reflect an *actual* overall ability to pay.

Suppose taxpayers in a comparable internal situation are taxed on their actual overall ability to pay. In that case, it is not unreasonable to examine whether the difference in treatment regarding the consideration of taxpayers' overall ability to pay constitutes discrimination or a restriction on the free movement unilaterally caused by one Member State and, therefore, forbidden under the EU law.

Before entering into that examination, which is carried out in Chapter 7, the CJEU's decisions on cases where taxpayers' ability to pay was undermined in the process of eliminating double taxation are analysed in Chapter 6 in order to shed some light on whether there is room for the Court to adopt a different perspective regarding the lack of elimination of international juridical double taxation.

CHAPTER 6
Relief from International Juridical Double Taxation: Compatibility with EU Law

– Examination of the CJEU's decisions on cases in which taxpayers' ability to pay was undermined in the process of eliminating international juridical double taxation.

– Analysis of the discriminatory and restrictive treatment arising from the lack of consideration of taxpayers' personal and family circumstances when applying the credit method or the exemption method to eliminate international juridical double taxation.

– Analysis of the State responsible for such discriminatory and restrictive treatment: the State of residence or the source State.

As seen in Chapter 4, personal and family circumstances must be taken into account *somewhere* within the EU at least once, preferably no more than once, without prejudice to disparities.

In Chapter 5, the analysis of the CJEU's case law made clear that international juridical double taxation does not need to be taken into account *anywhere* because its adverse consequences are a disparity arising from the exercise in parallel of Member States' tax sovereignty. Therefore, according to the Court's case law, the Member States are not obliged to eliminate international juridical double taxation.

However, it follows from the CJEU's case law that if the Member States decide to eliminate international juridical double taxation, they must comply with EU law.[494] In other words, the Member States cannot constrain free movement through discriminatory or restrictive tax measures when eliminating double taxation.

494. CJEU, Case C-168/11 (*Beker*), para. 34: 'As far as concerns the exercise of the power of taxation so allocated by bilateral conventions to prevent double taxation, the Member States must comply with European Union rules'- *See also* Case C-385/00 (*De Groot*), para. 94; Case C-527/06 (*Renneberg*), para. 51; Case C-303/12 (*Imfeld and Garcet*), para. 42; Case C-20/16 (*Bechtel*), para. 66; Case C-174/18 (*Jacob and Lennertz*), para. 25.

The Court's case law shows that applying the exemption and credit methods to eliminate international juridical double taxation may lead to cases of discriminatory or restrictive tax treatment regarding the consideration of taxpayers' personal and family circumstances. Moreover, *(i)* whether or not taxpayers obtain income in their Member State of residence, and *(ii)* the particular method applied by this State to avoid double taxation has a significant impact on which Member State must bear the obligation of taking those taxpayers' personal and family circumstances into account.

This chapter aims to examine these cases where taxpayers' ability to pay was undermined in the process of eliminating international juridical double taxation. For that, the cases will be grouped as per the origin of the total income of taxpayers – i.e., whether it is derived partially from the source Member State and partially from the residence Member State (section 6.1.), or, instead, whether it is derived (almost) exclusively from the source Member State (section 6.2.), and they will be analysed as per the concrete method used.

6.1 INCOME DERIVED PARTIALLY FROM THE SOURCE MEMBER STATE AND PARTIALLY FROM THE RESIDENCE MEMBER STATE

6.1.1 Credit Method

The credit method's basic premise is that resident taxpayers who earn both domestic and foreign income and resident taxpayers who earn only domestic income are exposed to the same taxation in the residence State. All their income will be subject to tax in the residence State similarly.[495]

From the perspective of the taxation borne in the residence Member State, a taxpayer exercising an EU freedom of movement and a taxpayer not exercising it are treated equally.

Nevertheless, applying the ordinary credit method may entail compatibility issues with the EU law regarding the consideration of taxpayers' personal and family circumstances, as will be discussed below. So far, no compatibility issues have arisen regarding the full credit, so this method is not addressed.

6.1.1.1 Ordinary Credit Method

a) The problem

When applying the ordinary credit method to eliminate international juridical double taxation, the taxpayer's residence State will contrast *(i)* the tax paid in the State of source with *(ii)* the tax due in the residence State regarding, specifically, the foreign income. The taxpayer will only be entitled to the lowest of the two amounts as a tax credit.

In order to determine *(ii)* – i.e., *the tax due in the residence State on the foreign income* – it is common to use a formula according to which the total theoretical tax due

495. *See supra* section 2.2.1.

in the residence State on the taxpayer's worldwide income is multiplied by the ratio between the taxpayer's foreign income and the taxpayer's worldwide income.[496]

The problem arises because the taxpayer's tax benefits for personal and family circumstances are included in *the total theoretical tax due in the residence State on the taxpayer's worldwide income,* but they are not included in the second part of the formula (in the ratio), regarding the *taxpayer's worldwide income.*

Consequently, these tax benefits will reduce *the total theoretical tax due in the residence State on the taxpayer's worldwide income*, but the same reduction will not be made on the *taxpayer's worldwide income*. Because the taxpayer's personal and family circumstances were not considered in the second part of the formula (i.e., in the ratio), the taxpayer will lose part of these benefits proportionally to his/her foreign income.

The loss of personal and family circumstances due to the application of the ordinary credit may be illustrated through the simplified example of two resident taxpayers carrying out the same activity, earning the same income and having the same personal and family circumstances. One of them (Taxpayer A) exercises such an activity in a purely internal situation, while the other (Taxpayer B) exercises it in a cross-border situation, deriving income from the State of residence and another State (the source State) in equal parts. The total income derived by each taxpayer amounts to 200, and the personal and family circumstances they are entitled to amount to 20. Consequently, their taxable income in the residence State is 180. The tax rate applicable is 30%; hence, the tax due in the residence State is 54 (180 × 30%).

In the case of Taxpayer B, one-half of his/her income is derived from the other State (the source State), meaning the amount of 100 will be subject to tax there. The source State applies the same 30% tax rate on the income derived from its territory, and it does not have to grant Taxpayer B tax benefits for personal and family circumstances since that taxpayer is not resident there. Thus, Taxpayer B will pay 30 (100 × 30%) on the source State.

Suppose the two States involved entered into a tax treaty to eliminate international juridical double taxation, and the residence State applies the ordinary credit method to that effect. Taxpayer B will be entitled to a tax credit granted by the residence State for the tax paid in the other State. Such a tax credit, as said, will be the lowest of the following two amounts: *(i)* the tax paid in the source State (i.e., 30); or *(ii)* the tax due in the residence State regarding the foreign income.

If the residence State uses the formula described above to determine the amount *(ii)*, it will multiply the (theoretical) tax due on the worldwide income of Taxpayer B (i.e., 54) by the ratio between his/her foreign income and his/her worldwide income (i.e., 100/200). Consequently, *(ii)* will amount to 27, which is lower than the tax paid in the source State (i.e., 30).

Taxpayer B is entitled to a tax credit of 27, which will be deducted from the tax due in the residence State (i.e., 54). The tax to be paid in the residence State is 27 (54–27).

496. The formula may be illustrated as follows:

$$\begin{array}{c}\text{Tax due in the residence}\\ \text{State on foreign income}\end{array} = \begin{array}{c}\text{Total theoretical tax due in the residence}\\ \text{State on taxpayer's worldwide income}\end{array} \times \frac{\text{Taxpayer's foreign income}}{\text{Taxpayer's worldwide income}}$$

See also CJEU, Case C-168/11 (*Beker*), para. 12, where this formula is described.

The overall tax Taxpayer B is liable to pay in the source State and in his/her residence State amounts to 57 (27 + 30), which is higher than the overall tax Taxpayer A is liable to pay (i.e., 54).

The difference between the overall tax Taxpayer A and Taxpayer B are liable to pay cannot be explained through differences in their income, differences in their personal and family circumstances or differences in the tax rates applied by both countries at stake. All these factors are the same in both cases. Therefore, all these factors being identical, eliminating international juridical double taxation should have led to an equal overall tax in the case of Taxpayer A and Taxpayer B. Both should have been liable to pay 54.

As mentioned, the origin of the problem lies in the fact that the benefits for personal and family circumstances are only partially considered in the case of Taxpayer B. Those benefits were considered in the proportion of the income he/she derives from his/her residence State. Having earned half of his/her income in the residence State, Taxpayer B is entitled to half of the benefits for personal and family circumstances.

Indeed, the difference between the overall tax Taxpayer A is liable to pay (i.e., 54) and the overall tax Taxpayer B is liable to pay (i.e., 57) is explained through a simple calculation:

- In the case of Taxpayer A, his/her worldwide income (200) is multiplied by the residence State tax rate (30%), the result being 60. Then, the full benefit for his/her personal and family circumstances (20) is multiplied by the same tax rate (30%), resulting in 6. Finally, if the first result (60) is reduced from the second (6), we reach the overall tax for which Taxpayer A is liable: 54.
- In the case of Taxpayer B, his/her worldwide income (200) is also multiplied by the residence State tax rate (30%), and the result is the same, 60. However, the benefit for his/her personal and family circumstances is not fully considered; it is considered only in the proportion of the income derived from the residence State. So, half of the income derived from the residence State (i.e., 100) corresponds to half of the benefit for personal and family circumstances (i.e., 10). When multiplying his/her benefit for personal and family circumstances by the said tax rate, the result is necessarily different, amounting to 3 (10 × 30%). If the first result (i.e., 60) is diminished from the second (i.e., 3), we reach the overall tax for which Taxpayer B is liable to pay: 57.

Table 6.1 outlines the example explained.

Table 6.1 Consequences of the Ordinary Credit on the Consideration of Personal and Family Circumstances when Taxpayers Derive Income from Both the Residence State and the Source State

	Taxpayer A	*Taxpayer B*
Worldwide income	200	200
Income derived from the State of residence	200	100
Income derived from the other State (source State)	–	100

	Taxpayer A	Taxpayer B
Tax due in the source State (30% tax rate)	–	30
Benefits for personal and family circumstances	20	20
Taxable income in the State of residence	200 – 20 = 180	200 – 20 = 180
Tax rate in the State of residence (30%)	30%	30%
Tax due in the State of residence	54	54
Tax credit to eliminate double taxation	–	54 × 100/200 = **27** > 30
Overall tax	**54**	(54 – 27) + 30 = **57**
Origin of the difference	200 × 30% = 60 20 × 30% = 6 60 – 6 = 54	200 × 30% = 60 10 × 30% = 3 60 – 3 = 57

b) Tax obstacle caused by the residence Member State

Within the EU framework, the residence Member State in the case described above is creating the tax obstacle for taxpayers making use of free movement.

The restrictive tax treatment arises from the fact that the Member State grants, in principle, a tax benefit to all its resident taxpayers derived from their personal and family circumstances. However, such a tax benefit is reduced whenever resident taxpayers obtain income from another State. The tax benefit reduction is made in the proportion of the foreign income they derive.

The residence Member State differentiates two groups of taxpayers: resident taxpayers who carry out exclusively economic activities within the borders of that State, obtaining only domestic income, and resident taxpayers who carry out the same economic activities also in another Member State and, thus, obtain foreign income. These two groups of resident taxpayers are in a comparable situation, as both are exercising the same economic activities, both are subject to full tax liability in the residence Member State, and both have the same personal and family circumstances.

The restrictive tax treatment is embedded in the ordinary credit method to avoid international juridical double taxation, which – if applied in the terms described above – leads to the limited consideration of taxpayers' personal and family circumstances when determining the final tax due in the residence Member State. Since the ordinary credit method is, by its nature, only applied in cross-border situations, the limited consideration of taxpayers' personal and family circumstances will only affect taxpayers engaged in cross-border activities. Taxpayers exclusively engaged in domestic activities – to whom the credit method does not apply – will have their personal and family circumstances fully considered.

Consequently, resident taxpayers exercising an EU freedom of movement are treated worse than the resident taxpayers not exercising it.

The restrictive tax treatment created by the Member State of residence is manifested in the overtaxation of resident taxpayers exercising an EU freedom of movement compared to resident taxpayers not exercising it.

The overtaxation is not attributable to international juridical double taxation as it was eliminated through the ordinary credit method.

c) Tax obstacle caused by the source Member State

In the case described above, the fact that the source Member State does not grant non-residents personal and family tax benefits granted to its own residents does not constitute, under EU law, a forbidden obstacle to free movement.

It is settled case law that resident and non-resident taxpayers are not, as a rule, in a comparable situation regarding the consideration of their personal and family circumstances.[497]

Since non-resident taxpayers only derive part of their total income from the source State, this State is not placed in the best position to ponder the taxpayers' overall ability to pay. Taxpayers' overall ability to pay must be considered in the residence Member State because it is there where taxpayers are usually subject to full tax liability. It is, thus, easier to gather in this State information on the resident taxpayers' aggregate income and personal and family circumstances to assess their overall ability to pay taxes.[498]

Therefore, the source Member State is not discriminating against non-resident taxpayers if it does not consider their personal and family circumstances because those circumstances are to be considered, as a rule, in the residence Member State.

d) Case law from the CJEU

The compatibility of the credit method with EU law was brought to the CJEU in the *Beker* case involving German residents.[499] The CJEU considered that the national way to determine the tax credit to be granted constituted a restriction on the free movement of capital enshrined in Article 63 of the TFEU.

---

497. *See supra* section 4.2.2.1.
498. *See, e.g.*, CJEU, Case C-279/93 (*Schumacker*), paras 32 and 33: '32. Income received in the territory of a Member State by a non-resident is in most cases only a part of his total income, which is concentrated at his place of residence. Moreover, a non-resident's personal ability to pay tax, determined by reference to his aggregate income and his personal and family circumstances, is more easy to assess at the place where his personal and financial interests are centred. In general, that is the place where he has his usual abode. Accordingly, international tax law, and in particular the Model Double Taxation Treaty of the Organization for Economic Cooperation and Development (OECD), recognizes that in principle the overall taxation of taxpayers, taking account of their personal and family circumstances, is a matter for the State of residence. 33. The situation of a resident is different in so far as the major part of his income is normally concentrated in the State of residence. Moreover, that State generally has available all the information needed to assess the taxpayer's overall ability to pay, taking account of his personal and family circumstances.'
499. CJEU, Case C-168/11 (*Beker*). Mr and Mrs Beker, residents in Germany, were subject to worldwide taxation there. In addition to their German income, they received dividends from minority capital holdings in various foreign corporate enterprises (namely, France, Luxembourg, the Netherlands, Switzerland, the USA and Japan). Under the relevant tax treaties for the avoidance of double taxation, the dividends were taxed in the source States and in the State of residence. Germany, as the State of residence, applied the credit method, by which the foreign withholding tax on those dividends was offset against the income tax due according to the income tax scale, up to the level of the German income tax charged on that income. The dispute stemmed from the method used to calculate the maximum amount of foreign withholding tax which could be offset against the income tax due in Germany. That method, as explained above, did not fully take account of the costs relating to personal and family circumstances of the taxpayers (cf. CJEU, Case C-168/11 (*Beker*), paras 36-39).

According to the Court, resident taxpayers in Germany receiving one part of their revenue abroad were at a disadvantage compared with those who received all their revenue in Germany. While resident taxpayers who obtained only domestic income benefited from all allowances corresponding to personal and family circumstances, resident taxpayers who exercised the EU free movement of capital, deriving income from another Member State, only benefited from those allowances in proportion to the income they received in the Member State of residence.[500]

The Court emphasised that 'it is a matter for the State of residence, in principle, to grant the taxpayer all the tax allowances relating to his personal and family circumstances because that State is best placed to assess the taxpayer's personal ability to pay tax since that is where his personal and financial interests are centred'.[501]

The CJEU did not accept that such restrictive tax treatment could be justified by the need to safeguard the balanced allocation of the power to impose taxes among the Member States.[502] That justification could only be accepted 'where the system in question is designed to prevent conduct capable of jeopardising the right of a Member State to exercise its powers of taxation in relation to activities carried out in its territory'. However, it was not what happened in the case at stake: fully granting tax benefits related to personal and family circumstances does not undermine that right. As explained by the Court, the income received in Germany by Mr and Mrs Beker was not less taxed than if it constituted the only income received by them.[503]

Additionally, the fact that the credit method system was optional did not render the formula for calculating the amount of tax credit less incompatible with EU law.[504]

Therefore, according to the CJEU's case law, the application of the ordinary credit method by the residence Member State cannot undermine the consideration of taxpayers' personal and family circumstances.

6.1.2 Exemption Method

The exemption method's basic premise is that the residence State does not tax its residents' foreign income. Income derived from another State will only be taxed in the State where it was obtained.

500. *Ibid.*, paras 50 and 51.
501. *Ibid.*, para. 43.
502. *Ibid.*, para. 55: The argument concerning the balanced allocation of the power to impose taxes between the Member States implies that it is possible to deduct expenses or costs only when they are directly linked to the tax revenue coming under a Member State's power to impose taxes under the allocation of powers between States provided for by the conventions for the avoidance of double taxation. The State of residence is not therefore obliged to compensate for disadvantages linked to the failure to take into account the taxpayers' personal circumstances during the taxation of foreign income in the State in which that income originates.'
503. *Ibid.*, paras 57 and 58.
504. *Ibid.*, para. 62. On the fact that the existence of an alternative system that the taxpayers may choose is not capable of remedying the restrictive effects of one of the systems, *see also* CJEU, Case C-446/04 (*Test Claimants in the FII Group Litigation*), paras 162 and 195; Case C-440/08 (*Gielen*), paras 50-53; Case C-632/13 (*Hirvonen*), para. 41.

However, the income so exempted in the State of residence may still be relevant to determine the tax rate to be imposed on the rest of the domestic income taxpayers receive, as it happens when the State of residence avoids international juridical double taxation through the application of the exemption with progression or the modified exemption.

From the perspective of the taxation borne in the residence Member State, the taxpayer engaged in cross-border activities is not treated worse than a taxpayer involved in purely domestic activities since the former taxpayer is only subject to tax in the residence State on his/her domestic income. Even when the residence State takes income derived from other States into account to determine the tax rate applied to domestic income, the resident who carries out cross-border activities is not treated worse than the resident not carrying them out since, in that case, the average tax rate applied to the domestic income of both is the same.

Nevertheless, applying the exemption method may entail compatibility issues with the EU law concerning the consideration of taxpayers' personal and family circumstances. The compatibility issues vary depending on whether the exemption with progression (section 6.1.2.1.) or modified exemption (section 6.1.2.2.) applies. The full exemption does not raise any compatibility issues since the residence Member State completely ignores the income obtained in the other State to establish the tax due on the domestic income.

6.1.2.1 Exemption with Progression

a) The problem

In its form of exemption with progression, the exemption method entails determining the average tax rate that would apply to the taxpayers' worldwide income to apply that tax rate to their domestic income, excluding taxpayers' foreign income from taxation.[505]

The exemption with progression becomes problematic when its application is combined with apparently neutral domestic tax rules.

These domestic tax rules seem neutral, making no distinction between resident taxpayers carrying out purely internal activities and resident taxpayers carrying out cross-border activities. However, when those rules are combined with the exemption with progression to eliminate double taxation – which, by nature, is only applicable to cross-border situations – they lead to a more burdensome treatment of these situations.

That more burdensome treatment stems from the lack of full consideration of the personal and family circumstances of residents engaged in cross-border activities, while such consideration occurs in the case of residents engaged in purely internal activities. Indeed, the lack of full consideration of personal and family circumstances leads to residents engaged in cross-border activities having their domestic income taxed heavier than that of residents engaged in purely internal activities.

Therefore, in these cases, taxpayers who exercise an EU freedom of movement are treated worse than those who do not exercise it.

505. *See supra* section 2.2.2.

This situation may be illustrated with the following example. Consider a married couple residing in a Member State, subject to joint assessment for income tax purposes there. One member of the couple works in their residence State, and the other works in another Member State. The couple's income is earned in equal parts and derived exclusively from their employment. Under the tax treaty in force, the residence Member State exempts the income derived from the other Member State despite considering it for determining the tax rate applied to the domestic income.

Suppose the residence Member State accepts the deductibility of expenses related to taxpayers' personal and family circumstances, subject to the condition that such expenses have no direct economic link with tax-exempt income. The spouse working in their residence State may deduct those expenses entirely, while the spouse working abroad cannot deduct any personal and family expenses as his/her income is tax-exempt in the residence State due to the method applied for avoiding double taxation.

The tax disadvantage will arise when calculating the couple's aggregate taxable income in the residence State since the lack of consideration of the personal and family expenses of the spouse working abroad will inflate the couple's worldwide income. Consequently, the average tax rate applied to their income derived from the residence Member State will be higher than that which would apply to a couple in an identical situation (or even to themselves) earning the same total income exclusively in the residence Member State.

b) Tax obstacle caused by the residence Member State

Within the EU law framework, the residence Member State in the case described above is creating the tax obstacle for taxpayers making use of free movement.

The restrictive tax treatment arises from the fact that the Member State of residence must, in principle, consider all its residents' personal and family circumstances. However, residents' personal and family circumstances are not fully considered when they obtain income from another Member State.

That restrictive tax treatment results from the interaction between an apparent neutral national rule and the method to eliminate double taxation.

The national rule establishes that when tax benefits are associated with tax-exempt income, they are not considered because neither is income considered. That rule is supposedly neutral, as it establishes the same regime for all resident taxpayers without differentiating between those who carry out their activities domestically and those engaged in cross-border activities.

Nevertheless, in cross-border cases, income that would typically be subject to tax in the residence Member State may be tax-exempt but still considered to determine the tax rate applicable due to the method used for eliminating international juridical double taxation.

In such a case, when double taxation is eliminated through the exemption with progression, that supposedly neutral national rule always puts resident taxpayers carrying out cross-border activities at a disadvantage compared to resident taxpayers carrying out purely internal activities since their personal and family circumstances are not fully considered.

The restrictive tax treatment created by the Member State of residence entails an overtaxation of resident taxpayers exercising an EU freedom of movement. That overtaxation occurs despite those taxpayers exercising an EU freedom of movement and those not exercising it being subject to full tax liability in the residence Member State, performing the same activity and having the same personal and family situation.

Besides, the overtaxation is not attributable to international juridical double taxation as it was eliminated through exemption with progression.

c) Tax obstacle caused by the source Member State

In the case described above, the source Member State does not discriminate against non-residents deriving income from its territory. The fact that the source Member State does not grant them the personal and family benefits it grants to its own residents does not constitute a forbidden obstacle under EU law because the two groups of taxpayers are not in a comparable situation.[506]

The incomparability of their situation derives from the fact that the non-residents only derive part of their total income from the source Member State, the other part being earned in their residence Member State. As non-residents are not subject to full tax liability in the source Member State, this State is not, as a rule, in a position to consider their personal and family circumstances.

Assessing taxpayers' overall ability to pay taxes is, in principle, more effortless in the Member State in which taxpayers are subject to full tax liability because that State has, as a rule, all the information regarding those taxpayers' aggregate income and personal and family circumstances.

d) Case law from the CJEU

The CJEU analysed the compatibility with EU law of the exemption with progression for avoiding double taxation in the *Bechtel* case, which concerned the tax deduction of pension and health insurance contributions. The deduction was subject to the condition that such contributions have no direct economic link with tax-exempt income.[507]

The Court noted that deducting those contributions when calculating the taxpayer's taxable income amounts to a tax advantage since it reduces the taxable income and, consequently, the rate applicable to that income.[508]

506. *See supra* section 4.2.2.1.
507. CJEU, Case C-20/16 (*Bechtel*). Mr and Mrs Bechtel were residents in Germany, where they were subject to joint assessment for income tax purposes. Mrs Bechtel worked in France, while her husband worked in Germany. Under the applicable tax treaty, her French remuneration was tax-exempt in Germany; however, it was taken into account when establishing the tax rate applied to the rest of the couple's taxable income. Certain pension and health insurance contributions levied on Mrs Bechtel's French remuneration were considered special expenses under German tax law. The deduction of special expenses is subject to the condition that they have no direct economic link with tax-exempt income. This condition was not met, as her remuneration was tax-exempt in Germany due to the exemption with progression method applied to eliminate double taxation in Germany.
508. *Ibid.*, para. 43.

The condition of the absence of a direct economic link with the exempt income could indiscriminately apply to cross-border and purely internal situations. Notwithstanding, the CJEU noted that in purely domestic situations, the contributions comparable to those at issue withheld from salaries paid in consideration of work were deductible. Hence, 'the condition relating to the absence of a direct economic link with exempt income may have a greater impact on resident taxpayers receiving wages in a Member State other than that of their residence, which are exempt in their Member State of residence'.[509] The Court thus found the condition laid down in German law to constitute a restriction on the free movement of workers.

When analysing the possible *justifications* for the restrictive tax treatment, the Court addressed the *comparability*[510] of the cross-border situation with the internal situation, classifying those contributions as tax advantages relating to personal and family circumstances. The CJEU concluded that those situations were comparable. It further stressed that granting those tax advantages is, in principle, a matter for the State of residence because that State is better placed to assess the taxpayer's personal ability to pay tax since that is where resident taxpayers' personal and financial interests are centred.[511]

The Court did not accept the German Government's justification of the unfavourable treatment based on the balanced allocation of taxation powers between Germany and France and the need for fiscal coherence in its national tax system.

On the one hand, the Court considered that Germany does not surrender part of its tax jurisdiction to the other Member States by allowing the deduction of those contributions, as it does not affect its power to tax activities carried out on its territory.[512] Furthermore, the Member State of residence cannot invoke the balanced allocation of powers to impose taxes to evade its responsibility to grant the personal and family allowances to which the taxpayers are entitled. The Member State of residence may only be released from this responsibility by way of an international agreement with the other Member State (in this case, the Member State of employment) or even in the absence of that agreement if it finds that the other Member State is granting tax advantages based on the personal and family circumstances of taxpayers who earn taxable income there. In this latter case, the tax legislation of the residence Member State must establish a correlation between the non-attribution of tax advantages relating to personal and family circumstances and the attribution of those tax advantages in the other Member State.[513]

On the other hand, the Court rejected the argument based on the need to maintain the cohesion of the tax system as the effectiveness of the progressivity of the income tax in the Member State of residence, intended by the exemption with progression method,

509. *Ibid.*, para. 48.
510. As already noted, the limits between *comparative analysis* and *justification grounds* are somehow blurred in the Court's case law. *See supra* section 3.4.1.1.
511. CJEU, Case C-20/16 (*Bechtel*), para. 55.
512. *Ibid.*, para. 70.
513. *Ibid.*, paras 71-74. *See supra* section 4.2.2.2.

is not conditional upon the consideration given to the personal and family circumstances of the taxpayer being limited to expenses connected with income taxed in that Member State.[514]

Another example of the blocking effect of the exemption with progression regarding personal and family circumstances is provided by the *Imfeld and Garcet* case.[515]

The issue, in this case, was the consideration of the tax-free income allowance for dependent children. Under Belgian law, such a tax advantage was granted to couples as a unit, but it was set off against the higher taxable income of one of the two spouses. In the case of the applicants, the higher income was earned by Mr Imfeld in Germany, against which the tax-free allowance was set off. However, Mr Imfeld's income, reduced from the tax-free allowance, was then taken away from the couple's taxable amount due to the exemption with progression applied to eliminate international juridical double taxation. So, in the end, the couple did not benefit from that tax advantage granted to them for dependent children.

The CJEU noted that the Belgian tax rule at issue, combined with the exemption with progression method to avoid double taxation, places resident couples who exercise an EU freedom of movement and earn most of their income in another Member State at a disadvantage compared to resident couples who earn all or almost all their income in Belgium.[516]

The rule for setting off the supplementary tax-free allowance for dependent children is neutral, as it applies to all resident taxpayers in the same way. Its purpose is to maximise the advantage: as the tax scale is progressive, attributing the tax-free allowance to the spouse with the higher income is more advantageous to the couple than its allocation in equal parts or even proportionally. Paradoxically, when applied in cross-border situations, that rule may lead to the opposite effect, where the spouse with the highest income earns all his/her income in another Member State.[517]

The CJEU found the Belgian tax rule to constitute a restriction on the freedom of establishment and did not accept the Belgian Government's justification of the unfavourable treatment based on the need to safeguard the balanced distribution of the power of taxation between the Member States. The Court considered that by granting personal and family tax benefits to those taxpayers, Belgium does not surrender part of its fiscal jurisdiction to another Member State since it may tax the activities carried out in its territory. The disadvantage lies in Mrs Garcet's income, which is entirely subject to Belgian tax, without receiving the family benefits she would be entitled to.[518] The Court explained that the mechanisms used to eliminate international juridical double

514. *Ibid.*, para. 77.
515. CJEU, Case C-303/12 (*Imfeld and Garcet*). Mr Imfeld and Ms Garcet were married with two children. They resided in Belgium, where they would be taxed jointly. Mrs Garcet worked in Belgium, while Mr Imfeld was a self-employed in Germany and earned all his income there. His income was tax-exempt in Belgium under the Belgium–Germany tax treaty; however, it was taken into account when establishing the tax rate applied to the rest of the couple's taxable income in Belgium.
516. *Ibid.*, para. 49.
517. *Ibid.*, para. 55.
518. *Ibid.*, paras 75 and 76.

taxation could not deprive taxpayers of their personal and family circumstances. Such benefits must be duly considered, regardless of how the Member States involved have allocated that obligation amongst themselves.[519]

As the residence Member State is, in principle, responsible for granting to resident taxpayers the personal and family allowances to which they are entitled, this responsibility may only be avoided by way of an international agreement or if the other Member State involved grants such advantages to taxpayers earning taxable income in its territory.[520]

In the present case, there was no international agreement on that matter, but Germany did grant Mr Imfeld a tax exemption for dependent children. Nevertheless, the Court did not consider that fact relevant because there was no correlation between tax advantages granted in Germany and the loss of the tax advantages in Belgium. According to the Court, 'the applicants in the main proceedings failed to benefit from the supplementary tax-free income allowance for dependent children, not because they benefited from an equivalent advantage in Germany, but only because the benefit of it was nullified by the rules for its offsetting'.[521] In other words, the automatic loss of tax advantage in cross-border situations constitutes a hindrance to free movement.[522]

The case law from the CJEU entails other cases concerning the exemption with progression and the consideration of resident taxpayers' ability to pay taxes. However, these cases differ from those analysed previously for two main reasons.

First, they do not concern the consideration of taxpayers' personal and family circumstances. Conversely, they regard only the assessment of their taxable income. In such cases, the residence Member State established different – and more burdensome – criteria to determine the worldwide income of resident taxpayers involved in cross-border situations than the criteria used to determine the worldwide income of those resident taxpayers engaged only in domestic activities.

Second, the exemption with progression does not lead to the disadvantageous tax treatment of resident taxpayers exercising an EU freedom of movement. On the contrary, the tax disadvantage stems directly from the national tax rule that establishes different criteria depending on whether or not resident taxpayers obtain income from abroad. However, these different and more burdensome criteria are, to some extent, dissimulated by exemption with progression, as the adverse effects of those criteria are only perceptible in the increase of the tax rate applied to domestic income.

The dissimulation of the differentiated and unfavourable tax treatment established through the exemption with progression method can be observed in the *Verest and Gerards* case.[523]

In this case, Belgium subjected all its resident taxpayers to tax on their immovable property not rented out. It differentiated between immovable property situated in its territory and abroad to determine the notional immovable property income.

519. *Ibid.*, para. 70.
520. *Ibid.*, para. 69.
521. *Ibid.*, para. 73.
522. *See supra* section 4.2.2.2.
523. CJEU, Case C-489/13 (*Verest and Gerards*).

Regarding immovable property situated in its territory, the notional income was determined based on the cadastral income. Instead, regarding immovable property situated in another State, the notional income was determined based on the rental value, which is, as a general rule, higher than the cadastral income.

The appellants were residents in Belgium and owned immovable property not rented in France. According to the applicable bilateral tax treaty, income derived from Belgian residents from immovable property in France was not taxed in Belgium. However, due to the exemption with progression applied in the case, the Belgian authorities considered such exempt income to determine the tax rate applicable to the appellants' domestic income.

The notional immovable property income determined based on the rental value, if higher than the cadastral value, increases those taxpayers' worldwide income, which leads to an increase in the average tax rate applied to those taxpayers' domestic income.

The mentioned difference in treatment provided by the residence Member State does not imply an overt disadvantage for resident taxpayers who have an immovable property not rented out abroad, as that income is exempt from tax in their residence Member State. Nevertheless, that disadvantage exists whenever the property's rental value exceeds its cadastral income.

In this regard, the CJEU considered that the difference in treatment was likely to dissuade resident taxpayers from investing in immovable property in a Member State other than their residence State, giving rise to a restriction on the free movement of capital.[524]

The Court then analysed whether the cross-border situation was comparable with the internal situation. It was true that income from immovable property in France was not taxed in Belgium, whereas income from immovable property in Belgium was included in the basis of the assessment. Notwithstanding, the income from immovable property in France was also considered in determining the tax rate applicable to income taxable in Belgium of those residents who own property in France.[525]

Consequently, taxpayers exercising an EU freedom of movement (i.e., owning property in France) and those not exercising it (i.e., owning property only in Belgium) were subject to the same tax rate. After all, the exemption with progression operates precisely to ensure that taxpayers exercising a cross-border activity do not escape the rule of progressivity in their residence State.[526]

Despite being in a comparable situation, the Belgian residents owning non-rented property in France, whenever the rental value of their property was higher than its cadastral value, were subject to a higher tax rate on their taxable income than the Belgian residents owning not rented property in Belgium.[527]

524. *Ibid.*, para. 24.
525. *Ibid.*, para. 29.
526. *Ibid.*, paras 30-31.
527. *Ibid.*, para. 32.

Any justification based on overriding reasons in the public interest was presented regarding this difference in treatment.[528]

6.1.2.2 Modified Exemption

a) The problem

The modified exemption is a variation of the exemption with progression method to eliminate international juridical double taxation, being placed halfway between the exemption and the credit method.[529]

As it happens in the exemption with progression, applying the modified exemption implies that resident taxpayers' foreign income will be considered to determine the tax rate applied to their domestic income. However, after the tax rate is determined, the foreign income is not simply excluded from the taxable income, as it happens with the exemption with progression. Instead, the residence State calculates the total domestic tax that would be due on the taxpayers' worldwide income, granting them a deduction equivalent to that part of the total tax corresponding to the domestic tax due on their foreign income.

The formula used to calculate the amount of tax to be exempt is the same formula used in the ordinary credit method. As described *supra*, in section 6.1.1.1.a), that formula consists of multiplying the total theoretical tax due in the residence State on the taxpayer's worldwide income by the ratio between the taxpayer's foreign income and the taxpayer's worldwide income.[530]

This way, the problem for EU law raised by the modified exemption is the same as observed when analysing the credit method in section 6.1.1.1.a).

Indeed, the problem is that *the total theoretical tax due in the residence State on the taxpayer's worldwide income* includes the taxpayer's benefits for his/her personal and family circumstances, which does not happen in the second part of the formula (in the ratio), regarding the *taxpayer's worldwide income*. Consequently, because the taxpayer's personal and family circumstances were considered in the first part of the formula but not in the second part (i.e., in the ratio), the taxpayer will lose part of these benefits proportionally to his/her foreign income.

b) Tax obstacle caused by the residence Member State

Within the EU framework, the residence Member State is, in this case, creating a tax obstacle to free movement.

The restrictive tax treatment arises from the fact that the Member State grants, in principle, a tax benefit to all its resident taxpayers derived from their personal and family circumstances. However, such a tax benefit is reduced whenever resident taxpayers obtain income from another State. The benefit reduction is made in the proportion of the foreign income the resident taxpayers earn.

528. *Ibid.*, para. 33.
529. *See supra* section 2.2.2.
530. The formula is illustrated in *supra* n. 495.

Because the modified exemption, by nature, is only applied in cross-border situations, the residence Member State is, de facto, treating differently resident taxpayers carrying out activities only domestically and resident taxpayers exercising an EU freedom of movement. The latter group of resident taxpayers is offered worse tax treatment, as their personal and family circumstances are not fully considered.

This unfavourable tax treatment occurs even though the two groups of resident taxpayers are comparable: both are subject to full tax liability in the residence Member State, both exercise the same activity and have the same personal and family situation.

The restrictive tax treatment created by the Member State of residence is reflected in the overtaxation of resident taxpayers exercising an EU freedom of movement compared to resident taxpayers not exercising it.

The overtaxation is not attributable to international juridical double taxation, as it was eliminated through the modified exemption.

c) Tax obstacle caused by the source Member State

As observed in sections 6.1.1.1.c) and 6.1.2.1.c), the fact that the source Member State does not grant non-residents personal and family tax benefits granted to its own resident taxpayers does not constitute a forbidden obstacle under the EU law since the two groups of taxpayers are not in a comparable situation.[531]

The incomparability of their situation derives from the fact that resident taxpayers are, as common practice, subject to full tax liability, while non-residents are subject to limited tax liability in that State. As non-residents are not subject to full tax liability in the source Member State, this State is not in a position to consider their personal and family circumstances.

As already mentioned, assessing taxpayers' overall ability to pay taxes is more effortless in the Member State, where taxpayers are subject to full tax liability because that State has all the information regarding taxpayers' aggregate income and personal and family circumstances.

d) Case law from the CJEU

The CJEU analysed the compatibility of the modified exemption with EU law in the *De Groot* case.[532]

The *De Groot* case concerned a resident in the Netherlands who derived income from his residence State and from other Member States. International juridical double taxation was eliminated through a modified exemption.[533] The way the amount of tax relief from double taxation was determined led to the loss of part of the tax personal and family benefits he was entitled to in proportion to the income he derived from

531. *See supra* section 4.2.2.1.
532. CJEU, Case C-385/00 (*De Groot*).
533. In the case, the method for eliminating double taxation is not referred to as a modified exemption. However, the description of the relief from double taxation provided does not permit to conclude otherwise. The exemption was applied by granting a reduction of income tax, computed by multiplying the tax on total income by the proportionality factor. This factor was represented by a fraction, in which the numerator was the foreign gross income and the denominator the total gross income.

abroad. Instead, if the taxpayer had earned his entire income in the Netherlands, he would have benefited fully from his personal and family circumstances.

The CJEU noted that the Dutch rules on the avoidance of international juridical double taxation entailed a tax disadvantage liable to discourage a resident taxpayer from leaving the country to take up paid employment in another Member State, concluding that those rules constituted an obstacle to freedom of movement for workers.

When analysing the possible justifications for the restrictive tax treatment, the Court stressed that the taxpayers' ability to pay, determined by reference to their aggregate income and personal and family circumstances, is easier to assess at the place where their personal and financial interests are centred. In general, that is their State of residence.[534]

The Member State of residence may be released from its obligation of considering its resident taxpayers' personal and family circumstances entirely through an international agreement or because the source Member States unilaterally grant such tax advantages to non-residents.[535] Notwithstanding, the Member States concerned must ensure taxpayers in a cross-border situation that, 'as the end result, all their personal and family circumstances will be duly taken into account, irrespective of how those Member States have allocated that obligation amongst themselves'.[536]

Furthermore, the CJEU did not consider it disproportionate to place on the State of residence the burden of granting all personal and family tax benefits to resident taxpayers, even where they have received part of their income in other Member States, which, according to the allocation rules in force, have the power to tax them. In this regard, a loss of tax revenue can never be relied upon to justify a restriction on freedom of movement within the EU.[537]

The loss of personal and family tax benefits proportional to the income the resident taxpayer obtained abroad was also analysed in the *Jacob and Lennertz* case[538] and in the *BJ v. État belge* case,[539] in which a system of exemption similar to that applied in the *De Groot* case was at issue. The CJEU reached the same conclusion about the restrictive tax treatment.

534. CJEU, Case C-385/00 (*De Groot*), para. 98.
535. *Ibid.*, paras 99 and 100. *See supra* section 4.2.2.2.
536. *Ibid.*, para. 101.
537. *Ibid.*, para. 103.
538. CJEU, Case C-174/18 (*Jacob and Lennertz*). Mr Jacob and Mrs Lennertz were residents in Belgium, where they were subject to joint assessment for income tax purposes. Mr Jacob received two pensions, one from Belgium and the other from Luxembourg. The pension from Luxembourg was exempt from taxation in Belgium under the relevant tax treaty. The couple were entitled to tax benefits in Belgium. However, due to the elimination of double taxation, part of those benefits was lost, being granted in a smaller proportion than they would be granted if the taxpayer had only received domestic income.
539. CJEU, Case C–241/20 (*BJ v. État belge*). BJ was a Belgian resident employed in Luxembourg. BJ also owned properties in Luxembourg and Belgium, which were rented. BJ's income from employment and immovable property in Luxembourg was exempt from tax in Belgium under the relevant tax treaty in force. However, due to the elimination of double taxation, the tax benefits BJ was entitled to under Belgian law were lost in proportion to his exempted income.

6.2 INCOME DERIVED (ALMOST) EXCLUSIVELY FROM THE SOURCE MEMBER STATE

6.2.1 Full Exemption and Exemption with Progression

a) The problem

Applying the full exemption or the exemption with progression for eliminating double taxation when taxpayers engaged in cross-border activities derive their income exclusively, or almost exclusively, from source Member States may lead to compatibility issues with EU law regarding the consideration of their personal and family circumstances.

Those issues arise from the fact that the residence Member State has the power to tax the worldwide income of its resident taxpayers, irrespectively from where it is derived. However, due to the elimination of international juridical double taxation, the foreign income is ignored (in the case of full exemption) or excluded from the tax base once the average tax rate corresponding to the taxpayers' worldwide income has been determined (in the case of the exemption with progression).

As these taxpayers do not have any domestic income or their domestic income is so low, there is - in practice - no taxable income in the residence Member State on which the benefits for personal and family circumstances may be applied.

This way, resident taxpayers who earn (almost) all of their income in another Member State do not have their personal and family circumstances considered in their residence Member State whenever international juridical double taxation is eliminated through full exemption or exemption with progression.

b) Tax obstacle caused by the residence Member State

In the case described above, the residence Member State does not treat resident taxpayers engaged in an EU cross-border situation worse than those in a purely internal situation. Thus, the Member State of residence does not hinder free movement within the EU.

The loss of tax advantages related to personal and family circumstances by the resident taxpayers who earn (almost) all their income in another Member State results from the fact that those residents do not have any taxable income in their residence Member State on which such tax advantages may be applied. Likewise, neither may resident taxpayers in a purely internal situation without relevant taxable income benefit from those tax advantages.

In these cases, the lack of consideration of personal and family circumstances by the residence Member State is a de facto impossibility.

c) Tax obstacle caused by the source Member State

As a rule, the fact that the source Member State does not grant non-residents personal and family tax benefits it grants to its own resident taxpayers does not constitute a forbidden tax obstacle under EU law because the two groups of taxpayers are not in a comparable situation.

The incomparability of their situations arises from the fact that, as common practice, resident taxpayers are subject to full tax liability, while non-residents are only subject to limited tax liability. In other words, as a general rule, the Member States subject their residents to worldwide taxation and non-residents to taxation on the income they earn in their territory.

There is a correlation between worldwide taxation and the consideration of taxpayers' personal and family circumstances. Usually, the State better positioned to consider taxpayers' personal and family circumstances is the State that subjects them to worldwide taxation since – due to, precisely, the worldwide taxation – that State has all the information about them and their aggregate income and, consequently, it becomes easier to assess their overall ability to pay tax. Therefore, in principle, the Member State of residence is responsible for taking all its resident taxpayers' personal and family circumstances into account.

However, as studied in more detail *supra* in section 4.2.2.1., the situation is different whenever taxpayers derive no significant income in their Member State of residence, obtaining their taxable income from another Member State.

Regarding those cases, on the one hand, the Member State of residence cannot grant taxpayers any tax advantage resulting from considering their personal and family situation, as no significant taxable income exists on which those advantages may be applied.

On the other hand, in the source Member State, the incomparability between its resident and non-resident taxpayers fades away in those cases. Non-residents indeed have only a territorial attachment with the source State. However, in the case of those taxpayers, a significant part of their vital interests is centred in that State, having a closer economic relationship with the source Member State than they have with their residence Member State.

The economic relation of those non-resident taxpayers with the source Member State is similar to the economic relation that State has with its own residents because despite those non-resident taxpayers are not formally subject to worldwide taxation in the source Member State, such worldwide taxation ends up happening in practice, all their income being subject to taxation in the source State, as they do not derive income other than from that State.

This way, in such cases, the grounds to treat resident and non-resident taxpayers differently disappear, and the source Member State incurs discrimination when it does not consider the personal and family circumstances of non-resident taxpayers' earning almost all their income from its territory whenever those personal and family circumstances are not considered elsewhere. Because those non-resident taxpayers derive (almost) all their income from the source Member State, this State is actually able to gather all the information needed to assess their overall ability to pay taxes.

As observed *supra* in section 4.2.2.1., even if non-residents taxpayers do not derive (almost) all their income from a source Member State, this Member State can be held responsible for taking into account (at least in part) their personal and family circumstances whenever those non-residents do not earn significant income in their residence Member State.

Therefore, the discrimination against non-resident taxpayers caused by the source Member State has a *relative* nature: the tax treatment the source Member State provides is not discriminatory to all non-resident taxpayers deriving income from its territory. Instead, those taxpayers' specific situation, whose personal and family circumstances cannot be considered in their residence Member State, leads to discriminatory tax treatment in the source Member State.

d) Case law from the CJEU

The landmark case in this regard is the *Schumacker* case.[540] Mr Schumacker resided in Belgium with his wife and children. He was employed in Germany, his German wages being the household's sole income. Under the Belgium–Germany tax treaty, his wages were taxed in Germany and tax-exempt in his State of residence.[541] Contrary to resident taxpayers in Germany, Mr Schumacker, as a non-resident, could not benefit from the splitting regime or deduct certain expenses related to his personal and family circumstances.

In light of the free movement of workers, the CJEU concluded that not granting such tax advantages to non-residents in such a situation constituted a discriminatory tax treatment.

In this regard, the Court clarified that the situation of residents and non-residents is not, as a rule, comparable because the income derived by a non-resident from the territory of a Member State is, in most cases, only part of his total income. Usually, taxpayers' personal and economic interests are centred in their State of residence, that State being better placed to assess their overall ability to pay tax, which mainly depends on worldwide income and personal and family circumstances. Therefore, the overall taxation of taxpayers, taking account of their personal and family circumstances, is a matter of the residence State.[542] Since residents and non-residents are not in a comparable situation, as a rule, the fact that a Member State does not grant non-residents the same personal and family tax benefits it grants its residents is not discriminatory.[543]

However, when taxpayers do not have significant income in their residence State, deriving the major part of their income from the source State, there is no objective difference in that State between the non-residents and resident taxpayers such as to justify the difference in treatment concerning taking into account taxpayers' personal and family circumstances for taxation purposes.[544]

540. CJEU, Case C-279/93 (*Schumacker*).
541. According to Art. 15(1) of the Double Taxation Treaty concluded between Belgium and Germany on 11 April 1967, when the employment is exercised in a State other than the State of residence, the remuneration derived therefrom may be taxed in that other State. In order to avoid double taxation of that income, exemption with progression was provided by Belgium under Art. 23(2)1* of the said Treaty.
542. CJEU, Case C-279/93 (*Schumacker*), paras 31-32.
543. *Ibid.*, para. 34.
544. *Ibid.*, paras 36-37.

In this regard, the Court concluded that discrimination arose because Mr Schumacker's personal and family circumstances were taken into account neither in his State of residence nor in his State of employment.[545]

Justification for this discriminatory tax treatment was based on the need for the cohesion of the tax system, as there is a link between taking into account personal and family circumstances and the right to tax worldwide income, which the source State does not have. The Court rejected this argument, repeating that the EU principle of equal treatment requires the source State to provide the same tax benefits as residents enjoy to taxpayers deriving almost all their income from its territory and whose residence Member State is not in conditions to grant them those tax benefits.[546]

Furthermore, the CJEU stressed that the source Member State could not argue administrative difficulties in ascertaining the total income of non-residents and their personal and family circumstances.[547] The Directive concerning mutual assistance provides ways of obtaining that information.[548]

The Court's position in the *Schumacker* case was followed in several other cases, which has allowed the unveiling of the scope and limits of this doctrine.

However, the lack of taxation in the residence Member State that led to discrimination in the source State due to disregarding taxpayers' personal and family circumstances does not arise from a bilateral tax treaty application in all Schumacker-like cases.[549]

In what concerns the cases where the lack of taxation in the residence Member State results from applying a tax treaty, the following cases may be highlighted.

The *Wielockx* case[550] concerned a Belgian resident self-employed in the Netherlands, where he earned his entire income. Under the relevant tax treaty, his income was taxable in the Netherlands and Belgium eliminated international juridical double taxation through the exemption with progression.[551]

The dispute arose because, under Dutch law, only resident taxpayers in the Netherlands could deduct from business income pension-reserve contributions.

Stressing that, as a rule, resident and non-resident taxpayers are not in a comparable situation, the Court stated that the lack of comparability between them

545. *Ibid.*, para. 38.
546. *Ibid.*, paras 40-42.
547. *Ibid.*, para. 45.
548. Currently, Council Directive 2011/16/EU of 15 February 2011 on administrative cooperation in the field of taxation and repealing Directive 77/799/EEC.
549. For instance, in the *Wallentin* case, the taxpayer received only a minor part of his overall income from the source State, the rest of his income being derived from Germany, his State of residence. However, his German income was tax-exempt under German domestic tax law. This way, all his taxable income was derived from the source Member State, being in a situation comparable to resident taxpayers in that State. *See* CJEU, Case C-169/03 (*Wallentin*). Other examples are the *Zurstrassen* case and the *Meindl* case, in which the source Member State did not create the Schumacker-like tax obstacle. Instead, as those cases addressed couples residing in different Member States, the tax obstacle was created by the Member State of the spouse earning the central part of the household's income. *See* CJEU, Case C-87/99 (*Zurstrassen*); CJEU, Case C-329/05 (*Meindl*).
550. CJEU, Case C-80/94 (*Wielockx*).
551. Belgium–Netherlands tax treaty to avoid double taxation of 19 October 1970, Arts 14(1) and 23(2)(1); CJEU, Case C-80/94 (*Wielockx*), para. 9.

ends when the non-resident taxpayers, whether employed or self-employed, receive all or almost all of their income in the State where they work. In such a case, the non-resident taxpayer 'is objectively in the same situation in so far as concerns income tax as a resident of that State who does the same work there. Both are taxed in that State alone and their taxable income is the same'.[552]

The Court explained further that, 'If a non-resident taxpayer is not given the same tax treatment as regards deductions from his taxable income as a resident, his personal situation will be taken into account neither by the tax authorities of the State where he works - because he is not resident there - nor by the State of residence - because he receives no income there. Consequently, his overall tax burden will be greater and he will be at a disadvantage compared to a resident.'[553]

This way, the CJEU considered Mr Wielockx was suffering discriminatory tax treatment because his situation - receiving all his income in the State where he worked - was entirely comparable to a resident's situation. However, his pension-reserve contributions were not deductible under the same conditions.[554]

Regarding the justifications for discriminatory tax treatment, the Netherlands' Government argued the principle of fiscal cohesion, according to which a correlation between deductibility and taxable income must exist. Under the relevant double taxation treaty, the Netherlands could not tax pensions received by non-residents; thus, pension-reserve contributions should not be deductible.[555]

However, the CJEU did not accept this argument, noting that the fiscal cohesion set in the relevant double taxation convention was not established 'in relation to one and the same person by a strict correlation between the deductibility of contributions and the taxation of pensions but is shifted to another level, that of the reciprocity of the rules applicable in the Contracting States'.[556]

---

552. CJEU, Case C-80/94 (*Wielockx*), para. 20. However, it has been argued that the CJEU may have misinterpreted the nature of the deduction. It should have been treated as a business deduction rather than a personal deduction, which implies that residents and non-residents are in a comparable situation, regardless of the percentage of non-residents derived from the source State. *See* K. Van Raad, *The Impact of the EC Treaty's Fundamental Freedoms Provisions on EU Member States' Taxation in Border-Crossing Situations – Current State of Affairs*, 4(4) EC Tax Rev. 190 (1995), 196 DOI: 10.54648/ecta1995031, with further references; *see also* A. Cordewener (D. Weber ed., Kluwer Law International 2007), 42.
553. CJEU, Case C-80/94 (*Wielockx*), para. 21.
554. *Ibid.*, para. 22.
555. *Ibid.*, para. 23.
556. *Ibid.*, paras 24-25. In contrast, the CJEU accepted the need to preserve the *internal* cohesion of the tax system as a justification for restrictive tax treatment in the Bachmann case [CJEU, Case C-204/90 (*Bachmann*)]. In this case, the national rule provided for the possibility of deducting life insurance premiums as long as they were paid to insurance companies established in Belgium. The Court saw in this tax treatment a restriction on the freedom of movement but accepted it because there was a correlation between the deductibility of insurance contributions and the liability to tax of sums payable by the insurers under pension and life assurance contracts. Conversely, those sums would be exempt from tax if such contributions were not deducted (paras 22-23). In contrast, in the *Wielock* case, the CJEU did not accept the argument based on the cohesion of the tax system because the State at issue had voluntarily withdrawn its taxing powers over those pensions.

The same reasoning was applied *mutatis mutandis* in the *Turpeinen* case.[557] This case concerned a Spanish resident receiving Finnish-source retirement pension payments from her earlier employment in public service there. The Finland–Spain tax treaty prevented international juridical double taxation of her pension by allocating the exclusive power to tax to Finland.[558] As Ms Turpeinen was a non-resident taxpayer, she was taxed at the flat rate of 35%, whereas residents were taxed on a progressive scale and with tax allowances to take their ability to pay tax and their personal and family circumstances into account.[559]

The Court stated that 'the objectives of simplification and transparency of the Finnish tax system for non-resident taxpayers could be achieved by measures less restrictive of the freedom of movement of citizens of the Union than a tax which could, in certain cases, prove to be higher than that applicable to resident taxpayers who receive the same income'.[560]

In the *Ritter-Coulais* case,[561] *Lakebrink and Peters-Lakebrink* case[562] and *Renneberg* case,[563] the same approach was adopted regarding the consideration of negative income from immovable property located in another Member State in the case of non-resident taxpayers deriving all their taxable income from the source Member State.

The *Ritter-Coulais* case and the *Renneberg* case concerned non-resident taxpayers employed in the source Member State as public servants, having that State's nationality. The relevant tax treaties prevented international juridical double taxation of their employment income by allocating the exclusive taxing power to the source State.[564] In the Lakebrink and Peters-Lakebrink case, both States could tax the income derived by

557. CJEU, Case C-520/04 (*Turpeinen*).
558. *Ibid.*, para. 4; *see also* Finland–Spain tax treaty to avoid double taxation of 15 November 1967, Art. 19(1).
559. CJEU, Case C-520/04 (*Turpeinen*), para. 30.
560. *Ibid.*, para. 34.
561. CJEU, Case C-152/03 (*Ritter-Coulais*). This case concerned immovable property situated in the taxpayers' Member State of residence and it addressed the recognition of rental income losses relating to taxpayers' own use of a private dwelling for the purpose of determining the tax rate applicable in the Member State of employment.
562. CJEU, Case C-182/06 (*Lakebrink and Peters-Lakebrink*). This case concerned immovable property situated in the taxpayers' Member State of residence and it addressed the consideration of negative rental income for the purpose of determining the tax rate applicable in the Member State of employment.
563. CJEU, Case C-527/06 (*Renneberg*). This case addressed the deduction in the Member State of employment of mortgage interest paid on an owner-occupied dwelling situated in the residence Member State for the purpose of determining the taxpayer's taxable base.
564. *Ritter-Coulais* case: Art. 14(1) of the Germany-France tax treaty for the avoidance of double taxation signed in Paris on 21 July 1959, as amended; Opinion of the AG Philippe Léger in Case C-152/03 (*Ritter-Coulais*), para. 5. *Renneberg* case: Art. 19(1) of the Netherlands-Belgium tax treaty for the avoidance of double taxation signed in Brussels on 19 October 1970; CJEU, Case C-527/06 (*Renneberg*), para. 5. In both cases, under the State of employment's national law (Germany in the *Ritter-Coulais* case; the Netherlands in the *Renneberg* case), these taxpayers were considered residents in that State. However, domestic provisions on residence were disregarded in favour of the tax treaties' provisions, being deemed residents in the place where they lived (France in the *Ritter-Coulais* case; Belgium in the *Renneberg* case). *See* CJEU, Case C-152/03 (*Ritter-Coulais*), para. 3; Opinion of the AG Philippe Léger in Case C-152/03 (*Ritter-Coulais*), para. 4; Case C-527/06 (*Renneberg*), para. 18.

the taxpayers from the State of employment. International juridical double taxation was avoided by the residence State through exemption with progression.[565]

In the *Ritter-Coulais* case and the *Lakebrink and Peters-Lakebrink* case, the discriminatory tax regime stemmed from the State of employment's national provisions applied to these non-residents.

In the *Ritter-Coulais* case, the domestic law prevented negative income derived from immovable property situated abroad from being considered to determine the tax rate applicable to domestic income in the absence of positive income of the same kind. Consequently, while resident taxpayers could benefit from the consideration of losses related to their own use of a private dwelling, non-residents - even when earning (almost) all their income in that State, and thus, in a comparable situation regarding resident taxpayers - could not benefit from the same tax advantage, as their private dwelling is always situated abroad.[566] The CJEU found such a tax treatment contrary to the free movement of workers and did not accept the German Government's justification of the unfavourable treatment based on the need for fiscal coherence in its national tax system.[567]

The Court did not invoke the Schumacker doctrine in the *Ritter-Coulais* case at any moment.[568] However, its reasoning implies that the appellants' situation was

565. Article 20(2) of the Germany–Luxembourg tax treaty for the avoidance of double taxation signed in Luxembourg on 23 August 1958, as amended. Because Mr and Mrs Lakebrink, residents in Germany, earned most of their taxable income in the State of employment (Luxembourg), they could apply to be taxed as resident taxpayers. What is called into question is Luxembourg's national provision extending the tax assessment for resident taxpayers to non-residents earning the majority of their income in that State.
566. CJEU, Case C-152/03 (*Ritter-Coulais*), para. 35.
567. In this regard, the Court pointed out that 'since the German tax system takes into account positive income deriving from the use of a dwelling in another Member State for the purposes of determining the rate of taxation, fiscal coherence is not a suitable justification on any ground for refusing to take into account, for the same purposes, income losses of the same kind arising in the same State' - CJEU, Case C-152/03 (*Ritter-Coulais*), para. 40. Conversely, Weber defends that 'Germany took negative income into account only for owner-occupied dwellings in Germany. Germany applied the territoriality principle equally to both resident and non-resident taxpayers', and Meussen argues that 'This is primarily a matter of consumption and a tax incentive granted in respect of a personal dwelling in one Member State should not be extended to a personal dwelling in another Member State' - D. Weber, *Cross-Border Losses: From Ritter-Coulais via Renneberg Back to Futura Participations?*, in *A Vision of Taxes Within and Outside European Borders* (L. Hinnekens & P. Hinnekens eds, Kluwer Law International 2008), 957; G. Meussen, *The Ritter-Coulais Case – A Wrong Decision in Principle by the ECJ*, 64(7) Eur. Tax'n 335 (2006), 338.
568. The Court did not follow the AG's reasoning presented in his Opinion, which was based on the implications to be drawn from the Schumacker decision. *See* Opinion of AG Léger in Case C-152/03 (*Ritter-Coulais*), para. 82-84, 94-98. AG Mengozzi considered this an 'undoubtedly deliberate omission', presenting two reasons for it. On the one hand, personal and family benefits were not at issue in this case, but rather the consideration of income losses, which are linked with a broader concept of ability to pay. On the other hand, the German tax treatment of foreign immovable property income losses was apparently neutral, as it was applied to resident and non-resident taxpayers in the absence of positive income. However, income losses relating to taxpayers' own use of a private dwelling abroad only occur, obviously, in the case of non-residents. *See* Opinion of AG Mengozzi in Case C–527/06 (*Renneberg*), paras 48-49. According to Lang, the Court did not apply the Schumacker doctrine and followed a slightly different approach because it did not establish a comparison between a non-resident and a

comparable to that of resident taxpayers in Germany, as the treatment of immovable property income received by resident taxpayers from abroad played a central role in the Court's decision. Furthermore, even if the appellants' residence Member State had the same tax regime, that State could never have considered their income losses, as all their income was derived from their employment State.

In the *Lakebrink and Peters-Lakebrink* case, the national provisions of the State of employment extending the residents' tax regime to non-residents who earned almost all their income in that State did not allow them to deduct rental income losses incurred abroad for the purpose of determining the tax rate applicable to their income. Contrary to what happened in the *Ritter-Coulais* case, the source State did not consider either positive or negative rental income when determining the tax rate applicable to those non-residents.

The Court considered the tax treatment provided to non-residents was less favourable than that to which resident taxpayers were entitled. It stressed that this disadvantageous tax treatment could not be compensated for by the fact that, in certain circumstances (for instance, when non-resident taxpayers earn positive rental income from abroad), such a tax treatment may offer a tax advantage to non-resident taxpayers.[569]

In this case, the Court expressly mentioned the Schumacker doctrine, noting that these non-residents received no income in their residence Member State, deriving all their income from the Member State of employment, and therefore, the tax treatment at issue was discriminatory since their ability to pay was not considered.[570] No justification was presented.

In the *Renneberg* case, the very interpretation of the applicable tax treaty to avoid international juridical double taxation led to discriminatory tax treatment.

Under the State of employment's tax regime, resident taxpayers could deduct the interest on debt taken on to finance a personal dwelling from their taxable income. This deduction was denied to Mr Renneberg, a non-resident who earned all his income in that State, because his dwelling was located in another Member State and, according to the relevant tax treaty, the power to tax immovable property located in that other Member State was allocated to that other State.[571]

The Court observed that the treatment of non-resident taxpayers was less advantageous than that of resident taxpayers, and the allocation of the power of taxation did not entitle the Member States to impose measures that contravene the freedoms of movement guaranteed by the EU Treaties.[572]

In this regard, the CJEU noted that the allocation of taxing powers between the States does not preclude, per se, the State of employment from taking into account

resident, but rather between a resident with foreign losses and a resident with only domestic losses – M. Lang, 18(3) EC Tax Rev. 98 (2009), 102-103. *See also* N. Bammens (C. Panayi et al. eds Elgar 2020), 170.

569. CJEU, Case C-182/06 (*Lakebrink and Peters-Lakebrink*), paras 19-24.
570. *Ibid.*, paras 33-34.
571. CJEU, Case C-527/06 (*Renneberg*), paras 39-40, 48-49.
572. *Ibid.*, 46, 50.

negative income relating to immovable property in the other State for the purposes of determining the taxable income of a non-resident who obtained all of his income in the State of employment. Indeed, regarding its residents, that State considered immovable property income (either positive or negative) derived from abroad on the taxable basis of those taxpayers, even though the power to tax is allocated to the other State.[573] Therefore, the difference in treatment provided by the State of employment depended on whether the taxpayers were residents or non-residents.

The Court then invoked the Schumacker doctrine, noticing that the appellant received no significant income in his Member State of residence, earning it exclusively from the State of employment. Consequently, his Member State of residence was not in a position to consider his negative income. Discrimination stemmed from the fact that his ability to pay was not considered in any of those States.[574]

The CJEU did not accept that this disadvantageous tax treatment arose from a disparity between the allowed deductions in the employment Member State and the residence Member State since even if both States had the same deduction system, the result would be the same: the taxpayer's ability to tax would not be considered anywhere.[575]

In turn, the *Ettwein* case[576] shows that the Schumacker doctrine also applies to Switzerland residents who earn most of their income in a Member State due to the EU-Switzerland agreement.[577]

Lastly, the Schumacker doctrine has evolved to cover the grey area cases (as it is the *X* case[578]) and borderline cases (as it is the *Commission v. Estonia* case[579]), as analysed in detail *supra*, in section 4.2.2.1.

573. *Ibid.*, paras 52-56. Welcoming the CJEU non-acceptance of the balanced allocation of taxing rights as a justification, Lang states that 'If a country voluntarily grants benefits that it was not obliged to grant under EC law to its resident taxpayers, it has to extend those benefits to all other taxpayers who are in a comparable situation. In such a case, that country may no longer refuse to do so by referring to the balanced allocation of taxing rights. If that Member State grants these benefits unilaterally in some circumstances, one may assume that it is not too concerned about preserving the balanced allocation of taxing rights' - M. Lang, 18(3) EC Tax Rev. 98 (2009), 103. Different opinion has Wattel, arguing that, in this case, 'the Court forced the non-location state (the Netherlands) where the non-resident employee did not have his personal dwelling and had not taken out a loan to finance that dwelling, to nevertheless allow for a deduction of the mortgage interest, which was totally alien to its taxing jurisdiction - obviously, the applicable tax treaty allocated, as always, all items of income in respect of real estate exclusively to the location state' - P. Wattel, 55(12) Eur. Tax'n 542 (2015), 551. According to this author, the case concerned a disparity rather than discrimination. Meussen takes the same opinion - G. Meussen, *European Union - Renneberg: ECJ Unjustifiably Expands Schumacker Doctrine to Losses from Financing of Personal Dwelling*, 54(4) Eur. Tax'n 185 (2009).
574. CJEU, Case C-527/06 (*Renneberg*), paras 65-68, 71.
575. *Ibid.*, para. 75.
576. CJEU, Case C-425/11 (*Ettwein*).
577. Agreement between the European Community and its Member States, of the one part, and the Swiss Confederation, of the other, on the free movement of persons (OJ L 114 30.4.2002, p. 6).
578. CJEU, Case C-283/15 (*X*).
579. CJEU, Case C-39/10 (*Commission v. Estonia*).

6.2.2 Ordinary Credit and Modified Exemption: Doubtful Cases

a) The problem

As observed in section 6.2.1., when taxpayers derive their income (almost) exclusively from the source Member State, and their residence Member State avoids international juridical double taxation through full exemption or exemption with progression, the source Member State is responsible for considering those non-residents' personal and family circumstances into account in the same terms as it does regarding its own residents. That obligation only arises because the residence Member State of those taxpayers cannot consider their personal and family situation due to the lack of a tax base there.

One may wonder whether the same solution is reached when the taxpayers' residence Member State eliminates international juridical double taxation through the ordinary credit or the modified exemption.

These cases are doubtful because applying those methods does not lead to the non-existence of a tax base in the residence Member State, even when taxpayers' income is derived exclusively from other Member States.

Indeed, such a tax base exists, and it includes the total income resident taxpayers earned, regardless of its origin, the domestic tax being calculated upon such a tax base. The residence Member State eliminates international juridical double taxation by granting taxpayers a deduction equivalent to the tax paid in the other State (in the case of ordinary credit) or equivalent to the part of domestic tax attributable to the income derived from the other State (in the case of the modified exemption or ordinary credit, whenever this amount is lower than the previous one).

Therefore, the application of the ordinary credit and the modified exemption to eliminate international juridical double taxation when resident taxpayers earn (almost) all their income from the source Member State does not lead to the impossibility of the residence Member State granting them benefits related to their personal and family situation.

In the residence Member State of those taxpayers, the tax base is assessed based on their worldwide income upon which the domestic tax is determined; only then is international juridical double taxation eliminated. Hence, because the benefits related to the personal and family situation are applied before the final tax determination, the residence Member State – strictly speaking – is in a position to grant those taxpayers all tax advantages related to their personal and family circumstances.

Nevertheless, this approach is remarkably *formal*. In the absence of domestic income, those resident taxpayers cannot effectively benefit from the tax advantages related to their personal and family circumstances, as the elimination of international juridical double taxation consumes the tax advantages granted.

The following example illustrates the *material loss* of benefits related to taxpayers' ability to pay whenever those taxpayers derive (almost) all their income from another Member State and the ordinary credit or the modified exemption is applied.

Two taxpayers reside in State 1, carrying out the same activity, earning the same income and having the same personal and family circumstances. One of them (Taxpayer A) exercises such an activity in a purely internal situation (in State 1), while the other (Taxpayer B) exercises it in a cross-border situation, deriving all his/her income from another Member State (State 2). A third taxpayer (Taxpayer C) resides in State 2, where he/she carries out the same activity, earns the same income and has the same personal and family circumstances as Taxpayers A and B. The total income derived by each taxpayer amounts to 100.

In State 1, the benefits regarding personal and family circumstances those resident taxpayers are entitled to amount to 10, the tax rate applicable to their taxable income is 10%, and the ordinary credit is applied to eliminate international juridical double taxation. State 2 provides the same benefits regarding personal and family circumstances and applies the same tax rate to its resident taxpayers in an equivalent situation.

The taxable income of Taxpayer A in the Member State of residence (State 1) amounts to 90 (i.e., 100 –10) and the tax due amounts to 9 (i.e., 90 × 10%). Taxpayer C has the same taxable income and pays the same tax in the Member State of residence (State 2).

In turn, Taxpayer B has a taxable income of 100 in the source Member State (State 2), as non-residents are not entitled to benefits regarding personal and family circumstances. The tax due in State 2 amounts to 10 (i.e., 100 × 10%). In the Member State of residence (State 1), the tax base is formed by his/her worldwide income (i.e., 100), being his/her taxable income of 90 (i.e., 100 –10). The tax due in State 1 is 9 (i.e., 90 × 10%). To eliminate international juridical double taxation, State 1 grants a deduction from the domestic tax due (i.e., 9) equivalent to the lower of the following amounts: the tax paid in the other Member State (i.e., 10) or the part of domestic tax attributable to the income derived from the other Member State (i.e., $9 \times \frac{100}{90}$),[580] which would amount to 9.99. Thus, in State 1, Taxpayer B has to pay a residual tax (i.e., 0.01) or even no tax (due to its residual value).

Therefore, despite international juridical double taxation being eliminated and the personal and family circumstances *formally* considered, Taxpayer B is subject to higher taxation than Taxpayers A and C. The difference in treatment derives from the fact that Taxpayer B's total income is earned in the other State, and his/her personal and family benefits were not effectively granted in his/her residence State, as no domestic income existed on which they could actually be applied.

The same result would be reached if the modified exemption had been used, as its formula is similar to the ordinary credit.

For the sake of clarity, the example is summarised in Table 6.2.

580. The ratio between the taxpayer's foreign income and the taxpayer's worldwide income was determined in a non-restrictive way by considering the taxpayer's personal and family circumstances in the denominator.

Table 6.2 Consequences of the Ordinary Credit and Modified Exemption on the Consideration of Personal and Family Circumstances when Taxpayers Derive All Their Income from the Source State

	Taxpayer A	*Taxpayer B*	*Taxpayer C*
Worldwide income	100	100	100
Personal and family benefits	10	10	10
Income derived from State 1	100 (his/her residence State)	- (his/her residence State)	-
Income derived from State 2	-	100 (the source State)	100 (his/her residence State)
Tax due in the source State (10%)	-	100 × 10% = **10**	-
Tax due in the residence State (10%);	100 – 10 = 90 90 × 10% = **9**	100 – 10 = 90 90 × 10% = **9**	100 – 10 = 90 90 × 10% = **9**
Tax deduction for the elimination of double taxation	-	The lower of the following amounts: - **10**; or - 9 × (100/90) = **9.99**	
Total tax paid	**9** (residence State)	0,01 (residence State) + 10 (source State) = **10.01** (in total)	**9** (residence State)

b) Tax obstacle caused by the residence Member State

In the case described above, the Member State of residence should not, in principle, be regarded as creating an obstacle to free movement. It does not grant different and more burdensome tax treatment to taxpayers engaged in an EU cross-border situation earning (almost) all their income abroad than the one it offers to resident taxpayers in a purely internal situation.

On the one hand, the residence Member State eliminates international juridical double taxation, not taxing again an income already taxed in another Member State. Consequently, the extra burden suffered by the resident taxpayers engaged in an EU cross-border situation earning (almost) all their income abroad cannot be attributed to double taxation.

On the other hand, the residence Member State formally grants those taxpayers all tax advantages related to their personal and family circumstances. However, they do not benefit effectively from such tax advantages, as there is no domestic income forming a tax base on which they could be applied. Therefore, the residence Member

State cannot be held responsible for the lack of material consideration of those taxpayers' ability to pay.

However, the case may differ when the residence Member State subjects married couples to joint taxation, and one household member derives income entirely from abroad while the other obtains domestic income. In such a case, the argument that there is no tax base on which personal and family circumstances may be fully considered ceases to be true if the couple has sufficient domestic income. In this case, the residence Member State restricts free movement when it does not fully consider the personal and family circumstances of the household members subject to joint taxation.

c) Tax obstacle caused by the source Member State

As explained above, residents and non-residents are not, as a rule, in a comparable situation. Consequently, as a rule, the Member States are not obliged to grant non-resident taxpayers benefits regarding their personal and family circumstances.

The situation is different whenever taxpayers derive most of their income from a Member State other than the one in which they reside.

In those cases, the incomparability between resident and non-resident taxpayers fades away in that State since those non-residents' worldwide income is subject to taxation in that State to the same extent as its resident taxpayers' worldwide income.

Under these circumstances, the source Member State incurs discrimination when it does not consider the personal and family circumstances of non-resident taxpayers' earning almost all their income from its territory, whenever those personal and family circumstances were not considered elsewhere.

This last requirement - i.e., lack of consideration of personal and family circumstances elsewhere - should only be regarded as met when such attribution occurs in material terms, allowing the taxpayer to effectively benefit from the tax advantages granted. Consequently, it should not be deemed fulfilled when there is no domestic tax base in the Member State of residence on which those tax advantages could *effectively* be applied.

d) Case law from the CJEU

Up to now, there is no case law from the CJEU explicitly addressing the issue of taxpayers earning (almost) all their income in another Member State and international juridical double taxation being eliminated through the ordinary credit or modified exemption, leading to merely formal consideration of those taxpayers' personal and family circumstances in the residence Member State.

Nonetheless, this issue seems to have caused, at least in part, the disadvantage suffered by the taxpayers in the *Gilly* case.[581] Indeed, Mrs Gilly did not earn any domestic income, deriving all her income from another Member State. In order to eliminate international juridical double taxation, her State of residence applied a 'tax credit mechanism', which was, in reality, equivalent to the modified exemption.[582] The application of this method led to the loss of personal and family circumstances Mrs

581. CJEU, Case C-336/96 (*Gilly*). *See supra* section 5.1.3.
582. *See supra* n. 448.

Gilly was entitled to in her residence Member State, despite these circumstances being formally granted to her. However, in this case, this disadvantage was not self-evident because, on the one hand, the tax rates in the other Member State were higher than in the residence Member State, and, on the other hand, the spouses were subject to joint taxation in the residence Member State, meaning that the loss of personal and family tax benefits occurred in the proportion of Mrs Gilly's income.[583]

As mentioned in section 5.1.3., the CJEU did not approach this issue in the *Gilly* case because the preliminary question was on the compatibility with EU law of the credit mechanism per se.

One may wonder what would be the stance of the CJEU on the case of a taxpayer earning all his/her income in another Member State and international juridical double taxation being eliminated through the ordinary credit or modified exemption, leading to merely formal consideration of that taxpayer's personal and family circumstances in the residence Member State.

It is settled case law that 'in the case of a non-resident who receives the major part of his income and almost all his family income in a Member State other than that of his residence, discrimination arises from the fact that his personal and family circumstances are taken into account neither in the State of residence nor in the State of employment'.[584]

For the EU freedoms of movement to be effectively guaranteed, tackling tax obstacles cannot be done through formal approaches. It is difficult to believe that the Court could admit that a taxpayer who exercises the right to free movement would be prevented from benefiting from the tax advantages related to his/her personal and family situation simply because those tax advantages were *theoretically* granted somewhere.

In such cases, the taxpayer does not benefit from the personal and family allowances he/she is entitled to, as those allowances are neutralised by the elimination of double taxation in the residence Member State. Therefore, the taxpayer's intangible economic strength is disregarded in the absence of *material* consideration of his/her personal and family circumstances somewhere, which seems inadmissible in light of human dignity, which is one of the fundamental values of the EU.[585]

6.3 THE RELEVANCE OF INDIVIDUALS' ABILITY TO PAY TAXES

Throughout the previous sections, it becomes clear that despite not being obliged to eliminate international juridical double taxation, the Member States cannot undermine

583. *See* P. Wattel, 60(6) Eur. Tax'n 210 (2000), 218-222, and N. Bammens (IBFD 2012), 615-618, who calculate the disadvantage suffered in the *Gilly* case for the loss of personal and family tax benefits.

584. CJEU, Case C-279/93 (*Schumacker*), para. 38; Case C-169/03 (*Wallentin*), para. 17; Case C-182/06 (*Lakebrink and Peters-Lakebrink*), para. 31; Case C-527/06 (*Renneberg*), para. 62; Case C-9/14 (*Kieback*), para. 26; Case C-632/13 (*Hirvonen*), para. 34; Case C-283/15 (*X*), paras 38-39.

585. *See supra* section 4.2.2.1.

the consideration of taxpayers' personal and family circumstances when they decide to eliminate double taxation.

In the cases analysed, the discriminatory or restrictive tax treatment arises from disregarding personal and family circumstances of taxpayers exercising an EU freedom of movement when those circumstances are considered in comparable purely internal situations.

Those cases confirm that the CJEU gives absolute priority to having taxpayers' personal and family circumstances considered *somewhere* within the EU, as previously analysed in Chapter 4.

The obligation to consider taxpayers' personal and family circumstances belongs, as a rule, to the residence Member State.

However, when that Member State is not in a position to consider these due to the lack of a taxable base on which the personal and family tax benefits may be applied, the source Member State must assume that obligation.

After all, the consideration of personal and family circumstances entails the protection of taxpayers' intangible economic strength intended to satisfy personal and family existential needs. The CJEU aims to ensure that when all the Member States involved in a given situation protect that intangible economic strength at a tax level, the exercise of an EU freedom of movement does not jeopardise that protection.

Therefore, the CJEU adopts an overall approach,[586] accepting that the discrimination caused by the source Member State due to the lack of consideration of non-residents' personal and family circumstances has a relative nature. That obstacle to free movement attributable to the source Member State depends on the concrete situation of the taxpayer in his/her Member State of residence.

6.4 CONCLUDING AND SUMMARISING REMARKS

After examining in Chapter 5 that international juridical double taxation is compatible with EU law despite undermining taxpayers' ability to pay, this chapter addresses the CJEU's decisions on cases in which taxpayers' ability to pay was undermined in the process of eliminating international juridical double taxation.

In effect, EU Law does not require the elimination of international juridical double taxation, but if the Member States decide to eliminate it, they must comply with EU Law, meaning they cannot hinder free movement in a discriminatory or restrictive way.

In the cases analysed, the discriminatory and restrictive treatment arose from the lack of consideration of taxpayers' personal and family circumstances when applying

586. E. Kemmeren (L. Hinnekens & P. Hinnekens eds, Kluwer Law International 2008), 561-562 and 568; A. García Prats (I. Richelle et al. eds, Springer 2013), 9; M. C. Barreiro Carril (Instituto de Estudios Fiscales 2012), 374-375; S. van Thiel, 48(7) Eur. Tax'n 339 (2008), 340. As synthesised by Barreiro Carril, 'per-country' and 'overall' approaches generally refer to the methodologies adopted by the CJEU when analysing discrimination and restrictions under the EU Treaties, although other names may be used to refer to these approaches – cf. M. C. Barreiro Carril, 38(2) Intertax 105 (2010), 105.

the credit method or the exemption method to eliminate international juridical double taxation.

It is observed that *(i)* the fact of whether or not taxpayers obtain income in the State of residence and *(ii)* the particular method applied by this State to avoid double taxation have a significant impact on which State must bear the obligation to take into account taxpayers' personal and family circumstances. If that State does not consider personal and family circumstances in cross-border situations when it considers them in purely internal situations, it breaches EU Law by hindering free movement.

In principle, as already analysed in Chapter 4, considering taxpayers' personal and family circumstances is a matter of the residence State.

Therefore, the Court does not accept that by applying the credit and the exemption methods to eliminate double taxation, the Member State of residence may avoid its obligation to take full account of personal and family circumstances when taxing residents engaged in cross-border activities.

This restrictive tax treatment contrary to EU law was addressed by the CJEU in cases involving the application of ordinary credit, exemption with progression and modified exemption.

The CJEU dealt with the restrictive tax treatment arising from the application of the ordinary credit in the *Beker* case and the application of the modified exemption in the *De Groot* case, the *Jacob and Lennertz* case and the *BJ v. État belge* case. In these cases, the formula used to calculate the amount of tax credit/the amount to be exempt led to the loss of personal and family tax benefits in proportion to taxpayers' foreign income.

The Court addressed the restrictive tax treatment arising from the application of the exemption with progression in the *Bechtel* case and the *Imfeld and Garcet* case. In these cases, the restrictive tax treatment resulted from the combination of this method to eliminate double taxation with apparently neutral domestic tax rules. Although the domestic rules at stake did not distinguish between resident taxpayers who carried out purely internal activities and those who carried out cross-border activities, the regime they established led to the loss of personal and family benefits when the exemption with progression was also applied, which, by nature, only applies to cross-border situations.

In parallel, in the *Verest and Gerards* case, it is also noted that the application of the exemption with progression – although not creating the restrictive tax treatment – dissimulated the adverse effects of national tax rules that established different and more burdensome criteria for resident taxpayers who obtain income from abroad than those applied to resident taxpayers who obtain only domestic income. In such a case, the disadvantageous tax treatment was perceptible in the increase in the tax rate applied to the domestic income of those taxpayers who also obtain income from abroad.

In all these cases of restrictive tax treatment deriving from the application of ordinary credit, exemption with progression and modified exemption, the residence Member State limits its tax jurisdiction by not taxing income resident taxpayers obtain in another Member State. Nonetheless, the residence Member State is still responsible for considering those residents' personal and family circumstances. In other words, the obligation to consider residents' personal and family circumstances remains even when the residence Member State does not tax their worldwide income.

That may be explained by the simple fact that although there is a correlation between being subject in a Member State to taxation on worldwide income and having personal and family circumstances considered in that State, personal and family tax benefits are not connected with the income derived by taxpayers but rather with their personal and family situation. And taxpayers' personal and family situation does not vary according to the origin of their income.

As seen in Chapter 4, as residents who exercise free movement and residents who do not are comparable to each other, the residence Member State must fully consider all their personal and family circumstances, regardless of the source of their income.

The residence Member State may be released from such an obligation in only a few situations: *(i)* in the case of an international agreement allocating that obligation to another Member State; *(ii)* in the case of the source Member State unilaterally considering personal and family circumstances of non-residents; and *(iii)* in the case the residence Member State being de facto prevented from considering residents' personal and family circumstances.

The third scenario occurs when taxpayers derive their total income (almost) exclusively from the source Member State, and there is not enough income in their residence Member State to which tax benefits for personal and family circumstances may be applied.

As examined in Chapter 4 and confirmed in the present Chapter, the CJEU gives absolute priority to the consideration of taxpayers' personal and family circumstances. Therefore, the source Member State incurs discrimination when it does not consider the personal and family circumstances of non-resident taxpayers deriving almost all their income from its territory whenever those circumstances are not considered elsewhere.

We notice that the discrimination against non-resident taxpayers caused by the source Member State, in this case, has a *relative* nature, as it is the particular situation of those taxpayers in the residence Member State that leads to discriminatory tax treatment in the other Member State. In other words, because those taxpayers do not derive income from the residence Member State, the source Member State breaches EU law when taxing them without considering their personal and family circumstances.

The CJEU has already addressed this discriminatory tax treatment in cases involving the application of full exemption and exemption with progression, as has been observed in the *Schumacker* case, *Wielockx* case, *Turpeinen* case, *Ritter-Coulais* case, *Lakebrink and Peters-Lakebrink* case, *Renneberg* case, *Ettwein* case and *X* case.

In those cases, the fact that those taxpayers had earned no income in the residence Member State, together with the application of the full exemption or exemption with progression, led to the complete absence of taxable income in the residence Member State.

However, we wonder whether the CJEU would reach the same conclusion if international juridical double taxation had been eliminated through the ordinary credit or the modified exemption.

In such cases, there is a tax base in the residence Member State, which includes the total income resident taxpayers earned, regardless of its origin. The residence Member State's tax is calculated based on that tax base, and double taxation is only eliminated once the domestic tax attributable to the income derived from the other State has been determined. Consequently, when a taxpayer earns all his/her income from the source Member State, the application of the ordinary credit and the modified exemption to eliminate double taxation does not imply the non-existence of a tax base in the residence Member State on which tax benefits related to personal and family situation may be applied.

Nevertheless, we argue that this approach is remarkably *formal*. In the absence of domestic income, the resident cannot effectively benefit from the tax advantages related to his/her personal and family circumstances, as the elimination of double taxation consumes the tax advantages granted.

It is hard to believe that the CJEU could admit that taxpayers exercising their right to free movement would be prevented from benefiting from the tax advantages related to their personal and family situation simply because their personal and family circumstances were *theoretically* considered somewhere. After all, personal and family circumstances represent taxpayers' intangible economic strength, and the free movement ensured within the EU internal market cannot jeopardise taxpayers' human dignity, which is one of the fundamental values of the EU.

We sustain that in those cases, the source Member State must take into account the personal and family circumstances of taxpayers earning (almost) all their income from its territory because the residence Member State cannot consider those circumstances *effectively*. However, the situation is different in cases where the residence Member State subjects couples to joint taxation, and one household member derives income entirely from abroad while the other obtains domestic income. If the couple has sufficient domestic income in the residence Member State, that State restricts free movement when it does not fully consider the personal and family circumstances of the household members subject to joint taxation.

CHAPTER 7
Final Assessment

– Reframing the problem of international juridical double taxation by adopting an ability-to-pay perspective of the issue.

– International juridical double taxation as resulting from a Member State's exercise of taxing powers in a discriminatory or restrictive way.

– Assessment of the consequences and challenges of perceiving international juridical double taxation from an ability-to-pay perspective.

7.1 REFRAMING THE PROBLEM OF INTERNATIONAL JURIDICAL DOUBLE TAXATION

Throughout this research, we have come across a paradox. The Member States do not breach EU law if they do not eliminate international juridical double taxation, even though it undermines taxpayers' ability to pay. However, the Member States breach EU law if they undermine taxpayers' ability to pay in the process of eliminating international juridical double taxation.

Notwithstanding, there is no contradiction in the reasoning followed by the CJEU in its case law.

Regarding direct taxation, the EU Treaties do not constrain the Member States' power to tax. This power to tax is only limited by a few Directives in particular areas and by the general EU Treaty provisions that forbid discrimination and restrictions on free movement.

Therefore, the Member States are sovereign in defining their tax jurisdiction and configuring their tax systems.

International juridical double taxation is a consequence of the overlap of tax jurisdictions. Since the Member States are not bound by any general EU provision regarding the definition of their tax jurisdiction, that overlap is not contrary to EU law. Furthermore, the definition of tax jurisdiction only sets *to what extent* a State may exercise their taxing power over taxpayers. It says nothing about *how* those taxing powers will be *exercised*. Therefore, the definition of tax jurisdiction does not imply the exercise of taxing powers in a discriminatory or restrictive way against taxpayers making use of an EU freedom of movement.

Thus, the CJEU, by adopting a jurisdictional perspective of the problem as observed in Chapter 5, concludes that the overtaxation suffered by taxpayers engaged in cross-border activities, in the case of international juridical double taxation, stems from the cumulative effect of being subject to tax in a non-discriminatory way in two Member States on the same item of income. Although undermining taxpayers' ability to pay, that disadvantage does not constitute a forbidden obstacle to free movement because it is a consequence of Member States' definition of tax jurisdiction and does not entail a discriminatory or restrictive tax treatment.

In turn, the Member States are also sovereign to limit their taxing powers to eliminate international juridical double taxation. The problem for EU law arises only when the elimination of international juridical double taxation implies disregarding tax benefits related to personal and family circumstances when those benefits are granted in purely internal situations.

The EU Treaty provisions prevent the Member States from hindering free movement by exercising their taxing powers in a discriminatory or restrictive way. Discriminatory or restrictive tax treatment is deemed to occur when a Member State treats worse taxpayers exercising an EU freedom of movement than taxpayers not exercising it when they are in a comparable situation. That is to say, if a Member State decides to grant taxpayers certain tax benefits, it cannot deny them just because taxpayers have exercised their right to free movement.

Accordingly, the CJEU maintains that the overtaxation derived from the loss of tax benefits related to personal and family circumstances in the process of eliminating double taxation constitutes a discriminatory or restrictive tax treatment because these tax benefits are granted to taxpayers engaged in purely internal activities in a comparable situation. Such a tax disadvantage thus entails a forbidden obstacle to free movement under EU law.

From the analysis carried out in Chapter 6, a particularity is evident concerning these cases in which taxpayers' ability to pay is undermined in the process of eliminating double taxation.

On the one hand, when taxpayers derive their total income partially from their Member State of residence and partially from another Member State, the disadvantage they suffer is created by the intentional and unilateral action of the Member State of residence by applying the methods for eliminating double taxation in a way meant to reduce the consideration of their personal and family circumstances.

On the other hand, when the taxpayers derive their total income from (a) source Member State(s), the disadvantage they suffer is not caused by any Member State's intentional and unilateral action. Indeed, the residence Member State cannot consider those taxpayers' personal and family circumstances because it has eliminated international juridical double taxation and, consequently, there is no taxable base on which personal and family tax benefits may be applied. The source Member State(s) is(are) only obliged to consider those non-resident taxpayers' personal and family circumstances because those circumstances cannot be considered in their residence Member State.

In this last case, it is the fact that the Member State of residence eliminates international juridical double taxation, combined with the factual situation of a taxpayer (i.e., deriving no domestic income), that leads to discriminatory tax treatment in the source Member State(s).

As explained in Chapter 4, the decision to consider the source Member State responsible for taking into account taxpayers' personal and family circumstances whenever they cannot be duly taken into account in the residence Member State proves the CJEU attributes absolute priority to having taxpayers' personal and family circumstances taken into account *somewhere*.

That may be explained by the fact that expenses related to personal and family circumstances represent what each Member State defines as taxpayers' intangible economic strength intended to satisfy existential needs. When all the Member States involved in a given situation protect that intangible economic strength at a tax level, the CJEU aims to ensure that the exercise of taxpayers' right to free movement does not jeopardise that protection.

By the same token, one wonders why, when all the Member States involved in a given situation tax taxpayers according to their overall ability to pay, the consideration of their overall ability to pay may be disregarded when taxpayers exercise free movement. For instance, that is the case whenever international juridical double taxation is not eliminated within the EU.[587]

Suppose there are no unilateral measures nor a tax treaty to avoid international juridical double taxation between two Member States. The residence Member State subjects all its residents to worldwide taxation, taxing all their income even when derived from abroad, while the source Member State subjects non-residents to tax on the income derived from its territory. Their tax jurisdictions overlap, leading to double taxation of a taxpayer residing in the first State and deriving income from the second State.

That taxpayer exercises his/her right to free movement by carrying out an activity cross-border. His/her economic strength is the same as a taxpayer who derives the same income by carrying out the same domestic activity in any of those Member States.

Each Member State taxes that taxpayer's income according to the ability to pay they consider it represents. The tax due in each State represents a burden on that income derived, reducing the taxpayer's economic strength.

As the Member States involved ignore the tax that is also due in the other Member State by the taxpayer, each Member State is taxing an artificial economic strength, as they are not considering the decrease in his/her economic strength caused by the tax liability in the other Member State.

587. García Prats has already highlighted the 'need to confront whether in some cases it is possible to deepen the possible theoretical analysis of legal constraints under EU Law to alleviate international double taxation'. According to this author, 'some EU Member states consider that imposing double tax on the same taxable fact without proper mechanisms to alleviate it violates the ability to pay principle. Extending such mechanism at a cross-border level would allow the ECJ to evaluate whether a specific country inflicts a restrictive treatment contrary to the consolidation of a single market' – A. García Prats (I. Richelle et al. eds, Springer 2013), 23.

This way, the taxpayer in the comparable purely internal situation bears a total tax according to his/her overall ability to pay, determined based on his/her actual economic strength. In contrast, the taxpayer in the cross-border situation bears a total tax that does not match his/her overall ability to pay because the loss of economic strength is not considered in any of the Member States involved.

There is, thus, a tax disadvantage suffered by taxpayers exercising free movement that does not occur in the case of taxpayers not exercising it. Nevertheless, ascertaining whether the unequal tax treatment may be attributable to one of the Member States involved is more delicate.

In such a situation, the source Member States is not, in principle, in a position to take those taxpayers' overall ability to pay into account because non-residents are only subject to limited tax liability. According to the CJEU's case law, as long as non-residents are not comparable to residents, the source Member State is not obliged, under EU law, to consider their overall ability to pay in the same way it does regarding its residents.[588]

By contrast, the residence Member State is, as a rule, responsible for taking its residents' overall ability to pay into account because that State generally has available all the information needed to assess it since that is where those taxpayers' personal and financial interests are centred.[589]

It may be argued that in the case at stake, the residence Member State does not treat the taxpayer engaged in the cross-border activity worse than the taxpayer pursuing the same activity domestically, *at least formally*. In that State, all residents are taxed on the same terms, i.e., according to their ability to pay, which is defined based on their economic strength. The way taxpayers' ability to pay is ascertained is defined by the residence Member State and applied equally to all resident taxpayers, irrespective of the source of their income.

Therefore, in principle, it seems there is no unequal tax treatment in the residence Member State.

However, it is worth recalling the Court's settled case law, according to which discrimination can arise through *applying different rules to comparable situations or applying the same rule to different situations.*[590]

---

588. CJEU, Case C-279/93 (*Schumacker*), para. 34; Case C-80/94 (*Wielockx*), para. 18; Case C-107/94 (*Asscher*), para. 41; Case C-391/97 (*Gschwind*), para. 23; Case C-234/01 (*Gerritse*), para. 44; Case C-169/03 (*Wallentin*), paras 15-16; Case C-520/04 (*Turpeinen*), paras 26-27; Case C-329/05 (*Meindl*), para. 23; Case C-383/05 (*Talotta*), para. 19; Case C-182/06 (*Lakebrink and Peters-Lakebrink*), paras 28-29; Case C-527/06 (*Renneberg*), para. 59; Case C–39/10 (*Commission v. Estonia*), para. 49; Case C-425/11 (*Ettwein*), paras 45-46; Case C-9/14 (*Kieback*), para. 22; Case C-632/13 (*Hirvonen*), paras 31-32; Case C-283/15 (*X*), para. 31.
589. CJEU, Case C-279/93 (*Schumacker*), paras 32-33; Case C-391/97 (*Gschwind*), para. 22; Case C-87/99 (*Zurstrassen*), para. 21; Case C-385/00 (*De Groot*), para. 90; Case C-234/01 (*Gerritse*), para. 43; Case C-169/03 (*Wallentin*), para. 15; Case C-520/04 (*Turpeinen*), para. 27; Case C-329/05 (*Meindl*), para. 23; Case C-425/11 (*Ettwein*), para. 45; Case C-168/11 (*Beker*), para. 43; Case C-303/12 (*Imfeld and Garcet*), para. 43; Case C-9/14 (*Kieback*), para. 22; Case C-632/13 (*Hirvonen*), para. 31; Case C-283/15 (*X*), para. 30; Case C-20/16 (*Bechtel*), para. 55; Case C-174/18 (*Jacob and Lennertz*), para. 26; Case C–241/20 (*BJ v. État belge*), para. 25.
590. *See, e.g.*, CJEU, Case C-279/93 (*Schumacker*), para. 30; Case C-80/94 (*Wielockx*), para. 17; Case C-391/97 (*Gschwind*), para. 21; Case C-329/05 (*Meindl*), para. 22; Case C-383/05 (*Talotta*),

In the residence Member State, *the same rule* applies to *different situations*.

The *same rule* is that which establishes the standard taxation of resident taxpayers, under which their worldwide income is subject to tax and their ability to pay is considered accordingly.

The *different situations* to which the same rule is applied are that of residents deriving only domestic income and residents deriving income from abroad without relief from international juridical double taxation.

Regarding taxpayers deriving income domestically, the standard taxation of residents fits perfectly: all their income is subject to tax, and that tax is calculated according to their ability to pay. Because they are not subject to an equivalent tax burden elsewhere, their total income utterly mirrors their *overall ability to pay*.

However, the situation of taxpayers deriving income from abroad without relief from double taxation differs from the former because they are also subject to equivalent taxation in another Member State. The standard taxation of resident taxpayers - by which worldwide income is subject to taxation and tax is ascertained based on their ability to pay - leads to unequal treatment of those residents because the tax liability in another Member State is ignored. Those taxpayers' total income does not mirror their *overall ability to pay*, as their economic strength is reduced by the tax burden also due in another Member State.

Therefore, when a Member State taxes resident taxpayers deriving income from abroad without taking the tax burden borne in the other Member State into account, the Member State of residence is taxing an *artificial* economic strength that does not represent those taxpayers' overall ability to pay.[591] In contrast, resident taxpayers who do not derive income from abroad are taxed on their *actual* economic strength, and consequently, their overall ability to pay is fully considered.

The tax disadvantage the taxpayers engaged in cross-border activities suffer may thus be attributable to the residence Member State, and it stems from the application of the same rule to different situations, which leads to restricting free movement within the EU.

From this perspective, the issue is no longer whether international juridical double taxation is compatible with EU law but whether disregarding taxpayers' overall ability in cross-border situations is in accordance with EU law by entailing a Member State's exercise of taxing powers in a discriminatory or restrictive way.

para. 18; Case C-182/06 (*Lakebrink and Peters-Lakebrink*), para. 27; Case C-440/08 (*Gielen*), para. 38; Case C–39/10 (*Commission v. Estonia*), para. 48; Case C-9/14 (*Kieback*), para. 21; Case C-632/13 (*Hirvonen*), para. 30; Case C-283/15 (*X*), para. 29.

591. *See*, in the same sense, H. Kube (A. Rust ed., Kluwer Law International 2011), 65, who, adopting a constitutional perspective, affirms that 'it appears inadequate to simply ignore the source state taxation of foreign source income when taxing in the state of residence. In other words, the source state taxation does constitute a relevant difference between foreign source income and domestic income that has to be taken into account in order to comply with the constitutional guarantee of equality. A resident taxpayer who has foreign source income and who has been subject to source state taxation therefore has an effectively lower ability to pay in the sense of the constitutional law principle than a taxpayer who has the same gross income domestically'.

As observed throughout this research, the CJEU's case law on the consideration of expenses related to economic activity and expenses related to taxpayers' personal and family circumstances shows that the Court seeks to ensure that individuals are taxed on their net income within the EU, provided that internal situations are taxed in the same way by the Member States involved.

Moreover, the concrete situation of the taxpayer in another Member State is not irrelevant in what concerns the consideration of taxpayers' ability to pay. For instance, the source Member State is deemed responsible for taking taxpayers' personal and family circumstances into account when the residence Member State cannot consider those circumstances.

This way, it is not unreasonable to sustain that the residence Member State cannot disregard the taxpayer's situation in the other Member State when assessing his/her overall ability to pay. In other words, the residence Member State cannot ignore another Member State's tax on the taxpayer's income to the extent that it decreases his/her economic strength.

Nevertheless, this ability-to-pay perspective of the issue of unrelieved double taxation does not seek to foster an EU concept of ability to pay; quite the opposite. Each Member State has the power to implement it and to adopt the configuration and techniques they consider the most appropriate to tax fairly. The fair amount of tax due must always be found in the interaction of the ability-to-pay principle with other constitutional principles, values and purposes. Consequently, ascertaining which should be the fair amount of tax due by each taxpayer may only be defined by each Member State alone.

Therefore, the ability-to-pay perspective proposed regarding the cases of unrelieved international juridical double taxation within the EU does not intend to interfere with Member States' criteria for establishing the fair amount of tax due by each taxpayer but to ensure that those criteria are applied substantively in an EU context.

In this regard, when establishing each resident taxpayer's fair amount of tax due, the Member State sets a ceiling for its own taxation.[592] As a self-imposed limit for taxation, that ceiling must have relevance in the EU context, meaning that it must be computed as also comprising the equivalent tax due in the other Member States. As Lang and Englisch point out, 'each national concept of ability to pay must be reconsidered from a cross-border perspective'.[593]

However, when the tax due in the other Member State is higher than that due in the residence Member State, this State must not be obliged to reimburse the taxpayer, as it is only bound to not tax beyond the self-imposed limit. In such a case, that overtaxation does not stem from a breach of said obligation.

Perceiving international juridical double taxation from an ability-to-pay perspective presents other challenges.

592. In a similar sense, J. Englisch, 33(8/9) Intertax 310 (2005), 352.
593. J. Lang & J. Englisch (A. Amatucci ed., Kluwer Law International 2d ed. 2012), 279. *See also* S. van Thiel, *Removal of Income Tax Barriers to Market Integration in the European Union: Litigation by the Community Citizen Instead of Harmonisation by the Community Legislature*, 12(1) EC Tax Rev. 4 (2003), 13 DOI: 10.54648/ecta2003002.

On the one hand, the obstacle to free movement caused by the residence Member State not considering taxpayers' overall ability to pay due to disregarding the tax burden in the other Member State is not triggered by a concrete tax provision. It is a restriction caused by that State's tax system, i.e., a systemic restriction to free movement.

By entailing a restriction on free movement, this systemic tax obstacle may be subject to the CJEU's scrutiny, which is competent to assess its compatibility with EU law, weighing the possible justification reasons put forward by the Member States and their proportionality.

Nevertheless, due to the enormous complexity inherent to a systemic tax obstacle, it is necessary to acknowledge that the most operational way of dealing with it and ensuring, at the same time, legal certainty is through positive regulation at the EU level.

Therefore, this matter should be regulated through a Directive that imposes a subsidiary method for eliminating international juridical double taxation whenever it is not effectively eliminated within the EU. In other words, where there is no tax treaty in place, there are no applicable unilateral measures, or those means fail to avoid double taxation, the Member States should be obliged to apply the ordinary credit method[594] or the exemption method. That choice should be left to the Member State responsible for overcoming the restrictive tax treatment, as both methods ensure that the tax disadvantage is overcome.

On the other hand, there is a substantial difference between requesting a Member State to take into account taxpayers' ability to pay in cases concerning expenses related to economic activity and personal and family circumstances and to take into account taxpayers' overall ability to pay in cases concerning unrelieved international juridical double taxation.

Considering expenses related to economic activity and personal and family circumstances, in principle, does not preclude taxation; at most, it decreases the tax burden in that Member State. Conversely, considering taxpayers' overall ability to pay in cases of unrelieved double taxation may prevent that Member State from taxing income derived from abroad.

It is arguable whether this substantial difference could justify different handling of cases of unrelieved double taxation at the EU level.

According to the settled case law, the loss of tax revenue can never be relied upon to justify measures contrary to exercising an EU freedom of movement.[595] Moreover, the need to safeguard the balanced allocation between the Member States of the power

594. The full tax credit may also be applied to overcome double taxation. Under this method, taxpayers are entitled to deduct from the tax determined in their residence State an amount equal to the income tax paid in the other State, which may be higher than the tax due in their residence State. The Court has already noted that the Member States cannot be required to grant a tax credit greater than the fraction of their national tax corresponding to the income from abroad because, otherwise, they would have to reduce their tax in respect of the remaining income. *See* CJEU, Case C-336/96 (*Gilly*), para. 48.

595. *See, e.g.*, CJEU, Case C-385/00 (*De Groot*), para. 103; CJEU, Case C-446/03 (*Marks & Spencer*), para. 44; CJEU, Case C-386/04 (*Centro di Musicologia Walter Stauffer*), para. 59; CJEU, Joined Cases C-436/08 and C-437/08 (*Haribo Lakritzen Hans Riegel*), para. 126.

to tax may only be invoked as a justification when the tax treatment in question is designed to prevent conduct capable of jeopardising the right of a Member State to exercise its fiscal jurisdiction concerning activities carried out in its territory.[596] Considering taxpayers' overall ability to pay in cases of unrelieved international juridical double taxation does not restrict, in any way, the Member States' power to tax activities carried out in their territory.

596. *See, e.g.*, CJEU, Case C-168/11 (*Beker*), para. 57; CJEU, Case C-303/12 (*Imfeld and Garcet*), para. 75.

General Conclusions

The present research aimed to ponder whether international juridical double taxation may be perceived as entailing a tax disadvantage for taxpayers engaged in cross-border activities stemming from Member States' exercise of taxing powers in a discriminatory or restrictive way. Such a tax disadvantage consists of disregarding those taxpayers' overall ability to pay within the EU context.

In order to conduct this study, the research was organised into seven chapters. Chapter 1 addressed the phenomenon of international juridical double taxation, followed by the analysis in Chapter 2 of how it is eliminated in general terms and, in particular, within the EU. In Chapter 3, the EU legal framework was explored to ascertain how EU law limits the exercise of Member States' taxing powers, and in Chapter 4, the relevance of individuals' overall ability to pay in light of EU law was assessed. Chapters 5 and 6, respectively, highlighted the CJEU case law on cases in which international juridical double taxation is not eliminated and in which taxpayers' ability to pay is undermined in the process of eliminating international juridical double taxation. Lastly, in Chapter 7, a final assessment was carried out on whether international juridical double taxation may be perceived from an ability-to-pay perspective in light of EU law, weighing the challenges of such an approach.

The general conclusions of this research are presented as follows:

(1) The OECD MC adopts the traditional notion of international juridical double taxation developed by scholars over time. More recently, the Directive on tax dispute resolution mechanisms introduced a definition of double taxation that is not entirely coincident with the traditional notion enshrined in the OECD MC. For instance, it only covers cases in which the Member States have not successfully eliminated double taxation through bilateral or multilateral agreements. Moreover, it includes a quantitative element related to the tax burden increase derived from the overlap of taxing jurisdictions.

In this regard, the two definitions differ because they delineate a different problem for which they seek a solution. The traditional notion formulates the problem in its original form, i.e., based on the assumption that there are no measures in force to avoid international juridical double taxation.

Its purpose is to pave the way for adopting substantive measures to eliminate it. In contrast, the notion foreseen in the Directive on tax dispute resolution mechanisms describes a second-layer problem: the occasional failure of bilateral or multilateral substantive measures adopted by the Member States to avoid the imposition of comparable taxes on the same taxable object within the EU. It aims to provide a solution for those cases of unrelieved double taxation through the adoption of procedural measures.

(2) Like those notions, the relevant notion of double taxation for the present research purposes is built around the specific problem for which it seeks a solution. That problem is the occasional failure or non-existence of substantive and procedural measures in place within the EU to avoid international juridical double taxation experienced by individuals. Therefore, the relevant notion of double taxation in this research is the effective imposition within the EU of comparable taxes by different Member States on the same individual regarding the same taxable object and tax period without providing any relief.

(3) International juridical double taxation is a consequence of the juxtaposition of States' tax jurisdictions. Defining tax jurisdiction implies determining to what extent a State may exercise its taxing powers. There is no unanimity in the doctrine on whether international law limits the States when defining their tax jurisdiction. However, the fact that the States never tax beyond certain limits indicates that there must be some connection between the State and the person performing the taxable event for that State to exercise its taxing powers over that person.

The lack of uniform criteria among States to determine the connecting factors may give rise to the juxtaposition of tax jurisdictions, causing international juridical double taxation. Moreover, the establishment of tax liability – which varies according to the connecting factors – increases those cases of the juxtaposition of tax jurisdictions.

(4) States eliminate international juridical double taxation because they aim to promote foreign investment, safeguard their taxing rights over such foreign investment and prevent tax evasion. Protecting the taxpayer against international juridical double taxation is a consequence of attaining those aims but not an end in itself.

International juridical double taxation is not deemed illegal or illegitimate under international law, and States are not obliged to eliminate it. However, analysing the legality or legitimacy of international juridical double taxation under international law amounts to observing the issue only from the perspective of tax jurisdiction: insofar as a State does not exceed its own tax jurisdiction – whose limits are not clearly defined under international law – the taxation imposed on a taxpayer is legitimate even if it overlaps with the taxation levied by another State following its tax jurisdiction.

(5) Tax jurisdiction only establishes *the extent to which* States may exercise their taxing powers, i.e., what persons they may tax and with what intensity such

taxation may be exercised. Tax jurisdiction says nothing about *how* the taxing powers are exercised, an issue outside the scope of international law.

The understanding of international juridical double taxation as implying the overall taxation of taxpayers discrepant from their overall ability to pay taxes may comprise a problem regarding *how* the States' taxing powers are exercised. The particular context of the EU is a breeding ground for exploring this hypothesis since, within the EU, the exercise of taxing powers by the Member States is not entirely free, as they have to comply with EU law.

(6) Within the EU, the tax treaties network on income taxes is vast, and only a small number of Member States have not concluded or have terminated them: Denmark–Spain, Finland–Portugal and Sweden–Portugal. The situation is different regarding inheritance and gift taxation, in which the network of bilateral tax treaties among the Member States is far from completion.

As far as EU law is concerned, it provides measures to eliminate international juridical double taxation in specific areas of corporate taxation within the EU, covering only certain operations carried out by certain undertakings resident in different Member States. In particular, the Parent-Subsidiary Directive applies to the distribution of profits involving companies (or their permanent establishment) of different Member States, provided a minimum holding requirement is met; the Interest and Royalty Directive applies to interest and royalty payments made between associated companies of different Member States; and the Merger Directive applies to mergers, divisions, partial divisions, transfers of assets and exchanges of shares concerning companies of different Member States.

No EU law substantive provision in force promotes the elimination of international juridical double taxation regarding individual taxpayers, nor does it oblige the Member States to adopt and maintain substantive provisions on the elimination of double taxation.

Therefore, although the Member States have been promoting the elimination of international juridical double taxation, individual taxpayers engaged in cross-border situations within the EU cannot always count on the elimination of double taxation since substantive measures on this matter may not exist. The elimination of international juridical double taxation within the EU depends on the willingness of the Member States to adopt unilateral measures or conclude tax treaties between them. It is also subject to the possibility of Member States revoking those measures or terminating those tax treaties discretionarily.

Procedural measures to avoid international juridical double taxation are applicable only when substantive measures have failed their purpose. Indeed, procedural measures are unavailable when no substantive measures to avoid double taxation are in place. Whenever Member States' unilateral substantive measures fail their purpose, taxpayers may only rely on procedural measures provided domestically. Conversely, when Member States' bilateral or multilateral measures fail their purpose, the taxpayers may rely on the mutual agreement procedure and arbitration foreseen in legal instruments such as the tax treaties applicable to the case, the BEPS MLI, the EU Multilateral Arbitration Convention and the Directive on tax dispute resolution mechanisms.

(7) The EU Treaties lack specific provisions regarding direct taxes. Outside the particular areas of corporate taxation covered by a few Directives, the Member States are sovereign to design their direct tax systems. However, taxation is an internal market matter because taxes may be used as a protectionist tool to deter intra-Union cross-border trade, employment, services and investment, driving taxpayers to remain in their home markets to avoid additional tax burdens. This way, the prohibitions laid down in the general provisions of the EU Treaties constrain the exercise of Member States' taxing powers. As the CJEU has repeatedly affirmed, *although direct taxation does not, as such, fall within the purview of the EU, the powers retained by the Member States must nevertheless be exercised consistently with EU law.*

(8) Articles 18, 45, 49, 56 and 63 of the TFEU forbid discrimination or restrictions on free movement. It follows that the Member States cannot constrain in an unjustified or (if justified) disproportionate way the taxpayers' right to free movement by treating them worse than taxpayers in a comparable purely internal situation.

In their pure form, the prohibition of discrimination and the prohibition of restrictions entail a different approach to the treatment of cross-border activities. While the prohibition of discrimination has a relative structure, requiring a comparative assessment, the prohibition of restrictions has an absolute structure linked to the right to freedom of movement. In this sense, the prohibition of restrictions is much more far-reaching than the prohibition of discrimination, even though restrictions may be justified by overriding reasons in the public interest, whereas discrimination may not. Nevertheless, in the field of direct taxation, the distinction between the prohibition of discrimination and restrictions has been relativised in its practical application, and the CJEU, in its decisions, never dispenses with the comparative assessment.

(9) In contrast with discrimination and restrictions, the EU Treaties do not forbid disparities. Disparities are distortions arising from the very existence of the Member States' power to tax, which allows them to define their tax jurisdiction and configure their tax systems. Any Member State is not bound to the tax policy choices of any other Member State, nor is it obliged to mimic another Member State's tax system configuration nor to coordinate the limits of its tax jurisdiction with another Member State.

Even though the Member States are sovereign in the definition of their tax jurisdiction and configuration of their tax systems, the prohibition of discrimination and restrictions foreseen in the EU Treaties limit the exercise of that power whenever the Member States create a unilateral disadvantage to taxpayers, making use of free movement. In such cases, the CJEU becomes competent to examine Member States' provisions that set additional burdens to the detriment of cross-border situations.

(10) Ultimately, the prohibition of discrimination and restrictions laid down in the EU Treaties embody a prohibition of arbitrariness in the treatment of cross-border situations within the EU internal market. The Member States' power to tax remains intact insofar as it does not unilaterally hinder free movement.

(11) This prohibition of arbitrariness in the treatment of cross-border situations within the EU also covers the determination of taxpayers' ability to pay.

It is observed that the ability to pay is embedded in the structure of most Member States' tax systems, regardless of the political choices and the concrete technical configuration employed by each State. However, adopting and implementing the ability to pay is not an EU law imperative; it only demands that the Member States comply with the prohibition of discrimination and restrictions laid down in the EU Treaties.

(12) Regarding expenses related to economic activity, the CJEU has stressed that there is no objective difference between taxpayers exercising an EU freedom of movement and those not exercising it. The comparability of their situation lies in the fact that, in any case, taxing a gross income amounts to taxing an artificial economic strength that does not represent an actual ability to pay. Consequently, under the EU Treaties, the Member States are forbidden to adopt different and more burdensome criteria and techniques for determining the objective net income of taxpayers exercising free of movement than those for determining the objective net income of taxpayers not exercising it.

(13) In its case law, the CJEU uses the expression 'expenses directly linked' to refer to expenses related to economic activity. Accordingly, such expenses must have a direct economic connection to the activity giving rise to taxable income in a Member State and, therefore, are inextricably linked to that activity. Furthermore, such expenses must be necessary, which does not mean that those expenses must be unavoidable.

The concept of expenses directly linked provided by the CJEU – which is independent of the Member States' legal classification of expenses – seeks to set the base for differentiation between expenses related to economic activity and expenses related to personal and family circumstances, as the Member States do not classify expenses similarly.

(14) The notion of 'personal and family circumstances' adopted by the CJEU covers all tax advantages not linked to economic activity granted by the Member States to taxpayers. It is not necessary for the tax advantages granted to have a social purpose. Even tax benefits designed mainly to encourage taxpayers to spend and make investments are considered linked to the taxpayer's personal and family situation insofar as they impact their ability to pay taxes.

The decision to protect taxpayers' personal and family circumstances at a tax level falls within the Member States' power to configure their tax systems. EU law only requires that the Member States do not treat taxpayers who exercise an EU freedom of movement worse than those who do not, as far as their situation is comparable.

(15) According to the CJEU's case law, comparability is assessed in these cases, based on factual circumstances. Due to the worldwide taxation taxpayers are subject to in their residence State, it is in this State where it is easier to consider their overall ability to pay because worldwide taxation implies further report obligations, such as a tax return containing all the taxpayers' aggregate income and their personal and family situation.

This way, it is apparent from the CJEU's case law that residents engaged in cross-border activities and residents engaged in purely internal activities are in a comparable situation regarding the consideration of their personal and family circumstances. All of them are subject to worldwide taxation in their residence State, this State being able to know their personal and family situation, as well as all the income they earned, regardless of its source. Moreover, the fact that residents obtain income from abroad does not prevent the residence Member State from being the best placed to assess their overall ability to pay.

Conversely, it follows from the CJEU's case law that, as a rule, resident taxpayers (subject to worldwide taxation) and non-residents (subject to source taxation) are not in a comparable situation because, among other reasons, the Member States have, in general, limited information on non-residents' aggregate income or on their personal and family situation. Due to their lack of comparability, the Member States do not breach EU law when considering residents' personal and family circumstances while not considering those of non-residents.

(16) The incomparability between residents and non-residents is not absolute. It gives in whenever taxpayers' personal and family circumstances are not duly considered in any Member State because taxpayers have exercised an EU freedom of movement.

It follows from the CJEU's case law that absolute priority is given to considering taxpayers' personal and family circumstances. That priority emerged with the exception introduced in the Schumacker case, and it was further enhanced with the *X* case and the *Commission v. Estonia* case, which set the path to be followed in the grey area and borderline cases.

The Court's approach to taxpayers' personal and family circumstances may be explained by the fact that expenses related to personal and family circumstances represent what each Member State defines as what we call taxpayers' 'intangible economic strength' intended to satisfy their existential needs. Thus, free movement ensured within the internal market must not jeopardise taxpayers' human dignity, which is one of the fundamental values of the EU.

(17) The Court's case law on personal and family circumstances is not entirely devoid of doubts. Van Raad and Wattel, among other scholars, have proposed fractional taxation as an alternative route for considering personal and family circumstances within the EU. According to this proposal, all taxpayers – residents and non-residents – should be subject in all Member States where they carry out economic activities to progressive taxation

determined based on their worldwide income and taking into account their personal and family circumstances. However, effective taxation in each Member State would only occur in proportion to the income obtained therein, which would lead, at the same time, to the pro rata attribution of personal and family tax benefits granted by that State.

It seems too ambitious to implement a fractional taxation system through negative integration when, within the EU, the elimination of international juridical double taxation is not mandatory, and this system, to work properly, implies such elimination.

(18) Since eliminating international juridical double taxation is not mandatory within the EU, the CJEU regards this problem as deriving from the *definition* of Member States' tax jurisdiction and not from the *exercise* of Member States' taxing powers. According to the CJEU case law, the overtaxation derived from international juridical double taxation does not constitute a forbidden obstacle to free movement because it does not entail a discriminatory or restrictive tax treatment unilaterally created by a Member State.

(19) As international juridical double taxation is not forbidden under EU law, the Member States are not obliged to conclude tax treaties with each other or adopt unilateral measures to avoid double taxation.

At the same time, because EU law does not lay down any general criteria to allocate taxing rights among the Member States, the CJEU cannot oblige the Member States to avoid international juridical double taxation, even when such obligation is foreseen in a bilateral tax treaty.

(20) It is unclear whether the Directive on tax dispute resolution mechanisms applies in situations of tax treaty override. Accepting that tax treaty override may be overcome by the action of tax authorities and independent persons of standing, countering a Member State's legislative power, may lead to a severe breach in that State's rule of law.

(21) Although EU law does not require the elimination of international juridical double taxation if the Member States decide to eliminate it, they must comply with EU law, meaning that they cannot hinder free movement in a discriminatory or restrictive way. This way, the Member States cannot disregard taxpayers' personal and family circumstances when applying the credit or the exemption methods to eliminate international juridical double taxation.

(22) The CJEU dealt with the restrictive tax treatment arising from the application of the ordinary credit in the *Beker* case and the application of the modified exemption in the *De Groot* case, the *Jacob and Lennertz* case and the *BJ v. État belge* case. In these cases, the formula used to calculate the amount of tax credit/the amount to be exempt led to the loss of personal and family tax benefits in proportion to taxpayers' foreign income.

The Court addressed the restrictive tax treatment arising from the application of the exemption with progression in the *Bechtel* case and the *Imfeld and Garcet* case. In these cases, taxpayers lost tax benefits related to their personal and family circumstances because their household income was partially tax-exempt due to applying the said method to eliminate double taxation.

(23) In all these cases of restrictive tax treatment deriving from the application of ordinary credit, modified exemption and exemption with progression, the residence Member State limited its tax jurisdiction by not taxing income resident taxpayers obtained in another Member State. Nevertheless, the CJEU held that the residence Member State is still responsible for fully considering those taxpayers' personal and family circumstances. In other words, the obligation to consider residents' personal and family circumstances remains even when the residence Member State does not tax their worldwide income.

That may be explained by the simple fact that although there is a correlation between being subject to taxation on the worldwide income in a Member State and having personal and family circumstances considered in that State, personal and family tax benefits are not tied to taxpayers' income but rather to their personal and family situation. Taxpayers' personal and family situation remains unchanged regardless of whether their income is obtained domestically or cross-borders.

(24) According to the CJEU's case law, the residence Member State may be released from the obligation of considering its residents' personal and family circumstances in just a few situations: *(i)* in the case of an international agreement allocating that obligation to another Member State; *(ii)* in the case of the source Member State unilaterally considering personal and family circumstances of non-residents; and *(iii)* in the case the residence Member State being de facto prevented from considering residents' personal and family circumstances.

(25) In the second scenario, not considering personal and family circumstances in the residence Member State *must be due* to the unilateral and not merely fortuitous granting of equivalent benefits in the other State. In the residence Member State's tax legislation, there must be a correlation between the refusal of granting personal and family tax advantages that residents are, as a rule, entitled to and the granting of such tax benefits to those taxpayers in another Member State.

(26) The third scenario occurs when taxpayers derive their total income (almost) exclusively from one or more Member States other than their residence Member State. Suppose the residence Member State eliminates international juridical double taxation through full exemption and exemption with progression. In that case, it cannot consider those taxpayers' personal and family circumstances because there is no taxable base on which personal and family tax benefits can be applied.

In such cases, the CJEU considers that the source Member State incurs discrimination when it does not consider the personal and family circumstances of non-resident taxpayers earning almost all their income in its territory whenever their personal and family circumstances are not considered elsewhere.

The discrimination against non-resident taxpayers caused by the source Member State(s) has a *relative nature*, as is the particular situation of those taxpayers in their residence Member State that leads to discriminatory tax treatment in the source Member State.

(27) In these cases, in which the taxpayers derive their total income (almost) exclusively from one or more Member States other than the residence Member State, if international juridical double taxation is eliminated through the ordinary credit or the modified exemption, we wonder whether the CJEU would reach the same conclusion mentioned in the previous point.

In such a case, at least *formally,* there is a tax base in the residence Member State on which personal and family tax benefits may be applied. However, in the absence of domestic income, resident taxpayers cannot *effectively* benefit from the tax advantages related to their personal and family circumstances, as the elimination of international juridical double taxation consumes the tax advantages granted.

We sustain that taxpayers exercising their right to free movement should not be prevented from benefiting from the tax advantages related to their personal and family situation just because their personal and family circumstances were *theoretically* considered elsewhere. After all, personal and family circumstances represent taxpayers' intangible economic strength, and the free movement ensured within the EU internal market should not jeopardise taxpayers' human dignity, which is one of the fundamental values of the EU.

(28) As a final assessment, it is observed that there is no contradiction in the reasoning followed by the CJEU in its case law.

The overtaxation suffered by taxpayers in a cross-border situation arising from international juridical double taxation does not constitute a forbidden obstacle to free movement because it is a consequence of Member States' definition of tax jurisdiction and does not entail a discriminatory or restrictive tax treatment.

Instead, the overtaxation suffered by taxpayers in a cross-border situation arising from the lack of full consideration of those taxpayers' personal and family circumstances is a consequence of a Member State's exercise of taxing powers in a discriminatory or restrictive way and, thus, it constitutes a forbidden obstacle to free movement.

Therefore, as mentioned above, the CJEU regards the obstacle to free movement arising from international juridical double taxations as deriving from the *definition* of Member States' tax jurisdiction while regarding the obstacle to free movement arising from the disregard of personal and family circumstances as resulting from the *exercise* of Member States' taxing powers.

(29) Nevertheless, as a result of the analysis conducted throughout this research, it is possible to clearly conclude that from an ability-to-pay perspective, the tax disadvantage deriving from international juridical double taxation may also be perceived as resulting from a Member State's exercise of taxing powers in a discriminatory or restrictive way.

The unequal tax treatment stems from applying the same rule to different situations. The rule that is applied in the same way is the standard taxation of resident taxpayers, under which their worldwide income is subject to tax, and their ability to pay is considered accordingly. The different situations to which the same rule is applied are that of residents deriving only domestic income and residents deriving income from abroad without relief from international juridical double taxation.

Regarding residents who derive their income domestically, the standard taxation of resident taxpayers fits perfectly: all their income is subject to tax, which is calculated according to their ability to pay. Because they are not subject to an equivalent tax burden elsewhere, their overall income utterly mirrors their *overall ability to pay*.

The situation of residents deriving income from abroad without relief from international juridical double taxation differs from the former, as they are also subject to equivalent taxation in another Member State. The standard taxation of resident taxpayers – whereby their worldwide income is subject to taxation and tax is ascertained based on their ability to pay – leads to unequal treatment of those residents because their tax liability in another Member State is ignored. Those taxpayers' overall income does not mirror their *overall ability to pay*, as their economic strength is reduced by the tax burden also due in another Member State. Therefore, in these cases, the residence Member State is taxing an *artificial* economic strength that does not represent those taxpayers' overall ability to pay.

(30) This perspective presents some challenges.

First, it entails accepting the taxpayers' ability to pay, as determined by each Member State according to its rules, as a ceiling or a self-imposed limit for taxation. That ceiling or self-imposed limit for taxation must have relevance in the EU context so that equivalent tax burdens due in the other Member States can be considered.

Secondly, since the disregard for taxpayers' overall ability to pay in the cases of unrelieved international juridical double taxation is not triggered by a Member State's concrete tax provision, that disregard constitutes a systemic tax obstacle to free movement. By entailing a restriction on free movement, this systemic tax obstacle may be subject to the CJEU's scrutiny, which is competent to assess its compatibility with the EU law, weighing the possible justification reasons put forward by the Member States and their proportionality. Nevertheless, due to the enormous complexity inherent to a systemic tax obstacle, it is necessary to acknowledge that the most operational way of dealing with it is through positive regulation at the EU level. Therefore, this matter should be regulated through a Directive that imposes subsidiary norms for eliminating international juridical double taxation whenever it is not effectively eliminated within the EU.

Finally, it also encompasses accepting that overcoming this systemic tax obstacle necessarily leads to the loss of tax revenue. However, according to the CJEU's settled case law, the loss of tax revenue can never be relied upon to justify measures that hinder free movement.

Bibliography

Agulló Agüero A., *Una reflexión en torno a la prohibición de confiscatoriedad del sistema tributario*, 36 REDF 555 (1982).

Agulló Agüero A., *Estructura de la imposición sobre la renta y el principio de capacidad contributiva*, 37 REDF 23 (1983).

Agulló Agüero A., *El Impuesto de Sociedades ante el Derecho Comunitario*, 2 Impuestos 895 (1986).

Akehurst M., *Jurisdiction in International Law*, 46 Brit. Y.B. Int'l L.145 (1972-1973).

Alarcón García G., *La determinación de los rendimientos netos en el ordenamiento alemán: relevancia para España y utilidad como modelo de armonización fiscal en la Unión Europea*, 1 Impuestos 1158 (1997).

Albrecht A. R., *The Taxation of Aliens under International Law*, 29 Brit. Y.B. Int'l L. 45 (1952).

Allix E., *La condition des étrangers au point de vue fiscal*, 61 Recueil des Cours 545 (1937).

Avery Jones J., *Carry on Discriminating*, 36(2) Eur. Tax'n 46 (1996).

Avery Jones J., *What Is the Difference Between Schumacker and Gilly?*, 39(1) Eur. Tax'n 2 (1999).

Avery Jones J., *A Comment on 'Progressive Taxation of Non-residents and Intra-EC Allocation of Personal Tax Allowances'*, 40(8) Eur. Tax'n 375 (2000).

Avery Jones J., *Avoiding Double Taxation: Credit Versus Exemption – The Origins*, 66(2) Bull. Int'l Tax'n 67 (2012).

Avi-Yonah R., *International Tax as International Law*, 57(4) Tax L. Rev. 483 (2004).

Bammens N., *The Principle of Non-discrimination in International and European Tax Law* (IBFD 2012).

Bammens N., *Free Movement of Citizens and Family Taxation*, in *Research Handbook on European Union Taxation Law* (C. Panayi et al. eds, Elgar 2020).

Bardini C., *Ability to Pay in the European Market: An Impossible Sudoku for the ECJ*, 38(1) Intertax 2 (2010).

Barents R., The Single Market and National Tax Sovereignty, in *Fiscal Sovereignty of the Member States in an Internal Market: Past and Future* (S. Jansen ed., Kluwer Law International 2011).

Barnard C. & Peers S., *European Union Law* (Oxford University Press 2014).

Barreiro Carril M. C., *National Tax Sovereignty and EC Fundamental Freedoms: The Impact of Tax Obstacles on the Internal Market*, 38(2) Intertax 105 (2010).

Barreiro Carril M. C., *Los impuestos directos y el Derecho de la Unión Europea: la armonización negativa realizada por el TJUE* (Instituto de Estudios Fiscales 2012).

Barthel F. et al., *The Relationship Between Double Taxation Treaties and Foreign Direct Investment*, in Tax Treaties: Building Bridges Between Law and Economics (M. Lang et al. ed., IBFD 2010).

Beale J. H., *Jurisdiction to Tax*, 32 Harv. L. Rev. 587 (1919).

Beretta G., *Cross-Border Mobility of Individuals and the Lack of Fiscal Policy Coordination among Jurisdictions (Even) After the BEPS Project*, 47(1) Intertax 91 (2019).

Berliri L. V., *El Impuesto justo* (F. Vicente-Arche Domingo trans., Instituto de Estudios Fiscales 1986).

Birk D., *Besteuerungsgleichheit in der Europäischen Union*, in *Steuerrecht im europäischen Binnenmarkt* (M. Lehner ed., Verlag Dr. Otto Schmidt 1996).

Bizioli G. & Reimer E., *Equality, Ability to Pay and Neutrality*, in *Research Handbook on European Union Taxation Law* (C. Panayi et al. eds, Elgar 2020).

Bizioli G. & Sacchetto C., *European Constitutional Integration: The Case of Direct Taxation*, in *Comparative Fiscal Federalism* (R. Avi Yonah & M. Lang eds, Kluwer Law International 2d ed. 2016).

Blum D. W., *The Relationship Between the OECD Multilateral Instrument and Covered Tax Agreements: Multilateralism and the Interpretation of the MLI*, 72(3) Bull. Int'l Tax'n 131 (2018).

Borras A., *La doble imposición: problemas jurídico-internacionales* (Instituto de Estudios Fiscales 1974).

Bravo N., *A Multilateral Instrument for Updating the Tax Treaty Network* (IBFD 2020).

Bühler O., *Les accords internationaux concernant la double imposition et l'évasion fiscale*, 55 Recueil des Cours 433 (1936).

Bühler O., *Principios de Derecho internacional tributario* (F. Cervera Torrejón trans., Editorial de Derecho Financiero 1965).

Calvo Vérgez J., *El papel de los CDI ante la doble imposición internacional en el ámbito del ISD*, in *La tributación de las sucesiones transfronterizas en España y en la Unión Europea: problemas actuales* (J. Ramos Prieto et al. eds., Aranzadi 2018).

Calvo Vérgez J., *Últimas actuaciones en materia de arbitraje tributario dentro de la Unión Europea: la Directiva (UE) 2017/1852 del Consejo, de 10 de octubre de 2017, relativa a los mecanismos de resolución de litigios fiscales*, 11(2) Econ. Analysis L. Rev. 3 (2020).

Casalta Nabais J., *O dever fundamental de pagar impostos* (Almedina 1998).

Cerioni L., *Double Taxation and the EC Internal Market: Reflections on the ECJ's Decisions in Block and Damseaux and the Potential Implications*, 63(11) Bull. Int'l Tax'n 543 (2009).

Cerioni L., *Guido Imfeld and Nathalie Garcet v Belgian State: A Continuation of the Schumacker Doctrine?*, 2 Brit. Tax Rev. 128 (2014).

Cerioni L., *The Never-Ending Issue of Cross-Border Loss Compensation Within the EU: Reconciling Balanced Allocation of Taxing Rights and Cross-Border Ability-to-Pay*, 24 EC Tax Rev. 268 (2015).

Cerioni L., *Case Note: X v Staatssecretaris van Financiën: A Step Forward in a Proper Application of the Ability-to-Pay Principle in Cross-Border Situations?*, 2 Brit. Tax Rev. 162 (2017).

CFE ECJ Task Force, Opinion Statement ECJ-TF 1/2016 on the Decision of the European Court of Justice in Joined Cases Miljoen (Case C-10/14), X (Case C-14/14) and Société Générale (Case C-17/14) on the Netherlands Dividend Withholding Tax, 56 Eur. Tax'n 255 (2016).

Checa González C., *Medidas y métodos para evitar la doble imposición internacional*, 5 Anuario Fac. Derecho Universidad de Extremadura 151 (1987).

Cordewener A., *The Prohibitions of Discrimination and Restriction Within the Framework of the Fully Integrated Internal Market*, in *EU Freedoms and Taxation: 2004 EATLP Congress* (F. Vanistendael ed., IBFD 2006).

Cordewener A., *Personal Income Taxation of Non-residents and the Increasing Impact of the EC Treaty Freedoms*, in *The Influence of European Law on Direct Taxation: Recent and Future Developments* (D. Weber ed., Kluwer Law International 2007).

Cordewener A. et al., *The Clash Between European Freedoms and National Direct Tax Law: Public Interest Defences Available to the Member States*, 46 Common Market L. Rev. 1951 (2009).

Cors Meya F. X., *Las tasas en el marco de un sistema tributario justo*, 51 REDF 325 (1986).

Cortés Domínguez M., *El principio de capacidad contributiva en el marco de la técnica jurídica*, 60 Revista de Derecho Financiero y Hacienda Pública 975 (1965).

Cortés Domínguez M., *Ordenamiento tributario español* (Civitas 1985).

Daxkobler K. & Huisman E., *Levy & Sebbag: The ECJ Has Once Again Been Asked to Deliver Its Opinion on Juridical Double Taxation in the Internal Market*, 53(8) Eur. Tax'n 400 (2013).

De Broe L., *Relief of Double Taxation of Cross-Border Dividends Within the Union and the Principle of Loyal Cooperation*, 21(4) EC Tax Rev. 180 (2012).

De Juan Casadevall J., *El principio de no discriminación fiscal como instrumento de armonización negativa* (Aranzadi 2010).

De La Feria R., *The EU VAT System and the Internal Market* (IBFD 2009).

De Pietro C., *Tax Treaty Override and the Need for Coordination Between Legal Systems: Safeguarding the Effectiveness of International Law*, 7(1) World Tax J. 73 (2015).

Debelva F., *International Double Taxation and the Right to Property: A Comparative, International and European Law Analysis* (IBFD 2019).

Debelva F. & Luts J., *The European Commission's Proposal for Double Taxation Dispute Resolution: Turning the Tide?*, 71 Bull. Int'l Tax'n 5 (2017).

Di Pietro A., *Justice fiscale et intégration européen: le rôle des juges fiscaux*, 2 Cluj Tax Forum Journal 7 (2019).

Dorn H., *Diritto finanziario e questioni fondamentali sulle doppie imposizioni*, 2(1) Rivista di Diritto Finanziario e Scienza delle Finanze 115 (1938).

Douma S., *The Three Ds of Direct Tax Jurisdiction: Disparity, Discrimination and Double Taxation*, 46(11) Eur. Tax'n 522 (2006).

Dourado A. P., *Free Movement of Capital: The European Union Anti-Tax Avoidance Package and Brexit*, 44(12) Intertax 870 (2016).

Dourado A. P., *The EU Free Movement of Capital and Third Countries: Recent Developments*, 45(3) Intertax 192 (2017).

Dourado A. P., *Governação Fiscal Global* (Almedina 2d ed. 2020).

Dziwiński K., *Dual Residence and Treaty Entitlement of Individuals*, in *Tax Treaty Entitlement* (M. Lang et al. eds, IBFD 2019).

Ehlermann, C., *The Internal Market Following the Single European Act*, 24(3) Common Market L. Rev. 361 (1987).

Einaudi L., *La coopération internationale en matière fiscale*, 25 Recueil des Cours 1 (1928).

Englisch J., *The European Treaties' Implications for Direct Taxes*, 33(8/9) Intertax 310 (2005).

Englisch J., *Taxation of Cross-Border Dividends and EC Fundamental Freedoms*, 38(4) Intertax 197 (2010).

Englisch J., *VAT and General Principles of EU Law*, in *Traditional and Alternative Routes to European Tax Integration* (D. Weber ed., IBFD 2010).

Englisch J., *Ability to Pay*, in *Principles of Law: Function, Status and Impact in EU Tax Law* (C. Brokelind ed., IBFD 2014).

Farmer P., *Direct Taxation and the Fundamental Freedoms*, in *The Oxford Handbook of European Union Law* (A. Arnull & D. Chalmers eds, Oxford 2015).

Fibbe G. & De Graaf A., *Is Double Taxation Arising from Autonomous Tax Classification of Foreign Entities Incompatible with EC Law?*, in *A Tax Globalist – Essays in Honour of Maarten J. Ellis* (H. Van Arendonk et al. eds, IBFD 2005).

Freyer D., *The Proportionality Principle under EU Tax Law: General and Practical Problems Caused by Its Extensive Application (Part 1)*, 57(9) Eur. Tax'n 384 (2017).

Freyer D., *The Proportionality Principle under EU Tax Law: General and Practical Problems Caused by Its Extensive Application (Part 2)*, 57(10) Eur. Tax'n 428 (2017).

Gadžo S., *Nexus Requirements for Taxation of Non-residents' Business Income: A Normative Evaluation in the Context of the Global Economy* (IBFD 2018).

Gadžo S., *The Principle of 'Nexus' or 'Genuine Link' as a Keystone of International Income Tax Law: A Reappraisal*, 46(3) Intertax 194 (2018).

Gammie M., *Double Taxation, Bilateral Treaties and the Fundamental Freedoms of the EC Treaty*, in *A Tax Globalist – Essays in Honour of Maarten J. Ellis* (H. Van Arendonk et al. eds, IBFD 2005).

Gammie M., *Non-discrimination and the Taxation of Cross-Border Dividends*, 2(2) World Tax J. 162 (2010).

García Prats A., *Imposición directa, no discriminación y derecho comunitario* (Tecnos 1998).

García Prats A., *La jurisprudencia del TJCE y el artículo 33 de la Ley del Impuesto de la Renta de no Residentes (De la asunción del principio de capacidad económica como principio del ordenamiento comunitario)*, 117 REDF 61 (2003).

García Prats A., *Revisiting 'Schumacker': Source, Residence and Citizenship in the ECJ Case-Law on Direct Taxation*, in *Allocating Taxing Powers Within the European Union* (I. Richelle et al. eds, Springer 2013).

García Prats A., *Subjective Ability to Pay: Schumacker*, in *Landmark Decisions of the ECJ in Direct Taxation* (W. Haslehner et al. eds, Kluwer Law International 2015).

García Prats A., *El 'prorrateo' de las ventajas fiscales personales y familiares, según el TJUE*, 1-2 Quincena Fiscal 103 (2018).

Giardina E., *Le basi teoriche del principio della capacità contributiva* (Giuffrè 1961).

González García G., *Una aproximación al contenido de los conceptos de discriminación y restricción en el derecho comunitario*, 8 Documentos IEF 1 (2004).

Gormley L., *The Genesis of the Rule of Reason in the Free Movement of Goods*, in *The Rule of Reason: Rethinking Another Classic of European Legal Doctrine* (A. Schrauwen ed., Europa Law Publishing 2005).

Govind S. & Turcan L., *Cross-Border Tax Dispute Resolution in the 21st Century: A Comparative Study of Existing Bilateral and Multilateral Remedies*, 19 Deriv. & Fin. Instruments 5 (2017).

Griziotti B., *L'imposition fiscale des étrangers*, 13 Recueil des Cours 1 (1926).

Griziotti B., *Principios de política, derecho y ciencia de la hacienda* (E. Mata trans., Editorial Reus 2d ed. 1958).

Guggenheim P., *L'imposition des successions en droit international et le problème de la double imposition* (Mémoires publiés par la Facultéde droit de Genève 1928).

Gutmann D., *How to Avoid Double Taxation in the European Union?*, in *Allocating Taxing Powers Within the European Union* (I. Richelle et al. eds, Springer 2013).

Helminen M., *The Principle of Elimination of Double Taxation under EU Law – Does It Exist?*, in *Principles of Law: Function, Status and Impact in EU Tax Law* (C. Brokelind ed., IBFD 2014).

Helminen M., *EU Tax Law – Direct Taxation* (IBFD 2017).

Herrera Molina P., *Capacidad económica y Sistema fiscal: análisis del ordenamiento español a la luz del derecho alemán* (Marcial Pons 1998).

Herrera Molina P., *The Restrictive Impact of the Principles of EU Law on Tax Sovereignty and the Concept of Tax in the EU Member States*, in *The Concept of Tax: 2005 EATLP Congress* (B. Peeters et al. eds, IBFD 2005).

Herrera Molina P., *Convenios de Doble Imposición y Derecho Comunitario* (Instituto de Estudios Fiscales 2009).

Herrera Molina P., *STJCE 4.11.2006, Kerckhaert-Morres, As. C-513/04: ¿es discriminatoria la doble imposición jurídica internacional?*, 148 Crónica tributaria 248 (2013).

Herrera Molina P. & Villar Ezcurra M., *Ayudas fiscales y Derecho comunitario: un ejemplo de armonización fiscal negativa*, in *Estudios de derecho financiero y tributario: en homenaje al profesor Calvo Ortega* (I. Martín Dégano et al. eds, Lex Nova, 2005).

Heydt V., *Juridical Double Taxation: Kerckhaert and Morres*, in *Landmark Decisions of the ECJ in Direct Taxation* (W. Haslehner et al. eds, Kluwer Law International 2015).

Hinnekens L., *Basis and Scope of Public Interest Justification of National Tax Measures Infringing Fundamental Treaty Freedoms*, in *EU Freedoms and Taxation: 2004 EATLP Congress* (F. Vanistendael ed., IBFD 2006).

Hinnekens L., *The Uneasy Case and Fate of Article 293 Second Indent EC*, 37(11) Intertax 602 (2009).

Hofmann H., *Double Tax Agreements: Between EU Law and Public International Law*, in *Double Taxation Within the European Union* (A. Rust ed., Kluwer Law International 2011).

Hofstätter M., *Who Is Competent to Issue Measures for the Elimination of Double Taxation Within the Community?*, in *Tax Treaty Law and EC Law* (M. Lang et al. eds, Kluwer Law International 2007).

Hongler P., *Justice in International Tax Law: A Normative Review of the International Tax Regime* (IBFD 2019).

Ismer R. & Ruß J., *What Is International Double Taxation?*, 48(6/7) Intertax 555 (2020).

Jeffery R., *The Impact of State Sovereignty on Global Trade and International Taxation* (Kluwer Law International 1999).

Kaldor N., *An Expenditure Tax* (Allen & Unwin 1955).

Kemmeren E., *Source of Income in Globalizing Economies: Overview of the Issues and A Plea for an Origin-Based Approach*, 60(11) Bull. Int'l Tax'n 430 (2006).

Kemmeren E., *Non-application of DTCs: Inconsistent with Community and EEA Loyalty*, in *The EU and Third Countries: Direct Taxation* (M. Lang & P. Pistone eds, Kluwer Law International 2007).

Kemmeren E., *After Repeal of Article 293 EC Treaty under the Lisbon Treaty: The EU Objective of Eliminating Double Taxation Can Be Applied More Widely*, 17(4) EC Tax Rev. 156 (2008).

Kemmeren E., *The Internal Market Approach Should Prevail over the Single Country Approach*, in *A Vision of Taxes Within and Beyond European Borders* (L. Hinnekens & P. Hinnekens eds, Kluwer Law International 2008).

Kemmeren E., *Legal and Economic Principles Support an Origin and Import Neutrality-Based over a Residence and Export Neutrality-Based Tax Treaty Policy*, in *Tax Treaties: Building Bridges Between Law and Economics* (M. Lang et al. eds, IBFD 2010).

Kemmeren E., *Double Tax Conventions on Income and Capital and the EU: Past, Present and Future*, 21(3) EC Tax Rev. 156 (2012).

Kemmeren E., *The CJEU and the Internal Market Concept in Direct Taxation*, in *EU Tax Law and Policy in the 21st Century* (W. Haslehner et al. eds, Kluwer Law International 2017).

Kiekebeld B. & Smit D., *EU Free Movement of Capital and Corporate Income Taxation: The Relationship Between the Free Movement of Capital and the Other TFEU Freedoms and Justification Grounds in a Third Country Context*, in *Fiscal Sovereignty of the Member States in an Internal Market: Past and Future* (S. Jansen ed., Kluwer Law International 2011).

Kleist D., *Methods for Elimination of Double Taxation under Double Tax Treaties – With Particular Reference to the Application of Double Tax Treaties in Sweden* (Iustus Förlag AB 2012).

Knechtle A. A., *Basic Problems in International Fiscal Law* (Kluwer 1979).

Knoll M. S. & Mason R., *Wynne: It's Not About Double Taxation*, 75 ST. Tax Notes 413 (2015).

Kobetsky M., *International Taxation of Permanent Establishments: Principles and Policy* (Cambridge University Press 2011).

Kofler G., *Double Taxation and European Union Law: Analysis of the Jurisprudence*, in *Double Taxation Within the European Union* (A. Rust ed., Kluwer Law International 2011).

Kofler G. & Schindler C. P., *'Dancing with Mr D': The ECJ's Denial of Most-Favoured-Nation Treatment in the 'D' Case*, 45(12) Eur. Tax'n 530 (2005).

Kofler G. & Mason R., *Double Taxation: A European 'Switch in Time'?*, 14 Colum. J. Eur. L. 63 (2007).

Kruse H. W., *Derecho tributario: parte general* (P. Yebra Martul-Ortega & M. Izquierdo Macías-Picavea trans., Edersa 3d ed. 1978).

Kube H, Double *Burdens Within the European Union: Solutions in Other Areas of Law: Constitutional Law*, in *Double Taxation Within the European Union* (A. Rust ed., Kluwer Law International 2011).

Lang J., *Tributación familiar*, 94 Hacienda Pública Española 407 (1985).

Lang J., *Steuergerechtigkeit und Globalisierung*, in *Steuerzentrierte Rechtsberatung* (W. Spindler et al. eds, Verlag Dr. Otto Schmidt 2009).

Lang J. & Englisch J., *A European Legal Tax Order Based on Ability to Pay*, in *International Tax Law* (A. Amatucci ed., Kluwer Law International 2d ed. 2012).

Lang M., *Direct Taxation: Is the ECJ Heading in a New Direction?*, 46(9) Eur. Tax'n 421, (2006).

Lang M., *Double Taxation and EC Law, in Comparative Fiscal Federalism: Comparing the European Court of Justice and the US Supreme Court's Tax Jurisprudence* (R. Avi-Yonah et al. eds, Kluwer Law International 2007).

Lang M., *Recent Case Law of the ECJ in Direct Taxation: Trends, Tensions, and Contradictions*, 18(3) EC Tax Rev. 98 (2009).

Lang M., *Introduction to the Law of Double Taxation Conventions* (Joint publication of IBFD & Linde 2013).

Lang M., *Double Taxation Conventions in the Case Law of the CJEU*, 46(3) Intertax 181 (2018).

Lazarov I., *The Relevance of the Fundamental Freedoms for Direct Taxation*, in *Introduction to European Tax Law on Direct Taxation* (M. Lang et al. eds, Linde Verlag 2018).

Lehner M., *Avoidance of Double Taxation Within the European Union: Is There an Obligation under EC Law?*, in *Tax Treaty Law and EC Law* (M. Lang et al. eds, Kluwer Law International 2007).

Lehr M. E., *Quelques mots sur les doubles impositions en droit international*, 31 Revue de Droit International et de Législation Comparée 554 (1899).

Lenaerts K., *'United in Diversity' – Also in Fiscalibus?*, in *A Vision of Taxes Within and Beyond European Borders* (L. Hinnekens & P. Hinnekens eds, Kluwer Law International 2008).

Lyal R., *Nondiscrimination and EU Direct Tax Law*, in *Comparative Fiscal Federalism* (R. Avi Yonah & M. Lang eds, Kluwer Law International 2d ed. 2016).

Malherbe J. et al., *Direct Taxation in the Case-Law of the European Court of Justice* (Larcier 2008).

Mann F. A., *The Doctrine of Jurisdiction in International Law*, 111 Recueil des Cours 1 (1964).

Mann F. A., *The Doctrine of International Jurisdiction Revisited after Twenty Years*, 186 Recueil des Cours 9 (1984).

Manzoni I., *Il Principio della capacità contributiva nell'ordinamento constituzionale italiano* (Giappichelli 1965).

Marchgraber C., *Double (Non-)Taxation and EU Law* (Kluwer Law International 2018).

Martha R., *The Jurisdiction to Tax in International Law: Theory and Practice of Legislative Fiscal Jurisdiction* (Kluwer Law and Taxation 1989).

Martín Delgado J. M., *Los principios de capacidad económica e igualdad en la Constitución española de 1978*, 60 Hacienda Pública Española 61 (1979).

Mason R., *Made in America for European Tax: The Internal Consistency Test*, 49 Bost. Coll. L. Rev. 1277 (2008).

Mason R. & Knoll M., *What Is Tax Discrimination?*, 121(5) Yale L.J. 1017 (2011).

Mattsson N., *Does the European Court of Justice Understand the Policy Behind Tax Benefits Based on Personal and Family Circumstances?*, 43(6) Eur. Tax'n 186 (2003).

Meussen G., *The Ritter-Coulais Case – A Wrong Decision in Principle by the ECJ*, 64(7) Eur. Tax'n 335 (2006).

Meussen G., *European Union – Renneberg: ECJ Unjustifiably Expands Schumacker Doctrine to Losses from Financing of Personal Dwelling*, 54(4) Eur. Tax'n 185 (2009).

Monsenego J., *Double Taxation in the EU: The Future after Block*, 54(3) Tax Notes Int'l 215 (2009).

Monsenego J., *Réflexions sur les conséquences de l'abrogation de l'article 293, alinéa 2 du Traité CE*, 9 Revue de Droit Fiscal 15 (2011).

Monsenego J., *Taxation of Foreign Business Income Within the European Internal Market* (IBFD 2012).

Moschetti F., *El principio de capacidad contributiva* (J. Calero Gallego & R. Navas Vazquez trans, Instituto de Estudios Fiscales 1980).

Musgrave P., *United States Taxation of Foreign Investment Income: Issues and Arguments* (Harvard Law School 1969).

Musgrave R., *Criteria for Foreign Tax Credit, in Taxation and Operations Abroad: Symposium* (R. Baker et al. eds, Princeton: Tax Institute 1960).

Musgrave R. & Musgrave P., *Inter-nation Equity*, in *Modern Fiscal Issues: Essays in Honour of Carl S. Shoup* (R. Bird & J. Head eds, University of Toronto Press 5th ed. 1972).

Musgrave R. & Musgrave P., *Public Finance in Theory and Practice* (McGraw-Hill 1989).

Neumark F., *Principios de la imposición* (L. Gutiérrez Andrés trans., Instituto de Estudios Fiscales 2d ed. 1994).

Niboyet J. P., *Les doubles impositions au point de vue juridique*, 31 Recueil des Cours 5 (1930).

Niesten H., *Growing Impetus for Harmonisation of Personal and Family Allowances: Current State of Affairs of the Schumaker-Doctrine after Imfeld and Garcet*, 24(4) EC Tax Rev. 185 (2015).

Niesten H., *Personal and Family Tax Benefits in the EU Internal Market: From Schumacker to Fractional Tax Treatment*, 55(3) Common Market L. Rev. 819 (2018).

Nogueira J. F., *Direito Fiscal Europeu – o paradigma da proporcionalidade* (Wolters Kluwer Portugal 2010).

Norr M., *Jurisdiction to Tax and International Income*, 17(3) Tax L. Rev. 431 (1962).

O'Shea T., *European Tax Controversies: A British-Dutch Debate: Back to Basics and Is the ECJ Consistent?*, 5(1) World Tax J. 100 (2013).

Offermanns R., *Restrictions on Treaty Override Resulting from EU Law*, 53(9) Eur. Tax'n 430 (2013).

Oxman B., *Jurisdiction of States*, in *Max Planck Encyclopedia of Public International Law* (R. Wolfrum ed., Oxford University Press 2012).

Palao Taboada C., *Apogeo y crisis del principio de capacidad contributiva*, in *Estudios jurídicos en homenaje al profesor Federico de Castro* (Tecnos 1976).

Palao Taboada C., *Nueva visita al principio de capacidad contributiva*, 124 REDF 767 (2005).

Palao Taboada C., *Capacidad contributiva, no confiscatoriedad y otros estudios de Derecho constitucional tributario* (Thomson Reuters Aranzadi 2018).

Papadopoulou R., *Principes généraux du droit et droit communautaire: origines et concrétisation* (Bruylant 1996).

Peeters B., *Mobility of EU Citizens and Family Taxation: A Hard to Reconcile Combination*, 23(3) EC Tax Rev. 118 (2014).

Perrou K., *Taxpayer Rights and Taxpayer Participation in Procedures under the Dispute Resolution Directive*, 47(8/9) Intertax 715 (2019).

Pescatore P., *Some Critical Remarks on the Single European Act*, 24 Common Market L. Rev. 9 (1987).

Pires M., *International Juridical Double Taxation of Income* (Kluwer Law and Taxation Publishers 1989).

Pistone P., *The Impact of Community Law on Tax Treaties: Issues and Solutions* (Kluwer Law International 2002).

Pistone P., *Double Taxation: Selected Issues of Compatibility with European Law, Multilateral Tax Treaties and CCCTB, in Double Taxation Within the European Union* (A. Rust ed., Kluwer Law International 2011).

Pistone P., *The Requirements of the EU Internal Market: Steering the Development of Direct Taxes Towards a Fair Mix of Positive and Negative Integration*, in *Horizontal Tax Coordination* (M. Lang et al. eds, IBFD 2012).

Pistone P. & Szudoczky R., *Coordination of Tax Laws and Tax Policies in the EU*, in *Introduction to European Tax Law on Direct Taxation* (M. Lang et al. eds, Linde Verlag 2018).

Pistone P. et al., *Fundamentals of Taxation: An Introduction to Tax Policy, Tax Law and Tax Administration* (IBFD 2019).

Pit H. M., *Arbitration under the OECD Multilateral Instrument: Reservations, Options and Choices*, 71(10) Bull. Int'l Tax'n 568 (2017).

Pit H. M., *Dispute Resolution in the EU: The EU Arbitration Convention and the Dispute Resolution Directive* (IBFD 2018).

Poiares Maduro M., *We the Court: The European Court of Justice and the European Economic Constitution* (Hart Publishing 1998).

Poulsen M., *Freedom of Establishment and the Balanced Allocation of Tax Jurisdiction*, 40(3) Intertax 200 (2012).

Qureshi A. H., *The Freedom of a State to Legislate in Fiscal Matters under General International Law*, 41 Bull. for Int'l Fiscal Documentation 14 (1987).

Qureshi A. H. & Kumar A., *The Public International Law of Taxation: Text, Cases and Materials* (Kluwer Law International 2d ed. 2019).

Reimer E., *The Abolition of Article 293 EC: Comments on Hofmann's Analysis*, in *Double Taxation Within the European Union* (A. Rust ed., Kluwer Law International 2011).

Reimer E. & Rust A. eds, *Klaus Vogel on Double Taxation Conventions* (Kluwer Law International 4th ed. 2015).

Ribeiro de Sousa P., *Tax Treaty Override*, in *Fundamental Issues and Practical Problems in Tax Treaty Interpretation* (M. Schilcher & P. Wenignger eds, Linde Verlag 2008).

Rust A., *Double Taxation*, in *Double Taxation Within the European Union* (A. Rust ed., Kluwer Law International 2011).

Rust A., *How European Law Could Solve Double Taxation*, in *Double Taxation Within the European Union* (A. Rust ed., Kluwer Law International 2011).

Rust A., *Germany II: Case C-20/16 (Bechtel & Bechtel)*, in *CJEU – Recent Developments in Direct Taxation 2016* (M. Lang et al. eds, Linde Verlag 2017).

Sáinz de Bujanda F., *Hacienda y Derecho* 3 (Instituto de Estudios Políticos 1963).

Sáinz de Bujanda F., *Reflexiones sobre un sistema de derecho tributario español*, 7 (16/17) Rev. Fac. Derecho Universidad de Madrid 7 (1963).

Santa-Bárbara Rupérez J., *La no discriminación fiscal* (Edersa 2001).

Schaumburg H., *Das Leistungsfähigkeitsprinzip im internationalen Steuerrecht*, in *Die Steuerrechtsordnung in der Diskussion: Festschrift für Klaus Tipke* (J. Lang ed., Verlag Dr. Otto Schmidt 1995).

Schön W., *International Tax Coordination for a Second-Best World (Part I)*, 1(1) World Tax J. 67 (2009).

Schön W., *Persons and Territories: On the International Allocation of Taxing Rights*, 6 Brit. Tax Rev. 554 (2010).

Schön W., *Neutrality and Territoriality – Competing or Converging Concepts in European Tax Law?*, 68(4/5) Bull. Int'l Tax'n 271 (2015).

Schön W., *Free Movement of Capital and Freedom of Establishment*, 17(3) Bus. Org. L. Rev. 229 (2016).
Schonewillet P., *Eliminating Tax Barriers via the Infringement Procedure of Article 226 of the EC Treaty*, 15(3) EC Tax Rev. 147 (2006).
Schrauwen A., *In Defence of Public Interest: The Rule of Reason; Genesis of a Principle of Law*, in *The Rule of Reason: Rethinking Another Classic of European Legal Doctrine* (A. Schrauwen ed., Europa Law Publishing 2005).
Seer R., *The Jurisprudence of the European Court of Justice: Limitation of the Legal Consequences?*, 46(10) Eur. Tax'n 470 (2006).
Seligman E., *Progressive Taxation in Theory and Practice*, 9(4) Am. Econ. Ass'n Q. 1 (1908).
Seligman E., *Essays in Taxation* (The Macmillan Company 1921).
Seligman E., *La double imposition et la coopération fiscale internationale*, 20 Recueil des Cours 460 (1927).
Simonek M., *Tax Coordination Between Cantons in Switzerland – Role of the Courts*, in *Horizontal Tax Coordination* (M. Lang et al. eds, IBFD 2012).
Smet P. & Laloo H., *ECJ to Rule on Taxation of Inbound Dividends in Belgium*, 45(4) Eur. Tax'n 158 (2005).
Smit D., *The Relationship Between the Free Movement of Capital and the Other EC Treaty Freedoms in Third Country Relationships in the Field of Direct Taxation: A Question of Exclusivity, Parallelism or Causality*, 16(6) EC Tax Rev. 252 (2007).
Smit D., *International Income Allocation under EU Tax Law: Tinker, Tailor, Soldier, Sailor*, 26(2) EC Tax Rev. 67 (2017).
Snell J., *Who's Got the Power? Free Movement and Allocation of Competences in EC Law*, 22(1) Y.B. Eur. L. 323 (2003).
Snell J., *Non-discriminatory Tax Obstacles in Community Law*, 56(2) Int'l & Compar. L.Q. 339 (2007).
Spitaler A., *Das Doppelbesteuerungsproblem bei den direkten Steuern* (Reichenberg 1936).
Steichen A., *La Justice dans l'impôt* (Centre Universitaire de Luxembourg 1994).
Steward M., *The Tax State, Benefit and Legitimacy*, in *Studies in the History of Tax Law* (P. Harris & D. Cogan eds, Hart Publishing 2015).
Tipke K., *Die Steurrechtsordnung* (Verlag Dr. Otto Schmidt 2d ed. 2000).
Tipke K., *Moral tributaria del Estado y de los contribuyentes (Besteuerungsmoral und Steuermoral)* (P. Herrera Molina trans., Marcial Pons 2002).
Tipke K. & Lang J., *Steuerrecht* (Verlag Dr. Otto Schmidt 10th ed. 2010).
Tipke K. & Yamashita D., *Justiça fiscal e princípio da capacidade contributiva* (Malheiros 2002).
Traversa E., *Objective Ability to Pay: The Gerritse Case*, in *Landmark Decisions of the ECJ in Direct Taxation* (W. Haslehner et al. eds, Kluwer Law International 2015).
Traversa E. & Pirlot A., *Tax Sovereignty and Territoriality under Siege: How Far Should the EU Freedoms of Movement Impact on the Territorial Allocation of Taxing Powers Between Member States?*, in *Principles of Law: Function, Status and Impact in EU Tax Law* (C. Brokelind ed., IBFD 2014).
Udina M., *Il diritto internazionale tributario* (CEDAM 1949).

Van de Vijver A., *International Double (Non)taxation: Comparative Guidance from European Legal Principles*, 24(5) EC Tax Rev. 240 (2015).

Van de Vijver A., *International Double Taxation in the European Union: Comparative Guidelines from Switzerland and the United States*, 26(1) EC Tax Rev. 10 (2017).

Vanistendael F., *Case C-336/96, Mr and Mrs Robert Gilly v. Directeur des Services Fiscaux du Bas Rhin*, 37(1) Common Market L. Rev. 167 (2000).

Vanistendael F., *The ECJ at the Crossroads: Balancing Tax Sovereignty Against the Imperatives of the Single Market*, 46(9) Eur. Tax'n 413 (2006).

Vanistendael F., *General Report on the Fundamental Freedoms and National Sovereignty in the European Union*, in *EU Freedoms and Taxation: 2004 EATLP Congress* (F. Vanistendael ed., IBFD 2006).

Vanistendael F., *Denkavit Internationaal: The Balance Between Fiscal Sovereignty and the Fundamental Freedoms?*, 47(5) Eur. Tax'n 210 (2007).

Vanistendael F., *Does the ECJ Have the Power of Interpretation to Build a Tax System Compatible with the Fundamental Freedoms?*, 17(2) EC Tax Rev. 52 (2008).

Vanistendael F., *In Defence of the European Court of Justice*, 62(3) Bull. Int'l Tax'n 90 (2008).

Vanistendael F., *Is Fiscal Justice Progressing?*, 64(10) Bull. Int'l Tax'n 526 (2010).

Vanistendael F., *Ability to Pay in European Community Law*, 23(3) EC Tax Rev. 121 (2014).

Van Raad K., *The Impact of the EC Treaty's Fundamental Freedoms Provisions on EU Member States' Taxation in Border-Crossing Situations – Current State of Affairs*, 4(4) EC Tax Rev. 190 (1995).

Van Raad K., *Fractional Taxation of Multistate Income of EU Resident Individuals – A Proposal*, in *Liber Amicorum Sven- Olof Lodin* (K. Andersson et al. eds, Kluwer Law International 2001).

Van Raad K., *Non-residents – Personal Allowances, Deduction of Personal Expenses and Tax Rates*, 2(2) World Tax J. 154 (2010).

van Thiel S., *Removal of Income Tax Barriers to Market Integration in the European Union: Litigation by the Community Citizen Instead of Harmonisation by the Community Legislature*, 12(1) EC Tax Rev. 4 (2003).

van Thiel S., *Why the European Court of Justice Should Interpret Directly Applicable Community Law as a Right to Most-Favoured-Nation Treatment and a Prohibition of Double Taxation*, in *The Influence of European Law on Direct Taxation: Recent and Future Developments* (D. Weber ed., Kluwer Law International 2007).

van Thiel S., *Justifications in Community Law for Income Tax Restrictions on Free Movement: Acte Clair Rules That Can Be Readily Applied by National Courts – Part 1*, 48(6) Eur. Tax'n 279 (2008).

van Thiel S., *Justifications in Community Law for Income Tax Restrictions on Free Movement: Acte Clair Rules That Can Be Readily Applied by National Courts – Part 2*, 48(7) Eur. Tax'n 339 (2008).

van Thiel S., *Justifications in Community Law for Income Tax Restrictions on Free Movement: Acte Clair Rules That Can Be Readily Applied by National Courts*, in *The Acte Clair in EC Direct Tax Law* (A. P. Dourado & R. Borges eds, IBFD 2008).

van Thiel S., *Avoiding a Double Burden Within the European Union: Comments on Kofler and Rust's Analysis*, in *Double Taxation Within the European Union* (A. Rust ed., Kluwer Law International 2011).

van Thiel S., *Double Burdens on Cross-Border Economic Activity Within the European Union*, in *Comparative Fiscal Federalism* (R. Avi Yonah and M. Lang eds, Kluwer Law International 2016).

Vasques S., *Capacidade Contributiva, Rendimento e Património*, 23 Fiscalidade 15 (2005).

Vasques S., *O Princípio da Equivalência como Critério de Igualdade Tributária* (Almedina 2008).

Vogel K, *Observaciones acerca de la teoría de la justificación del impuesto*, 100 Hacienda Pública Española 149 (1986).

Vogel K., *Double Tax Treaties and Their Interpretation*, 4(1) Int'l Tax & Bus. Law 1 (1986).

Vogel K., *The Justification for Taxation: A Forgotten Question*, 33 Am. J. Juris. 19 (1988).

Vogel K., *Worldwide vs. Source Taxation of Income: A Review and Re-evaluation of Arguments (Part I)*, 8/9 Intertax 216 (1988).

Vogel K., *Worldwide vs. Source Taxation of Income: A Review and Re-evaluation of Arguments (Part II)*, 10 Intertax 310 (1988).

Vogel K., *Some Observations Regarding Gilly*, 7(3) EC Tax Rev. 150 (1998).

Vogel K., *Which Method Should the European Community Adopt for the Avoidance of Double Taxation?*, 56 Bull. for Int'l Fiscal Documentation 4 (2002).

Wathelet M., *The Sovereignty of the Member States and the European Court of Justice: New Trends or Confirmation?*, in *A Vision of Taxes Within and Outside European Borders* (L. Hinnekens & P. Hinnekens eds, Kluwer Law International 2008).

Wattel P., *Progressive Taxation of Non-residents and Intra-EC Allocation of Personal Tax Allowances: Why Schumacker, Asscher, Gilly and Gschwind Do Not Suffice*, 60(6) Eur. Tax'n 210 (2000).

Wattel P., *Red Herrings in Direct Tax Cases Before the ECJ*, 31(2) Legal Issues Econ. Integration 81 (2004).

Wattel P., *Fiscal Cohesion, Fiscal Territoriality and Preservation of the (Balanced) Allocation of Taxing Power; What Is the Difference?*, in *The Influence of European Law on Direct Taxation: Recent and Future Developments* (D. Weber ed., Kluwer Law International 2007).

Wattel P., *Passing the Buck Around: Who Is Responsible for Double Taxation?: Comments on Profs. Kofler and Rust's Analysis*, in *Double Taxation Within the European Union* (A. Rust ed., Kluwer Law International 2011).

Wattel P., *Non-discrimination à la Cour: The ECJ's (Lack of) Comparability Analysis in Direct Tax Cases*, 55(12) Eur. Tax'n 542 (2015).

Wattel P. et al., *Terra/Wattel European Tax Law* I (Kluwer Law International 7th ed. 2018).

Weber D., *In Search of a (New) Equilibrium Between Tax Sovereignty and the Freedom of Movement Within the EC*, 34(12) Intertax 585 (2006).

Weber D., *Cross-Border Losses: From Ritter-Coulais via Renneberg Back to Futura Participations?*, in *A Vision of Taxes Within and Outside European Borders* (L. Hinnekens & P. Hinnekens eds, Kluwer Law International 2008).

Weber D., *An Analysis of the Past, Current and Future of the Coherence of the Tax System as Justification*, 24(1) EC Tax Rev. 43 (2015).

Wöhrer V., *Data Protection and Taxpayers' Rights: Challenges Created by Automatic Exchange of Information* (IBFD 2018).

Xavier A., *Direito tributário internacional* (Almedina 2d ed. 2011).

Zalasiński A., *The Role of the European Court of Justice in Taxpayer Protection in the Field of Direct Taxation*, in *Protection of Taxpayer's Rights: European, International and Domestic Tax Law Perspectives* (W. Nykiel & M. Sek eds, Wolters Kluwer Polska 2009).

Zalasiński A., *The Limits of the EC Concept of 'Direct Tax Restriction on Free Movement Rights', the Principles of Equality and Ability to Pay, and the Interstate Fiscal Equity*, 37(5) Intertax 282 (2009).

Zalasiński A., *The Principle of Proportionality and (European) Tax Law*, in *Principles of Law: Function, Status and Impact in EU Tax Law* (C. Brokelind ed., IBFD 2014).

Table of Cases

Index

EUCOTAX Series on European Taxation

(1) Peter HJ Essers, Guido JME de Bont & Eric CCM Kemmeren (eds), *The Compatibility of Anti-Abuse Provisions in Tax Treaties with EC Law*, 1998 (ISBN 90-411-9678-1).
(2) Gerard TK Meussen (ed.), *The Principle of Equality in European Taxation*, 1999 (ISBN 90-411-9693-5).
(3) Michael Lang (ed.), *Tax Treaty Interpretation*, 2001 (ISBN 90-411-9857-1).
(4) Pasquale Pistone, *The Impact of Community Law on Tax Treaties: Issues and Solutions*, 2002 (ISBN 90-411-9860-1).
(5) René Offermanns, *The Entrepreneurship Concept in a European Comparative Tax Law Perspective*, 2002 (ISBN 90-411-9887-3).
(6) Michael Lang & Mario Züger, *Settlement of Disputes in Tax Treaty Law*, 2002 (ISBN 90-411-9904-7).
(7) Carlo Pinto, *Tax Competition and EU Law*, 2003 (ISBN 90-411-9913-6).
(8) Michael Lang, Hans-Jörgen Aigner, Ulrich Scheuerle & Markus Stefaner, *CFC Legislation, Tax Treaties and EC Law*, 2004 (ISBN 90-411-2284-2).
(9) Mattias Dahlberg, *Direct Taxation in Relation to the Freedom of Establishment and the Free Movement of Capital*, 2005 (ISBN 90-411-2363-6).
(10) Michael Lang, Judith Herdin & Ines Hofbauer, *WTO and Direct Taxation*, 2005 (ISBN 90-411-2371-7).
(11) Dennis Weber, *Tax Avoidance and the EC Tray Freedoms: A Study of the Limitations under European Law for the Prevention of Tax Avoidance*, 2005 (ISBN 90-411-2402-0).
(12) Félix Alberto Vega Borrego, *Limitations on Benefits Clauses on Double Taxation Conventions*, 2005 (ISBN 90-411-2370-9).
(13) Michael Lang, Josef Schuch & Claus Staringer, *ECJ-Recent Developments in Direct Taxation*, 2006 (ISBN 90-411-2509-4).
(14) Reuven S. Avi-Yonah, James R. Hines Jr. & Michael Lang, *Comparative Fiscal Federalism. Comparing the European Court of Justice and the US Supreme Court's Tax Jurisprudence*, 2007 (ISBN 978-90-411-2552-1).
(15) Christiana HJI Panayi, *Double Taxation, Tax Treaties, Treaty-Shopping and the European Community*, 2007 (ISBN 978-90-411-2658-0).
(16) Dennis Weber, *The Influence of European Law on Direct Taxation: Recent and Future Developments*, 2007 (ISBN 978-90-411-2667-2).
(17) Michael Lang & Pasquale Pistone, *The EU and Third Countries: Direct Taxation*, 2007 (ISBN 978-90-411-2665-8).
(18) Oskar Henkow, *Financial Activities in European VAT: A Theoretical and Legal Research of the European VAT System and Preferred Treatment of Financial Activities*, 2007 (ISBN 978-90-411-2703-7).
(19) Michael Lang (ed.), *Tax Compliance Costs for Companies in an Enlarged European Community*, 2008 (ISBN 978-90-411-2666-5).

(20) Michael Lang (ed.), *Source versus Residence. Problems Arising from the Allocation of Taxing Rights in Tax Treaty Law and Possible Alternatives*, 2008 (ISBN 978-90-411-2763-1).

(21) Ioanna Mitroyanni, *Integration Approaches to Group Taxation in the European Internal Market*, 2008 (ISBN 978-90-411-2779-2).

(22) Rolf Eicke, *Tax Planning with Holding Companies. Repatriation of US Profits from Europe: Concepts, Strategies, Structures*, 2008 (ISBN978-90-411-2794-5).

(23) Peter Essers et al. (ed.), *The Influence of IAS/IFRS on the CCCTB, Tax Accounting, Disclosure and Corporate Law Accounting Concepts: 'A Clash of Cultures'*, 2008 (ISBN 978-90-411-2819-5).

(24) Tonny Schenk-Geers, *International Exchange of Information and the Protection of Taxpayers*, 2009 (ISBN 978-90-411-3142-3).

(25) Raymond Adema, *UCITS and Taxation: Towards Harmonization of the Taxation of UCITS*, 2009 (ISBN 978-90-411-2839-3).

(26) Michael Lang, Jianwen Liu & Gongliang Tang (eds), *Europe–China Tax Treaties*, 2010 (ISBN 978-90-411-3216-1).

(27) Michael Lang, Pasquale Pistone, Josef Schuch & Claus Staringer (eds), *Procedural Rules in Tax Law in the Context of European Union and Domestic Law*, 2010 (ISBN 978-90-411-3376-2).

(28) Sjaak J.J.M. Jansen, *Fiscal Sovereignty of the Member States in an Internal Market: Past and Future*, 2011 (ISBN 978-90-411-3403-5).

(29) Dennis Weber & Bruno da Silva, *From Marks & Spencer to X Holding: The Future of Cross-Border Group Taxation*, 2011 (ISBN 978-90-411-3399-1).

(30) Claus Bohn Jespersen, *Intermediation of Insurance and Financial Services in European VAT*, 2011 (ISBN 978-90-411-3732-6).

(31) Sabine Heidenbauer, *Charity Crossing Borders: The Fundamental Freedoms' Influence on Charity and Donor Taxation in Europe*, 2011 (ISBN 978-90-411-3813-2).

(32) Michael Lang, et al., *The Future of Indirect Taxation: Recent Trends in VAT and GST Systems around the World*, 2012 (ISBN 978-90-411-3797-5).

(33) Harm van den Broek, *Cross-Border Mergers within the EU: Proposals to Remove the Remaining Tax Obstacles*, 2012 (ISBN 978-90-411-3824-8).

(34) Michael Lang, et al. (eds), *Tax Treaty Case Law around the Globe – 2011*, 2012 (ISBN 978-90-411-3876-7).

(35) Dennis Weber (ed.), *CCCTB: Selected Issues*, 2012 (ISBN 978-90-411-3872-9).

(36) Daniël Smit, *EU Freedoms, Non-EU Countries and Company Taxation*, 2012 (ISBN 978-90-411-4041-8).

(37) Rita de la Feria, *VAT Exemptions: Consequences and Design Alternatives*, 2013 (ISBN 978-90-411-3276-5).

(38) Karin Simader, *Withholding Taxes and the Fundamental Freedoms*, 2013 (ISBN 978-90-411-4842-1).

(39) Madeleine Merkx, *Establishments in European VAT*, 2013 (ISBN 978-90-411-4554-3).

(40) Carla De Pietro, *Tax Treaty Override*, 2014 (ISBN 978-90-411-5406-4).

(41) G.K. Fibbe & A.J.A. Stevens (eds), *Hybrid Entities and the EU Direct Tax Directives*, 2015 (ISBN 978-90-411-5942-7).
(42) Gerard Staats, *Personal Pensions in the EU*, 2015 (ISBN 978-90-411-5953-3).
(43) Michael Lang & Ine Lejeune (eds), *VAT/GST in a Global Digital Economy*, 2015 (ISBN 978-90-411-5952-6).
(44) Massimo Basilavecchia, Lorenzo del Federico & Pietro Mastellone (eds), *Tax Implications of Environmental Disasters and Pollution*, 2015 (ISBN 978-90-411-5611-2).
(45) Cristina Trenta, *Rethinking EU VAT for P2P Distribution*, 2015 (ISBN 978-90-411-6137-6).
(46) Marie Lamensch, Edoardo Traversa & Servaas van Thiel (eds), *Value Added Tax and the Digital Economy: The 2015 EU Rules and Broader Issues*, 2016 (ISBN 978-90-411-6612-8).
(47) Raffaele Petruzzi, *Transfer Pricing Aspects of Intra-Group Financing*, 2016 (ISBN 978-90-411-6732-3).
(48) Mario Grandinetti (ed.), *Corporate Tax Base in the Light of the IAS/IFRS and EU Directive 2013/34: A Comparative Approach*, 2016 (ISBN 978-90-411-6745-3).
(49) Bruno da Silva, *The Impact of Tax Treaties and EU Law on Group Taxation Regimes*, 2016 (ISBN 978-90-411-6905-1).
(50) Michael Lang, Alfred Storck & Raffaele Petruzzi (eds), *Transfer Pricing in a Post-BEPS World*, 2016 (ISBN 978-90-411-6710-1).
(51) Marta Papis-Almansa, *Insurance in European VAT: Current and Preferred Treatment in the Light of the New Zealand and Australian GST Systems*, 2017 (ISBN 978-90-411-8360-6).
(52) Wolfgang Speckhahn, *Real Estate Investment Trusts In Europe: Europeanising Tax Regimes*, 2017 (ISBN 978-90-411-8360-6).
(53) Frank J.G. Nellen, *Information Asymmetries in EU VAT*, 2017 (ISBN 978-90-411-8837-3).
(54) Erik Ros, *EU Citizenship and Direct Taxation*, 2017 (ISBN 978-90-411-8584-6).
(55) Werner Haslehner, Georg Kofler & Alexander Rust (eds), *EU Tax Law and Policy in the 21st Century*, 2017 (ISBN 978-90-411-8815-1).
(56) Claudia Sanò, *National Legal Presumptions and European Tax Law*, 2018 (ISBN 978-90-411-6613-5).
(57) Christoph Marchgraber, *Double (Non-)Taxation and EU Law*, 2018 (ISBN 978-90-411-9410-7).
(58) Dennis Weber & Jan van de Streek (eds), *The EU Common Consolidated Corporate Tax Base: Critical Analysis*, 2018 (ISBN 978-90-411-9233-2).
(59) Werner Haslehner (ed.), *Investment Fund Taxation: Domestic Law, EU Law, and Double Taxation Treaties*, 2018 (ISBN 978-90-411-9669-9).
(60) Jérôme Monsenego, *Selectivity in State Aid Law and the Methods for the Allocation of the Corporate Tax Base*, 2018 (ISBN 978-90-411-9413-8).
(61) José Manuel Almudí Cid, Jorge A. Ferreras Gutiérrez & Pablo A. Hernández González-Barreda (eds), *Combating Tax Avoidance in the EU: Harmonization and Cooperation in Direct Taxation*, 2019 (ISBN 978-94-035-0154-3).

(62) Werner Haslehner, Georg Kofler & Alexander Rust (eds), *Time and Tax: Issues in International, EU, and Constitutional Law*, 2019 (ISBN 978-94-035-0354-7).

(63) Nathalie Wittock, *Sales Promotion Techniques and VAT in the EU*, 2019 (ISBN 978-94-035-0861-0).

(64) Carla De Pietro (ed.), *New Perspectives on Fiscal State Aid: Legitimacy and Effectiveness of Fiscal State Aid Control*, 2019 (ISBN 978-94-035-1415-4).

(65) Giorgio Beretta, *European VAT and the Sharing Economy*, 2019 (ISBN 978-94-035-1435-2).

(66) Claudio Cipollini, *Special Tax Zones and EU Law: Theory, Implementations, and Future Challenges*, 2020 (ISBN 978-94-035-1885-5).

(67) Gianluigi Bizioli, Mario Grandinetti, Leopoldo Parada, Giuseppe Vanz & Alessandro Vicini Ronchetti (eds), *Corporate Taxation, Group Debt Funding and Base Erosion: New Perspectives on the EU Anti-Tax Avoidance Directive*, 2020 (ISBN 978-94-035-1170-2).

(68) Ronald Hein & Ronald Russo (eds), *Co-operative Compliance and the OECD's International Compliance Assurance Programme*, 2020 (ISBN 978-94-035-1951-7).

(69) Jeffrey Owens & Jonathan Leigh Pemberton, *Cooperative Compliance: A Multi-stakeholder and Sustainable Approach to Taxation*, 2021 (ISBN 978-94-035-3193-9).

(70) Christina Pollak, *Platforms in EU VAT Law: A Legal Analysis of the Supply of Goods*, 2022 (ISBN 978-94-035-1026-2).

(71) Shu-Chien Chen, *Towards a Neutral Formulary Apportionment System in Regional Integration*, 2023 (ISBN 978-94-035-3276-9).

(72) Maria Júlia Ildefonso Mendonça, *International Juridical Double Taxation from an Ability-to-Pay Perspective under EU Law*, 2024 (ISBN 978-94-035-0298-4).

www.ingramcontent.com/pod-product-compliance
Lightning Source LLC
Chambersburg PA
CBHW071244230926
51849CB00001B/226
9789403502984